THE RISE OF THE BRITISH PRESIDENCY

MICHAEL FOLEY

The rise of the British presidency

MANCHESTER UNIVERSITY PRESS
MANCHESTER AND NEW YORK

distributed exclusively in the USA and Canada by St. Martin's Press

Copyright © Manchester University Press 1993

Published by Manchester University Press
Oxford Road, Manchester M13 9PL, UK
and Room 400, 175 Fifth Avenue, New York, NY 10010, USA

Distributed exclusively in the USA and Canada
by St. Martin's Press, Inc., 175 Fifth Avenue, New York, NY 10010, USA

British Library Cataloguing-in-Publication Data
A catalogue record for this book is available from the British Library

Library of Congress Cataloging-in-Publication Data
Foley, Michael, 1948–
    The rise of the British presidency / Michael Foley.
        p.   cm.
    ISBN 0-7190-3621-6 (cloth). — ISBN 0-7190-4010-8 (pbk.)
    1.Prime ministers—Great Britain. 2. Great Britain—Politics and
government—1979– 3. Thatcher, Margaret. 4. Presidents—United States.
I. Title.
JN406.F65   1993
354.4103'13—dc20   92-37304

ISBN 0-7190-3621-6 hardback
ISBN 0-7190-4010-8 paperback

Set in Aldus
by Koinonia Ltd, Manchester
Printed in Great Britain
by Biddles Ltd., Guildford and King's Lynn

CONTENTS

ACKNOWLEDGEMENTS

I am indebted to numerous individuals for their help and advice with this project. In particular, I would like to thank all those who provided encouragement and constructive criticism when I first tried out these ideas at a seminar at Nuffield College, Oxford. Nigel Bowles, Richard Hodder-Williams, Des King, Peter Madgwick, Gillian Peele, Byron Shafer and Alan Ware all made very useful contributions that strongly influenced my research. At Manchester University Press, I was fortunate enough to have the benefit of both Bill Jones's lucid critique of my original proposal and Richard Purslow's perceptive appraisals. I would also like to thank Anthony Mughan for sending me some of his work from the United States: his excellent research helped me to clarify a number of ideas. My colleagues in the Department of International Politics are also owed a debt of gratitude. Apart from providing a very stimulating environment in which to work, they tolerated my various forms of preoccupation with great forbearance. I appreciate the opportunities afforded to me by John Garnett and David Steeds, whose leadership of the department has made it into a place that is highly conducive to serious research.

Special mention must be made of Anthony King. He has always given encouragement and practical support to me in my various endeavours. This time was no exception. In addition to his very helpful comments, I was furnished with armfuls of opinion polls and other materials from his files. Without his peerless work on the British prime minister, this study would have had no foundation of contemporary scholarship upon which to proceed. It is wholly appropriate, therefore, that this book should be dedicated to him.

For their technical support in the prodigious task of transforming my research into publishable form, I am grateful to Stephen Ball, Kim Hardy and Jane Hammond Foster.

Very special thanks are reserved for my wife, Frances, who produced both the finished typescript and the index, and to my daughter, Jo, for her help with some of the diagrams. My son, Nicholas, and younger daughter, Louise, made it into a family affair by giving me a host of original insights into the highly precarious nature of all leadership.

TO TONY

CHAPTER 1

Prime ministerial government and the presidential analogy

In recent years, the British public has become acutely aware of the potential, and arguably the need, for personal leadership in the midst of its political system. This represents a major change in perceptions and values, for the British form of government has traditionally been distinguished by its collegiate and impersonal nature. The British system is based upon the constitutional doctrine of parliamentary sovereignty, the political principle of a representative democracy drawn from a mass electorate, and on an operational ethos of party loyalty, collective cabinet responsibility and a professional civil service. As a consequence, British government is usually noted for its high level of institutional and individual integration. In these circumstances, personal prominence comes only with close team work. Just as the way to power in such a system is by a slow and graduated route of collective appraisal, so the exercise of power is cautious, sensitive and above all, collaborative in nature. Leadership in such conditions could almost be said to be a contradiction in terms – i.e. a leadership bound by the need to maintain party loyalty, cabinet unity and electoral support, and to comply with the moral code of constitutional conventions that always required government at the highest level to be a matter of consultation rather than direction. As a consequence, the British system, at least until recently, was 'always held to be stronger than any particular man (or woman)'.[1]

It is true that there have been occasions in the past when the collaborative properties of British government have come under severe strain. David Lloyd George in World War I and Winston Churchill in World War II were propelled into positions of ascendancy during their wartime administrations. They became national figures in a society whose interests and organisation were being directly threatened by an enemy with highly destructive forces at its disposal. The leadership positions of both Lloyd George and Churchill were very much the product of the intense national solidarity aroused by wartime mobilisation, and of the related recognition that focal points of leadership

1

amounted to an unavoidable feature of directing total warfare. The extent to which the political drives, skills and sheer willpower of these respective leaders were responsible for maximising the extraordinary opportunities that were made available to them remains a matter of debate. What is clear is that the scale of personal power exercised by these two leaders was confined to the abnormal circumstances of World War I and World War II. After both these wars, the principles of the British liberal tradition were revived; politicians and government reverted to the valued normality of argument and persuasion, of negotiation and reconciliation, and of party division, electoral competition and corporate assertion breaking power down in both senses of the word. Highly centralised government and highly personalised leadership consequently became closely associated with the peculiar conditions of massive international conflict. As Lloyd George and Churchill were duly honoured as national heroes, their great individual powers melted in peace. Such concentrated leadership became recognised as a grim coercive necessity – as a wholly exceptional response to the utterly aberrational conditions of warfare.

It is important to bear this historical context in mind, in order to grasp the significance of what occurred in British politics during the 1980s. In essence, the country witnessed the emergence of a peacetime prime minister whose pre-eminence in government was comparable only to that of Winston Churchill in World War II. In her attempt to change the face of Britain, Margaret Thatcher in effect became the face of Britain. She not only transformed that nature and vocabulary of political debate and drastically altered the priorities of the British political agenda, but centralised the government and its objectives so much around the motivating force of her own convictions that government largely became synonymous with Margaret Thatcher's persona. This was an impression that strengthened as the decade progressed until she became the longest continually serving prime minister this century and the only one to win three successive general elections. In the same way that she was said to be 'the personal embodiment of a political idea',[2] so it was plausible to claim that the government was the institutional embodiment of her personal ideas and drives.

In challenging the post-war political consensus on economic management and the welfare state, Mrs Thatcher also assaulted the established customs and beliefs concerning the distribution and exercise of power in British government. She may not have been able to induce the formation of a new social consensus in support of her policy programme, but, in seeking to produce one, she did succeed in drawing opinion together on the extraordinary scale of her power. Her supporters and her opponents may have been bitterly divided over what she sought to do with the authority at her disposal, but nearly all were agreed on the fact of its existence.

2

To her sympathisers, Margaret Thatcher had revived the quality of personal leadership in an increasingly collectivist and anonymous age. In 1987, S. E. Finer concluded that while she may have fallen short of greatness, there could be no doubt that she had acquired a position of dominance.

> She has towered over all her contemporaries, inside her party as well as outside. Her courage – intellectual, psychological, and in the face of physical danger – is quite out of the ordinary. It is her unwavering purpose that has kept her governments on their fixed course through the troughs as well as the crests of party and personal popularity ... Mrs Thatcher evokes admiration and detestation for one identical reason: she is 'big'. She has impressed herself on government as nobody has done since the war years of Churchill.[3]

As a consequence of this 'bigness', she was able to confront and to prevail over powerful adversaries (e.g. Arthur Scargill and General Galtieri) in a singular deployment of individual authority and sustained intransigence. In the view of Kenneth Minogue, 'her opponents in the notable dramas which it had been her vocation to provoke were none of them insignificant, but each served merely to exhibit her mettle'.[4] It was a testament to the belief in the force of her personality and the zeal she instilled into her loyalists that Mrs Thatcher was assumed capable both of diminishing the social intrusion of the state and of reversing Britain's post-war decline. Her supporters felt in no way deluded in thinking that the force of Mrs Thatcher's missionary vision and personal willpower could match and even prevail over the characteristics of established institutions and policies.

To her opponents, Margaret Thatcher was a reactionary enemy of public expenditure and social welfare, and an ideological extremist intent on using authoritarian means to release market forces, to defend property rights and to maintain law and order – even at the expense of civil liberties and established social conventions. If Thatcher's opponents could rarely agree on which aspects of her programme or personality they deplored most, they were at least united on the magnitude of her influence upon government and society. To Hugo Young, Margaret Thatcher gave 'her name to the age in which we live'.[5] None of her predecessors 'more voraciously dominated a peacetime government with their personal impact and commitment than Margaret Thatcher'. He continued:

> She was a leader of lurid style and risky habits, especially in the field of personal relations. Aggressive to a fault, she spent years scorning not only consensual policies but the consensual demeanour. With nerveless indifference, she was prepared to see the larger proportion of her friends as well as her enemies in high places depart the scene as a direct result of her behaviour.[6]

In Young's view, the Thatcher era was different and 'nowhere more so than in

3

the evidence it offers that personality can be the single most potent contribu-
tor to the pattern of events'.[7] And on the occasion of Mrs Thatcher's resignation, Andrew Gamble of *Marxism Today* summed up her premiership in the
following terms

> Thatcher's fall is the end of an era in British politics as turbulent and eventful as
> any in the 20th century. Quieter times lie ahead. As Thatcher's preferred
> successor, John Major represents continuity. But he also represents the
> routinisation of charisma, and the dissipation of the energy, the radicalism, and
> the conviction that suffused the Thatcher decade. Thatcher's resignation is more
> than just the end of one political leader. It signals the end of a regime. Thatcher
> was not only a dominating political personality like Churchill, but also the focus
> of a distinctive political project. It is the future of this project that is now in
> doubt.[8]

It was the radicalism of Thatcher's programme and leadership that
essentially radicalised the perspectives on the relationships between the state
and society, and between government and its own inner hierarchy. For good
or ill, therefore, Thatcher's administrations were seen as governments that
necessarily had Thatcherite policies, which in their turn were building a
Thatcherite society. The interconnections appeared so close and durable that
the conclusions drawn from them seemed irrefutable. In the same way that
Margaret Thatcher's pervasive influence in government characterised her
administration as Thatcherite, so government policy and social change were
reduced as a matter of course to derivatives of Thatcherism. As a result, the
authority of what was after all only a prime minister, in the context of the
British constitution, appeared well nigh complete.

At the very least, it can be said that during her premiership, Margaret
Thatcher performed the 'minor miracle' of making 'the study of government
and public administration interesting again'.[9] In particular, she made leadership an acceptable and even an unavoidable subject of analysis and evaluation.
Thatcher's conception of politics and the nature of her policy objectives were
refracted through the lens of her leadership style. The manner of Thatcher's
leadership was dramatically different to that of her predecessors in that it was
highly substantive in content and directly confrontational in approach. Mrs
Thatcher not only had an agenda of her own, she had one that was not shared
by most of her party – let alone by much of the country. While other prime
ministers may have concerned themselves with keeping the cabinet united at
all costs and with maintaining the electoral appeal of an integrated party,
Thatcher had to impose herself and her agenda upon the party and the
government. Tough, relentless and even inspirational leadership was actually
required for Thatcher to *remain* prime minister, given that she was committed

to a programme designed to produce a radical change in political attitudes.

Margaret Thatcher had to lead from the front – so far out in front that she was often in danger of losing contact with her troops. She saw teaching and instruction as essential to her role as prime minister.

> In public and private, she is a relentless educator. An important task of leadership in her view is to win the battle of ideas, and this done, by frequently expressing basic beliefs and principles… . Colleagues are impressed (and sometimes alarmed) by her willingness to link large philosophical issues with day to day matters.[10]

She had embarked on a crusade against what she saw as moribund structures, anachronistic attitudes and decadent behaviour. According to her outlook, those who opposed her in government merely damned themselves as part of the dead wood. They had to be argued into submission or cut down.

This leads to another element in Thatcher's leadership – namely her compulsive drive to prevail by the sheer strength of her personality. Whether it was senior civil servants, or cabinet ministers, or members of Parliament, or councillors, or representatives of industry, commerce or labour, Mrs Thatcher would lose no opportunity to imprint her view firmly, perhaps forcibly – even emotionally – upon her audience. It is well known that Margaret Thatcher was a formidable figure to confront on a personal basis. Anthony King describes the power of what was called 'fear at first hand'.

> Mrs Thatcher has a formidable personality, and she is capable of hectoring, cajoling, threatening, wrong-footing, bullying, embarrassing and even humiliating her ministers and officials. She is, in this respect, the Lyndon Johnson of modern British politics. Johnson discovered that people will take a lot from as powerful a person as the President of the United States; Mrs Thatcher has made the same discovery about the British Prime Minister. She puts the fear of God into people, and they usually respond well.[11]

This more visceral leadership complemented the mobilising force of her doctrinal leadership to produce a totally unprecedented level of individual hegemony in British government.

During the Thatcher years, it became second nature to make sweeping statements about the place of leadership in modern British politics. Thatcher swiftly acquired the reputation of having resolved the 'ungovernability problem' of British society – even to the extent of rendering the notorious inertia of the bureaucratic state to the conscious direction of individual leadership. As long as the person's temperament and power of reason were appropriate to the role, then leadership appeared to be a thoroughly plausible political option.

Reactions to her revealed the extent to which perceptions over the possibility of such leadership in the British system had changed. It became

5

commonplace to read or to hear that the government was 'in simple truth, *her* government'.[12] As she became more established in office, 'she was increasingly taken at her own valuation as a prime minister who towered alike over colleagues and opponents'.[13] It was widely concluded that 'to an extent more than any other peacetime prime minister, Mrs Thatcher used power to further a personal conception of what needed to be done'[14] both within government and in society as a whole. As a consequence, government was increasingly seen as being personally motivated by Mrs Thatcher to serve her personal objectives. To Joe Rogaly, for example, it was clear that for eleven years Britain had been

> governed by a prime minister who, whatever her faults, has been infused with a vision. She had been a driven woman, always urging ministers forward, terrifying them, tiring them out one by one, disposing of them, nagging them, politicising their senior officials, popping in on this or that issue, scrawling her comments on everything, vetoing this, insisting on that, overshadowing all.[15]

Whether government action was applauded or denounced, it was judged on the assumption of being Thatcherite policy. Whether or not Margaret Thatcher actively encouraged such an impression, whatever government did or did not do in these years was done in her name. As a consequence of this beguiling imagery of leadership, the era generated a renewed interest in the nature of individual leadership and in the relationship between personality, government and history. Margaret Thatcher had broken down many of the barriers to such considerations in the normal run of British politics. With her record in mind, it suddenly became so much easier to conclude that only her government would have undertaken certain policies; and without Margaret Thatcher as prime minister the government's agenda and performance would have been radically different. Even a cautious political scientist like Dennis Kavanagh sensed that a leadership role now existed in British politics and that Margaret Thatcher could be said to have successfully fulfilled it. She offered

> to successors, and to students of British government, a model of what was probably the most successful peacetime premiership this century, measured in electoral success and policy initiatives.[16]

The problem with public prominence is that it is two-edged. Just as a dominant prime minister is recognised as someone able to 'achieve things which would not otherwise have been achieved', so he or she is also identified as a person able to 'make mistakes which would not otherwise have been made'.[17] Margaret Thatcher's dominion over her administrations had precisely this effect. Her pre-eminence was reciprocated in responsibility. She was held accountable for practically every social ill, economic disappointment and political setback on the grounds of her sprawling personalisation of government and her electoral strategy of going 'to the country as herself' on the basis of 'her style of doing things and her ideological intentions made as clear as could be'.[18]

After the 1983 election, the political opposition arrayed against Mrs Thatcher began to sense how this prominence could be turned to its advantage.

> If she stood head and shoulders above her contemporaries, then all faults, all miseries, all shortcomings could be laid at her door. Quite who decided to crucify her is not known, but intelligent minds saw her as the perfect material for psychological warfare. She was stubborn, inflexible, callous, uncaring, divisive, it was said, and not only by the Opposition. Such single-issue propaganda, ably and constantly directed, became the focus of the anti-Thatcher consensus of the mid-1980s, united round personal hostility rather than a doctrine.[19]

Of course, this strategy not only capitalised upon the Thatcher phenomenon of a 'highly personal and frequently arbitrary style of governing',[20] but had the effect of doubly reinforcing the public impression of Thatcher's individual command of government. Once the pattern was set, it was persistently repeated until Thatcher's centrality to government acquired the status of a self-evident fact and the point of departure for any analysis or evaluation of British government. In the introduction to his book *Misrule* (1987), Tam Dalyell made it quite clear that his criticism of British government was reducible to the figure of Margaret Thatcher.

> What this book is about is the personal behaviour on public matters of one particular Party leader and Prime Minister... . And for being 'personal' in this matter I offer no apology. Never in recent times has the highest level of British Government been run on such a personal basis.[21]

It was common for her opponents to equate government with Margaret Thatcher and, as a consequence, to project their criticism of it in purely personal terms. This habit even extended to members – or rather ex-members – of her own government. Ian Gilmour, for example, complained of 'Thatchocracy' and the 'Thatchocratic state'.[22] And when Michael Heseltine resigned from the cabinet over the Westland affair he complained of the prime minister's autocratic handling of the cabinet.

The Thatcher era was a time of easy-going constructions of British government and even of British society based upon the individual properties of Margaret Thatcher's leadership. It was also a time when, in high places and over high policy, personal attacks upon the prime minister were not merely common but habitual. Mrs Thatcher's domineering political style was widely regarded to be a political issue in its own right.[23] In October 1989, for example, the *Observer* began an editorial in the following terms.

> Mrs Thatcher's style in Downing Street is beginning to resemble the Upas Tree, a venomous Javanese bush so powerful that it destroys everything it touches. A generation of Conservative politicians – Messrs Prior, Pym, Biffen, Heseltine, Tebbit and now Lawson, to mention but a few – have all fallen victims to its poison.[24]

What is so surprising is that such indictments were in no way exceptional or out of the ordinary. They were thoroughly conventional and continually endorsed the impression of an imperious prime minister and of a politics dominated by a vocabulary of personal accusation and indictment.

It is possible to see the Thatcher premiership as some sort of aberration in British government. According to this view, Margaret Thatcher's ascribed excesses ultimately brought about her own downfall. Some saw her enforced retirement in November 1990 as a form of natural justice. Others interpreted it as the inevitable consequence of aroused countervailing political forces working their natural dynamics through the system. But what these types of explanation overlook is the question of how Margaret Thatcher was ever able to acquire and to sustain such a degree of personal influence over such an extended period in such an ostensibly collective and corporate framework of government. In challenging the political consensus, she also assaulted the general understandings surrounding what could be accommodated within the British system. Thatcher may have changed the political agenda, but in doing so she also changed the agenda of questions on British government requiring explanation. Central to these were the issues of how she secured such a leadership position and maintained it as a workable political instrument and what her tenure revealed about the deeper forces at work in British government.

It is a feature of British political analysis that such questions are almost invariably reduced to the classic dispute between cabinet government and prime ministerial government. This debate has provided the context for the study of executive power in Britain since the early 1960s. It was initiated in the main by John P. Mackintosh and Richard Crossman[25] who both asserted the existence of long-term trends that had progressively inflated the power of the prime minister and correspondingly diminished the position of the cabinet as the supreme agent of government in the British constitution. They drew attention to the growth of prime ministerial authority over the cabinet by virtue of his or her capacity to choose its members, to allocate portfolios, to alter jurisdictions, to determine the cabinet's agenda, to chair meetings, to select the subject matter and composition of cabinet committees, and to interpret and declare cabinet decisions. The prime minister had developed other overwhelming advantages. The office allowed its occupants to control government and party patronage; to have first access to the formidable network of government information, political intelligence and administrative direction embodied in the Cabinet Secretariat; to have the prior claim to speak for the government; and represent government to the public and through the mass media. The prime minister's strategic position set amidst the rising monoliths of parliamentary party machines and of a centralised civil service was thought to have provided the office with a structural pre-eminence and compelling political superiority. It was no longer feasible to expect the cabinet to deliberate and to decide upon the weighty matters of the day. It had become a panel providing political clearance and official sanction for decisions taken elsewhere. Although cabinets still provided the arena where serious disputes were raised and settled, it was no longer a governing body. In Mackintosh's view, 'the role of the cabinet and the way decisions were taken had changed and changed in a manner which left more influence and power of initiative with the prime minister'.[26] He went on to conclude that the lines of political development had undergone such changes that they had 'led contemporary British government to be described as prime ministerial rather than cabinet government'.[27]

Richard Crossman sought to press the point home in his celebrated introduction to the 1963 edition of Walter Bagehot's *The English Constitution*. He adopted Bagehot's terminology to demonstrate that the 'immense accretion of power to the prime minister'[28] was the consequence of those self-same modern conditions that had changed the cabinet from one of the 'efficient' elements of the constitution into one of its 'dignified' parts like the monarchy and the House of Lords. The change towards 'prime ministerial government'[29] had been so dramatic that Crossman felt there was no alternative but to resort to presidential allusions, in order to convey the magnitude of power that was now lodged in the prime minister's position.[30] The modern prime minister was now at 'the apex not only of a highly centralised political machine, but also of an equally centralised and vastly more powerful administrative machine'.[31] The 'voluntary totalitarianism'[32] of British society in World War II had been retained with dramatic consequences that could only be adequately conveyed through the use of the presidential analogy. 'If we mean by presidential government, government by an elective first magistrate then,' Crossman declared, 'we in England have a president as truly as the Americans'.[33]

Although Mackintosh felt that to compare the British prime minister directly to the American presidency was an overstatement, both books were responsible for disseminating the idea that prime ministerial power had become so prodigious that it could only be satisfactorily grasped by reference to some feature lying beyond the scope of the traditional framework of the British constitution. The association of the personal authority of the prime minister as the 'focal point of the modern cabinet'[34] and the evident individual stature of an American president proved too close and too appealing a linkage to ignore. In many respects, there appeared to be no other way of adequately assessing and accounting for the process by which 'British government had become more and more a matter of a prime minister governing absolutely'.[35] As a result, the comparability of the prime minister and the presidency became a regular feature of political analysis.

As the political developments originally described by Mackintosh and Crossman appeared to intensify during the 1960s and 1970s, the presidential analogy accordingly became more common. Whether it was used merely as a figure of speech or as an analytical statement, its usage appeared to be logically commensurate with the further development of governmental centralisation.

By the late 1970s, the comparison had achieved a resonance in the wider sphere of public discussion. Even James Callaghan, who cut a genial and avuncular figure amongst the general public, was accused by members of his own party and his own cabinet of diminishing parliamentary democracy and collegiate government in favour of enhancing his own personal authority within government. With such enhancement came the need for protection on the self-same grounds of personal position. James Callaghan was no exception to the habit of regarding criticism of the prime minister as an attack on him as a person and, therefore, as a direct challenge to his personal power base. In *The Secret Constitution* (1980), Brian Sedgemore observed at close hand what he described as Callaghan's tendency 'to personalise situations which should not be personalised'.[36] To illustrate the point, Sedgemore described 'Callaghan at his most brutal'[37] at a meeting of the Parliamentary Labour Party held in 1978 to discuss a proposed guillotine motion on the issue of direct elections to the EEC.

> The Leader of the House, Michael Foot, began the meeting by saying, almost in tears, that loyalty to the Prime Minister came before loyalty to party and Parliamentary democracy. Michael Foot is one of our great democrats and Parliamentarians for whom my admiration remains undiminished. I am sure he did not mean what he was implying. I only record the point to show what pressures Cabinet ministers are under and how they can reduce themselves to ashes. And then ... the Prime Minister said that he did not care how M.P.s voted at the meeting because he was going to go through with the guillotine motion whether they liked it or not. He made it absolutely clear that not only did he have the power to dissolve Parliament but also that democracy as we used to know it had to give way to government by trust in the Prime Minister based on an understanding of the brutal use to which patronage could be put.[38]

Tony Benn himself had attempted to generate interest in the presidential dimension of prime ministerial power in a controversial lecture entitled 'The Case for a Constitutional Premiership' (1979). In it, he sought to use the issue of prime ministerial power in the British system to lever open to public scrutiny the secrecy and unaccountability of Whitehall, and especially the sweeping national security powers afforded by crown prerogative to the highest level of the British executive. To Benn, the confidentiality and private coercion of government was embodied by the prime minister whose 'centralisation of power' amounted to a 'system of personal rule in the very heart of our parliamentary democracy'.[39]

The progressive enlargement of prime ministerial power was not lost either on thoughtful journalists like James Margach whose book, *The Anatomy of Power* (1979) traced the transfer of power from Westminster to the 'secret corridors of Whitehall'[40] during the twentieth century. Margach also acknowledged the recent academic debate on prime ministerial and cabinet power and, like Sedgemore, was convinced that the dispute signified a deep underlying acceleration in the distribution of political resources.

> There has been much speculation among academics who study such developments from the outside about whether prime ministers have become more presidential in style. Those whose job it has been to report at first hand contemporary events as they unfold every day in Washington and London are under no illusions. Prime ministers have in fact become more powerful than even Presidents.[41]

The modern thesis of prime ministerial power, therefore, is not new. Prompted initially by the public appeal and political style of Harold Macmillan and developed subsequently from the careers of Alec Douglas-Home, Harold Wilson, Edward Heath and James Callaghan, the issue of prime ministerial government had percolated into the attentive margins of political reflection well before Mrs Thatcher's accession to the premiership. It may not have been exactly a live political issue or a serious political debate but the question of prime ministerial power had been raised. There was an increased awareness that an alternative frame of reference was available for an understanding of the modern British executive. And there was a growing susceptibility towards regarding the American presidency not only as directly comparable to the British premiership, but as the likely end point of its development.

Colourful though these analogies and assertions were, they were for the most part neutralised into a grey conformity of three basic counterarguments which rested upon a conventional view of the British constitution. *First*, they were condemned on formal and structural grounds. These critiques were based upon the selection of criteria like institutional arrangements and party organisation which would be guaranteed to produce no substantial points of comparison whatsoever. The most obvious and overt differences between the British prime minister and the American president would be alluded to, in order to dispense with such a comparison as quickly as possible. Since the American presidency could be shown to operate in a strict separation of powers system with a national constituency, a fixed term of office and an electoral and political independence from the legislature, then the impulse was to conclude that there was little point in proceeding further in any comparison. The case for a presidential analogy, therefore, was normally dismissed at the outset.

A *second* supporting argument against such an Anglo-American comparison being made was based on the grounds of cultural prejudice and intellectual tradition. Attempts to impute the existence of another constitutional order within the British system of government, or to claim that particular prime ministers had personally transmuted the British constitution into a different entity, were seen as inflammatory allegations of an alien intrusion into the British style of politics. And what was regarded as inflammatory was normally regarded as being false as well. Furthermore, such charges suffered from the British disposition towards a conception of politics based upon historical experience and unconscious evolution. Questions on the relative power of cabinets and prime ministers, and the extent to which they conformed either to some underlying pattern of relationships or to some anchorage of constitutional principles, were not matters that sober-minded British citizens normally felt the need to dwell upon. They were usually jettisoned accordingly as abstract 'meta-questions (almost metaphysical questions)'[42] that had no place in the British study of British politics. Anthony King's comments illustrate this outlook.

> Much of the academic writing about the cabinet is woolly and confused. Some writers chase constitutional will-o'-the-wisps and others search for 'inner cabinets', like small boys searching for mealie-worms. Since they never specify in advance what an 'inner cabinet' would look like if they found one, they tend to find them everywhere or, alternatively, cannot find them at all.[43]

According to this view, it was much better simply to study what cabinets and prime ministers actually did rather than worry about what they were or what they were supposed to be. This was especially so, given the British system's mutability, in which a new prime minister could transform any previous pattern of conventions surrounding the office at a single stroke. Accordingly, generalisations were seen as being more appropriate to the United States with its written constitution and its subsequent fascination for textual meanings, constructions of intent, and interpretation of institutional forms and transcendent balances.

The *third* reason why the presidential allusion was so swiftly refuted was because it was invariably seen as a politically motivated form of criticism of the office-holder and, by extension, of the government and its policies. In the tradition of Britain's 'political constitution' in which government and law are assumed to be reducible to the content and effects of contemporary power relationships, references to a British presidency were immediately interpreted as a set of spuriously contrived attacks upon the current government's pro-gramme of policies. It was seen as a device for introducing an alternative constitutional dimension for the sole purpose of undermining the authority of the legitimate government by sleight of hand. As a result of this reaction, and of the critics' own inconsistencies and variable interest in the charge, the presidential allusion was normally demolished as simply rhetoric, or journal-istic licence, or a form of political sharp practice disguised as constitutional fiction.

All three strands of opinion were woven into the stock defences of conventional cabinet government. Harold Wilson, for example, in his book *The Governance of Britain* (1976) directly refuted the 'predominantly aca-demic verdict of overriding prime ministerial power'.[44] Such a view 'ignored the system of democratic checks and balances in parliament, in the cabinet, and not least in the party machine'.[45] Wilson clearly believed that 'academic onlookers'[46] looked too much at historical epochs and not enough at the day to day conditions of political counter-pressures. 'Constitutional rationalists'[47] failed to see that government is not static but highly mutable and responsive to the essentially human differences between different prime ministers and different sets of cabinet ministers. With this in mind, Wilson could not resist using Richard Crossman's career in Labour administrations to counter Crossman's own allegations of prime-ministerial-cum-presidential govern-ment. Whatever may have been the case in Harold Macmillan's cabinet was, in Wilson's view, not true of his own cabinet.

> For me, the classical refutation of this 1963 assertion was Richard Crossman as a minister, and his unfailing, frequently argumentative, role from 1964 to 1970 in ruthlessly examining every proposal, policy or projection put before Cabinet by departmental ministers – or by the prime minister.[48]

Contrary to Wilson's belief, by no means all academics subscribed to the thesis of prime ministerial government. Some were attentive to changes towards centralisation in British government, but still held to the basic belief that 'a prime minister was not the chief executive of government' and that 'unlike an American president, a prime minister could not make decisions by himself.'[49] The academic most scornful of the prime ministerial government argument and most active in the attempt to demolish it was George Jones. He it was who originally challenged Mackintosh's work when it was first published and he it was who continued to attack the thesis relentlessly, thereby ensuring that the 'cabinet versus prime ministerial government' argument remained a live dispute in constitutional circles. Jones argued that the 'prime minister's power had been exaggerated and that the restraints on his ascendancy were as strong as ever, and in some ways even stronger'.[50] Jones believed that for every interpretation supporting the thesis of prime ministerial dominance, there was a contrary interpretation denying the validity of such a thesis. The prime minister was not the symbol of his party in the country so much as 'the prisoner of the image of his party'.[51] Television did not help the prime minister to retain his prominence as much as it helped his opponents to become public figures and potential challengers to his position. What might appear to be an exercise of prime ministerial authority over the cabinet was in reality a demonstration of the fact that a prime minister can only be 'as strong as his party, and in particular his chief colleagues, let him be'.[52] Jones believed that many of the assertions of prime ministerial power were not only politically motivated, but were based upon a fundamental misunderstanding of political reality. It required the horse sense of a practising politician like Ian Macleod to correct such lavish misconceptions.

> Mr Macmillan set a new standard of competence in the business of forming, controlling and guiding a cabinet. It was because the whole Cabinet worked so well and so smoothly that people formed the impression of an absolute personal ascendancy, and the notion grew up that we were changing from a cabinet to a presidential system of Government. In fact the reverse was happening. Mr Macmillan by his skill, restored a great deal of vitality to the cabinet as a body.[53]

Prime ministerial or presidential government, therefore, was a fabrication of the mind, or rather of overactive minds. As an intellectual construction it failed to take account of the solid realism of internal conflict, of leadership rivals, of possible revolts and of prime ministerial consensus building.

By the time Margaret Thatcher moved into Downing Street, the arguments about cabinet government, prime ministerial power and the onset of presidentialism had become an established feature of those observers and analysts who thought about such things. In many respects it had become too established and too esoteric in the process. It was difficult to ascertain whether the respective proponents of cabinet and prime ministerial government were talking about two forms of the same phenomenon, or two reference points that between them could embrace a full range of different variants. It was argued on the one hand that cabinet government represented the base norm of the British system, and that while prime ministers may come and go the varied nature of their administrations was ultimately reducible to the limits imposed by the cabinet. On the other hand, it was asserted that individual prime ministers could and had exerted such force from the centre that it had led to a fundamental change in the balance of power within the British government. The debate went on and on, and round and round. A fatigued Anthony King provided a succinct summary of its main points. 'The two sides contend furiously (and interminably); but it is rather like the old argument about whether the bottle is half full or half empty. The evidence is there to support either contention.'[54]

It might be thought that given the evident nature of Mrs Thatcher's influence upon government, the ground rules of the debate would have changed to accommodate such an iconoclastic figure. Mrs Thatcher might have been expected to have precipitated a break with the past and to have stimulated the use of a range of more appropriate categories of analysis and evaluation that would transcend the old framework of cabinet claim and prime ministerial/presidential counterclaim.

Dramatic and controversial though Mrs Thatcher's administrations were, they did not lead to any thorough revision of perspective, or to any recognition that she may have represented some deep qualitative change in British executive power that might require different ways of looking at it and of seeking to understand it. Even though it is true that Mrs Thatcher ignited public interest over the nature and scale of her office in government, and made the British executive a live political issue, the vocabulary and concepts used in the revived debate were drawn almost exclusively from the old debate. It was as if the question of Thatcher's power slipped through a grill and fell into the old channels of dispute.

Mrs Thatcher was seen to be engaged in 'a gradual strengthening and accretion of prime ministerial influence over and against the cabinet'.[55] As a consequence she gave the impression of being 'an exponent more of presidential than of cabinet government'.[56] This view intensified and hardened during her premiership. It became thoroughly conventional to declare that Britain was 'moving towards a presidential system';[57] that the prime minister had acquired a 'quasi-presidential role'[58] in the British constitution; that her cabinet reshuffles were 'a powerful demonstration of presidential government';[59] even that the powers of the British prime minister had come to 'exceed those of an American president'.[60] George Jones himself, who had always defended the interpretation of British government as cabinet government against such fanciful neologisms as presidential style leadership, was forced to concede that Mrs Thatcher had tipped the balance from 'collective to presidential government'.[61]

The earnestness of these 'allegations' brought in their wake a set of equally forceful and equally predictable counterarguments. It led to an instinctive reiteration of the formal principle that 'government decisions in Britain are made in the name of the cabinet, in contrast to the United States where they are made in the name of the president'.[62] Others pointed out that Mrs Thatcher had been 'an imperial prime minister', but had done 'little to increase the power of her office'.[63] Writing in February 1989, Peter Jenkins came to the following conclusion.

> She has shown not the slightest interest in constitution mongering and very little in tinkering with the machinery of government. Since her re-election in June 1987 her manner of governing has become more intensely personal than ever. Yet, as far as I can judge, or discover from the people close to her, there has been no lasting development in prime ministerial government and no reason why, when she eventually goes, Cabinet government – such as it was – will not take up again where she left off. In that sense, 'Thatcherism' will have been a personal *tour de force* which will end with her.[64]

As Mrs Thatcher declined in power George Jones was revitalised and, like a revivalist preacher strengthened by temptation, fulminated against seeing Thatcher as anything other than a creature of collective cabinet government. The old faith still held. It was now clear that the office was 'like an elastic band'. Mrs Thatcher had 'stretched the elastic' and had 'established her ascendancy',[65] but her pre-eminence could not extend to the physical properties of rubber. In April 1990, Jones concluded that

> As long as her style brings success to her party it will be accepted, but if her luck runs out and she appears a liability, she will be dropped. The elastic will snap back on her.[66]

What appeared to be a visionary and prophetic statement was in reality nothing more than a fatalistic declaration of cabinet predestination. If Mrs Thatcher was a temporary aberration, then she could only be seen as such against the permanent ground rules ascribed to cabinet government, and in terms of her necessary and inevitable return to base. A comet is not a star, but it can only be confirmed as a comet when it starts to come back.

When Mrs Thatcher unexpectedly fell from power in November 1990, the presidential analogy suddenly fell with her. Even though the cabinet as a collective body was not instrumental in her dramatic downfall, the fact of her enforced resignation was taken to represent a restoration of cabinet government. This impression was strengthened by the apparently collegiate inclinations of her successor and by his explicit avowal of cabinet decision-making. As George Jones revelled in the fact that 'the elastic snapped back on her',[67] British politics appeared to return to a more 'normal' course of party politics and policy debates. In this atmosphere of practical realism, uncluttered by constitutional self-consciousness, the allusions to presidentialism seemed peculiarly inappropriate; merely part and parcel of the Thatcher *divertissement*. Given the fact that even 'cabinet government' was to many 'a term of art belonging to the textbooks of political science',[68] the notions of 'presidential government' had been quite an intolerable affront to the British way of politics.

This reaction was quite evident in many of the post-mortems of the Thatcher years, but nowhere more so than in an article by Frank Johnson suggestively entitled 'The Cabinet was in charge all along'. In it, he makes it quite clear that rule by cabinet ministers was the satisfactory norm until the early 1960s when 'something ominous happened: political scientists, a new profession, got control of the subject'.[69] Johnson has very little time for the breed.

> They persuade education ministers to give them large sums of our money in order – deep in their sinister plate-glass universities – to lock themselves into their equivalent of the laboratory, brood over their equivalent of the Bunsen burner, and conjure up clouds of hot-air and noxious gases, to the terror of the civilian population.[70]

In the early 1960s, they released the vapour of prime ministerial power. They were joined by Crossman who also 'liked things to be not as they seemed'[71] and together they popularised the idea of the prime minister possessing a presidential pre-eminence. To Johnson, the theory, for such it was, ' fell with Thatcher ... disproved by events'.[72] With the benefit of hindsight it was crystal clear to Johnson that Mrs Thatcher had been

> constantly outwitted or forced to change her mind, or go against her natural inclinations, by crafty ministers or officials.[73]

With this 'fact' solidly re-established, it is clear that Johnson hoped that normal British politics could be resumed and mischievous questions over the distribution of power at the highest levels could satisfactorily be left to the dynamic interplay of cabinet ministers. The point was not to prove or to disprove the arguments over prime ministerial power so much as to suspend them and, thereby, to prevent the needless disturbance to government and public confidence occasioned by them.

One of the chief consequences of these debates over the position of the British premiership during the Thatcher era is that both sides have tended to use the example of the American presidency, but in such a way as to undermine its value as an instrument of analysis. Those wishing to oppose the proposition that Mrs Thatcher had become 'presidential' in the style and effect of her leadership employed the presidency as a rigid frame of reference that bore little relationship to the reality of the office. The presidency in these hands became something akin to a Roman emperor or Turkish sultan – a figure of supreme authority whose personal autocracy was permanent, un-equivocal and beyond dispute. Using this gargoyle of a caricature as the fixed point of comparison, it was a simple matter to refute the analogies with presidentialism made by Mrs Thatcher's critics.

The irony here was that in defending her premiership, Mrs Thatcher's supporters then tended to define her position in terms that were in reality not dissimilar to the authentic characteristics of the modern presidency. Many of the arguments deployed to counter the assertions of a presidential prime minister were in effect arguments supporting the original allegations. Con-trary to the impression prevalent in this country, the American presidency, like the British premiership, is noted for the elasticity of its power, for its numerous constraints, for its dependence upon social conditions and political issues, for its transformation with different incumbents and for the contingent nature of its authority. Those seeking to use the presidency to rebut the charges of prime ministerial power, therefore, come perilously close to refuting their own arguments. George Jones, for example, states that Mrs Thatcher's

> dominance was not structural but political and contingent, dependent on her will, the responses of her ministerial colleagues, the issues under consideration, and the standing of the government and of herself at a particular moment.[74]

Anyone who has ever worked in the White House would wonder how this differed from the position of a president. Inaccurate though these comparisons may be, they nevertheless have the effect of reinforcing and perpetuating this country's misreading of American government. As a consequence, they help to close off many potentially valuable avenues of analysis that could be provided by a more sensitive, and realistic perspective of the modern presi-dency.

Those who supported the thesis of a presidential Margaret Thatcher tended to distort their own terms of reference. The word 'presidential' was openly used as a polemical device in the Thatcher years. The worst that could be said of Thatcher was that she had become *even* more powerful than a president. Some of this usage of the presidency as the hallmark of personal power was drawn from the anti-Americanism of the 1980s and, in particular, from President Reagan's restrictive social policies and virulent anti-commu-nism. But much of the usage of the presidential analogy came from the same misreading of American politics that afflicted those opposed to attaching the presidential label to Mrs Thatcher. Presidentialism implied supreme power and that in turn implied the potential for, and the probability of, its abuse. Presidentialism, therefore, offered the opportunity to turn policy issues and political argument into a personalised debate about the individual usage of governmental authority. The presidential analogy made governmental power and policies altogether more accessible to political argument by transforming the perspective into *her* policies, *her* power and *her* government.

This outlook introduced another characteristic into Thatcher's presidential associations and one that served to undermine still further the real comparison of the modern British premiership with the American presidency. The characteristic in question was the belief that Margaret Thatcher was so exceptional, she warranted an exceptional term like 'presidential' being attached to her. In other words, she was out of the ordinary and, therefore, required an extraordinary appellation. This understanding generated an analytical dynamic, which is still prevalent in the way Margaret Thatcher is seen and interpreted. The dynamic runs as follows. First, Margaret Thatcher's formidable personality is viewed as having infused government with a particular style and approach. Second, the government (1979-1990) is then seen as having been her government, in which its major features were reduced to the personalised leadership of Margaret Thatcher. Third, Thatcher is subsequently converted into 'a force, an elemental force of nature'[75] and, thereby, into a wholly idiosyncratic figure in British political history. Lastly, as she is seen as having been a phenomenon in her own right and entire to herself, she acquires a status that is not directly comparable to any other prime minister. Hers becomes an exceptional and unrepeatable administration that does not offer any grounds for generalisation. With the establishment of this outlook, there is an increased disposition to taking the first step in the cycle of seeing Thatcher as a formidable personality in government and then proceeding again through the remaining three stages.

The circular dynamic tightens with time and usage. As Margaret Thatcher is elevated into a personal phenomenon unrepresentative of anything other than herself and her government, then her departure is seen as marking both the abandonment of the presidential government allegation and the consequent reinstatement of cabinet government. Even if the allegation could ever be proved true, therefore, Thatcher's fall from government rendered it meaningless as an instrument of analysis. Nothing could be drawn from it since it had been based wholly on the notion of the abnormality of Thatcher's leadership. Similar to the idea of being 'King for a day', Mrs Thatcher could be dismissed as having been a 'president for a decade'. When she returned home to Dulwich, it was assumed that British government had returned to normal, leaving presidentialism in British politics as a freakish idea connected to a freakish woman in freakish times.

It can be seen both from the general debate over prime ministerial power and from the enriched dispute over Mrs Thatcher's power that in their different ways the various proponents and opponents of the presidential analogy in British politics have threatened to devalue, and to dismiss the relevance of, presidentialism in Britain. The highly inaccurate and even distorted view of the American presidency combined with the gross misuse of the term for political purposes risks a state of affairs in which every feature associated with the presidential analogy will be wantonly discarded as devoid of useful analytical content.

The purpose of this book is firstly to arrest this trivialisation of the presidency before the point of comparison becomes completely discredited, and secondly to channel the interpretive and explanatory properties of the comparison into an altogether more productive sphere. The aim is not to reverse the passage of time and return to the original assertions of Mackintosh and Crossman. Still less is it an attempt to participate in the misleading and sterile arguments of the 'cabinet government versus prime ministerial government' debate. It is a demonstration that when the presidential analogy is correctly used, especially in relation to the development of the contemporary presidency, it can provide a very promising set of perspectives on the development of British government since the late 1970s. It can throw fresh light on the nature of the prime minister's position not only in general terms, but also in relation to the new opportunities for leadership that have been generated in recent times. Correctly used, the presidential analogy can open up fields of discovery rather than close them down.

This study is an invitation to pause for thought – to interpose a period of careful reflection between the point when the presidential allusion is raised and the point when it is subjected to its customary rejection or grotesque misrepresentation. The need for consideration is based on the premise that the various references to presidential power and politics are altogether too lightly dismissed. In refuting what are all too often seen as 'allegations', there is insufficient attention given to what is being discarded or misused. The desire to reject the usefulness of the presidential proposition raises serious doubts as to what insights, perspectives and interpretive possibilities are being needlessly jeopardised by sheer carelessness or cultural prejudice.

The claim here is that the presidential allusion has a deeper significance than is normally recognised. It can, for example, lead to an improved understanding of both the American presidency and the British premiership and, in particular, of those new conditions and forces which now make the analogy so much more apposite than it once was. Correctly employed, the presidential allusion not only permits but encourages the use of the analytical perspectives associated with the presidency to gain a deeper insight into the contemporary nature of prime ministerial power. Furthermore, the presidential analogy alerts us to the possibility of general trends in the underlying properties of political leadership and to the existence of new resources and strategies of leadership that may well signify deep and comparable changes in two, ostensibly different, political systems. In sum, the presidential analogy can generate a rich mixture of concepts and approaches which can provide a variety of ways of comprehending the underlying position of both the president and prime minister – and of understanding the real nature of the links between them.

The study does not seek to deny the magnitude or the significance of the structural differences between the American and British systems. On the other hand, it does challenge the view that because these differences exist they constitute a sufficient reason in themselves for abandoning any analytical insights that might be drawn from a comparison between the White House and Number 10 Downing Street. Given that the British grasp of the American presidency is so poor, it is even more important to challenge this view of incomparability. At present, British analogies with the presidency are normally based on an 'inside-out' view of the American executive. This is a perspective which relies upon the projection of indigenous preconceptions and convictions about American government onto the office of the presidency. A basic requirement, therefore, is an 'outside-in' view of the presidency that can correct many of the misconceptions associated with the office and clear the ground for a more sensitive and productive set of comparisons that not only acknowledge the real differences, but recognise the real similarities between the two positions.

By developing a more discriminating view of the presidency, it is possible to prevent the erosion of serious thinking about the British premiership that has been one of the effects of John Major replacing Mrs Thatcher as prime minister. There is a danger that the insights afforded by the Thatcher years will be lost through the simple means of a new leader who is, by definition, considered different in every possible respect and who, therefore, invalidates every generalisation and conclusion drawn from the Thatcher era.

To many, the political issue of prime ministerial power was satisfactorily resolved by Mrs Thatcher's removal from office. But the nature of that power and what it revealed about British government is, as a result, also in danger of being swept aside by the novelty of John Major. It is important not to personalise the analysis of personalisation to this extent. Such a short-sighted attitude can lead us to overlook the degree to which Mrs Thatcher altered the content and evaluation of political leadership in this country. It would be premature to dismiss these changes as limited solely to the figure of Mrs Thatcher. It is one thing to acknowledge Mrs Thatcher's personal pre-eminence in government; it is quite another to claim as a consequence that it was in some way unexaminable or not susceptible to any general categories of explanation. This assumption can all too often lead to a damaging tautology in which personal leadership is not reduced to general scrutiny because it is regarded as individual in nature; and that because it is not subjected to structural examination, the leadership in question is thereby assumed to be self-evidently personal and transient in nature.

An informed understanding of the United States presidency can break this circle and reveal the true significance of leadership to general conditions of political activity and development. By employing perspectives drawn from the American presidency, it is possible to show that prime ministerial leadership has undergone changes since the late 1970s of such profundity that they amount to a qualitative shift in the type of leadership that is now viable in the British system of government. These changes have been due partly to the effect of Thatcher's long tenure of office as a conditioning agent and guiding precedent for future leaders. But the changes have deeper roots than these. The significance of Mrs Thatcher's premiership lies more in the way that it brought to the surface new and fundamental sources of leadership that had previously been associated with the American presidency, but which have since been shown to be not limited to that office.

The contention is that Mrs Thatcher's period in office marked the presence of motive forces, structural dynamics and required strategies which are now central to leadership in Britain and which are far deeper in substance than the personality and temporary circumstances of one incumbency. In effect, Thatcher's premiership was probably less significant for its personal idiosyncrasy and more noteworthy as a visible outlet and register of a set of underlying and previously concealed dynamics. The usefulness of the United States presidency is that, when it is properly understood, it can help to illuminate and explain the nature of these underlying forces and deep-set changes in the character of the British political system that helped give rise to such prominent leadership.

The properties and concepts associated with the presidency reveal deeper foundations to the presidential analogy in Britain and deeper reasons for taking the comparison seriously. Personal leadership is now a feature of, and an issue in, British politics and it is very likely to remain so. The explanatory potential of the Thatcher period of leadership should be considered very carefully before it is designated as dated and consequently lost to serious contemporary consideration. By understanding what Mrs Thatcher was responding to, how she exploited the opportunities afforded to her, and how she changed the character of leadership around her, it will be possible to comprehend not just her premiership but the personalised styles of such leaders as Neil Kinnock, David Owen, Paddy Ashdown, Michael Heseltine and John Major. The contention is that the old conventions of prime ministerial leadership have not only been stretched out of recognition, but that if the insights afforded by the presidential analogy continue to be overlooked, these changes will remain unobserved and unacknowledged.

The intention of this study is to reveal the nature and extent of those changes to both the conditions and expectations of political leadership in Britain that have made the prime minister's position amenable to presidential terms of description. My objective is not to pursue every allusion to presidential politics made by British commentators. Many of these references are superficial, eclectic, trivial and even spurious in character. The objective is rather to disclose those deep-set and barely discernible changes in British politics that provide the conditions for the many impulsive and popular references to a presidential form of political leadership.

In order to achieve this aim, it will be necessary to examine and to appraise the fundamental characteristics of the presidency in the United States, along with the subtle changes experienced in the nature and style of presidential politics over the past quarter century. It is only by understanding the inner properties of the contemporary presidency and by assimilating the analytical perspectives generated by the office, that it becomes possible to grasp the scale and significance of the recent changes to political leadership in Britain. In this way, the presidential analogy opens up the prospect of being able to track the underlying trends in the forms and substance of political leadership, and to establish the existence of new resources and strategies of leadership. Together, they represent such a profound transformation of the structure of British politics that it amounts to far more than an analogy of the American presidency; it represents nothing less than the emergence of a British presidency.

CHAPTER 2

Outsiders and spatial leadership in modern American politics

In order to understand the real points of comparison between the American presidency and the British premiership, it is necessary to look away from those features that are usually employed to characterise political systems. Comparisons normally dwell upon such factors as institutional structures, operational procedures, relationships between the constituent parts of governmental systems, and established conceptions of authority, control and consent. Nevertheless, it is often more revealing to examine the less explicit and often obscure elements of government which provide evidence of underlying forces at work within a political system. It is these deeper developments which not only provide insights into the American presidency, but also into the development of the British prime minister's office. In this way the American presidency can be used as a lever to open up some of the less visible, but arguably more important, properties and dynamics of the British premiership. In doing so, it will become clear that a number of features central to the American presidency are now shared by the premiership in this country. These features are highly significant, for they can illustrate the scale and substance of the changes occurring behind the apparently imperturbable edifice of British cabinet government. They can also draw attention to the full implications of such changes and, in particular, to the way that *de facto* presidential politics has been altering British perspectives of parties and elections and British evaluations of public authority and political performance.

The first feature of modern presidential politics in the United States to be considered is the practice of what can be called 'spatial leadership'. This refers to the way that recent presidents have sought to enhance their position in Washington by creating as much distance between it and the presidency. Physical distance and political distance become synonymous with one another in this form of leadership. The strategy allows a president to remain an integral and even a central part of government, whilst at the same time affording him

24

the opportunity of detaching himself from government and, thereby, relinquishing responsibility for much of what it does. Paradoxically, it might even be said that this sort of spatial detachment has become one of the most effective ways for a president to maintain his central position in government.

It is often remarked that Ronald Reagan began his term of office with the declaration that 'Government is not the solution to our problems. Government is the problem.'[1] What is overlooked is the fact that he was still convincingly claiming this to be true eight years later, and without a hint of self-contradiction. President Reagan exploited to the full those opportunities that had grown up over the previous 25 years for leadership to become detached from government. Reagan revealed the extent to which it had become possible to open up space between the presidency and the branch of executive government over which he was expected to preside. He managed to retain and to develop throughout his two full terms of office the role of outsider that he had so assiduously cultivated as a candidate before his election. The extent of his popularity at the end of his administration represented a triumphant affirmation not merely of Reagan himself, but of the extraordinary potential of a leadership style that was at one and the same time both self-denying and self-promoting in nature.

Spatial leadership is quite alien to the traditional conception of leadership in the modern presidency – a form of leadership that made the presidency into the formidable office it is still reputed to be. The central theme of the 'modern presidency' has traditionally been one of inspired leadership forcefully and skilfully imposing itself upon a congenitally fragmented system of entrenched interests, political enclaves and dispersed authority. The character of presidential activism has been dominated by the simple imperative of a need being met. It was Franklin Roosevelt's New Deal programme in the 1930s and his leadership in World War II that set the precedent that subsequently provided the standard upon which succeeding presidents would be judged. After Roosevelt, it was not merely a hope that presidents would counteract the dissonance of America's government and provide a central form of public purpose. It was an expectation.

The structure and role of the presidency became progressively institutionalised in the period following Roosevelt's term of office. The American system became dependent upon the presidency for direction, coordination, decisiveness and a sense of national vision. It was widely recognised that 'the contributions that a president could make to government were indispensable'.[2] In Thomas Cronin's words,

> only the president could be the genuine architect of U.S. public policy, and only he, by attacking problems frontally and aggressively and by interpreting his

power expansively, could slay the dragon of crisis and be the engine of change to move this nation forward.[3]

As a result, the modern presidency was acknowledged to be '*the* strategic catalyst for progress in the American system'.[4] In this guise, the presidency was America's 'instrument of twentieth century government'[5] – an instrument that had facilitated the full and irreversible establishment of both the 'positive state' and the 'national security state' in the ostensibly anti-statist culture of the American republic. The presidency was the chief promoter, beneficiary and trustee of both these modern developments. It was the president's responsibility to attend to the open-ended nature of governmental commitments, to be an agent of adaptation to new conditions and to make the best of the government's potential for concerted action at home and abroad. If the United States still did not have the coherence of a party government, or the anchorage of a formal centre, then at least it had a workable alternative to both. Commentators referred instinctively to the existence of 'presidential government' and to the fact that 'in presidential government Americans had established one of the most powerful institutions in the free world'.[6] Accordingly, the presidency came to be considered 'the nearest thing to a concrete embodiment of the state'[7] in the scheme of American politics.

The motivating idea of the modern presidency was that of maximising power in order to take *on* the government, and wherever possible to take *over* the government; even at times to be the government. The presidency had grown into such a functional necessity in modern American government, it had become indistinguishable from it. Executive activism and presidential self-promotion were accepted as being mutually inclusive and as being minimal requirements in a governmental system otherwise disposed to disarray and immobilism. The presidency was permeated by a morality of power that would save the American system from its own prodigious self-restraint. The means to power were legitimated firstly by the fact of its acquisition in a system of limited powers, and secondly by the contemporary presumption that presidential power was intrinsically beneficial to the citizenry. These developments and these beliefs led to the presidency's occupation of an exclusive dimension in American society. Presidents increasingly claimed, and the American public increasingly affirmed, the office to be an extraordinary 'agency of popular representation',[8] the 'democratic symbol of national unity, and the necessary instrument of national action'.[9] The growth of government programmes and bureaucratic structures provided physical evidence of the success that past presidents had had in evoking the interest of the public and the nation. Moreover, it was widely assumed that future presidents would look upon this inheritance as the basis for further government action and additional social improvement.

Since the end of the 1960s, this pattern of presidential hegemony over American government and its accompanying ethos of executive authority and social benefit has undergone a profound change. In one sense, the notion of presidential government had always been something of an illusion – albeit a very powerful and functionally productive one. By the late 1960s and early 1970s, however, it was becoming clear that the federal government and its budget was becoming a political problem in its own right. Instead of regulating and resolving society's ills through rational planning and efficient administration, the federal government began to re-awaken America's traditional anxieties over the bias, waste and injustice of state action. As government programmes, budgets and taxes multiplied, the presidency began to look less like a beneficent magistrate and more like the sorcerer's apprentice, overwhelmed by the self-perpetuating and self-replicating properties of government activity. The problem of public expenditure may have been acknowledged, but the political arguments and forces favouring further expansion were usually so compelling that entitlements, benefits and subsidies proceeded apace. Given that the United States was also committed to a highly expensive war in South East Asia, the net effect of this guns and butter policy was an inflationary syndrome of increased government expenditure unmatched by larger revenues or by greater economic growth.

Even with the wars in Vietnam and Cambodia at an end, the upward pressures on the federal budget were immense. Furthermore, they were accompanied by a pronounced cultural reaction against what were now seen to be the excesses of social reform and innovation that had been introduced through President Kennedy's New Frontier programme and President Johnson's Great Society programme. The Great Society, in particular, exemplified to many Americans the perils of redistributive and egalitarian legislation. According to popular opinion, it led to more government and to worse government. It led not to the alleviation of social problems but to their exacerbation, and through it, to a deterioration in the social conditions of all. Just as Vietnam became known as a liberal war, and especially as Johnson's war, so the violent disruption inside the United States became known as Johnson's society. Rightfully or not, crime, pornography, drug abuse, racial conflict, campus revolts, street demonstrations and political assassination all became associated with liberal reform brought about by the exercise of presidential power. Although the dislocation of American society prompted the election of a Republican administration, it did not resolve the underlying problem of a political economy susceptible to inflation through the stimulus of entrenched public spending by government. With the onset of an economic recession in 1973-4, the stock of the federal government fell even further and the basic pattern was set for the next two decades. Presidential candidates, committed to exercising control over the government by balancing the budget, were confronted in the White House with 'uncontrollable' government expenditures, irreversible contractual obligations, statutory commitments, rising entitlements, integral cost of living adjustments and growing financial deficits – all set in a context of the United States's relative decline as an industrial, commercial, financial and military power.[10]

The upward thrust of government expansion was accompanied by an equally fierce down-draught of forces limiting the presidency's scope for action. The reputation of the federal government changed from that of an instrument of progress into a burden of unmanageable complexity dominated by self-serving bureaucratic interests. The chief challenge confronting presidents became one of restraining and controlling government, rather than using its powers in any innovative and creative way. But even this challenge was seen as being insurmountable because at the same time that government was growing, the structures of political authority capable of subjecting it to concerted direction were breaking down. The supportive struts of presidential centralism were being eroded away. Parties, for example, were in an advanced state of internal decomposition. The rise of primary elections allowing interested members of the public to recruit party leaders, the onset of new campaign finance laws that channelled money directly to candidates, and the lack of continuity in the ranks of party officials and workers were all leading to the decline of parties as national organisations.[11]

Their plight was made worse by the increased volatility in the public's voting behaviour. The large electoral blocs, that had afforded such a powerful base for public mobilisation and government action during the New Deal era, were being disrupted by lower electoral turnouts, by more discriminatory voting behaviour like ticket-splitting and by an enhanced electoral pluralism featuring candidate-based campaigns with widely differing combinations of issue concerns.[12] The 'New Deal coalition' that had made the Democrats into the natural party of government for a generation experienced the full weight of these disintegrative forces. The south was no longer as solid as a Democrat stronghold, the labour unions were losing their members and their ability to deliver strategic groups of votes, and the farmers had relinquished their basic attachment to the party that had rescued them from the Great Depression. Although blacks and members of ethnic minorities remained faithful Democrats, they tended to deepen the party's popular image of impulsive national radicalism which was not to the benefit of the general public.[13]

In an era when the New Deal's bequest was being widely discredited, the capacity of any Democrat president to assemble both a winning electoral coalition and an effective governing coalition was very limited. New issues like environmental protection, abortion, women's rights, drug abuse and energy costs together with new ideological interest groups cut across and further disoriented old party divisions and voting loyalties. As a result, anything resembling the old New Deal coalition had become a practical impossibility. The point was that while one coalition had effectively collapsed, there was no sense in which it had been replaced by another under either Republican or Democratic party colours. Moreover, there was no prospect that an electoral assemblage comparable in organisation and durability to the old New Deal coalition would ever be viable in the new fluidity of American politics. Presidents simply had to work with multiplying centres of power, with rapidly changing agendas of issues, with surges of 'dealigned' and independent voters, and with improvised techniques of matching candidate-centred products to current electoral markets.[14] The United States Congress followed the same pattern of fragmentation. Congress had always been an institution noted for its lack of corporate identity, broken as it was into a host of semi-autonomous committees. Nevertheless, its conventions had supported an internal hierarchy of status which provided sets of leaders who could be highly influential in the coalitional nature of Congressional politics. Presidents could negotiate effectively with Congress by reaching accommodations with key party leaders and committee chairmen. Over the 1960s and 1970s, this informal oligarchy gave way to a far more undisciplined and decentralised style of Congressional decision-making. Members of Congress became more constituency oriented, better informed and more independent. Power in both chambers was redistributed more widely through a range of committee reforms and procedural changes. Committees were broken down into powerful sub-committees where even freshmen members could become chairpersons and use their panels to publicise issues and to promote their political reputations both inside the chamber, but importantly, outside Washington as well.[15]

As Congress became more unpredictable, growing numbers of professional lobbyists swarmed into the corridors of the Capitol building. And as members of Congress became ever more hard-pressed for money to finance their expensive candidate-centred re-election drives, 'political action committees' competed with one another to press their campaign contributions upon hungry Congressmen and Senators. The net effect of all these developments was that members not only had the institutional opportunities, the professional facilities and financial backing to become political activists and policy entrepreneurs, they also had the constituency and electoral motivations to break down Congressional hierarchies and to arouse personal followings of supporters in their home bases. The independence and assertiveness of members was now no longer confined merely to resisting the chief executive and his legitimate lieutenants. It extended to the point of outright confrontation. Congress went so far as to challenge the presidency in what had been the most revered field of executive primacy – i.e. foreign policy. It even sought to establish itself as a senior policy-making partner, in such sensitive areas as national security, intelligence operations, and military policy. This lack of inhibition typified the new Congress and the new political attitudes that supported it. It was now good local politics for members of Congress to exercise their rights of legislative participation, even if it meant that Congress as a whole was in danger of becoming unmanageable.

All these disabling conditions served to undermine the centrality of the presidency and nowhere was this more evident than in the chief executive's relationship with the federal government. Because the political resources available to a president had become so scattered and diffuse, it was difficult to draw a sufficient amount together to confront the bureaucracy with an agenda of new priorities. When the government itself was so fragmented in form and so mercurial in nature, it was hard enough even to locate its presence – let alone to catch it and direct its operations.

This ethereal quality of the federal government was partly a result of its grand scale and poor organisation. But it was also due to its extensive connections to outside interests and to those specialised committees in Congress, which authorised the statutory responsibilities of executive agencies and funded their activities. Commentators drew attention to the intense interactions and collective self-interest of these combinations of executive agencies, Congressional committees and political interest groups. It was widely suggested that these triangular relationships represented forms of private self-government within the main body of the federal bureaucracy.[16] Because they had access to formidable reserves of political, economic and electoral resources, they were able to evade efforts at central control and to preserve their influence inside government. Whether or not Theodore Lowi is correct in claiming that past liberal reform did not so much exercise power as parcel it out to special interests,[17] the fact remains that private interests had achieved so much penetration into government that it was difficult to differentiate the private sector from the public sector.

These 'issue networks' which had insinuated their way into the fabric of government exemplified the central problem confronting presidents in their task of presiding over the executive branch of government. In essence, it was that by highlighting government itself as a challenge and by dramatising their credentials to meet that challenge, presidential candidates raised expectations that could not be fulfilled for a host of political, economic, international and structural reasons. Nothing underlined the chronic nature of the problems facing the American political system more emphatically than the onset of a sustained period of 'divided government' in Washington. The Republican party regularly won presidential elections, but never enough Congressional seats to dislodge the solid Democratic majorities on Capitol Hill. This electoral disjunction was the inevitable outcome of the party system's decomposition. Even as early as 1968, a quarter of voters were 'splitting their tickets' by voting for different parties in presidential and Congressional elections. The result was a pattern of divided control which gave 'each branch of government an electoral incentive to work for the failure of the branch held by the other (party)'.[18]

The failures incurred in Washington further decreased public trust in government and further increased the public's cynicism towards the political process. Presidents were left to explain that in a system of shared and divided powers, they were only one centre of influence. But they were also the most publicised and the most prominent centre and, as such, their failures were the most conspicuous and the most damning. They in effect drew attention to the one problem they could not resolve and, in doing so, they not only underlined the subsequent failure to realise their own performance standards, but deepened the public's consciousness of the issue of government management.

Government now crippled presidencies instead of invigorating them.[19] Presidents were deemed to be in a 'no-win' situation.[20] They were expected to do more and more, but they were not afforded the authority commensurate with the job at hand. Failure was practically assured, intensifying the 'crisis of competence' in American government and generating ever more fervent cries for political leadership. The presidency had become 'impossible because the gap between public illusions and reality as well as between expectations and performance was so massive that no one could bridge it any longer'.[21] According to this view, presidential government had become a nullity because the problems of government were intractable, the interests served by government were unassailable, the political structures capable of exerting control were lying broken in pieces, and the public's interest in political issues was narrow, unstable and unpredictable. Presidents were confronted by a range of prodigious difficulties, but none seemed more chronic than the uncomfortable proposition that government itself had become ungovernable.

It was during this period that presidents first began to turn the vice of multiple weakness into the virtue of a single strength. In being forced to 'go public' as the only practicable method of overcoming the frustrations of office and to bring pressure to bear on their opponents in Washington, presidents came to appreciate the implicit advantages of spatial leadership. They assiduously sought to cultivate the outsider image over and against a Washington portrayed – by the presidency's own insistence upon distance – as an unresponsive fortress of insider exclusiveness and privilege.

Presidents built upon the constitution's prima facie separation of the chief executive as a single entity distinct from the institutionalised nature of the rest of the federal government. They also capitalised upon America's ever available tradition of popular sovereignty which emphasises the primacy of a participant political culture, arouses a concomitant suspicion of government, and translates democracy primarily into a device for preventing the abuse of power. Furthermore, presidents were able to use the very prominence of their public position to attract attention to themselves as outsiders whenever it was in their interests to convey this impression.

The strategy of spatial leadership was not used then and has not been used since as simply a new way to achieve an old goal. It is not deployed to achieve – by means of innovative ways of engaging public support – the modern presidency's traditional objective of executive dominion. On the contrary, it is an overtly self-denying form of leadership that uses the public to maintain a distance between the presidency and 'the government'. As a result, spatial leadership helps to generate an imagery of government that is differentiated from the public. It transforms 'government' into a populist issue that in its turn can protect the presidency from Washington and even from the consequences of a president's own actions.

As presidents engage in such a strategy, they will no doubt have become aware of the marvellously self-fulfilling and self-perpetuating properties to such 'outsiderdom'. For example, in resorting to public assistance which – according to the precepts of the modern presidency, no chief executive would need to do without good reason or wish to do through choice – a president can verify his own case of government unresponsiveness. He can do so by casting himself in an outsider role and implying that he had been coerced into such a position by the conditions encountered in Washington. There again, by distancing himself from Washington, a president can use his public position to portray the rest of government as an undifferentiated bloc of undemocratic power, and the rightful object of popular prejudice. By creating space between his position of central leadership and the other political and institutional components of Washington, a president can also provide himself with the very defeats required to prove his outsider status and to substantiate the claims of an intractable government. Lastly, by encouraging a temperamental reaction against 'governmental power' *per se*, a president can increase the security of his political position as a focal point of insurgency and popular disenchantment. At the same time, he can avoid responsibility for government, and retain a political licence to exploit his outsider status, as an embodiment of popular insurgency, to challenge further the legitimacy of 'the government'.

Despite its evident attractions, this sort of leadership is a politically difficult and even a dangerous game to play. It is in essence a device for running with both the hare and the hounds. While political defeats can be an effective way of generating public sympathy for a president's construction of reality in Washington, he runs the risk of associating detachment with weakness or incompetence. Defeats have to be chosen with care, in order to ride the wave of such self-inflicted populism. What is significant is that the incentives and opportunities for such leadership clearly exist and are regularly tapped by besieged presidents. They provide welcome means to maintain the chief source of presidential authority – namely the electoral process during which a president's original appeal was formed. Most contemporary presidents start as outsiders in a pack of party hopefuls. They are seen to win the nomination against the odds by a series of public appeals and, subsequently, to secure the presidency in an extended campaign outside Washington and against Washington. Spatial leadership, therefore, becomes a way of retaining in government – albeit in diminished form – the drama of popular acclamation that accompanied the original elevation of inexperience and public contact to the presidential office.

Richard Nixon was probably the first president to secure the possible benefits of such self-generated disengagement. His belief in being an outsider led him to identify his presidency with what he called the 'silent majority' – i.e. those whom he thought shared his resentments against the 'liberal establishment' in Washington. Through this device, Nixon wanted to appeal to those who were *not* vociferous and militant minorities and who were *not* publicly critical of American values and commitments. Nixon surmised that there was a vast untapped source of forgotten people who could be encouraged to see Nixon as one of their own. He hoped to arouse a populist movement, centred on 'middle America', that would accept Nixon as its natural leader and support him in a patriotic confrontation against the critics and innovators that appeared to occupy the commanding heights of Washington.[22]

In particular, Nixon targeted what had become known as the 'new class'. It typified the power structure he was pledged to oppose. The class was composed of those intellectuals and professionals who had flocked to Washington during the 1960s, intent upon demonstrating that there were rational and administrative solutions to social problems. As a consequence, their careers and professional self-interest were thought to have became firmly wedded to the state. According to Irving Kristol, these 'bright young aggressive people from universities, whose job it was to dream up programmes which no one had ever thought of before', were motivated by a desire to 'shift power or influence away from the private sector and towards the government ... [and] a highly regulated society.'[23] They were reputed to have built up a formidable network of influence, connected as they were to the various client groups who were dependent upon social welfare programmes. They were also assumed to have allies in universities, foundations and the media, who were similarly

sceptical of America's traditional capitalist ethos and who were similarly supportive of the need for a high level of protection for the poor and oppressed. Nixon felt
that this professionalisation of social concern had generated an elitist bureaucracy
dependent upon increasing government expenditures. It had also produced a
bureaucratic establishment that was contemptuous of the middle class whose
productive enterprise and taxation dollars funded the new class's provocative
programmes.[24]

Although Nixon had touched upon a rich vein of popular resentment, he
was not really the person to mobilise and translate it into a movement. His
background in the black arts of anti-communist witchcraft during the late
1940s, and his reputation as an aggressive and unscrupulous politician since
that time, had always cast a shadow over his credentials for leadership. After
losing both the 1960 presidential election and the 1962 election for the gover-
norship of California, Nixon retreated into private life and was said to have
undergone a metamorphosis during these wilderness years. A key debate in
1968 was whether there was in fact a new Nixon or not.[25] In the end, either
enough people believed the change to be genuine, or were indifferent towards
the dispute for Nixon to be elected president.

Nixon won the presidency but he had not won the silent majority. He
only scraped into office with 43% of the national vote. This was the lowest
proportion of the vote to be acquired by a winning candidate since 1912. To
make matters worse, Nixon became the first president since 1848 to enter the
White House without a Congress controlled by his own party. Large numbers
of voters were hedging their bets by opting for a Republican president but
balancing it with a Democratic Congress. Furthermore, Nixon's level of public
approval was significantly lower than the norm for incoming presidents. The
politician who won the presidency under the banner of the ordinary men's
champion had to adjust to the fact that he was not held in great affection or
trust by the silent majority.[26]

Nixon's period of office was characterised by frustration. Much of this
was caused by the fact that he was a radical in a minority party surrounded
by entrenched political interests. Nixon felt himself to be an outsider not
just politically but by birth and background and by personality and temperament.

> Nixon the politician ... concealed Nixon the man and the man was, even to some
> of his close friends, an unbelievably complex, shy, remote and tense figure
> whose iron control seldom permitted anyone to glimpse the tumult inside. He
> was also a man cursed to live without the appearance of charm. ... At the root of
> this incapacity was his loneliness, and the loneliness was partly an inheritance of
> birth in a poor and undistinguished family, partly his environment as a poor
> boy, partly the harsh way politics had dealt with him. Having never attached

himself to powerful causes, he lacked the political intimacies and camaraderies that so often joined politicians in common undertakings.[27]

It was difficult for Nixon to be a champion of the middle class outsiders of America if he could not communicate with them. It was even more difficult when it became clear that Nixon's main objective was to gain admittance to Washington's 'inside'. Nixon had grown up with the modern presidency. He had observed the office at close quarters as vice-president in the 1950s. He remained a zealous defender of vigorous presidential leadership and its role in purposefully directing the nation. He now wished to claim his Rooseveltian inheritance. But times had changed. Nixon's personality seemed quite unable to cope with the fact that presidential power, which had always been provisional in nature, was now highly contentious and more dependent than ever upon the skills and subtlety of the man in the White House. Nixon's political frustrations, together with his propensity for self-pity and for feeling the subject of unwarranted victimisation, led him to resort more to private means to confront government. He found the 'silent majority' too shapeless and self-limiting a weapon to use effectively in his drive to make government come to heel.

As the Nixon administration became increasingly insular and ingrown, its resentments and aggression also became more conspicuous. Nixon's relationship with the media – his lifeline to what fashionable Washingtonians referred to disdainfully as 'out there' – suffered accordingly. To the Nixon White House, the media were not merely uncooperative in their manner, they were the leading element of the resistance movement confronting the government itself. As Pat Buchanan, one of Nixon's White House staff, explained,

> This hasn't been our town. They live in Georgetown, with their parties; they never invited us, they ignored us. We were the vanguard of Middle America and they were the liberal elite. It's a schism that's cultural, political, social, emotional. When we came in in 1968, they dominated all American society – the media, the Supreme Court, the bureaucracy, the foundations. They left us with our cities burning, and inflation going, our students rioting on the campus. And Nixon challenged all this.[28]

The Nixon team operated on the premise that there was a 'countergovernment' at work in American society and that its purpose was 'clearly aimed at the destruction of our traditional institutions' which it 'could not hope to eliminate through the elective process'.[29] This subversion justified exceptional forms of 'hardball' infighting. Tragically for Nixon, soon after winning the 1972 presidential election over the archetype of the 'new class' (George McGovern), his authority crumbled away in the Watergate scandal. His proposed campaign against government was undermined by charges that he had himself already usurped and corrupted government. Nixon's remoteness as a figure left his supporters surviving on the belief in his good faith, but as one revelation of duplicity and intrigue followed another, Nixon finally lost the respect of his silent constituency. He had lost touch with his public, and ultimately, betrayed them by being seen to be at the epicentre of 'Washington corruption'.[30] To the silent majority, Nixon had reached the heights of high government and the depths of depravity in the 'imperial presidency' – positionally and morally he was not one of them after all.

Nixon's excesses ultimately brought Jimmy Carter to Washington. Carter's whole campaign had been based on the proposition that he could provide a moral antidote to the power politics and duplicitous statecraft that had discredited Nixon's administration. To Carter, the answer to the 'imperial presidency' was to elect an individual so totally divorced from Washington that he could be regarded as its personal antithesis. On the basis of background, character and experience, Carter presented himself as the ideal candidate to correct America's disenchantment with itself and its government. Carter relished and cultivated the role of outsider. He would revive and redeem American government. To a secure and confident figure like Carter, being an outsider was a virtue and a mark of distinction to be exploited to the maximum political effect.

In many respects, Carter's attachment to the role of outsider was dictated to him by the circumstances of his elevation. He had begun his campaign as ex-Governor of Georgia, with no experience of Washington, no real links with the major elements of the Democratic party and no opportunity to impress the party cadres in any national arena. As a consequence, it is true to say that 'Jimmy Carter could only have won the Democratic Party's nomination and the ensuing general election by pursuing as he did the strategy of an "outsider".'[31] In a brilliant primary election campaign that was a model exercise in how an obscure politician could use the new channels of public participation and impose himself upon the national party, Carter defeated his more illustrious rival for the nomination. His direct appeal to the rank and file was based upon a visceral attack upon Washington and the need for the 'chasm between the people and government to be bridged'.[32] Carter openly deployed his outsider status to lend weight to his concept of an isolated and unresponsive government in Washington. Public confidence in the integrity and competence of government could only be renewed by wide-ranging reforms, through which the public might penetrate the edifice of a private state. In Carter's words:

> The natural opposition of special interests, selfish bureaucrats, and hidebound elected officials must be overcome. This is not so difficult as it might seem.

> These opponents simply cannot prevail against the truth and an aroused and
> determined public. I have often seen them retreat into their dark corners when
> exposed to public scrutiny and debate.[33]

This was an effective message and a successful electoral strategy. But it was
more than this. To Carter, the veracity of the message was reaffirmed by the
manner of his own rise to office. His self-image of a morally scrupulous
outsider acting as an agent of the people against its own government was
vindicated in his eyes by his popular passage to the White House against all
the odds.

The odds had indeed been considerable. Carter had no experience of the
federal government or of international affairs. He was even an outsider in his
own party. He depicted himself as someone outside the normally expedient
character of American politics and, in particular, outside the wheeler-dealer
character of Congressional decision-making. Furthermore, he was from the
South – America's outsider region. This was the area of the United States
traditionally most hostile to the federal government and traditionally the
subject of prejudice and ridicule from other parts of the union. Being a
Southerner had long been thought to be a disqualification for the White
House. Carter had overcome this disadvantage, but he was well aware of the
disparagement that remained.

> The local cartoonists had a field day characterizing us as barefoot country hicks
> with straw sticking out of our ears, clad in overalls, and unfamiliar with the
> proper use of indoor plumbing.... . Although many Southerners were angry at
> the regional ridicule, our family was too exuberant to have our spirits damp-
> ened. We were able to laugh at these articles and political cartoons.[34]

To Carter, and the 'Georgian Mafia' he brought with him to Washington, the
laughter was founded on the self-confidence that they had succeeded in
reaching Washington in spite of the establishment who lived and worked
there.

The Carter White House was committed to the same strategy in government as that which had succeeded in the election. In some respects, it was
forced into this position by its poor relationships with other power centres.
Whatever the reason, Carter tried to maintain that combination of moralism
and populism which had been the hallmarks of his rise to power, to establish
himself in office. This was always going to be a difficult strategy because it
entailed the president seeking to remain an outsider while situated inside the
centre of Washington. Carter saw the potential for using the sense of distance
between himself and the rest of Washington as an effective strategy for
maintaining the lustre of public contact and trust that had accompanied his
election. Unfortunately for Carter and his presidency, he was unable to con-

37

vert that potential into the desired effect.

Carter aggravated political leaders in Washington by his sense of moral superiority and intellectual detachment, and by his insistence that he owed nothing to anyone as he had secured the presidency through his own direct relationship with 'the people'. The cost of Carter's attachment with the public came to be measured by a commensurate deterioration in his links with the party, with the Congress and with the rest of Washington 'insiders'. Carter might have done better if he had not made it quite so obvious that he preferred an abstract affinity to the public rather than any tangible engagements with the public's other representatives.

Carter was poor at consulting with members of Congress or at giving adequate notification of his legislative proposals. He vetoed their pork barrel projects and was uninterested in their claims for patronage. He often refused to compromise and had a habit of publicly disclosing the contents of political negotiations while they were still under discussion.[35] Carter himself made no apologies for these failings.

> I was not part of the Wall Street business Establishment, the Washington political Establishment or the Hollywood entertainment Establishment in any way. I was a Southern peanut farmer populist type. That was fine with me.... . We were alien in some ways. There were ways I could have reached out. It was not an antagonistic attitude. It is just not part of my personality. I do not condemn the cocktail circuit. It is just not natural for me to be part of it.[36]

The unconventional nature of Carter's leadership mixed high intelligence with political amateurism; religious humility with personal disdain. It led to charges of arrogance. David Broder's accusation was typical of the genre.

> As an outsider, he often has failed to recognize the legitimacy of the complex system of constituency representation, reflected in Congress, the bureaucracy and the interest groups. He often has failed to involve other leaders, with constituencies of their own, in the common tasks of governing or to give them a substantial stake in the success of his policies.... . Too often in this term, Carter has been captured by the conceit that his own mystique and communion with the 'people' could substitute for the daily drudgery of coalition-building in Congress and the political realm.'[37]

The Carter White House tended to dismiss such criticism as anti-Southern snobbery. Carter for his part was 'determined to prove that he and his associates had not stepped straight out of Dogpatch'.[38] This attitude did lead at times to assumptions of omniscience by Carter and his lieutenants.

> They had done what no one else had known how to do. Why should they take pains to listen to those who had designed the New Deal, the Fair Deal, the Great Society? The town was theirs for the taking.[39]

38

But as James Fallows pointed out, 'the insiders were right to scoff at him for they understood how much he did not know'.[40]

Carter's evocation of Thomas Jefferson's ideal of wise innocence paled into public fatigue for a range of reasons. In one sense, it would have been difficult for any president to survive the body blows of continued stagflation, rising energy costs, high interest rates, budget deficits, pressure on the dollar and a full blown hostage crisis in Iran. But probably more critical to his presidency were two factors that disorientated and, ultimately, undermined his outsider status in Washington. First, as a 'populist who tried to run the U.S., [he] learnt to his sorrow that Washington politics is a complex profession'.[41] His attempts to master the administration almost single-handedly as a public champion of good government led him to be buried in detail and, as a result, to appear indecisive and even incompetent. As Carter became enveloped in government problems, he lost that sense of space between himself and the government that signified his attachment to the public.

Secondly, Carter used his own licence as an outsider to take upon himself the task of informing the American people about subjects that no previous president had ever dared to raise. Carter's candour, and his special relationship with the public, led him to tell his fellow citizens that America's social and economic problems were intractable; that there were many problems which government simply could not solve; and that there were even problems to which no solutions existed at all. He urged Americans to face the truth that there were limits to economic growth, limits to higher standards of living and limits to energy provision. Expectations had to be lowered.[42] America's relative economic and military decline had to be accepted. Americans in effect had to accustom themselves to painful changes.

Apart from the message itself being unpalatable and apart from the economic crises that plagued Carter's administration and gave credence to his warnings, the fact remains that Carter mishandled his own populist resources. He made the mistake of using his public position to tell Americans that they themselves were the problem – thereby turning populism on its head. He compounded this mistake with another by informing them that there were even more severe problems looming on the horizon and that no one could do anything about them apart from accepting their existence. Carter overplayed his outsider role to such an extent that he ended up outside the public itself.

It was Ronald Reagan who provided the master's touch to the strategy of spatial leadership. He it was who demonstrated its exceptional properties and the extraordinary uses to which it could be put. Like Carter, Reagan entered the White House by virtue of a campaign against government in Washington. But unlike Carter, Reagan insisted upon retaining his public distance from Washington even while centred emphatically in it. As a consequence, the

White House was run as if it were engaged in a permanent election campaign. In fact,

> governing according to a Reagan staffer, amounted to little more than an extension of the campaign that brought him into office. In early 1983 aides were urging him to announce his candidacy for re-election to strengthen his hand in Congress.[43]

Reagan refused to become entangled in complex issues or in the grind of government management. He almost took as a matter of pride the complaints that he was administratively lax and ran a 'hands off' style of organisation in the White House. What Reagan did take very seriously were the links with his public constituency outside Washington. This was where his chief political resource lay and he knew it could best be tapped by persistent and broad based ideological assertions of social optimism, national pride and a healthy scepticism of Washington politics. Instead of Carter's intellectual and fatalistic diagnoses of America's problems, Reagan offered the prospect of dramatic escapes through the sheer exertion of American will. The war for self-belief was more important than any lost battles over policy and administration. In fact, flaming defeats could even be politically useful.

Reagan was another self-proclaimed outsider. As an uncompromising apologist for the Republican right wing during the 1960s and 70s, Reagan had always been on the margins of national politics. He had served two terms as Governor of California. He clearly harboured ambitions for the White House but for many years he had been considered too extreme, too inexperienced, and too old to warrant consideration for such high office. As keeper of the pure faith of cold war fundamentalism and pre-New-Deal private enterprise, Ronald Reagan was not a serious contender for the presidency until the late 1970s. In the malaise of national decline and economic stagflation which marked the last two years of the Carter presidency, the public mood shifted progressively to the right. Eventually, it came upon the figure of Reagan and the strident optimism of his old doctrines.

In contrast to the technocratic realism and intellectual detachment of the self-effacing Jimmy Carter, Reagan offered the virtue of national self-assertion and the promise of economic revival. Reagan, and his audaciously simple economic formulas from the entrepreneurial culture of America's sunbelt, offered the prospect of a possible recovery. Through the sheer force of national self-belief and of inspirational leadership, America could be brought back from the brink to resume its position of economic fulfilment and social destiny.[44] According to Reagan, America could only be made great again by traditionally American means. That meant a fundamentalist crusade to release America's ancient impulses and autonomous energies from the dead hand of excessive government dependency and regulation. Reagan's own presidency was no exception. He had to lead, but he also had to symbolise the office's own emancipation from governing structures.

Reagan knew that the appeal of his message and his own appeal as president were grounded in his outsider status in Washington. In a prodigious electoral campaign between 1976 and 1980, in which he fought well over fifty primary elections, Reagan had hammered home his criticism of Washington politics and the federal government time and time again. In the end, he even managed to outflank Jimmy Carter's outsider status and cast him as an unreconstructed Washingtonian, enveloped in government and dithering in political decisions. It was essential to Reagan that he should retain in government his chief electoral assets: the integrity of inexperience, the freshness of detachment, and the honour of forthright commitment to publicly declared principles. The one affliction which the Reagan White House was intent upon avoiding at all costs was the leader being 'Carterised' – i.e. dragged down by detail and distraction to the point where the president's identity became indistinguishable from government.

Reagan's objectives posed many problems. Not the least of them were Reagan's doctrinal objections to the federal government and the flamboyance of his promises to confront and reduce it. Jimmy Carter had been a conservative Democrat who criticised the culture of Washington and tried to subject the federal government to critical review. Reagan was different. His whole career had been dominated by the desire to challenge the federal government. He was committed to a frontal assault upon the 'smothering hand'[45] of Washington and to a campaign to undermine its legitimacy and to reverse the scale of its operations in American society.

> We can make government again responsive to people only by cutting its size and scope ... Man is not free unless government is limited. There is a clear cause and effect here that is as neat and predictable as a law of physics: As government expands, liberty contracts.[46]

At the beginning of his administration when he was seeking to install the main framework of his economic reform programme, Reagan extended the confrontational and plebiscitary approach to the presidency that his recent predecessors had begun. When he encountered stiff opposition in Congress, Reagan recalled his time as Governor of California.

> In Sacramento, the most important lesson I learned was the value of making an end run around the legislature by going directly to the people on television or radio, I'd lay out the problems we faced and ask their help to persuade the legislators to vote as they wanted, not in the way special-interest groups did.[47]

41

This became the Reagan way in Washington. In his autobiography, Reagan recounts how the New Deal liberals in Congress constantly sought to frustrate his plans and then to pin the blame for the subsequent deadlock onto the president. In Reagan's view, Congress was especially susceptible to special interests and not to what he regarded as being the public will. To strengthen his identity with the public and thereby to substantiate his assumption that 'Reaganomics' reflected public demand, the president describes how he had 'to keep the heat on Congress'[48] by plunging himself into the American populace.

> I flew to Chicago in early July, ostensibly to speak at a fund-raiser for Governor Jim Thompson, but used my visit to the district of Dan Rostenkowski, chairman of the House Ways and Means Committee, to point out to his constituents that he held the fate of the tax-cut proposals in his palm. I urged them to write to him: 'If all of you will join with your neighbors to send the same message to Washington, we'll have that tax cut and we'll have it this year.' I was told that the speech generated hundreds of letters to Rostenkowski, who subsequently became something of a conciliatory voice among the Democratic leaders in the House as we approached the finish line in the battle over tax reduction.[49]

Trips, speeches, lobbying and televised broadcasts to the nation were all directed to the objective of asking 'the people to make their views known to their elected representatives'.[50] His efforts were successful and the reform package secured Congressional approval in July 1981. Reagan felt vindicated on all fronts. In his view, he had turned the tide of government by taking himself to the people and instilling in them a renewed sense of their own autonomy.

Despite the sweeping nature of his critique and the ambitiousness of his programme, Reagan, like Nixon and Carter before him, was confronted by the self-evident permanence of the government's infrastructure, its statutory obligations and committed expenditures. It is true that in 1981 Reagan did galvanise the public and the Congress behind a specific programme of dramatic tax cuts, expenditure cuts and increases in the military budget.[51] It is also true that this programme of 'Reaganomics' was intended to subject government to the discipline of a balanced budget. The programme certainly had widespread repercussions. It was blamed not only for having induced, or at least for having worsened, the severe recession of 1981-1983, but also for setting in motion the gross indiscipline of large federal deficits for the rest of the decade.

The problems of 'Reaganomics' also led to a change in the balance of Reagan's leadership. After 1981, Reagan found the forces amassed against him too formidable to engage in any further exercises of mass mobilisation directed against government. Reagan's own popularity was suffering from the effects of the recession and the deficit. He plummeted in the polls. His public approval rating had reached the level of 68% in May 1981, but by December 1982 it had slumped to 32%.[52] The issue of the budget, its content and priorities now became central to the viability of Reagan's presidency. In the wars of attrition that marked each year's budget cycle, Reagan found that his only real option was one of a rearguard action in defence of his 1981 priorities. With this objective in mind and with the need to restore his presidency's credibility, Reagan shifted his leadership emphatically towards a position of detachment from the budgeting process. This strategy evoked more clearly the outsider ethos of his election and provided a means through which he could portray the public interest over and against merely the special interests that fed openly on the budget.

After 1982, the public was regularly presented with the sight of a president who, while formally responsible for the federal government's budget, openly dissociated himself from the discussions over its substance. After reiterating his original principles of reduced taxation, diminished social spending and increased military expenditure, and offering a budget that was usually ignored by an incredulous Congress, Reagan would then bathe publicly in his own intransigence. He would affect not to negotiate on the key issues; he would threaten to take parts of the budget to the people through televised addresses; he would promise vetoes; and he would dissociate himself from the final outcome. In the judgement of Louis Fisher,

> Reagan was content to sit on the sidelines and tell Congress: 'You figure it out.'
> In matters of budgeting, it is difficult to find a more irresponsible President in
> the twentieth century.[53]

Behind the scenes, Reagan would make compromises and reach accommodations to facilitate the budget's passage into law. In public, the impression was quite different. It was of a feisty man of principle cowed only by the greater force of lesser men. As responsibility was offloaded either onto Congress for budgetary priorities, or onto members of his cabinet for unpopular decisions, Reagan was able to preserve his standing as a crusader committed to internal exile.

Reagan was particularly adept at using public occasions to renew his communion with the populace and to do it at the direct expense of another sector of the political system. The Democratically controlled Congress was a favourite target. In his 1983 State of the Union Address, Reagan said that 'we who are in government must take the lead in restoring the economy'.[54] At this point, the Democrats rose to their feet to applaud in an attempt to give emphasis to Reagan's apparent acceptance that he shared responsibility for the budget deficit. But Reagan turned the tables on them by making the following

43

aside: 'And here all the time, I thought you were reading the paper.'[55] Speaker Tip O'Neil's administrative assistant, Christopher Matthews, remembers that everyone laughed at what they thought was a joke.

> All the members thought he meant reading the script along with him which is a reasonable thing to be doing, ... At home everybody thought they were a bunch of Claghorns with their feet up on the desks reading the newspaper. He was able to portray the Congress as politicians and incumbents and himself as the American voice.[56]

This type of suggestiveness in Reagan's speeches was not unusual. In his 1986 State of the Union address, he again implied Congressional culpability for the condition of the government's finances. By doing so, he appeared to absolve himself from even partial blame. He reached out to the public by distancing himself from the ascribed myopia and self-seeking of ordinary politicians in Washington who were necessarily misrepresenting the public. In the view of Christopher Matthews,

> Reagan suggests that the government is the Congress and he is a citizen politician. He is the people's ombudsman, their spokesman. The responsibility for the deficits belongs in Congress. When he called upon the Speaker to do something about the deficit he wasn't saying that his own policies had quadrupled the deficit in five years. He was simply putting responsibility on the shoulders of the Speaker as he does when he holds rallies against the deficits which he had done twice on the Capitol grounds.[57]

Reagan's exemplary command of spatial leadership was based essentially upon acts of defiance. Instead of Carter's gloomy realism, Reagan had always preached a gospel of defiance against economic limits, intractable problems and national decline. As his presidency developed, Reagan extended this defiance to his own record. He defied the failures of his programme, the severity of its effects, the significance of the deficits, the divisiveness of his policies and the retreats from his stated positions. As a result, the Reagan years were marked by policy failures, U-turns, internal dissension and administrative disarray. And yet, President Reagan's stature with the public remained undiminished. His verbal gaffes, his intellectual deficiencies, his inattentiveness and even his indolence were celebrated as acts of defiance against the protocol of government. He was termed the 'Teflon' president to whom no charge ever stuck.

Reagan's public popularity for being both public and popular gave him an extraordinary dispensation from critical scrutiny. His ability to dissociate himself from his own administration baffled analysts and journalists alike. It was said that Reagan possessed 'formidable powers of denial'[58] even to the point of disputing the existence of evident failures and the validity of factual knowledge. To Garry Wills, American politics under President Reagan were 'shot through with unreality'.[59] It was said that the president not only stretched his convictions to the point of intentional self-delusion, but for the most part was encouraged to do so by a public infected by his outright optimism. When Reagan campaigned against Carter, he promised that a strong America would never be subjected to terrorist outrages. But when terrorists continued to take American hostages and to kill American service-men during his administration,

> Reagan attributed this to the lingering effects of Carterism and assured others (as well as himself) that it would not happen in the future (though it continued to) ... Reagan was consistent, in all such apparent contradictions, with his principled optimism. Even when untoward things happened on his 'watch' of responsibility (if not control), he was busy convincing people that the future would be different. That explained the energy with which he campaigned against the government even when he *was* the government.[60]

Reagan's powers of disengagement allowed him to build up a dichotomy in the public's mind between on the one hand the leadership, and on the other hand the president's own policy proposals and political conduct. The period of the Reagan administration, therefore, was marked by an extraordinary disjunction between a high public approval of his presidency and majority disapproval of his policies. Reagan's visceral relationship with the American public was witnessed at first hand and graphically conveyed by Jane Mayer and Doyle McManus.

> Reagan seemed to share a strange kind of alchemy with the American public. It was visible in the tear-streaked faces of the cheerleaders who lined his parade routes, in the hurting farmers who said they'd vote for him despite their economic devastation, and in the southern Democrats who set aside traditions held since the Civil War and flocked to the party of Lincoln. Reagan evoked the romantic myth of American superiority, as old and powerful as the country itself. Reagan was larger than life yet voters had an extraordinary affection for him as a man. They were inspired by his optimism, and they responded to his warmth and humor. They felt he was more trustworthy than other politicians. They thought he had backbone – whether they approved of his programs or not.[61]

This is precisely the point. While Reagan regularly received strong public approval ratings for his presidency, more people consistently disapproved of his policies than approved them. This was true even when his approval ratings were stretched to levels in excess of 65%. In 1985, Louis Harris observed that Reagan had 'never been so popular personally and his programs so little supported by the public'.[62] Reagan may have been able to draw on the public's negative disposition towards government in general terms, but he was quite unable to disturb the public's attachment to the tangible benefits, and even the ideals, of the New Deal's positive state. The position is summarised by Everett Carll Ladd.

> The popular sense of government as a 'problem' squared clearly with established Republican doctrine and thus contributed positively to the fortunes of the GOP. But at the same time, people had not stopped looking to government for solutions and assistance. Americans of all classes expected high levels of performance by government.[63]

Opinion poll evidence demonstrates, for example, that the electorate in the 1980s continued to favour high levels of spending on education, unemployment, public assistance and health care. In fact, after five years of the Reagan programme, Americans took 'a more positive view of the activist programs initiated by past Democratic presidents than they did just before he took office'.[64] Within this context of assured spending and basic provision, huge numbers of Americans seemed quite able to tolerate, and even to commend a president whose ideology of achievement, competition and a weaker state was pitted against the established assumptions of state benefit.

Reagan fought tenaciously against the pressures for increased social spending, higher taxes and lower military budgets. In some respects, his campaign may be said to have been effective in producing a government shakeout and shifting the onus of justification onto those seeking to preserve and extend public expenditure. But the campaign was characterised, in its most immediate sense, by defeat rather than success – highly publicised and conspicuous defeats following bouts of open confrontation with his opponents. Reagan, however, seemed to thrive on defeat. Many of them were dramatic in nature and comprehensive in scale. Sometimes they would be due to his failure to prevail in negotiations. On other occasions, they were due to his defiant support for such politically untenable causes as abortion reform, school prayer amendments, progressive tax reduction, increased assistance to the *contra* rebels in Nicaragua and a constitutional amendment mandating a balanced federal budget. These sorts of defeat seemed only to enhance his reputation by embodying social frustration over government in general and by maintaining the satisfying imagery of earnest confrontation against the impersonal forces of governmental power. They were the strategic defeats by which Reagan could further distance himself from government and even from the effects of his policies.

The high level of public approval which Reagan attracted was not just a measure of the economic recovery which began in 1983 and gathered pace in the mid-1980s. It was also a measure of Reagan's extraordinary skills in the use of the media to keep his guileless geniality and earnest integrity before the public. To a greater and greater extent as his presidency developed, he offered leadership at a more and more symbolic level. It was a leadership style that was eminently appropriate for the media to convey to the public. It acquired a considerable substance in its own right that could be converted into subtle forms of political leverage inside Washington. The leadership of public rhetoric and political acclaim became divorced from policy, and assumed an identity of its own. It also possessed its own dynamic. In the same way that Andy Warhol was said 'to be famous for being famous', Reagan appeared to be popular for being popular. Between 1984 and 1986, he was unassailable as president. He was

> identified with the presidency as perhaps no other President in recent times. By the middle of his fifth year in office, he [was] the most well-respected President at a comparable period since polling began, well surpassing Dwight Eisenhower. He [was] 'King Reagan'. And in the style of monarchies, while one may attack the ministers and the policies of the government, the person of the king remained inviolate. This 'rule' was respected even more by Reagan's detractors than his defenders. Detractors discovered that the best way to neutralize Reagan's influence was not to dispute his benevolence. People might love Ronald Reagan, but that implied nothing about his policies.[65]

It is a tribute to the remarkable qualities of Reagan's engagement with the public as an endearingly tough outsider, that he was able to survive the Iran–*contra* scandal in 1987. The deceiving, and even self-deluding, properties of Reagan's emphasis upon appearance and presentation were painfully exposed in this episode. The Reagan White House was seen to be in open disarray and guilty of breaking not only its own publicly declared policies, but also the rule of law. Reagan himself was revealed to be ill-informed, negligent, evasive and remote. It was a particularly serious crisis for the Reagan presidency because it threatened his public standing with the potentially deadly condition of hard realism and critical enquiry. Reagan's popularity never recovered to the levels he had achieved in the mid-1980s. Nevertheless, he did regain enough of his rapport with the public to leave office in a surge of national fervour. Astonishingly he was still as popular at the end of his presidency as he was at the beginning. He had played the role of outsider successfully for eight years. While confounded commentators and political opponents complained that Reagan and his public had been outside of reality itself, Reagan had showed that by playing to the public a president need not become tainted by Washington and could avoid failure by converting leadership into an effect on public spirits. After two full terms, Reagan left office as popular and as convincing a dissenter from government as he was when he entered it. In 1984, when Reagan was at the height of his power, his advisors were concerned that his successful status as an outsider was bound to be in jeopardy after Reagan's presence in Washington for four years. The public might begin to hold him responsible for the government he himself headed. Stuart Spencer, who had worked for Reagan since his entry into California politics in the 1960s and was now his chief strategist for the 1984 presidential elections, knew better: 'He can pull it off,' he said.

> In 1970 he pulled it off. He ran against the fucking government he was running. I mean he believes he's above it all. He believes it. That's why they believe it. I can't believe it. But they do.[66]

They still believed it in 1988 when Reagan stepped down from office.

Reagan had always insisted that the victories and successes ascribed to him were not his at all. In his final address to the nation, he reiterated this theme of the president as the people's agent.

> I've had my share of victories in the Congress, but what few people noticed is that I never won anything you didn't win for me. They never saw my troops, they never saw Reagan's regiments, the American people. You won every battle with every call you made and letter you wrote demanding action.[67]

The corollary to this proposition was that while Reagan accepted little of the credit for his reforms, he similarly accepted little of the blame for their effects. His message had been one of affirming his confidence in the people and of returning power back to the public domain. It was difficult to criticise the 'feel good' messages of a president who not only placed his trust in the audience's own view of American values and traditions, but who seemed to be situated at the centre of the auditorium itself as he did so.

Perhaps the most remarkable, if not wholly successful, attempt at spatial leadership came with Ronald Reagan's successor. George Bush had never been an outsider in his life. He was in fact the living epitome of America's East Coast establishment. Coming from a highly privileged background and educated at Andover and Yale, Bush followed his father in dedicating himself to the obligations of public service. Before being chosen for the vice-presidential nomination by Ronald Reagan in 1980, Bush had held a formidable array of public positions.[68] Although these achievements were impressive, they were tempered both by the knowledge that they were not jobs Bush had actually sought, and by the impression that Bush had had to ingratiate himself to several patrons, in order to acquire even these consolation prizes. The pattern was no different in 1980 when Bush sought the presidency but ended up a loyal team player in the Reagan administration.

In 1980, Bush had sought to make the transition from vice-president to president. For a vice-president to reach the Oval Office by way of an election after a president had served out two full terms of office is a rare event in American politics. To accomplish it after such an exceptionally popular and idiosyncratic president as Reagan would be very difficult – even more so, considering the personal and temperamental differences between the president and his vice-president. In many respects, it is necessary for a vice-president running for the presidency to show that he is his own man; to be loyal but also to distance himself from his previous superior and to offer a different style of leadership. Bush's problem was that his dissimilarities to Reagan were not to his benefit. They were not thought to be the ingredients of leadership. His loyalty to Reagan, for example, was widely seen to be self-deprecating, and even deferential, in nature. Whatever substance he possessed as a politician had arguably been eclipsed by Reagan and, thereafter, subsumed under the Reagan mantle.

Bush believed that his record of public office spoke for itself and that when he presented his 'curriculum vitae' to the American people it would be recognised for what Bush believed it to be – his evident qualification for high office. What was painfully evident in the early days of his campaign, however, was a conflict between what Bush regarded as credentials for the presidency (e.g. experience in matters of state, a background in diplomacy, an intimate knowledge of government hierarchies, party loyalty) and what many voters saw as his lack of qualification for the office. Bush was seen as a distant Washington insider who, as Reagan's chosen heir, was simply expecting to assume office through hierarchical succession. Bush was criticised as complacent, evasive and vacuous. Worst of all, he was described as a 'wimp'.[69]

The extraordinary aspect of Bush's rise to the presidency and his subsequent conduct in office is that in 1988 he was compelled to make every effort to change his status to that of an outsider. As a consummate insider, and vice-president for eight years, this metamorphosis was no easy task. Stung by the criticism coming from Republican rivals for the nomination, Bush's image had to be hastily reconstructed. He distracted attention away from his New England patrician background by playing up his connections to Texas and his early career as an oilman. He toughened up his language, became more aggressive and made every effort to accommodate himself to the legendary outsiders of the Republican right wing. Given that even a vice-president has to win the nomination through the levelling process of primary elections and given that Bush suffered some dramatic early reversals, he was able to demonstrate that he had some outsider credentials for leadership. In particular, he was able to show that he had the aggression to come from behind and to slog his way to the nomination in a public display of gritty determination and 'hardball' politics.[70]

Bush had the advantage of struggle in another respect. He began the election campaign for the presidency 17 points behind Michael Dukakis, the Democratic party's candidate. Dukakis had sound outsider credentials. He was a Greek American who, as Governor of Massachusetts, had modernised the state's economy and wiped out its budget deficit. He was leader of the financially weaker and more socially disadvantaged party which had been in the White House for only four out of the previous twenty years. Dukakis claimed that he was a moderate Democrat, committed to managerial competence, rather than to large-scale spending programmes.

In order to close the gap, Bush was advised to employ negative campaigning techniques and to shift publicly to the right. Bush dutifully smeared Dukakis for being unpatriotic and soft on defence. He criticised him as a mushy civil libertarian who wanted to flood the streets with 'cop killers, rapists and drug dealing thugs'.[71] Bush also made his notorious 'read my lips' pledge of no new taxes. As a member of the Reagan administration for eight years, with direct experience of the severity of the deficit problem, this was an outrageously irresponsible statement. It was, however, a measure of the lengths that a sober politician like Bush was prepared to go, in order to appease the Republican right and to affirm his posture against government. This piece of self-inflicted populism demonstrated that he was intent upon following Reagan's old route to the White House – even though Bush himself was already in the White House! The rashness of Bush's pledge – subsequently to be rescinded in 1990 – dramatised the issue of government spending. In particular, it cast doubt on Dukakis who was too responsible a challenger to make such a wild undertaking in reply.

Through these sort of tactics, Dukakis was effectively portrayed as the candidate of 'big government' and vested bureaucratic interests. Dukakis tried to counter by insisting that he was not a proponent of government, by emphatically denying that he was a liberal and by declaring that he had no innovative ideas to put forward.[72] This only lost him ground amongst his own supporters. It was very late in his campaign that Dukakis was stung into a populist style attack upon Bush's privileged background, and his insider status in the Washington establishment. It was too late. Dukakis had in effect already been stripped of his outsider credentials.

> In a masterpiece of temporal and spatial transference, Bush presented himself as the puritan dissenter committed to limiting government and fighting taxes. From his vantage point in the White House, it was Bush who plastered Governor Dukakis with the odium of government, and therefore, with the demonic chill of liberalism.[73]

Bush's presidency was very much the product of the 1988 campaign.

Although he had to distance himself from his predecessor by advocating 'a kinder and gentler society' he was in fact wedded to the exemplary outsider politics of the Reagan era. He inherited the spending constraints of the deficit and he made a theatrical pledge to imitate Reagan's anathema to increased taxation. At the beginning of his presidency, Bush had very little in the way of a domestic agenda. Given the persistent problem of the deficit and his own anxiety over the right wing of the Republican Party, Bush was committed to criticising the excess of government and to creating as much space as possible between his presidency and the consequences of political decision-making.

Like his predecessor, Bush's enthusiasm for dissociation even extended to the apparently self-denying ordinance of allowing the Democratic Congress to take the initiative with the federal budget, and with it, the final responsibility for its content and effect. *Time* reported in November 1990 that Bush

> takes the popular position that taxes need not rise, even on the wealthy, if only federal spending is cut – yet he insists that Congress make the tough choices on whose spending is cut. His attitude is that the buck stops there.[74]

Bush succeeded in persuading the public that Congress was largely to blame for the continued budget deficit crisis.[75] According to the president, the problems of domestic policy (i.e. those areas of political concern most closely associated in the public's mind with 'the government') were attributable to 'a Congress that has a different philosophical approach to many issues – most issues'.[76]

But in other respects, the president's assertions proved unconvincing and counterproductive. Unlike Reagan, Bush did not have the ideological zeal for a *jihad* against government. As a government careerist, he believed in it too much. It is true that Bush was not keen to launch new government programmes, but this was not because he was aggressively motivated against the idea of government. It was simply because he was not interested enough and found the politics of domestic policy-making distasteful.

> He has never had firm convictions on domestic issues; over the years he has altered his stance on abortion, civil rights and even supply-side economics when it was politically expedient to do so. Bush has always regarded domestic policy as 'deep doo-doo' not to be stepped in if at all possible.[77]

As a result, his presidency had been severely criticised for drift, remoteness and indecision before the high-risk venture of the Gulf War dramatically strengthened his claims to leadership.

It is impossible to know what the Bush presidency would have been like without the conditioning factor of the Reagan administration. It is just as impossible to determine the precise extent to which Bush had to change his style and agenda, in order to acquire the presidency. Nonetheless, it is not unreasonable to conclude that the opportunities and motivation for spatial leadership were too great even for George Bush to resist. Given Bush's predilection to government as a public service and his attachment to its institutional values and *esprit de corps*, it is significant that Bush of all people was prepared to resort to populist rhetoric and to distance himself conspicuously from government wherever this was possible. It was Bush, the archetypal Ivy League insider, who felt compelled to be an outsider and publicly exploit government as a term of abuse. It can, of course, be argued that Bush has never been particularly convincing as an outsider and has largely failed to translate the space he has created for himself into a form of public leadership. Nevertheless, what is significant is that Bush – even Bush – evidently felt that there was no alternative but to try and change his image from that of progressive Republican and team player to one of a maverick figure assuring public services whilst running down the 'government'.

The ambiguities inherent in Bush becoming heir to the Reaganite legacy had became fully evident by the end of his first term of office. Bush had acquired a reputation for caution and accommodation. Despite the success of the Gulf War and the fact that the collapse of communism and the end of the cold war had coincided with Bush's incumbency, the president was under attack for the general lack of direction and coherence in domestic policy. This was exemplified in the economic recession which gripped the United States in 1991 and which sent the president's popularity falling from 79% in January to 51% in December. By April 1992 he had slipped to 41%. In May, his level of approval stood at 37%.[78]

Bush's style of leadership began to attract critical scrutiny for its minimalist agenda, its emphasis on consensus, and its willingness to be suffused in the collective immobilism of Washington's brokerage politics. Bush was labelled an American Tory. He had neither a mandate, nor the desire for one. He appeared to be an emollient insider operating purely in reaction to events with the objective of accommodating interests and maintaining stability. To Bert Rockman, it was clear that Bush was 'addicted to insider politics'.[79] As a consequence, the question of what an authentic insider administration would look like in Washington had been answered by Bush's presence in the capital. Bush demonstrated a penchant for harmony, for working with small groups and for addressing problems reluctantly and incrementally. He showed that he was 'more able than most presidents to deal with other elites at the top of the system with confidence'.[80] Useful though these attributes were, they meant that Bush would have to live down his background, character and record all over again to win re-election.

In 1992 Bush had to confront an array of new outsiders from the

Democratic party, intent upon exploiting every variant of outsider politics to distance themselves from Washington, and its political culture, in an effort to lend legitimacy to their campaign for the party leadership. Indeed, it would be no exaggeration to say that the Democratic party in 1992 achieved a truly exotic level of outsider competition. Six minor runners contended the nomination after the party's heavyweight figures (e.g. Mario Cuomo, Albert Gore, Lloyd Bentsen, George Mitchell) had earlier refused to enter the race. They had been deterred from doing so when Bush's popularity in the afterglow of the Gulf War had given every indication that he could be assured of re-election to a second term of office. Senator Tom Harkin and Senator Bob Kerrey, who suffered the stigma of being Washington politicians, were clearly disadvantaged and were quickly dismissed as serious contenders. Douglas Wilder, the black Governor of Virginia, withdrew through lack of support. It was Paul Tsongas who first emerged from the pack as the winner of the influential New Hampshire primary election.

Tsongas typified the mood against establishment politicians and mainstream politics with a bold programme of economic reform and a style that was the antithesis of modern electioneering.

> His importance was symbolic as well as substantive: Tsongas possesses a power of glamourlessness, a nerdy, basset-hound anti-image that gives hope to some voters who despair of American politics as glib, empty, pointless – all sound bites and video bursts. Tsongas' astringent message was that Santa Claus in whatever extravagant forms (Ronald Reagan or the Great Society) is not coming back, and the U.S. can't afford any more toys. Tsongas succeeded, for the moment, by being virtually everything that Reagan was not.[81]

After a campaign of economic realism, and deliberate self-deprecation that implied a virtuous lack of charisma, Tsongas celebrated his win in New Hampshire with the following admonishment.

> Hello Washington … this is New Hampshire calling. Are you listening? We're sending you a message, just tell us the truth. We're grown-ups. We can live with it.[82]

Tsongas now relished the idea of a campaign against an established national politician – 'I'd love to run against a Washington-based power broker',[83] he said. His chances of winning the nomination, however, were limited. He was seen as too much of a regional candidate. Questions remained about his strength and the extent of his recovery from lymphatic cancer, which had forced him to retire as Senator for Massachusetts in 1983. But most significant of all, he was faced by the powerful figure of Governor Bill Clinton of Arkansas.

53

Unlike Tsongas, who had been a member of the U.S. Senate, Clinton was able to cast himself as a true outsider untainted by Washington not only from the point of view that he had never served in it, but also because Arkansas was much further away from it than Massachusetts. Clinton was the Democratic party's favoured candidate. He offered to secure the South, to draw the blue collar 'Reagan Democrats' back to the fold, and to appeal both to minorities and the middle class. He struck a familiar and popular chord in wishing to reduce the federal bureaucracy and 'to repair the damaged bond between the people and their government'.[84] But Clinton was hampered by personal revelations of marital infidelity, marijuana smoking in his youth, and draft dodging during the Vietnam war. He also appeared to be glitzy and packaged at a time when such considerations were not thought to be the attributes of a true outsider. Tsongas was able to exploit Clinton's reputation as a 'slick Willie' in New Hampshire, but once the campaign moved into the South and Mid-west Clinton was generally able to prevail.

Although Tsongas had withdrawn from the race by the end of March following his defeats in the Michigan and Illinois primaries, Clinton still had to contend with Jerry Brown whose outsider campaign had an almost surreal quality to it. The ex-Governor of California, who had, amongst many other things, taken up Zen Buddhism and worked in the past with Mother Teresa of Calcutta, used his disgust with the alleged corruption and systematic depravity of American politics as the basis of an attempt on the presidency. This ultimate figure in anti-politics ran what could be called an anti-campaign that retained a staff of only ten and refused any contribution over $100. As for the candidate, he adhered to no planned schedule, he slept on couches in supporters' houses rather than stay in hotels and could only be contacted by leaving messages at a friend's flat. Brown regarded Clinton as a symbol of machine politics and simply another false innovator in a corrupt system. Brown was a shock winner of the Connecticut primary in March. At a time when Clinton was hoping to be accepted as the heir apparent to the Democratic party and concentrating his energies upon George Bush, the party's chief outsider was having to defend himself against another outsider who was challenging the frontrunner's outsider status. In the big New York primary that followed the Connecticut upset, Clinton and Brown both sought to outmanoeuvre one another so that each might be better able to cast his opponent as an insider, leaving the soubriquet of outsider to himself. In one television debate, Brown summed up in one remark to Clinton the forces motivating the campaign for the party leadership: 'I don't think you can posture yourself as an outsider next to me.'[85] Although Clinton won the New York primary, Brown vowed to carry his damaging campaign to the party convention. Meanwhile, Paul Tsongas, who had earlier withdrawn from the race, won 20% of the votes in

New York and considered re-entering the leadership campaign. In the event he refused to do so, content with the position of 'double outsider' who would be available at a later date should the successive tabloid revelations of Clinton's private life make him unelectable.

President Bush was not able to draw much comfort from the undisciplined rush towards outsider politics in the opposition party. This was partly because there always existed the possibility that one such outsider could suddenly form a coalition capable of exploiting the high level of disenchantment with the federal government during a recession. It was also because Bush himself had been subjected to a direct challenge by Pat Buchanan for the Republican party's nomination. Although the Buchanan campaign was always likely to fail in its immediate objective of unseating Bush, it did constitute a threat to the presidency's credentials as a public leader set apart from Washington politics. Buchanan himself was another Washington insider, but one who relished the aggressive and combative spirit of the outsiders on the Republican right wing. He launched a blistering assault on Bush's presidency at the beginning of 1992. He accused Bush of reneging on Reagan's radical conservatism with insipid trade policies, concessions on environmental and civil rights measures, and damaging reversals in economic policy.

> My old friend Mr Bush, after promising no new taxes, has presided over the biggest tax increase in history. He is the highest spender in history and has run the three biggest deficits in history.[86]

Buchanan wanted to mobilise the disaffected behind a 'middle American revolution' against the Eastern establishment and its alleged preoccupation with international involvement and global philanthropy. His clearly expressed nativist prejudices against blacks, Jews, ethnic minorities, homosexuals, and impoverished 'freeloaders' made it unlikely that he would ever attract a majority of Republicans. Nonetheless, his uninhibited appeal for Americans to put themselves first threatened to embarrass Bush by giving the impression that the 'silent majority' was still in existence and still poorly served by presidents who had lost the will to remain in contact with ordinary people.

The criticisms, along with the attendant threat of being smeared as a Washington insider, stung Bush into moving sharply to the right, in order to prevent a host of protest votes falling into Buchanan's lap by default. From this standpoint, he tried to detach himself, not from conventional state provision, but from its alleged abuses in such areas as welfare, affirmative action, criminal law and arts subsidies which so infuriated middle class citizens. Bush suddenly abandoned his 'kinder and gentler' conservatism. He set about the Democratic Congress and the Democratic presidential challengers with unbridled hostility, sloughing off the image and language of Tory harmony for earthy plain speaking – Texas style.

> If I'd 'a listened to the leader of the United States Senate, George Mitchell, Saddam Hussein'd be in Saudi Arabia and you'd be paying 20 bucks a gallon for gasoline. Now try that one on for size. I'm getting sick and tired, I am, every single night, hearing one of those carping little liberal Democrats jumping all over my you-know-what... . I vowed I would come over here tonight and be calm – but I tell you something, I'm a little sick and tired of being the punching bag for a lot of lightweights around this country yelling at me day in and day out. And I'm *sick* of it. They want a fight – they're going to have one. And I mean it.[87]

The extent to which Bush was able to dissociate himself from Washington by resorting to roustabout vernacular and by blaming the Democratic Congress for the recession remains open to question at the time of writing. Paralysing inarticulateness can come perilously close to prevarication or to incompetence in a president defending the record of his administration. In the early primary elections, Bush appeared to be out of touch with the fears and anxieties of middle class Americans in particular. In New Hampshire, Buchanan was fond of saying that 'if George Bush came up here and looked these people in the eyes, he would see the consequences of his policies'.[88] But when Bush arrived at the front line, his attempts to eat pork rinds in 'greasy spoon' cafes, drive fork lift trucks and tell vomit jokes to Texans, in order to appear a man of the people, conveyed instead only insincerity and condescension. It seemed to confirm his reputation as president given more to *noblesse oblige* rather than to genuine care. While an upturn in the economy would probably secure a second term of office, his evident lack of interest in domestic issues and social policy together with his preoccupation with foreign policy had made him very vulnerable to an outsider challenge.

If such a challenge were not to be effectively mounted by the Democrats, Bush was left to contemplate the possibility of a challenge by the Texan billionaire folk hero H. Ross Perot. In April 1992, he was giving active consideration to entering the presidential role as an independent outsider candidate.

> 'I have to', he said. 'If someone as blessed as I am is not willing to pick up a shovel and clean out the barn, who will?'[89]

His anti-Washington credentials were impeccable.

> This city has become a town filled with sound bites, shell games, handlers and media stunt-men who posture, create images, talk and shoot off Roman candles but don't ever accomplish anything.[90]

Even though he was only contemplating such a course of action, a *Los Angeles*

Times poll a week later put him at 21% with Clinton at 35% and Bush at 37%.

These early conjectures about running for president quickly produced a mass movement to ensure that each of the 50 states would place his name on the ballot for the presidential election. By June 1992, a CNN-*Time* poll had Perot receiving 33% of public support, with Bush on 28% and Clinton on 24%. Perot's level of support served to vindicate his original message that the 'entire political system ... is run by insiders who do not listen to working people and are incapable of solving our problems'.[91] Perot insisted that American democracy could be revitalised through an outsider like himself introducing new techniques of government, which would allow the ordinary person to make a greater contribution to public affairs. He advocated the use of interactive technology to produce an 'electronic town-meeting', where the voters could give their unmediated response to important issues of the day without having to leave their living rooms. Such aids to decision-making would deliberately circumvent the established devices of representation and elections. Perot believed that his candidacy would pave the way for such radical populism. As the ultimate outsider, he would demonstrate that it was possible to go outside America's gargantuan structure of presidential selection – primaries, caucuses, conventions – and become president by public demand. 'This is America', he said. 'We don't have to take their candidates, we can nominate our own.'[92] Even though Perot withdrew and then re-entered the presidential race, he was able to amass over 19 million votes and secure a remarkable 19% of the popular vote. His lack of a party base was widely regarded to be not so much a handicap as a positive advantage in tapping the large constituencies of disaffection that were increasingly becoming evident in the United States.

To Bush, 1992 was a 'weird year' with a 'lot of crazy people running around'. He said it was a 'funny season where everyone wants to have the most populist appeal'.[93] To his challengers, it was not so much an unusual year, as one which thoroughly typified what had become the conventional means to acquire, cultivate and sustain positions of leadership. By making leadership at a distance from government synonymous with the effective engagement of public attention and support, outsiders could translate space into a political resource that could yield positions of leadership within government. Outsiders, therefore, had to be both professional and permanent outsiders to maintain even the impression of public contact and public leadership that was now required to survive deep inside government. While an outsider like Clinton had been able to demolish President Bush's pretensions to a common identity with a recession-hit public in the 1992 election, he was immediately confronted by the very same problem that had dogged his predecessor in the White House. This was the need to be firmly in government, but demonstrably not a captive of it; to remain linked to the people by being spatially removed from the privileges, abuses and entrenched interests of Washington government.

It was significant that during the campaign, Clinton had managed to live down his Washington connections – e.g. his Georgetown education, his employment in the Senate. He did so partly by juxtaposing himself with the manifestly establishment figure of George Bush, and partly by deliberate decisions to keep his candidacy at a distance from Washington and free from any adverse associations with previous 'tax and spend' Democratic administrations. For example, he insisted upon keeping his campaign headquarters stationed in Little Rock, in spite of the strategic handicaps that such a location entailed. He also kept important Democratic party interests like the unions and the black groupings on the outer fringes of the campaign. He knew the importance of the middle class vote and its suspicions of Washington's largesse to coercive minorities.

Unlike Bush, President Clinton is dedicated to an imaginative and purposive deployment of government in pursuit of a policy programme. Whether he will be able to succeed in relying upon government for economic and social regeneration, while at the same time working to reduce the disjunction between Washington and American society, remains open to question. Clearly, Clinton's schemes to 're-invent government' and transform it into frameworks of mutual obligation and non-bureaucratic forms of administration have been prompted by his desire to be both an activist and a populist president. The attempt to close the gap between the public and the federal government, by drawing the former to the latter on a communitarian basis, may not in the end be a feasible proposition. Nevertheless, what it shows is the driving force of a professional politician intent upon attending to the central problem of his own likely detachment from the public while serving in Washington. With the prospect of another Perot campaign in 1996, and the likelihood of other insurgency movements both inside and outside the Democratic party, it seem probable that Clinton will be hard-pressed to maintain his outsider credentials while being persistently and visibly located at the very centre of government.

CHAPTER 3

Outsiders and spatial leadership in modern British politics

In many respects, the perversities of spatial leadership are peculiarly American in nature. They seem perfectly consistent with a political culture that evidently possess a state but has 'no acceptable tradition of one'.[1] As a consequence, it is possible to turn political scepticism into a political conviction and to use it to compete for high political office. In the United States, a politician can run against government itself, in order to become not merely part of the offending structure, but its most central and active part. Once there, he can exploit America's populist anxieties, dissenting traditions and libertarian temperament to maintain a position inside government by being seen to be conspicuously outside of it and unaccountable for it. To many, this bizarre dissociation is unique to the United States. It is seen to be a derivative of America's own constitutional development, its characteristically fragmented system of government, its idiosyncratic forms of political mobilisation and the unique ancestry of its republican attachment to limited government. Plenty of arguments can be marshalled along these lines but they begin to look less secure when Margaret Thatcher's premiership is taken into account. Indeed, many parallels can be drawn between the nature of her leadership and the motives, objectives, and strategies of recent presidential leadership. And in the same way that presidential leadership can reveal deep-seated and long-term developments in the American polity, so the changes in the British premiership during the 1980s also signify the existence of political developments which, in all likelihood, will make spatial leadership a permanent feature of the British political landscape.

Margaret Thatcher's remarkable cultivation of spatial leadership was rooted in the most fertile soil for such a phenomenon. She considered herself, and was widely regarded by others, to be an outsider. This outlook was probably drawn first and foremost from her background as a tradesman's daughter in Grantham during the great depression and from the nonconformist environment of her Methodist upbringing. By all accounts, she was a

59

lonely girl at school and became a solitary woman at Oxford. Her seriousness and cold sense of purpose cut her off from many of her contemporaries. Margaret Roberts' prodigious zeal was directed towards a political career and after acquiring financial security through marriage, she rose through the party ranks to become the first woman member of a British cabinet. As Secretary of State for Education in Edward Heath's government (1970-1974), she was not expected to progress much further in the government hierarchy. In the view of James Prior,

> Margaret Thatcher had little experience of the higher levels of Government. She had always been cold-shouldered by Ted; she sat in Cabinet on his right side, carefully hidden by the Secretary of the Cabinet, who was always leaning forward to take notes. It was the most difficult place for anyone to catch the Prime Minister's eye, and I am sure that she was placed there quite deliberately.[2]

Mrs Thatcher herself said at the time that she did not believe there would be a woman prime minister in her lifetime.

But conditions changed dramatically in the mid-1970s. The chronic position of the Conservative party and of the country's economy generated a set of conditions that allowed an outsider with Margaret Thatcher's temperament and perspective to become a serious contender for high office. The manner of her advance would become the hallmark of her subsequent position. It would be a standing vindication of her outsider status and her outsider politics. Furthermore, it would stand as a guiding precedent to the style and operation of her leadership. Ultimately, she refined and cultivated her outsider status in government to such an extent that it became indistinguishable from her whole conception of leadership.

Three factors stand out as being instrumental in the development of Margaret Thatcher's reputation not only as an outsider but as an outsider who could exploit her weaknesses and disadvantages, and translate them into formidable political strengths.

First, were the circumstances surrounding her elevation to the party leadership in 1975. After two general election defeats in 1974 and a series of earlier policy reversals in government, there was a groundswell of opinion in the Conservative parliamentary party in favour of a leadership election. At the very least, it was thought that an election would help re-establish Edward Heath's authority. Although Heath's aloof and even arrogant style of leadership had embittered a large proportion of the party, it was assumed that he would prevail in any first election. It was thought that no one outside the cabinet had the requisite weight to displace him and that no one inside the cabinet would dare be so disloyal as to challenge him. Speculation surrounded Sir Keith Joseph, the maverick right-winger who had been Heath's minister for social services. But after being rash enough to make a number of inflam-matory speeches about social and economic policy, he refused to let his name go forward. Edward du Cann, chairman of the 1922 Committee, was another who had flirted with the idea of challenging Heath, but who subsequently refused to declare himself a candidate.

These wilting violets forced the dissidents to look elsewhere. Eventually, they came up with Margaret Thatcher, a middle ranking member of the shadow cabinet. According to James Prior,

> I don't think anyone at that time really thought that Margaret was a serious contender. After all it was quite clear that Airey Neave and a number of others were determined to get rid of Ted, and they were going to try to find almost anyone to take on, and that's why they first of all went to Keith Joseph, and when he dropped out for some reason or other, then they actually approached Edward du Cann and he dropped out for some reason or other, so they were getting pretty desperate by then. There was literally no one else within the Cabinet or anywhere near the Cabinet who was prepared to stand against Ted Heath, unless Ted Heath said he was going to go.[3]

Prior did not believe that even Thatcher 'thought of herself as a candidate for the leadership'.[4] The dissidents, however, needed her to test the waters and measure the vulnerability of Heath. They knew that if Heath could be suffi-ciently embarrassed in the first ballot to stand down as a candidate, then the rules allowed other candidates to enter for a second ballot. A heavyweight like Willie Whitelaw would no longer feel confined by his loyalty to Heath. Once the initial breach was made, he could step in and cruise to the leadership that many believed was his rightful inheritance.

Margaret Thatcher's position was a very exposed one. 'I know', she said, 'that if I lose, my political career is over'.[5] For her, it was the gambler's throw of an outsider who was no part of the inner club of senior Conservatives and Tory grandees.

> Questions were raised about the desirability of the party being led by a Grantham grocer's daughter with a second- class degree in Chemistry, only able to be in politics because she had a rich husband, and totally ignorant of foreign affairs.[6]

To Airey Neave, her own campaign manager, Thatcher was a stalking horse capable only of inflicting damage on Heath. In some respects, she was even limited as a stalking horse. She was a woman in a male-dominated profession and seeking to lead a notoriously hierarchical party. As Secretary of State for Education, she had also been associated with small but politically damaging issues like her widely condemned ending of free milk to primary school children between the ages of eight and eleven. On the credit side,

Neave had two things going for him. First, probably more than two-thirds of the parliamentary party wanted Edward Heath out. Second, his candidate was a conceivable, if not yet credible leader.[7]

The antipathy towards Heath was evident in the shock result of the first ballot. Thatcher defeated Heath by 130 votes to 119. Heath promptly withdrew. Others rushed in to fill his place (Willie Whitelaw, Geoffrey Howe, James Prior, John Peyton) but the momentum behind Thatcher was too great. She won the second ballot easily. The party had rallied to its new leader. To most Conservatives, it was enough that 'she offered something different'[8] – different that is from Heath.

Her supporters could hardly believe it and her critics within the Party reacted by speaking of her as a stop-gap or a temporary aberration which in due course would be corrected. That the Party had chosen such a dissident and outsider was phenomenon enough. But this outsider was a woman.[9]

Margaret Thatcher had become leader of a party that hardly knew her. She had toppled an incumbent party leader and former prime minister, but she was still an outsider. That was seen by many of her supporters and detractors as a handicap. It was seen by Margaret Thatcher as an opportunity to be exploited.

The *second* factor in the development of Margaret Thatcher's version of spatial leadership centred upon the content of her personal manifesto for the party. She not only stood outside the mainstream conventions on public policy which Conservatives had adhered to since World War II, but wished to use her position to challenge the premises and principles of that orthodoxy. The 'post-war settlement' represented an intuitive agreement between the two main parties on the basic ground rules for managing the political economy. It was rooted in the Conservative party's recognition of the welfare state, and, in its acceptance of the central objective of full employment, together with the need for Keynesian techniques of macro-economic management to finance these twin pillars of social stability. The Conservatives had no wish to risk the social upheaval of attempting to dismantle all the innovations of the 1945-51 Labour government. In their desire to bury the party's association with the mass unemployment of the 1930s, the Conservatives accommodated themselves to the principle of a permanent managerial state. As a result, Conservative governments in the 1950s and early 1960s were politically attuned to the need to cooperate with the trade unions, to intervene in the economy through planning, subsidies and incentives, to maintain a high level of public expenditure on social welfare programmes, and to exploit deficit financing in order to maintain demand in the economy, even if this was at the price of mild inflation.

By 1970, this pattern of consensus politics had become ossified into a controlling orthodoxy. Its effects on the size, the role and the responsibilities of the state were the cause of increasing concern to a large section of the Conservative party. It was troubled by what appeared to be the self-propelling dynamics of state intervention in which government action and provision led ineluctably to more and more of the same. The state had already become the largest single employer, spender and consumer in the economy – and the pace of its advance showed no signs of deceleration. Intervention was increasingly seen to be not merely a requisite response to an economy declining in productivity and competition, but also a direct material cause of the economy's poor performance. As the private sector diminished in relative size and wealth, the standard circular response was to increase state intervention even more, in order to correct for the lack of economic growth.

The incoming Heath government of 1970 was pledged to radical change that would break this circle of rising public expenditure and diminishing economic performance. Heath intended to reduce government spending, to curb trade union power and to restore competition. He wanted to dispense with prices and incomes policy. His intention of injecting the economy with the incentives and disciplines of the free market meant that the government would no longer bail out 'lame duck' companies. But within two years, the Heath government had had to engage in a series of humiliating U-turns. The *force majeure* of established political forces and expectations were too great even for the government to resist.

As the economy continued to falter – albeit as a result of a world recession resulting from a quadrupling of oil prices – public expenditure grew, companies were bailed out and a prices and incomes policy was imposed in a frantic effort to control inflationary pressures. After being defeated in a miners' strike in 1972 when the National Union of Mineworkers effectively destroyed the government's original policy of voluntary pay restraint, the Heath administration was confronted by another miners' strike in 1974. This time Heath went to the country for a mandate to renew the government's authority. Campaigning on the slogan of 'who governs the country', Heath lost the election. He lost another general election later in the same year on the same theme of industrial relations and social disorder. The Labour Party promised industrial peace. It claimed that only it knew how to deal effectively with the unions and that it was the only party which had a knowledgeable grasp of the corporate state. 'Heath had tried first to escape from the post-war settlement, then to prop it up'.[10] In the end, he was utterly defeated by it.

As the Labour government (1974-79) also proceeded to sink into double digit inflation, industrial strife and rising demands on public expenditure, the defeated Conservative party began a critical review not just of the Heath government but of the entire nature of the post-war settlement. There was no fixed group or firm philosophy, just a set of individuals intent upon critical scrutiny and motivated by an appetite for radical alternatives and robust action. Margaret Thatcher moved amongst these circles. She was particularly influenced by Sir Keith Joseph and Alfred Sherman's radical re-evaluation of the post-war economy. They in their turn were influenced by the monetarist doctrines of Milton Friedman and by the revival of interest in F.A. Hayek's stark dichotomy between state action and individual liberty. Assisted by the publications of the Institute of Economic Affairs, the 'new right' or the 'neo-liberals' generated an adventurism in heretical ideas in favour of economic liberty and against state intervention, high taxation, and inflation.

This reaching out for new solutions was set against a background of stagnation and inflation that provided an urgency and sense of licence to the search for alternatives. The pathological sense of social disintegration was heightened by the disclosure of several proposed 'private armies' of citizen vigilantes, dedicated to the preservation of 'law and order'. Britain was thought to be degenerating into an 'ungovernable' country.[11] Whether the post-war British state had always harboured irreconcilable contradictions, or whether the 'consensus' had simply deteriorated under the duress of 'stagflation', the net effect had been the abandonment of long term public policy in favour of short term pay-offs for specific interests. In one study suggestively entitled *Britain against Itself* (1982),[12] Samuel Beer pointed out that the unintended consequence of the collectivist state's responsibility for social services and economic management was the multiplication of pressure groups, scrambling for benefits, incentives and concessions. These groups were locked into a self-defeating process from which they could not escape. As parties competed, and outbid one another, for the electoral support of such groups, governments became hostages to the accumulation of their compound promises. As a result, they were compelled to increase public expenditure, to enlarge government borrowing and to accommodate inflationary wage settlements.

It was possible to go even further and to claim that the government's autonomy was not merely being compromised by pressure groups and private interests, so much as being physically and conceptually replaced by a system in which producer interests and trade unions were becoming fully incorporated into government decision-making. Governments were losing their identity and their authority as government policy was made explicitly dependent upon the consent and persuasive power of particular interests, and especially the interests of the burgeoning trade unions. In an effort to achieve the elixir of economic growth, whilst controlling inflation, successive governments offered trade unions additional powers, protections and resources to buy support for government pay policies. This strengthened the unions' ability to press for higher demands, thereby increasing the inflationary pressures on pay policies and threatening government plans for economic growth. The nature of this ensuing dynamic is encapsulated by Robert Skidelsky.

> The growth of state responsibility for making the economy work went hand in hand with the growth of union power to prevent it from working . . . In essence the bargaining position of the unions in industry was strengthened partly to win T.U.C. support for pay restraint, in turn seen necessary to secure the growth which would deliver greater benefits to the working class. When the growth and the benefits failed to materialise what was left was simply enhanced union power which could be turned against the state – either as employer or policy-maker.[13]

Peter Jenkins agrees that governmental authority was undermined but, in his view, the sort of corporatism employed by British governments did not deteriorate because it had never been sustainable.

> Too much was asked of the unions in this; in return they asked too much of government. Neither side could deliver. For each side the negative aspects of their too ambitious bargain came to outweigh the positive: the unions practised wage restraint according to their lights but full employment was abandoned none the less and social spending cut; the government conferred all manner of privileges upon the unions, enhancing their negative power, but wage inflation continued none the less and there was no bonus in productivity.[14]

In the same way that governments had been forced to rely upon the unions' power of political mobilisation, the unions themselves had been similarly entrapped into a denial of their natural functions. They were expected to share responsibility for economic management and in the process to limit free collective bargaining, in order to achieve economic growth, or at least to sustain their members' living standards. Predictably, the partnership of government ministers and union leaders fuelled suspicion that the arrangement was a device for limiting the value of wages. This belief limited the discretion of the union leadership in economic management at the same time that it aroused insurgent forces within the unions themselves. As the government lost control of its policy-making process, the union leadership lost control of its own members. Militant local action and unofficial strikes made industry increasingly unmanageable. Corporatism was seen not to have resolved the problem of ungovernability, so much as to have exacerbated it. Government had used corporatism to penetrate deeper into macro-economic management, but, in doing so, it had lost not only its authority but also its distance from micro-economic conditions and individual circumstances.

> The government came to be held responsible for what people were paid, not only for the general level of wages but for the disparities between the pay of a nurse and a miner, a general and a policeman. Government soon found itself carrying a can of worms marked 'social justice'.[15]

Government had inadvertently taken on an impossible agenda and had in the process acquired a reputation of vacuous prominence and extravagant sterility in British society.

Margaret Thatcher was part of a group of Conservatives who wanted the most thorough and comprehensive reconsideration of the assumptions behind the post-war settlement. The intellectual force was provided by Sir Keith Joseph who in a series of speeches and articles sought to articulate the need for a reconstruction of the political economy. He pointed out, for example, that inflation was becoming a structural feature of British society because of the government's inability to resist expanding economic demand in the hope that government spending would produce the cure-all of growth. To Sir Keith, it was necessary to proclaim that

> Keynes is dead, that no government can secure full employment irrespective of what people do, that it depends on each individual to a greater or lesser extent, that baling out threatens to sink the ship and should be stopped before the ship sinks.[16]

Mrs Thatcher joined the charge against the excessive state and the high tax economy that ignored not just the productive, but also the moral, elements of human motivations in working for personal advancement and self-esteem. She drew attention to the 'noble ideals of personal responsibility' and to the fact that 'in some respects the concepts of social responsibility had turned sour'.[17] At the risk of increasing inequality and even unemployment, Mrs Thatcher believed it was necessary to release human and social energies by relating rewards to effort, risk and wealth creation. Her economic vision, therefore, included

> the promotion of thrift, the defence of 'sound' rather than 'suitcase' money, the matching of effort to appetite, the provision of positive incentives rather than of negative cushioning, the privatization of state-owned industries, the encouragement of calculated risk-taking within the context of a market freely responsive to patterns of individual choice, and an increase in the number of those with a propertied stake in social order.[18]

These principles, unequivocally stated and proposed in deadly earnest irrespective of the consequences, were sweeping and highly controversial in nature. To many, they were positively inflammatory and quite contrary to the governing ethos of the post-war settlement. It was thought that she, and people like her, were intent upon marshalling popular support against the progressive achievements and civilising traditions of that settlement. They acquired the reputation of being

> less concerned simply to shift the balance between capital and labour within the crumbling framework of the 'post-war settlement' than to abandon the whole project in favour of a new edifice more favourable to capital.[19]

Such an indictment would not have perturbed an individual like Mrs Thatcher. This is because she not only had an outsider's flair for the unconventional, but possessed that element of moral certainty and inner righteousness that thrives in such a self-conscious outsider. To Margaret Thatcher, being an outsider was synonymous with being right, and to sustain that certainty it was necessary to remain an outsider. One of Mrs Thatcher's central convictions was that the rest of her convictions were dependent upon a zeal and passionate intransigence that were warranted in her eyes by the moral integrity of her outlook. Bearing in mind the compromises, reversals and defeats of the Heath government, the idea of a true faith and that of an unshakeable attachment to it, together with an absolute commitment to defend it, was part and parcel of her programme. It was integral to her *raison d'être* as a politician and to her style of leadership.

In this respect, Margaret Thatcher was doubly exceptional. She was outside the conventional mainstream of the party in terms of her policy positions. But she was also outside the party's traditions of pragmatism and aversion to philosophical speculation. She openly adhered to a set of iconoclastic economic principles and, to make matters worse, she did so with an intransigence that seemed to be as challenging to the Conservative party as it was to the Labour party.

The two elements of Margaret Thatcher's leadership mentioned so far – her outsider status and her unconventional proposals – were both instrumental in generating a *third* component. This was Mrs Thatcher's populist appeal to those who had come to feel marginalised by the convulsive events of the 1970s. To those who could only look upon the period with a mixture of anxiety, resentment and incomprehension, Mrs Thatcher offered the prospect of a tangible expression of private grievance and inner outrage. Whether it was an old-age pensioner whose savings had been eaten up by inflation, or families reduced to candlelight by industrial action, or skilled workers humbled by unskilled workers, Mrs Thatcher's sentiments and style evoked a widespread murmuring of acknowledgement. Her outsider status, her pugnacious temperament and her tough message of old economic disciplines, individual responsibility and social obligations aroused interest in her as an individual emblem of social unrest. Mrs Thatcher for her part saw the political advantages to be accrued from reciprocating the interest. In the highly volatile

67

political conditions of the 1970s and early 1980s when political allegiances were weakening and third parties could prompt sudden changes in electoral behaviour, Mrs Thatcher sought to establish her own direct links to the electorate. Like Richard Nixon, she wanted to identify with society's 'silent majority'.

Many of Mrs Thatcher's parliamentary colleagues in the Conservative party were very wary about her avowed rejection of the 'post-war settlement'. They approved of her performance as a blistering and unremitting critic of the Labour government. They condoned her crusade against socialism as a national disease, even though the tone of her attacks was strident and the possible repercussions of her ideas on social stability were serious. But many senior Conservatives proceeded on the assumption that she would inevitably have to accommodate the starker qualities of her vision to the prevailing forces and traditions of British politics. It was believed that she was enough of a politician to realise that persuasion, conciliation and concession were necessary to make any headway with a radical reform programme. Even one of her staunchest critics, Francis Pym, saw that 'although a populist by nature, she recognised the need to change the climate of intellectual opinion in the country'.[20] But this could only be done gradually and pragmatically.

Mrs Thatcher was certainly a politician and a far more adept one than her outspoken mentor, Sir Keith Joseph. But her political sense led her to appreciate the advantages of cultivating a public constituency. Negotiations could be reached discreetly. What was important was that they should not be seen to characterise her administration or to compromise the integrity of her public connections. Appearance was of central importance. The public image of a public leader, directly implicated in popular issues, could generate its own material benefits of enhanced influence and leverage inside the party and the government. For Margaret Thatcher, it was better to be up-front and calculatedly headstrong rather than to be collegiate, measured and impotent. Like Ronald Reagan, the strategy was one of defiance and theatrical bluff. Thatcher would seek the centre stage and ignore protocol and convention in pursuit of her radical ambitions. By conveying a picture of political determination and conspicuous personal resolve, the bluff could pay off with compromises overlooked, the programme advanced and her leadership secured.

There are many facets to, and interpretations of, Margaret Thatcher's populism. To some, it was confined to her new style or methods of political communication. This could include her positive ability to translate the intellectual critiques of the New Right into the easy accessibility of simple moral axioms, gut reactions and housewifely economies. It could also include her negative 'streetfighter' or 'fish wife' performances in the House of Commons or the hustings. The combination could generate mixed feelings from even her admirers. Her biographer, Kenneth Harris, for example, recalls that she could

> lay about her on the level of everyday argument, deliver personal attacks in the language of the market place and more than hold her own if a shouting match began. Her voice was refined, her appearance was elegant, her manner cool and calm, but the commonsense and basic values she expressed came from the grocer's daughter. Among the other qualities she now displayed was that of being the nearest thing to a demagogue the leaders of the Conservative Party had ever produced. She bid fair to become the first Conservative populist.[21]

Others give emphasis to the policy components of Thatcher's populism. They point to her continual public support of such right-wing back-bench issues as capital punishment and immigration control even after her election as party leader and her subsequent rise to the premiership. Julian Critchley observed at the time that 'her popularity increases the further down the party structure one goes'.[22] In many respects, this was because she remained one of the rank and file. Her affinity with the party workers was described by Edward Pearce in terms of physical and emotional compulsion.

> Mrs Thatcher – a lady in a petal hat made queen – genuinely loved her party, breathed in and out with it, and shared its hates and loves, especially its instincts for class war, for which members of a higher social class felt fastidious distaste. It was not nice to watch but it was authentic.[23]

In another sense, her populism could be seen as discreet rather than explicit – a conclusion drawn from her economic programme. John Vincent, for example, believed that her market economics appealed to the skilled working class whose position in the industrial hierarchy had been eroded during the 1970s.

> Thatcherism resembles trade unionism in that both are about differentials. The need which Mrs Thatcher intuited in 1975-80 was to give a moral meaning to latent anti-egalitarian feeling among those who had seen their differentials eroded.[24]

In yet another dimension, Thatcher's populism was interpreted as indicative of a major sociological change. Opinions vary on the nature of the change. One view sees Thatcherism as representing a conscious mobilisation of the British people against the social democratic state, in which political differences and identities were submerged into a more consensual and neutral polity. Another perspective sees Thatcher's populism as an 'authoritarian populism' which was essentially manipulative in its intentions and divisive in its nature:

> It is not concerned with an active populist mobilization – which would be threatening to the decisional autonomy of Thatcherism. Instead it is concerned

to outflank organized opposition from government backbenches (especially the so-called wets) as well as from the labour movement. For, if Thatcher represents the people directly, opposition can be presented as undemocratic.[25]

Whatever the relative merits of these various perspectives of Thatcher's populism, they all serve to substantiate the close relationship between the style of her leadership and the nature of her personal background and rise to prominence. Her position outside the mainstream of the party and outside the governing orthodoxies of post-war government lent weight to the radical credentials of her economic programme. Her conspicuous independence and her iconoclastic aims reflected and illuminated each other to the extent that they appeared, ultimately, to be analogous in nature. The dogmatic and populist style of her leadership was also closely interconnected with Thatcher's policy objectives and her outsider status. As an outsider, Mrs Thatcher was especially adept at risking the unconventional and circumventing the traditional intermediary structures that lay between government and the public. As an outsider and a populist politician, she was able to use intransigence not just as a means to acquire her policy aims, but as a functional objective in its own right. Through the spectacle of her intransigence, she sought to direct the force of public protest, to appeal to popular temperament and to rally a change in social attitudes.

Obduracy served Mrs Thatcher's interests because it inferred the existence of a cause that was simply too profound and indispensable to warrant even the consideration of compromise.

> Indeed, one of the dominant influences on the Prime Minister and her closest colleagues has been U-turn Psychosis, also known as Barber's Syndrome. She has been obsessed by the belief that what Tennyson called 'honest doubt' is the enemy of revolutionary political action. And it was on economic and political revolution, leading to a revival of Britain and the final defeat of socialism that Margaret Thatcher had set her heart.[26]

The revolution and revival, of course, were as much to do with radicalising public impulses as they were with government deregulation and reduced public expenditure. And to complete the circle, it was the visceral nature of the issues raised by Thatcher's leadership which helped in turn to serve that leadership – firstly by highlighting the importance of a leader's public prominence to radical change, and secondly, by legitimising the outsider qualities appropriate to providing such novel direction.

Mrs Thatcher's outsider origins, her radical programme and her populism were the key ingredients in her development of spatial leadership in British policies. Her premiership exhibited the full potential that existed for this type of leadership in a system which appeared to be quite unamenable to such a form of high-level dissociation. Although the story of Margaret Thatcher's period in office is a familiar one, it frequently overlooks the significance of her ability to occupy the centre of power whilst simultaneously distancing herself from it.

The conventional account of Mrs Thatcher's rise to power plots her progress from the periphery to the centre; from a flamboyant outsider to an apparently immovable insider. At the beginning of her premiership, she had had to resort to an aggressive style of public leadership and 'conviction politics'.

> Partly this was a matter of her personality . . . But it was at least as much a matter of the objective situation in which she found herself. She was forced to behave like an outsider for the simple reason that she was one.[27]

She was in a minority position in her party, in her cabinet and in the government at large. In contrast to her predecessors, Mrs Thatcher had her own policy agenda. Moreover, it was an agenda that was not shared by a majority of the Conservative party or even by a majority of Mrs Thatcher's own cabinet. For the sake of party unity, she had been forced to include several 'wets' in her cabinet, who were expected to defend the consensus approach of the 'post-war system' against the assault of the Thatcherites. As Mrs Thatcher established herself in office, she acquired a reputation for pre-eminence and even dominance. She substituted 'dry' ministers for 'wet' ministers, circumvented or pre-empted cabinet decision-making and exerted closer political control of the civil service. At the same time, she secured two re-election victories (1983 and 1987) that captivated the party rank and file, and which allowed her 'to produce a team of ministers loyal to her person and, more importantly, to her policy agenda'.[28]

And yet, in spite of the increased security of her position, Mrs Thatcher's outlook and leadership style did not change. It was neither to her taste nor to her advantage to be regarded as an established figure in the established streets of Whitehall and Westminster. To a populist politician who had benefited from and encouraged populist politics in Britain, Mrs Thatcher was keen to play down her position and to preserve that distance from government by which she could exert pressure upon it. Thatcher's *raison d'être* as a leader continued to be based upon the notion that government itself was the overriding issue in contemporary politics. This outlook was rooted in her self-image as an outsider standing apart from prevailing political ideas and practices. But it was also a direct consequence of her political instincts. Far from feeling dominant, Thatcher was more aware of the severity of the political constraints surrounding her, and the need to resort to negotiations and accommodation with other centres of political power. Even in her own cabinet, she was regularly in a minority position and frequently defeated. The feeling that she was nowhere near to being dominant could lead to an over-reaction. In Peter Jenkins's words:

> Her outsider mentality led her to regard government as a personal conspiracy against her. Her technique was to conspire against it. This she did by bringing in outsiders, by dealing directly with officials who took her fancy, by operating a network of trusties strategically placed in the departments.[29]

More important though than not feeling dominant was the need not to convey the impression of dominance. In other words, Thatcher's political instincts drove her to try and retain her initial outsider status in government, even during the very period when the force and centrality of her power was at its most formidable. To a remarkable extent and for an extraordinary length of time, Margaret Thatcher was effective in preserving that original sense of space between herself and the government, which characterised her rise to office. 'Government' could then remain the issue, with Thatcher located some distance away from its most negative associations of high taxation, wasteful spending and mass regulation. Accordingly, Thatcher could revel in her cabinet defeats, maintain her reputation as a non-appeaser, and engage in highly publicised interventions into government departments even to the extent of claiming individual policy areas (e.g. the national curriculum, local government finance, football supporters' identity cards) as her own. 'I am the cabinet rebel',[30] she once remarked with pride. It was important to her personally to be a rebel. But it was even more important for her political position and leadership style to be *seen* as a rebel.

Behaving as an outsider was a natural precondition to being seen and understood as an outsider. And being an outsider gave her the licence to engage in that form of leadership which suited her best. Her favoured role was that of beleaguered enlightenment facing dark forces of restrictive practices, moribund immunities and impregnable privileges. This was a conflict where righteousness was always viewed to be inversely proportional to size. Such leadership made her curiously dependent upon the existence of forces that were both plausible and threatening. She battled against inflation, taxation, government expenditure and public ownership in her crusade to rid the country of the scourge of socialism. She 'stood up' to Arthur Scargill and the National Union of Mineworkers, to General Galtieri and the Argentinian military in the South Atlantic, and to Jacques Delors and his sovereignty – sapping proposals for European union and social reform. Most of all, she tested her mettle, and that of her mission, against the public sector forces of the British establishment. By choice and temperament, hers was

> punctuated by set battles, sometimes broken off, but always resumed, against all

those forces which, in her view, had brought, or were bringing Britain low.[31]

Battling drew attention to her leadership, but it also highlighted what it was she could not control and why she needed such a belligerent approach.

Despite her reputed dominance of government, therefore, Thatcher was still dependent upon its reputed autonomy and inertia for her primary *raison d'être*. Her spiritual detachment from government allowed her to engage in a publicly fought holy war against government and to maintain the paradoxical position of increasing state powers, in order to decentralise government control. This form of detachment was not the same sort that had crippled Heath's premiership. His detachment denoted arrogance, isolation and weakness. Margaret Thatcher's detachment was consciously planned and founded securely on close ties with Conservative backbenchers and popular opinion. Margaret Thatcher, like Ronald Reagan, was often described as having the ability to give expression to the anxieties and prejudices of the lower middle class and, in particular, to the upper working classes. Thatcher's tough confrontational approach to issues was often deplored by professional people and by traditional Tory gentlemen, but it found approval amongst many in the C2 (skilled workers) stratum of society. To Peregrine Worsthorne, Thatcher's style

> conformed with much of their own experience; rang true to the realities of their own lives. On this point there is really no doubt about what C2s believe. They believe that it is a rough old world in which only the strong and bloody-minded have a chance of surviving.[32]

Worsthorne went on to add that 'the political class had no faith in Britain: disapproved of the bourgeoisie and sniffed at the working class. Mrs Thatcher attached legendary qualities to both'.[33]

Mindful of this sort of constituency and her pugnacious reputation, it was her practice to flout conventional opinion in Parliament on such sensitive issues as immigration, capital punishment and European integration, sure in the knowledge that defeats in these issues could be turned into discreet public victories for her strategy of 'spatial leadership'. Cabinet rows and splits could also be deployed to serve the same purpose. Thatcher's was a high-risk strategy, but it did possess the public glamour of high risk. It kept her both centre stage and peculiarly off-stage for eleven years. It produced charges of her being an imperious prime minister at the same time that it revealed her weaknesses, exposed her cabinet defeats and aroused concern over government disunity. The mixture of an apparently raw appetite for personal power and a public facility for melting away from the appearance of its possession baffled fellow politicians and political observers alike.

This insistence on being the active leader of the government – on leading it, as it were, from outside rather than inside – manifests itself in another, rather curious way: in the prime minister's penchant for talking about the government as though she were not a member of it. The customary pronoun used by prime ministers when speaking about their own government is 'we'; Thatcher's pronoun is usually 'we', but often 'they'. 'They' are making life difficult for for her; 'they' are having to be persuaded; 'they' are too concerned with defending the interests of their own departments. The language is not typically British. It is more like that used by American presidents when speaking about Congress. It is significant that the prime minister thinks in this way of her own cabinet as being, in effect, another branch of government. And, just as American presidents have to put up with hostility from Congress, so Thatcher has to put up with her not always amenable cabinet colleagues. (Anthony King)[34]

I'm sure that loyalty matters enormously to her. I think 'Is he one of us?' is one of the most remarkable phrases that has ever come out of a prime minister in Britain. In a sense it's almost as though she thought of herself as being one of a small band of pioneers and conspirators that found themselves in a kind of minority, an exposed position in Whitehall and Westminster, and that they had to stick together as a club in order to get the great machinery of state to be responsive to their new and radical approach. (Peter Shore)[35]

Her persona is, in part, that of the ordinary person: the tradesman's daughter, the person who talks of 'little' issues, housekeeping for example, expresses 'little' emotions, perpetually giving voice to the desires and anxieties of 'ordinary people', often to the point where she conveys the notion that she, like them, is not interested in politics, but is simply the woman we see bustling about with her handbag on her arm. (John Gaffney)[36]

What I think is her peculiar quality is that she manages at once to be a powerful leader of her government and to detach herself from her government – to be in a sense leader of the government and leader of the opposition at one and the same time. I was very struck, watching her dedicating the memorial in St James's Square to that poor policewoman who was shot in that terrible terrorist incident, when she said, 'These incidents must stop.' Now this was very interesting. It was detaching herself from the government, because if anybody can stop it . . . it's the government who can, not the county council or the opposition or whatever. It's the government who can do it, and yet she was saying, 'It's intolerable that this goes on. It ought to be stopped. It ought to be stopped by, not *my* government then, but *the* government. Why doesn't the government stop it?' She does have this curious capacity, which is clever. (Roy Jenkins)[37]

The oddity of Mrs Thatcher's position, is that she both is and is not the Government. Her personal brand of populism enables her to detach herself from government actions whenever it suits her to do so. Usually it is the Government's inactions from which she distances herself, so that when ministries actually do anything she can take the credit. In 1984 she said that she hoped that she had 'shattered the illusion that government could somehow substitute for individual performance'. Populism is thus identified with being anti-government. This means that it is ideally suited to radical Conservatives when they are in opposition. But what are they to do when they *are* the Government? The answer, for Mrs Thatcher, is all too easy: she can disown the lot of them whenever it suits her. (Noel Malcolm)[38]

Cabinet discussions were kept to a minimum, whilst she reserved the right to make public her disagreements with her own ministers. . . .[She] was notorious for keeping up a private running commentary on the failings of her ministers and their policies, as if the Government was in some way nothing to do with her. Stevas has describes how she once stood on a chair during a party in Downing Street and announced herself to be 'the rebel head of an establishment government'. (Robert Harris)[39]

Coinciding with Margaret Thatcher's remarkable distance from the government that she purportedly dominated was the emergence of an American-style distinction between leadership and policy. The differentiation in question is that between the public's assessment of a leader, based on the possession of various personal traits thought to be essential to leadership, and the public's disapproval of many of the policy objectives associated with that leadership. Survey evidence suggests that Mrs Thatcher's 'New Right' strictures on moral standards, censorship, tax cuts, free enterprise, market discipline, individual responsibility, privatisation and government dependency were not shared by a majority of respondents – even at the height of Mrs Thatcher's popularity. Attitudes on issues like health, housing, education and unemployment demonstrated that 'the public remained wedded to the collective, welfare ethic of social democracy'.[40] And yet, in spite of 'the failure of Thatcher's cultural crusade',[41] she was 'widely if grudgingly respected as a leader'.[42] She translated government and its role in British society into a full blown political issue. In doing so, Thatcher was able to compensate for her poor showing on social and economic issues by attracting widespread affirmation of her 'fitness to govern', exemplified more than anything else by Mrs Thatcher's own leadership. In the opinion of Ivor Crewe it was Thatcherism's 'statecraft' which was 'at least as distinctive as its economic and cultural prejudices' and which represented the 'neglected element of its electoral success'.[43] Even when Mrs Thatcher was deep in the doldrums of her third term in May 1990, William Rees-Mogg felt impelled to remind his readers that the complaints over her should be interpreted with great care.

Almost everyone I meet grumbles about some aspect of Mrs Thatcher's personality or policy, but most of them admire her strength of will and trust her determination to defend British interests. I suspect that people both complain about and vote for strength of character and, that she is in fact a greater electoral asset than the polls would imply.[44]

Like President Reagan, Mrs Thatcher was a highly prominent and successful leader whose policy programme was firmly rejected by the public. Nevertheless, they both won re-election by large margins. Mrs Thatcher did so on two occasions in 1983 and 1987. President Reagan regularly enjoyed a high public approval rating *in spite* of his political proposals. It is often pointed out that Mrs Thatcher was different in so far as she never achieved the public approval levels of either Reagan or any other post-war prime minister, apart that is from Edward Heath whose government collapsed in 1974. Her average approval between 1979 and 1987 was only 39% compared, for example, with Harold Macmillan (1957-1963) with 51%, Harold Wilson (1964-1970, 1974-1976) with 59% and 41%, and James Callaghan (1976-79) with 46%.[45] However, what has to be borne in mind is that such leaders embodied the programmatic and collegiate basis of their respective parties and drew support to themselves accordingly. Mrs Thatcher by contrast received an approval rating on the basis of her performance as Mrs Thatcher. Given the high level of public dissatisfaction with Thatcher's policies (average of 67.0%) reflecting the broadscale contempt in which her objectives were held, the figure of 39% for the public's satisfaction with Thatcher herself was a substantial one.[46] It denoted the capacity of a leader to transcend her own widely declared aims and to appeal to the electorate on grounds that were not solely confined to, or reducible to, social and economic policy.

In a parliamentary system whose chief characteristic is the fusion of the legislature and the executive through party discipline and collective responsibility, Mrs Thatcher's leadership was remarkable for the way that it allowed her to escape from her government's own record and to be judged on alternative criteria. It was itself a mark of her leadership that government management and style became as important as what a government did or intended to do. Reminiscent of the traditions and impulses of America's separation of powers system, 'leadership' under Thatcher had become a political issue in its own right. In effect, leadership had been translated into an objective function of government and, thereby, into a distinct object of political evaluation.

It is commonly asserted that Mrs Thatcher acquired an extraordinary pre-eminence over her cabinet and, to all intents and purposes 'presided' over government. Just as common is the proposition that Mrs Thatcher's leadership was wholly exceptional and peculiar to herself and to the particular circumstances that gave rise to her premiership. In one sense this is irrefutably self-evident and something of a truism. No prime minister is exactly the same as another prime minister. Nevertheless, in a different and more important sense such a proposition is needlessly self-limiting. In seeking to account for Thatcher's leadership by recourse to exceptionalism, it not only fails to offer any real explanation, but jeopardises the potentially deeper insights and generalisations that can be drawn from Thatcher's premiership. As has already been made clear, this study is predicated on the conviction that Thatcher's period in office is just as significant for what it discloses about underlying political pressures and developments as it is for what it reveals about a singular woman.

Mrs Thatcher may have been an exceptional prime minister but in many respects the forces she was responding to and the techniques she employed in her leadership were not confined to her alone. On the contrary, they were and have been apparent in other guises, in other parties, by other leaders. The public cultivation of public space between a leader and the party and its usage to make leaders look more like leaders, so that they can participate more effectively in the contemporary forum of leadership, has become a conspicuous feature of party competition. The sources of third parties over recent years, for example, has been due in no small part to their capacity for producing leaders with a built-in licence to compete politically at some distance from their party structures. Leaders from minor parties have been able to acquire a degree of public exposure for their political views and personal attributes that has been quite out of proportion to the scale of their organisational base. In many ways, such leaders have been able to compensate for the weaknesses of their own parties by developing the appearance of comparability with the major parties at the leadership level. This has entailed a widening of the gap between such leaders and their parties. It is a gap that parties have had to condone, and even to encourage, in order to compete at the high table and to maximise their political influence.

The modern conditions of political competition have progressively stretched the space between a leader and the party from an initial licence to engage other leaders on an equal footing to an altogether more marked and public detachment. Once leaders begin to compete with one another in public arenas they quickly find that they need more and more discretion to cultivate their standing outside the party and to attend to political strategies that have become increasingly leadership oriented in nature. Leaders in this position will insist upon the widening of space between themselves and the party's decision-making structures, in fact as well as in appearance. They will insist that such space is essential to pursuing the party's interests. The process continues with leaders finding that in order to compete effectively they have to spend more and more time away from the party, thereby strengthening the appearance of space and enhancing the impression of effective leadership. Leadership in these conditions is characterised by a leader who has been leader enough to detach himself or herself from the party, whose nominal unity in allowing such distance rests upon the benefits expected or imagined by way of such high-ranking political licence.

The Liberal party has traditionally been the home of protest politics and selected anti-statism. In many ways, it has been the archetypal outsider organisation and doomed to remain outside government.[47] This has often made it an undisciplined, and arguably an unmanageable, party. But starting with Jeremy Thorpe and continuing with David Steel and Paddy Ashdown, the party has risen to a third force in British politics.[48] It was David Steel, in particular, who sought to make himself a true outsider leader of the outsider party and, in so doing, turned its focus from that of pluralist dissent to one of active organisation in the pursuit of governmental power.

Steel did not share the party's traditional passion for community politics and protest voting. He was far more interested in precipitating a realignment of the non-socialist left in British politics. With this in mind, he managed to curb his fellow Liberals' disposition for internal disputes and multiple policy positions, in order to allow himself the room to compete for the party at the leadership level. He did not so much transform the party as distance himself effectively from it. It was said of him that he did not have policies, so much as party strategies. The Lib–Lab pact, for example, which kept the Callaghan government in power between 1977 and 1978, was devised and organised by Steel. It was his personal achievement. The same might almost be said of the Liberal party's impressive performance in the 1983 General Election when, in partnership with the recently formed Social Democratic party, it amassed 7.8 million votes amounting to 25.4% of the popular vote.

Steel's high profile – long-distance leadership – kept the Liberal party in a prominent position and conditioned it to the advantages of 'top down', or rather 'top off' leadership discretion. By the time Steel stood down, the party had learned the lesson of modern leadership politics. In considering who should succeed David Steel as leader, it chose the candidate with those flamboyant qualities most likely to open up a sense of public space between himself and the party. Paddy Ashdown was preferred to Alan Beith. Although Beith was 'a much more skilful and astute politician', Ashdown was selected

> by reason of his public attractiveness: that mixture of good looks, a striking manner and self-proclamation which is known dismally to the age as charisma.[49]

The Social Democratic party displayed a similar process of accelerated development in leadership politics. Its original conception of a collective leadership in which the various skills and power sources of Roy Jenkins, Shirley Williams, David Owen and William Rodgers were pooled together, quickly gave way to the norm of a single leader (i.e. Roy Jenkins). The nature of party competition at the national level had made a single identifiable leader, who could personify and publicise the party, into an indispensable requirement. After the 1983 general election, a considerable body of opinion in the new party felt that it was important not just to have a single spokesman, but a dynamic individual leader. This being so, Roy Jenkins, the founding father of the party, felt obliged to resign and make way for David Owen.

Owen was a young, vigorous and highly self-assertive leader who, despite leading a party with a self-consciously democratic organisation, gave the impression of being so replete with leadership potential that he was in effect a free agent. His public stature as a leader was so commanding and the opportunities for him to demonstrate it in innumerable television discussions, magazine interviews and newspaper articles were so many that he often had to live down the accusation of being a leader without a party. The Social Democratic party was of course there and functioning as an organisation, but it was a function of modern political conditions that a leader was only rarely seen with his or her party in any collective sense. With David Owen's reputation for urbane self-possession and forthright political judgement, the party was made to appear distant and even superfluous to its own chances of success. To all intents and purposes, sheer leadership had displaced party in image and policy substance. The party had knowingly selected as leader a domineering individual, who was described by a fellow founder of the SDP, William Rodgers, as 'not a man who works with a team . . . or who likes listening to his equals in politics'.[50] Owen was clearly irritated at the charge that his party was not up to much if it could be so emphatically eclipsed by its leader. Nevertheless, he could not deny his own dominance of a party ostensibly designed to prevent such personal pre-eminence from occurring. His position was a mark of his own achievement in having exploited the opportunities for spatial leadership so fully and effectively. However much he may have insisted to the contrary, Owen did his best for the Social Democratic party by leaving it to one side.

When David Steel's Liberal party and David Owen's Social Democratic party came together to form the Alliance to fight the 1987 general election, the combination exposed the perils of spatial leadership. The two parties wished to maximise their electoral advantages by joining forces, but, in doing so, they inadvertently jeopardised their most valuable assets. The sense of space around each leader was hopelessly compromised. As the 'two Davids' attempted to conduct a joint election campaign, each unavoidably undermined the position of the other. The dual leadership aroused tribal enmities between the two parties. Each saw the leader of the other party as being closer to their man than they themselves were. This rivalry generated all manner of suspicions. David Owen was charged with leading David Steel to the right. David

Steel, on the other hand, wanted to direct the campaign against Mrs Thatcher rather than against the Labour party and was subsequently accused of trying to push the Alliance to the left.

William Rodgers believed that the confusion over how the Alliance tried to win both Conservative and Labour voters to its ranks was closely connected to the 'two Davids' problem.

> Only David Owen and David Steel know precisely how far their wary relationship contributed to these errors. Both have rare talent for leadership, shrewdness of judgement and immense energy. . . . But the restraint of the relationship was unnatural for two ambitious men fighting to break the system. Both parties made a virtue out of necessity, arguing that the partnership was unique and a marvel to us all. It was unique and, at the time, inescapable. But marvel it was not.[51]

Even when there was unanimity between them, David Steel complained that their individual leadership qualities were undermined by being made to look like Tweedledum and Tweedledee. 'When the two Davids were asked by the planning group not to look bored on television when the other was speaking, one of them said, "But we are bored".'[52] At other times 'the pair did try to outscore one another, and the media inevitably inflated differences of emphasis into serious disagreements'.[53] In his memoirs, *Time to Declare* (1991), David Owen recognised that both he and David Steel were using their extensive leadership prerogatives to different ends. As a consequence, 'the coherence of our campaign disintegrated'.[54]

The Alliance campaign rotted from the head down because the two Davids' approach to leadership was wholly incompatible with the basic requirements of political competition at the leadership level. Loner leaders on licence to cultivate spatial leadership were much more likely to be distrusted when placed together in a partnership of 'co-leadership'. They exposed and even exaggerated the lack of unity beneath. David Steel found it all so intolerable that he launched his plan for a full merger of the two parties only days after their failure to gain a breakthrough in the 1987 general election. David Owen sensed a takeover by the Liberals and refused to jeopardise his position by even contemplating union. As a result, he was left in the end with a small rump of zealous Social Democrats who refused to join the new Social and Liberal Democrat Party. It was a mark of Owen's extraordinary leadership skills that he was able to command a high profile leadership position even with a visibly decaying party base. There seemed to be no difference between David Owen's public prominence before the merger and after it. It was widely remarked in the late 1980s that had Britain possessed a formal presidential system, then David Owen would have been a prime candidate for the post. What commentators failed to appreciate was the extent to which Britain already had enough of a presidential system of leadership politics to sustain a disengaged and even free-floating figure like Owen in a style to which he had become accustomed as a party leader.

The Labour party has long been considered to be immune from the sort of free-wheeling improvisation that has traditionally marked the Conservative party and led to the idiosyncratic individualism of its leaders. Labour leaders by contrast are seen to be set firmly in a matrix of party organisation built layer by layer according to formal rules and procedures designed to produce a democratically constituted hierarchy. Tensions have always existed between the leadership and the rank and file; between the leadership's need for discretion and patronage and the party's claims to sustained participation and accountability; between the leadership's need for party solidarity behind it and the party's traditions of democratic dispute and open debate; between the leadership's need to compete with the Conservative party's traditions of strong leadership and loyal followership and the need to accommodate Labour's roots as an organisation developed outside parliament.

After its general election defeat in 1979, the Labour party began an acrimonious post-mortem on the Wilson–Callaghan government (1974-1979). It was widely accused not only of betraying the general principles of the Labour party, but also of reneging on specific policy commitments affirmed by Labour Party conferences and pledged in the Labour manifesto. The premiership was accused of aiding and abetting the government's displacement of the rank and file's policies and priorities. It was evident to these dissidents that the solution lay in a reorganisation of the party structure. By exerting greater party control in such areas as the party leadership and the content of the manifesto, it was hoped to increase the responsiveness and accountability of the party's elected representatives and to widen the basis of a future Labour government. The centrepiece of these reforms which were adopted by the party in 1981 was the electoral college. The power to choose the party leader was stripped from the Parliamentary Labour Party (PLP) and lodged instead in this new college which was specifically constituted to select the leader. The trades unions possessed 40% of the electoral college's votes, the Constituency Labour Parties (CLPs) had 30% while the once dominant PLP was left with 30%.

The irony of this innovation was the same as that which affected the Democratic party in the United States. The Democrats' attempt to increase democracy inside the party, though various structural and procedural reforms including the extension of primary elections, weakened the hierarchical structure of the party organisation to such an extent that it allowed young inexperienced politicians to leapfrog into positions of leadership. They were able to exploit the new opportunities for electioneering within the party and to develop their skills in mobilising political resources over a wide area to present the party not just with ready-made leaders, but with market-related electoral strategies.

The same problem was repeated – albeit in a less exaggerated form – in the Labour party during the early 1980s. Michael Foot, who had replaced James Callaghan in 1980, won the party leadership under the old PLP system. In many ways, he embodied the traditional framework of parliamentary hierarchy. He had been an eminent back-bencher and respected rhetorician in support of socialist principles for much of his parliamentary career. In many ways, Foot represented the conscience and history of the Labour Party. He was steeped in the conflicts of the 1930s and 1940s and soaked in the spirit of Aneurin Bevan's flamboyant struggles with Toryism wherever it might be found on either side of the party divide. Being party leader may have been a just reward for past services, but even to an old ally like Anthony Howard it was a fatally misplaced honour.

> For, if ever there was a 'yesterday's man', it is Mr Foot. All his imagery, his political evocations, even his economic arguments, are drawn defiantly from a world not so much forgotten as not even capable of being remembered by the bulk of the British electorate. That presumably explains why the nickname of 'Worzel Gummidge' has stuck.[55]

Within a year, Foot's influence in the fracturing party was minimal. According to Gallup, his standing as leader of the Opposition was the lowest on record. Foot appeared old, weak, indecisive and out of touch. His personal eccentricities were cruelly exposed by television. Just as it was a reflection of Michael Foot that he did not see the need to tailor his appearance or speaking style to television, so it was also a reflection of the Labour party's complacency over the public's perception of leadership that it persevered with Foot for as long as it did. As the party stumbled towards and finally succumbed to an emphatic election defeat in 1983, it became clear that Foot would have to be replaced by a younger and altogether more modern politician. Foot stood down in October 1983 and effectively ended his generation's presence in the party leadership.

Under the old leadership selection system, it is generally agreed that Roy Hattersley would have been the choice of the PLP. Hattersley himself believed that his chances of securing the leadership even in the electoral college were still good. But he reckoned without Neil Kinnock. Kinnock had been cultivating the trade unions and constituency parties for years. While Hattersley had been serving in government during the 1970s, Kinnock had declined office and used the time instead to build up a formidable network of support and alliances that had secured him a strong place on the National

Executive of the party. Kinnock 'simply neglected parliament in favour of political activity outside and had failed, as a result, to build up a base of support in Westminster'.[56] He even told his local party in 1980 that he would attend outside political engagements even if it meant defying three-line whips. Between November 1981 and October 1982, for example,

> he did not ask a single oral question in Parliament, put down only twenty-eight written questions and voted in just seventy-nine out of a total of 332 divisions. Excluding those who died during the session or who represented Northern Irish seats, this gave Kinnock the tenth worst attendance record in the entire House of Commons – an astonishing performance for a Shadow Cabinet spokesman.[57]

Kinnock had been strongly in favour of the electoral college and in 1983 he became the first leader to benefit from the reform. With the unions and CLPs already sewn up, the PLP bowed to the inevitable and took the outsider as its leader with prudent good grace.

In becoming leader, Kinnock had won an impressive victory in a large and sprawling national organisation. It demanded the highest levels of personal commitment and campaign management. Kinnock had not only circumvented the PLP but had used the wider organisation to open up space between himself and the parliamentary party. In presenting himself as a young popular general to the hardened battle commanders of the parliamentary party, he was by his very presence implying that the nature of the war had changed. This was due to many factors including Labour's incompetent campaign and crushing defeat in the 1983 general election, Britain's victory in the Falklands war, an improving economy, and the demoralisation of the left. The changes were encapsulated in the need to come to terms with Margaret Thatcher's controversial and attention-grabbing leadership. Because she had made leadership into a political issue in its own right, she compelled the Opposition to compete with her on precisely this basis. Neil Kinnock was well placed and well qualified to respond to such a challenge. He was a very young outsider and an unlikely candidate for the party leadership. He won it by converting his outsider status into political advantage. After his accession to the leadership, he managed to retain his reputation for being his own man. He often jeopardised his party position and risked party splits by confronting the 'hard left' on the grounds of the public damage it was inflicting on the party's image and on Kinnock's own authority as leader. The division between Kinnock and the Militant Tendency even worked to his advantage. It allowed him openly to demonstrate his capacity to distance himself from a wing of the party and still remain effective as leader. Arguably it made him more effective because it improved his public standing and with it his position over the party as a whole.

Kinnock was as much an exemplar of leadership-centred politics as

Margaret Thatcher was. He not only changed his party into a formidable electoral organisation, but he was *seen* to have renovated and reformed it. In October 1989, the *Observer* gave recognition to Kinnock's achievements:

> Without the charisma of Gaitskell, or the intelligence of Wilson, Neil Kinnock has done more than either to march Labour, often backwards, to change. Unsaleable commitments shed, the Left neutralised, the party moved to the centre and all done democratically. A huge achievement.[58]

By May 1991, even a senior Conservative like John Biffen was prepared to concede that Kinnock had successfully led his party into a position of electoral contention.

> He has done more to bring the Labour party back to the centre ground of British politics than Hugh Gaitskell ever was able to succeed in doing, notwithstanding the intellectual brilliance of Gaitskell . . . When it came to sheer political sensitivity, knowing where to apply the pressures, Neil Kinnock has been quite outstanding in putting the Labour party into a better position politically than it has been in for decades. After so many years in the margins Labour now looks distinctly electable.[59]

Although Kinnock 'had taken care to carry his party with him',[60] the achievement was seen to have been Kinnock's in design and execution. He had made the party look as leader-led as the Conservative party. He had changed the party's style to conform to modern electioneering conditions. He had also been instrumental in turning its programme into a marketable centre-based socialism that was compatible both with the state of popular preferences and with the modern electoral imperative of protecting the party leader's claims to exterior public leadership.

Even the Labour party, therefore, had found it prudent to give its leader the level of discretion required to compete with other leaders and to enhance the party's appeal beyond Labour's contracting natural constituency and out towards an increasingly dealigned and independent electorate. Kinnock's style certainly produced criticism that he had betrayed socialist principles for the slick presentation of centrist policies, in support of a market economy and individual freedoms. On the other hand, he was also condemned for not being enough of an outsider in what has been described as 'the world's supreme insider culture'.[61] He was criticised for being too entrenched in a diminishing Labour heartland of big factories, large housing estates and old allegiances to state action. To a critic like Martin Jacques, Kinnock mobilised an outsider campaign from outside parliament, but it did not go far enough because Kinnock was not a true outsider. As a result, he was never able to compete with the spatial leadership of other outsiders. He was still locked firmly in 'the highly introverted and self-absorbed' characteristics of Labour's 'ghetto culture and its fixation with the mass production society'[62] of 1945.

In answer to these criticisms, Kinnock's defenders claim that in order to secure the party leadership, he had to confront and to defeat the left wing insurgency of Tony Benn. 'No politician in Britain had more enthusiastic and committed supporters outside the palace of Westminster than Tony Benn',[63] but they were almost invariably confined to that insider culture of trade unions and CLPs. It was Kinnock who had to appeal to these elements on the basis of a broader discipline that could yield electoral support. In effect it could be said that Kinnock defeated Benn by persuading the party to look outwards and to undertake a more realistic appraisal of its need to attract votes from outside the party.

In spite of the rumbling debate about the nature of Kinnock's leadership, he succeeded in making his leadership, the policy revision associated with it, into the focal point of unity for the party in its approach to the 1992 general election. Astonishingly for the Labour party, Kinnock had acquired a position in 1990 where, after seven years as leader, he could 'set his agenda . . . without looking permanently over his shoulder'.[64] Not only had the party's electoral college given a formal and unambiguous recognition of the office of Labour leader for the first time in its history, it had afforded it unprecedented authority and discretion.[65] Party traditions were cast aside in the face of the overriding need to compete effectively in the rapidly developing arena of leadership politics. Kinnock, for his part, took full advantage of his position. He, more than anyone else in the Labour party, was keenly aware of the central significance of leadership to the party's long-term prospects. As a consequence, he further enhanced the position and operating discretion of the leader by insulating himself as much as possible from the party. He and his office of dedicated assistants became 'a professional family (which) operated on the basis of exclusive, total loyalty'.[66] While the privilege and access afforded to this group caused friction in some sectors of the party, Kinnock gave every encouragement to his office to provide what he deemed to be the necessary protection, and even isolation, from the party. He required such independence in order to engage in long-range planning, but also to preserve the strategic prerogatives of his leadership. It was a measure of the Labour party's desperation to challenge its opponents on the grounds of political leadership that it was prepared to condone such a sweeping transfer of initiative to the leader's office.

The 1980s are usually noted for the leadership of Mrs Thatcher. But as we have seen the decade was also significant for the presence of other vigorous leaders. David Steel, David Owen, Paddy Ashdown and Neil Kinnock were all young professional politicians who had risen rapidly to acquire positions that used to be the prize of a lifetime's patient apprenticeship in parliament. They, along with Margaret Thatcher, were all unlikely figureheads. They were a far cry from the traditional structure of authority, rooted in status and deference, that was still evident in the post-war years. Kenneth O. Morgan notes that:

> In the Attlee era, the British people knew by whom they were led. The direct chain of command in central and local government alike, related both to recollections of wartime victory and older notions of authority embodied in the public-school, cricket-loving Edwardian philanthropist who occupied 10 Downing Street.[67]

In the 1960s, 'the stable base of British public leadership, the pivot of civic culture for generations, was being undermined'. Morgan laments that by 'the later phase of Mrs Thatcher's government, Britain was in danger of being rudderless as nothing very obvious came to succeed this older source of authority'.[68] But where there was adversity and even decay, so there was also opportunity. The decline in hierarchy fostered new possibilities for leadership which centred necessarily upon the exploitation of that self-same decline.

The leaders of the 1980s busied themselves in creating as much distance between their leadership and the stereotypical images of their respective parties. Some like Roy Jenkins and David Owen felt compelled to form an entirely new party, in order to escape from the traditional culture of the old. All the leaders in the 1980s advanced the trend in leadership towards a middle class professionalism based upon socially mobile and often self-made individuals who were attuned to the nature of social change and to the need for political adaptation.[69] These leaders had to carve out their own identities and, in doing so, they refashioned the identities of their parties, allowing them to appeal to an ever more fluid and unpredictable public. In order to achieve this flexibility of purpose, these individuals exploited the growing opportunities to engage in spatial leadership. They all distanced themselves from the organisation they purported to lead. They all either implicitly or explicitly turned on parts of their own organisation. And they all cultivated an outsider position in their own parties so that they could enhance their personal claims of public attention and popular representation.

It is true that Margaret Thatcher's premiership provides the fullest expression of this form of leadership. Nevertheless, it is not peculiar to Mrs Thatcher. Hers is not the only model of spatial leadership and her style is not the only means of acquiring it. On the contrary, there are many variations of spatial leadership and many different strategies in cultivating and sustaining it. The important point to grasp is that spatial leadership in Britain is not reducible either to Mrs Thatcher's character or to her New Right adventurism against government. There is of course a personality and policy 'push' to spatial leadership but there is also an extensive form of demand 'pull' that draws leaders away from their parties. Mrs Thatcher's political success as a leader now ranks as a factor on the side of demand pull. Her premiership constitutes a conditioning precedent. It has set the standard of leadership that her successors will try to emulate and upon which they will be judged by the public for their effectiveness.

John Major, for example, clearly felt the weight of the Thatcher precedent when he entered 10 Downing Street. Within weeks he was being criticised on the *issue* of leadership and had to make a number of dramatic interventions to try to stamp his premiership upon government (see pp.218–20). This was arguably out of character for John Major, but it was most emphatically in accordance with the modern imperatives of effective leadership.

Mrs Thatcher's leadership may exert a demand pull upon contemporary leaders, but it is just as significant for embodying the various demands that were made upon her to be the sort of leader she was. In other words, Mrs Thatcher may be said not so much to have broken the mould as to have emerged flawlessly from it. She exemplified the forces, dynamics and disciplines of modern leadership. She gave physical form to that which drives leaders into presidential solitude at the same time that it forces them into presidential prominence as a personalised intermediary between the government and the public. Leaders coming after her, therefore, are not merely following her. They are responding to the same demands that motivated her rise to power and characterised the presidential mannerisms of her premiership.

CHAPTER 4

Going public and getting personal in the United States and Britain

Prime ministers are increasingly drawn away from their parliamentary and cabinet colleagues. A premier's daily routine is filled to an ever greater extent with engagements, appointments and meetings that physically remove the prime minister from the ambit of his or her immediate allies. It is true that the prime minister's constitutional position remains rooted in a collective entity of fellow ministers and a broader assemblage of back-benchers. Nevertheless, the prodigious responsibilities and demands of the office push the incumbent out into an altogether larger environment that widens the gap between the prime minister and the corporate character of the premier's formal power base.

These demands come in two main varieties. First, there are the prosaic duties of unavoidable daily engagements. These include having to undertake trips abroad, to participate in ceremonies of state, to make speeches to organisations and to attend international conferences, EEC and Commonwealth meetings. A prime minister must be available to present awards, to plan the government's legislative business, to chair the cabinet, to welcome overseas leaders, to respond to constituency problems and to give press statements. The premier is also expected to represent the government at funerals and memorial services, to liaise with the party and fulfil a host of party obligations from fund raising to conference addresses.

The second type of demand that pulls the prime minister into a more individually conspicuous position is ostensibly less imposing than the first type, but, in reality, it amounts to an imperative which has now become central to the premiership in Britain. It is the need not merely to lead in public or to publicise one's leadership, but to make every effort to provide leadership that is supported by the public and is evocative of public confidence, and even occasionally, of popular acclaim. To acquire even the impression of this sort of leadership, a prime minister must continually cultivate his or her links with the public. The basis of appeal has to be progressively broadened. The public's interest has to be repeatedly aroused and issues have to be increasingly personalised for public consumption. This is no longer a personal option or an eccentric strategy. It has become a grinding imperative to all prime ministers and to all politicians who seek to be prime minister.

The need to establish and to sustain a personal engagement with the public has become an incessant, unremitting and overriding discipline in modern British politics. The requirement to provide leadership in public, for the public and of the public has now become indispensable not only to a leader's standing in the traditionally private arena of parliament, but also to a leader's capacity to prevail in his or her own party. While it is true that a prime minister is pulled away from the old moorings of parliament and party by a bulging diary of official appointments, there are less overt but more significant sources of detachment. Propulsion comes both from the party's own interest in, and judgement of, its leader's public status, and from the leader's own inner motivation to retain and develop the leadership according to the current evaluative criteria of public approval. It is these latter forces that help to enlarge the appointments still further and to transform many a public duty into a political opportunity. This emphasis upon public leadership in public arenas, which is now strong enough to politicise the most mundane of official engagements, has very clear parallels with the contemporary condition of the American presidency.

The American presidency: Mass media and public leadership

In the United States, commentators have repeatedly drawn attention to the way that presidents have sought to compensate for their weaknesses in Washington by appealing directly to the public for support. Presidents have exploited the individuality of the office to project themselves as the focal embodiments of popular concern and the public interest. In 'going public', it is claimed that presidents generate a personal following in the country which displaces the traditional need for political negotiation and accommodation within Washington.

> A White House faced with the prospect of fishing for the votes of hundreds of congressional minnows can turn to the publicity resources of the Oval Office to create public support for a proposal before it is discussed with Congress. If successful in this, a President need not bargain for votes; instead, members of Congress are forced to support a White House proposal by the tide of public opinion that the President has created.[1]

The increased incidence of public appearances, televised addresses and political trips have massively enhanced the presidency's centrality in American politics. It has reached the point where presidents are able not just to 'speak directly to voters over the heads of Congress and organised interests' but to 'overrule the influence of these traditional adversaries'.[2] This in turn projected presidents into

> the limelight of American politics, and citizens come naturally to organize their political thinking and focus their hopes for the future around the White House.[3]

The scale and depth of this trend towards a 'public presidency' has been so dramatic that it is widely regarded as being one of the most important and revealing developments in American politics over the last generation. Scholars and commentators do not question the existence of the phenomenon, so much as raise questions over its significance and express anxiety over wider consequences. Bruce Miroff, for example, points to the way that presidents have derogated the substance of leadership into a derivative of public spectacle in which actions are meaningful 'not for what they achieve but for what they signify'.[4] To Miroff, spectacles imply a passive audience whose attention is concentrated upon a central character engaged in an emblematic action designed to appeal to the senses of the onlookers, rather than to their reason. Because presidents are increasingly the subject of excessive and contradictory expectations, they use their centrality in the political process, in order to 'turn to the gestures of spectacle to satisfy their audience'.[5] If the spectacles are correctly orchestrated to magnify the appropriate qualities in the individual president, gesture can be made to supersede fact and accomplishment. Miroff believes that the Reagan administration exemplified the extent to which deliberately crafted symbolism on a mass scale can deflect the critical faculties and suffuse the president in benevolent affection devoid of policy content. As a result, 'the Reagan presidency largely floated above the consequences of its flawed processes or failed policies, secure in the brilliant glow of its successful spectacles'.[6]

In a seminal article entitled 'The Rise of the Rhetorical Presidency',[7] James Ceaser *et al.* underlined the importance, not of vision but of hearing in the presidency's penetration into the public's consciousness. They demonstrate that the use of popular rhetoric to attract public attention and to marshal political forces is a relatively recent phenomenon in the United States. It has replaced America's traditional fears of mass oratory and demagoguery, and challenged the country's republican ideal of enlightened reasoning through the medium of the written word. Popular rhetoric had its beginnings with Woodrow Wilson, whose progressivism embraced the idea that political leadership should aim for an active and restless public opinion in the search of a visionary new order. It gathered pace with advances in communications technology and the democratisation of party structures. By the

1980s, the United States had reached the point where 'popular or mass rhetoric, which presidents once employed only rarely, now serves as one of their principal tools in attempting to govern the nation'.[8]

A president is now expected as a matter of course to move the public, to inspire an allegiance to a common purpose, and to draw the ideals and interests of a mass public to his own person. As a consequence, presidents are increasingly measured by word rather than deed – or more accurately by the popular effects of words rather than by serious attempts at concrete achievements. To an increasing degree, presidential speech and action reflects the 'opinion that speaking *is* governing. Speeches are written to become the events to which people react no less than "real" events themselves'.[9]

To James Ceaser *et al.* the success of presidents in using rhetoric to enhance their own leadership threatens to make the mobilising property of rhetoric into a central objective of political leadership and even into an end in its own right. In the same vein, they see the prospect of the public being deceived by its own receptivity to presidential rhetoric. In their view, this misplaced 'reliance on inspirational rhetoric to deal with the normal problems of politics . . . leads us to neglect our principles for our hopes and to ignore the benefits and needs of our institutions for a fleeting sense of oneness with our leaders'.[10]

According to Samuel Kernell, who has done most to popularise the term 'going public', presidents now *have* to publicise themselves, in order to maintain their public visibility as leaders and, thereby, their influence over other Washington decision-makers. In doing so, however, they risk reducing the skills of governing to the techniques of campaigning and transforming policy into a device for substantiating the rhetoric of public statements. Moreover, the presidential strategies of public politics contribute further to the highly volatile nature of America's political agenda and its policy-making decisions. In essence, the 'effect of the president's own public standing on his ability to rally public opinion behind his policies exposes policy to extraneous and wholly unrelated events. Whatever affects the president's standing with the public will alter the prospects for those policies he sponsors.'[11] As a consequence, presidents have come to be obsessed not only with how the public view them, but with what can be done to influence still further the popular perceptions and judgements of their political leadership. These preoccupations have brought in their wake the extensive, and at times exotic, forms of political marketing that have come to characterise presidential politics in the United States. Presidents and presidential candidates now seek first to ascertain the condition of public opinion and then to promote themselves as expressions of popular anxieties and aspirations, and as such the rightful beneficiaries of consumer choice.[12]

It is Theodore Lowi who examines the full implications of these current trends. To Lowi, it is the president's ability to become the direct focus of popular demands which not only characterises the modern office, but marks the emergence of a new political order. He argues that what he terms the 'plebiscitary presidency' has mobilised public perceptions and political influence to the point where it is now a common assumption that 'the presidency with all powers is the necessary condition for governing a large democratic nation'.[13] To Lowi, the presidency's manipulative use of the mass media together with the exaggerated attention given to the president, both as a person and as a personification of mass demands and hopes, represents nothing less than a fundamental change in the character of American democracy.

The concerns enumerated above reflect the extent to which the identity of the modern presidency has become fused with that of the public. Whether the conclusions and prognoses derived from this duality are valid or not, they are indicative of the degree to which the presidential office has developed from a position whose influence was ultimately drawn from public support, to one whose influence is now drawn almost exclusively from a continuous intimate relationship with the public. The convergence of the presidency and the public to categories that are extensions of each other reflects a systemic change in the character of politics that has been beyond any single president to change – let alone to reverse. On the contrary, the intensification of the 'public presidency' is the product of a set of pressures, dynamics that presidents by and large defer to. In doing so, they strengthen still further the structural demands on their successors.

There can be little doubt that the most important facet of the relationship between the presidency and the public, and the one that exerts the most pressure upon the incumbent, is the linkage between the White House and the mass media. The basis of the connection is one of mutual need and support. The media not only need to report the news, they need news to report and the presidency is in a unique position to satisfy both requirements. The presidency is geared to satisfying the voracious demands for comments, briefings, speeches, interviews and pictures. This helps the presidency to be both the centre of government communications and the most newsworthy subject of popular interest. As a consequence, the White House is used by the media 'almost automatically because the president is looked at as the great explainer and a personified demonstration of today in government'.[14] The president for his part is similarly dependent upon the news organisations. They can supply him with information and advice on matters of current public concern. They can inform him about issues and conflicts inside his own administration, the progress or otherwise of his policy proposals, and the condition of his political status in Washington. More significantly, they can provide him with his point of contact with the public. They furnish him with the lines of communication through which he can convey his construction of world events and his interpretation of domestic needs. With the assistance of the electronic media, in particular, the president can carry his own news continuously to the public through the constant public exposure of his activities as president.

This relationship between the presidency and the media has led to a range of theories concerning the precise nature of their interdependence. There is a debate, for example, over the extent to which the media are merely passive receptors of news or whether they actively create news – or at least create the conditions in which their news perspectives become self-fulfilling propositions. The same point is often made in reverse. The president is accused of 'managing the news' through using his position to influence the content and timing of government information and to control the access of different journalists to the news-making facilities of the presidency.[15] The controversies surrounding the relationship between the presidency and the media are particularly fierce as there is no way of satisfactorily determining the nature of the connection. Indeed, there is often a circular quality to the categories of analysis that are drawn from the separate parties' dependence upon each other.

It is commonly asserted that the news coverage of the presidency tends to reflect and, subsequently, to reinforce the cycle of economic performance or the pattern of public opinion. By the same token the media itself responds to public opinion and changes its tenor of reporting in such a way as to encourage the public on its course.

> Low approval rating and negative media coverage feed each other, heightening the perception that the president is floundering, deepening the drumbeat of decline – dissolving one of his few persuasive resources, the notion that public opinion is on his side.[16]

The same collection of interrelated drives and responses can push a president's public approval and media image upwards to peaks as similarly exaggerated as the troughs. Even a president's own relationship with the media is couched in terms of a cycle in which a honeymoon period deteriorates into a competitive friction, which is followed by a third stage of detachment, before returning to the first stage with the campaign for re-election.[17]

Whether the exact mechanics of the media's relationship with the presidency are ascertainable or not, and whether the political effects of the media's coverage are intentional or unintentional, what cannot be disputed is the fact that presidents have to exist in a system increasingly saturated with media attention. This generates far-reaching consequences for presidents who find they are the subject of a whole series of dynamics that produce not merely opportunities and incentives, but also deeply driven imperatives over the style and manner of leadership.

For example, the media have a general reputation for reporting government as politics, and for characterising politics 'in its narrowest sense, the sense most akin to sports'.[18] It is said that journalists have a tendency to interpret

> events from a short-term, anti-historical perspective; see individual or group action, not structural or other impersonal long run forces, at the root of most occurrences; and simplify and reduce stories to conventional symbols for easy assimilation by audiences.[19]

Presidential politics are therefore seen as the perfect foil to the inherent complexities of government and the potential boredom of political news coverage. Presidential politics suits both the professional techniques of popular journalism and the low tolerance threshold of the market for news stories. The White House easily lends itself to the human interest of blunders and gaffes, and of who is 'in' and who is 'out' of favour. It fosters questions like how a new appointment is being handled by the president and whether the appointment will be confirmed or rejected. And it generates controversies such as what a new policy might mean to the president's ratings in public opinion polls. A president's press secretary learns very quickly that these journalistic appetites have to be attended to, in order to ensure that the president's position is not misrepresented, but most of all, to maintain the president's exposure to the public. Catering to such demands, however, leads to more and more of the same and, thereupon, to the White House's own complicity in the progressive personalisation of daily politics.

Since the prospect and aftermath of presidential elections now overshadow an entire term of office, the White House also provides a permanent dimension of electoral considerations that can cast virtually any presidential news story into the ubiquitous categories of a horse race for the White House. In this way, much of Washington can be simplified for the purpose of news into a contest between the president and his potential or actual challengers. As a result of this set of reactions, politics is represented by the media and consumed by the audience to an ever increasing extent as an easily digestible form of sporting endeavour. The emphasis becomes one of who is ahead, who is behind, who is the dark horse and what are the odds. Presidents in these circumstances cannot afford *not* to be part of the action.

If this dynamic of presidents seeking the news and in turn shaping the conception and purpose of news is present in the media in general, then it is endemic in the electronic media. Television, in particular, exaggerates and extends the characteristics and consequences of the print media. Television's presentation of politics is dominated both by the medium's dependency upon visual information and by the limited attention span and fickle viewing habits of its audience.[20] In a study of the networks' news coverage, Fred Smoller ascertained the existence of three main factors in television's portrayal of the White House.[21] First is the need not only for pictures, but for a format that can make use of them within a two minute time scale – i.e. the maximum length for a news story. Second, the use of images to present information leads television to cover issues entertainingly in terms of action and events. Third, the audiences's general lack of political interest extends still further the editorial tendency to concentrate on stories concerning scandal, conflict and presidential mistakes. The net effect is to make the news president-centred, to make the presidency into an object of public consumption and to transform conceptions of political leadership into a set of personal characteristics best suited to television, and best conveyed by television to a mass audience.[22]

Criticisms abound of the presidency's relationship with the electronic media. Television is said to shape categories of popular political judgement in accordance with television's own properties as a communications medium. It is said to persuade people not only that they can adjudicate between different candidates, but that they can do so on the basis of the visual impressions conveyed through television. The sober reflection of professional reputations and policy ideas supposedly gives way to personal immediacy and accessibility. Accordingly, 'the gestures of . . . spectacle are becoming more prevalent, and are coming to dominate the public's perception of leadership in the White House'.[23] Such assumptions have come to have a material effect in the United States. The emphasis on imagery and on its manipulation for political effect is now so central to political leadership, that media advisors, public relations consultants, and public opinion pollsters have come to occupy strategic positions in the White House. In the words of Michael Deaver, who was President Reagan's senior media advisor and Deputy Chief of Staff in his first administration, 'TV has changed everything so much. The visual image is all important.'[24] It is precisely this concern for presentation and personalisation which creates concern over the extent to which government and campaigning – political leadership and public exposure – have become indistinguishable from one another.

The Reagan administration, in particular, illustrated the centrality of television to the conduct of the presidency. The Reagan White House went to extraordinary lengths to structure the media's access to Reagan and to ensure that Reagan's messages reached the public, irrespective of the press corps' interest in them. Their efforts in these respects, however, paled in comparison to the resources expended upon Reagan's appearances on television. These occasions were seen as the centrepiece of the administration's strategy of public politics. Television was perfectly suited to Reagan's skills, experience and political predicament. His background in the cinema and visual arts had prepared him for politics in the television age, where complex argument could be displaced by visual associations, graphic assertions and sound bites. Kathleen Jamieson in *Eloquence in an Electronic Age* (1988) points out that because 'television is a visual medium whose natural grammar is associative, a person adept at visualizing claims in dramatic capsules will be able to use television to short-circuit the audience's demand that those claims be dignified with evidence'.[25] Reagan had an instinctive grasp of how a leader could use television on its own terms and through its own grammar. The Reagan White House not only produced speeches with the compulsory verbal nuggets for the attention of the media's newscasts, but staged the speeches to provide them with a visual dimension. The staging was chosen to coordinate with the message and place it in a concentrated context of dramatised images. Such staging was designed to intensify the effect of the words to such an extent that it would supersede their meaning with the comparatively emotional effect of a visual experience. Ronald Reagan was extremely successful at

> synopsizing an important sentiment in memorable visual and verbal form on an appropriate stage so that it could be telegraphed to a national audience by the news media.[26]

But it was precisely that success which provoked so much disquiet over the effect of television on the nature of politics. As the 'moving synoptic movement . . . replaced the eloquent speech'[27] of reason, analysis and argument, concern was expressed that Reagan had revealed the vulnerability of modern leadership to the sensory effects of television upon the public mind. In the view of Charles Dunn and David Woodward, Reagan's style matched his environment to perfection.

> The political skills of an impressionist painter in the Oval Office beautifully coincided with the dictates of the electronic media that rewards style over substance and symbolic impression over substantive impact.[28]

Critics believe that television has become such an integral part of American government, that it has a systemic effect on everything within the political structure. It is accused, for example, of turning Washington into a fishbowl in which all the many private arrangements for reaching public agreements are compromised by exposure. It allegedly 'constrains bargaining strategies, makes government look disorderly and heightens tendencies for personality and organizational clashes'.[29] It can be claimed that

> the media more than any other agency, have filled the vacuum left by the steady erosion of the mediating institutions that once bridged the gap between the understandings and desires of mass publics and the actions of government.[30]

By the same token, it can also be asserted that the media have advanced the decline of parties by allowing presidents and presidential candidates to appeal to the public for popular approval on precisely those grounds that are calculated to provide it. To James Ceaser *et al*, this produces a new form of constitutional government by assembly with 'television "speaking" to the president and the president responding to the demands and moods that it creates'.[31] They conclude that this combination of television and the presidency

> makes it increasingly difficult for presidents to present an appearance of stability and to allow time for policies to mature and for events to respond to their measures. Instead, the president is under more pressure to act – or to appear to act – to respond to the moods generated by the news.[32]

While this gives the presidency a position of public focus, it can lead the White House to 'confuse doing something about the media with doing something about a problem'.[33]

These criticisms are highly significant because they serve to highlight the extent of the media's penetration not merely into the framework of government but into the manner and operating assumptions of government, at the very highest levels. The condemnations bear witness to television's ubiquitous presence and to the opportunities and fears concerning how it can be exploited for political effect. For an aspiring politician, 'going public' is therefore something of a honey-trap. In order to reach the public, it is necessary to be a willing captive of television and of what it can communicate to a mass audience. Political leadership has at the very least to be compatible with the disciplines and priorities of television. And this means that for leadership to remain viable it must be continuously set in a public context by television and favourably assessed by the public through television.

Whether these critical observations are completely justified or not, they do throw into relief the overriding fact that television is now a structural component of American political life. Television is the primary source of news information for most Americans. For its part, television is habituated to the characteristics of its audience and to the properties of its subject matter. For good or ill, it is imprisoned by its own market conditions and by the very nature of the medium in producing news as a visual experience of visual events.

> Whatever the political desires of its producers may be, television is at its best picturing the concrete and at its worst explaining the abstract. Political leaders are much more telegenic as tangible, individual faces, voices, and personalities than as members of abstractions such as political organizations or coalitions.[34]

It is no longer possible for presidents merely to use the public to complement their other leadership facilities. A president has to be popular. Moreover, he has to be prominently and enduringly popular. It is not enough for presidents simply to resort to the communications media, in order to circumvent and weaken Washington's opposition to their policies. Presidents have to be incorporated into the media's handling of the news on a virtually permanent basis simply in order to maintain their position. Neither can presidents any longer merely claim to be the expression of the popular will. They need instead to be seen to be implanted physically within it. With this in mind, each president can do no other than to affirm and to intensify a process that progressively propels presidents into the public eye of television, while at the same time inducing them to adopt a style of leadership that will be amenable to the national networks. As television is such a potent vehicle of popular mobilisation, and as it inevitably defines the required characteristics of leadership in terms of its own visual and personal properties, so presidents are increasingly induced to exploit the mass media in order to cultivate a form of personalised leadership.

It can be argued that leadership is now the only satisfactory way of comprehending the relationship between a prominent politician and his or her public. Leadership is provided by leaders. Moreover, leadership is characterised and defined by the personal qualities of leaders. Television thrives in this logic because as a medium of people it can justify its interest in individuals by reference to 'leadership'. It can also justify its personalised treatment of politics and election campaigns through the same device. As television is people-centred, leadership likewise becomes person-centred, thereby giving television companies further encouragement to translate politics and government into projections of individual characteristics and personal conflict. The net effect is that presidents not only have to be popular; they have to be popular as highly individualised leaders. To be a leader, it is necessary to be seen first and foremost as an individual. To be solitary is the minimal precondition to being outstanding. Together the effect is to make the personalisation of the office the best, and perhaps the only, way of retaining the presidency's televised access to the public.

The need to attend to the media takes time and resources. For example, according to one of his aides, President Reagan spent two-thirds of his time in the White House on public relations and ceremony, and only a third on policy matters.[35] Much of the White House staff was also geared to what is called 'political outreach' by which the messages and images of the presidency are constantly disseminated to the public. All this effort is partly to ensure that the president's policies and objectives are properly conveyed. But it is also to maintain a high level of public prominence and public recognition for the brand name of the presidency. The accent is upon filling the many pathways to the public on a daily basis, in order to ensure that they are not filled by someone else. Presidents have to cultivate a continuous engagement with the public, which means that they have to maintain a capacity to displace other competitors for public attention. This is not an easy feat to achieve, as the American political system tends to arouse popular interest in potential presidential leaders. The electronic media's own inclination towards personalising political disputes gives particular encouragement to the cultivation of presidential aspirants. As a result, a successful president has to maximise his exposure simply to keep challenges at bay and to prevent the integrity of his administration from being compromised by the appearance of alternative leadership.

One of the most effective strategies employed by presidents, and one that they find growing incentives to use, is based less on content and more on style and suggestion. Because of the media's conjunction of personalisation with publicisation, and because many of the problems faced by presidents can be reduced to a lack of authority over competing power centres, presidents have sought to instil an impression which the media are particularly adept at conveying. The image is that of the man apart from the pack; the individual pitted against impersonal structures and forces; the tangible persona set against anonymous organisations. Presidents use the very intractability of Washington government as a counterpoint to their own individual distinction. This can have the effect of increasing a president's problems by making Washington even more intractable than before. But it can also ease them by confirming his publicly declared indictments of government and further enhancing the personal authority of his public touch.

The drives and disciplines of the presidency in such a media-centred system closely correspond with the incentives of 'spatial leadership'. They both complement and reinforce one another. Every successful contender for the presidency begins as an 'outsider' and knows the importance of protecting himself against the challenge of other potential leaders who, if nothing else, can always make substantial claims to being 'outsiders'. In the American system, the chief opposition to a presidency will come from a pack of prototype leaders – competing, or preparing to compete, in a primary election campaign. Each will try to differentiate himself from the other by making the personal and, therefore, televised qualities of leadership the main issue at stake. Each will seek to make a virtue out of the debilitating condition of being an outsider which all of them emphatically *are* by the very status of being presidential contenders. In this setting, the president is always at risk from appearing to represent the archetypal Washington insider. It is in the presidential interest, therefore, to protect his personal leadership by flavouring his activities and speeches with a sense of populist distance and aggravation. By going public through television, a president can propagate the suggestion that he is in a sense separate from government. He can sit in the voters' living rooms looking in on government with them. Part of Reagan's genius as a communicator on television was the way he could use the medium to talk to a mass audience as though he were having an intimate conversation with each one of its members. The familiarity of Reagan's speaking style 'identified him with his audience. He could speak for us, in part because he spoke as we did'.[36] This skill made his detachment from government even more credible.

A particularly effective way of arousing public opinion is through populist anguish, and one of the best ways of signifying the populist message of the diminutive in relation to the grand is through television imagery. With this in mind, presidents find that portraying the self-image of an honourable outsider, with whom people can most readily identify, and even admire, is an effective protective device. Even the highest in the land can be made to look extremely small and especially so when pitted against fearful abstract forces made more menacing by television's inability to depict them. Confronting adversity, and even suffering defeats by it, can be translated through careful media management into a defiant outsider standing up for principle and right in an amoral world. The dank impersonal force is usually 'government'. In the past, it has been the Soviet Union (cf. the 'evil empire'), the United Nations and OPEC. More recently, it has been terrorism, Libya and Iran. At present, it can vary from South American drug barons to the regime of Saddam Hussein in Iraq. Underlying them all is the fundamental anxiety of national decline.

In their efforts to counteract the fluctuations in public approval and favourable media attention, and to fight for their near monopoly of the televised coverage of domestic leadership, presidents have occasionally resorted to the supreme irony of attacking the media itself. They have used the media not just as an instrument of presidential populism, but as its chief target. When presidents have sought to generate public dissent against the media themselves as an elitist and intervening structure between the populace and its government, they have benefited from the self-fulfilling qualities of the proposition. The controversy is guaranteed to receive blanket coverage as news. If everything goes according to plan, the president will be presented as a beleaguered individual confronting a hostile press.

To turn the tables on the media in this way is a very risky strategy. President Nixon tried it with some initial success, but ended up as an isolated figure whose outsider status degenerated into purposeless detachment.[37] President Ronald Reagan kept the media press at bay by relying extensively upon his staff to provide carefully doctored briefings, stories and pictures. He supplemented this strategy of using the media on his own terms by giving stage managed performances, or 'spectacles', designed to command public attention, to dominate the news and to dispel doubts over his leadership capacity. This was the equivalent of 'going public' over the heads of the media themselves. Reagan was able to achieve this detachment from the media, not least because his outsider credentials were beyond reproach after so many years in the wilderness of the Republican right wing.

George Bush was different to both Nixon and Reagan in that he was a consummate Washington insider. But even he found a way of using the media to build up a sense of space between himself and Washington. Bush's relationship with the media has been particularly instructive in this regard because it shows how different presidents can use different strategies to produce the desired effect of enhancing their claims to public leadership. Instead of avoiding the press and television networks, as might have been expected from an insider who could in no way be regarded as any sort of communicator, Bush opened his doors to them. He did so in order to relieve his special problem as president.

Bush's chief difficulty upon entering the White House was that of needing to distance himself from the exemplary outsider politics of Reagan, but at the same time without giving the appearance of having defected to the inside of the Washington establishment. He was constantly monitored by the congenitally suspicious right-wingers of the Republican party. This appendage had long been the traditional focus of righteous detachment from contemporary American life. It was wary of George Bush, who was thought to be too closely identified with the 'Eastern establishment'. Bush himself was acutely aware of the right wing's capacity to damage his presidency, but he was also concerned about his reputation on a much broader front. He had the problem of living down his patrician background. It was also evident that he lacked those rhetorical skills which had allowed his predecessor to occupy the centre of government, whilst simultaneously inhabiting a separate dimension of emotive imagery, social symbolism and historical suggestion. As a consequence, Bush's presidency often suffered from drift and a lack of purpose. Bush attempted to emulate Reagan's bold, and even theatrical, objections to such evident imperatives as the need for higher government revenues. Nevertheless, he lacked the ideological conviction and endearing earnestness that would have allowed him to transcend the consequences of those inevitable adjustments to stark positions that come with political negotiation and economic realism.[38]

It was his very insecurity, however, that allowed him to devise his own strategy for distancing himself from the culture of government. In effect, Bush's lack of confidence prompted him to be exceptionally accessible to the media. He gave more press conferences in his first eighteen months than Reagan gave in his entire eight years in office. Moreover, Bush developed his own personal trade marks in speaking to the public. When Bush was in front of the cameras or talking to the press, it was his self-conscious awkwardness, his fractured syntax, his pauses and prevarications and his sheer ordinariness that are impressed upon his audience. Paradoxically, Bush's discomfort and inarticulateness became his chief assets in keeping his lines open to the public and keeping his distance from the sophisticated intellectualism of Washington bureaucracy. In 1990, Peter Pringle concluded that poor communication had become an established feature of the Bush presidency.

> It is not because he doesn't know what he is talking about, which was often the case with Mr Reagan . . . It is more that his strategy is not to tell you anything because he thinks that is the best way to keep ahead, and because he thinks that is actually what Americans want . . . He appears very earnest, with a permanently furrowed brow; he waves his arms a lot, points his forefinger and slaps the table and shifts his body from one side of his chair to another to strike a new pose for a new thought; but he says precious little.[39]

It is safe to assume that the excruciating nature of his extemporising was a technique which was approved as functionally productive by Bush's media advisers. Even so, the effect was to distance Bush from Reagan's set piece orations and to create the impression of a president having such an intimate familiarity with his audiences that he communicates with them in a spontaneously conversational style. This reduced the space between the president and the public, and by virtue of that fact strengthened Bush's claim to be apart from that abstract infrastructure of government that carries so many primal and negative connotations to so many Americans.

While it is true that Bush exploited the public presidency as much as any recent incumbent, it is equally true that this was not a style which naturally conformed to his character. Bush was the first to concede his lack of rhetorical flair. 'I'm not good at expressing the concerns of a nation – I'm just not very good at it'.[40] It is evident that what Reagan attempted to achieve by rhetoric, confrontation and polarisation, Bush sought to acquire by way of indirection, suggestion and quiet negotiation. Because Bush clearly preferred to work in an assimilative and diplomatic style within government, it made his periodic efforts to break out of the government and immerse himself in the people seem contrived and unconvincing.

By 1992, his character had once again come into question. Even after victory in the Gulf war, Bush was having to defend himself against renewed charges that he was a wimpish captive of government forces. He was pressed in particular by H. Ross Perot, who was not only running a campaign against Washington from a position outside both the federal government and the two party system, but was doing so by discarding the elite national television networks, based in Washington and New York, in favour of 'narrowcasting' through the multitude of 'people's channels' carried by cable television networks. In what was a vintage year for outsider challengers to Washington, Bush had to distance himself from government, and even from his own public persona as president, in an attempt to restore his connection with the public and its political implication. As a candidate in the Republican primaries, Bush had to engage in a public penance of apologising for not reacting earlier to social and economic anxieties and for violating his Reaganite pledge in 1988 of 'no new taxes'. Bush explained that the modest tax rise in 1990 sent the wrong signals about his presidency's association with 'big government'. In a radio broadcast from the White House Bush told listeners that it had in fact been the worst mistake of his presidency. 'Listen. If I had to do that over, I wouldn't do it. Look at all the flak it's taking.'[41]

Bush felt it was necessary to assure his restive audiences that the message was getting through and being registered. Most urgently of all, he had to change the impression of being a president who was thoroughly at home with the career bureaucracy to one that reflected George Bush the Texan, oilfield chancer and inarticulate populist. Bush knew that even for a sitting president to succeed, he would have to relocate himself away from Washington and, in the process, restore a sense of immediacy with the public. He imitated his chief rival Bill Clinton in following Ross Perot's initiative in ignoring the traditional mediating structures of the national news networks, in favour of the narrow but intensive formats of local news outlets, talk shows and 'phone-ins'. Like Perot and Clinton, the president felt obliged to demonstrate his geniality and accessibility in informal surroundings by appearing on CNN's *Larry King Live*. Bush was determined to reverse the reputation for remoteness and unresponsiveness that he had acquired as president. He was intent upon showing that his lack of verbal flair was compensated for by a sensitive capacity to turn on government in the measured, and largely unthreatening, way required by the modern American electorate. He had to display governmental competence, but at the same time he had both to symbolise the public's exasperation with the political process and to fulfil the public's demand for direct contact and responsiveness at the top.

The British premiership: Mass media and public leadership

In Britain, references to political leaders going public and to the subsequent 'presidentialisation' of British politics have grown with the rise of the broadcasting media, and especially television, as the pre-eminent vehicle of political information. Harold Wilson welcomed television with open arms because it gave him an opportunity to escape, or at least to circumvent, the effects of what he considered to be a hostile Tory press. Since television was governed by rules of fair balance and intended impartiality, Wilson felt that a Labour leader could not only compete equally on television but, with sufficient skill, overcome all the handicaps experienced elsewhere in the press. Marcia Williams, who was Harold Wilson's political advisor, notes that television had the effect of emancipating the Labour leader from the confines of Westminster and of the party organisation. It liberated him from the interpretive licence and political dispositions of the intermediary agencies lying between the leadership and the electorate.

> The television camera cannot lie, inasmuch as the viewer sees on his screen a man he either likes or dislikes on sight. He is able then to make the sort of judgement he makes daily in his ordinary life. He isn't being told by a newspaper writer that 'such and such' is ghastly. He is able to look at the figure directly, hear him speak and make up his own mind about what he thinks of him.[42]

According to Williams, it was only because of his performances on television that Harold Wilson was able to withstand the press assaults on his personal competence and integrity, and to retain his personal popularity in the party and amongst the general public between 1964 and 1967.

It was Harold Wilson who really gave rise to the comparisons between British politics and the American presidency. It is true that Harold Macmillan had adapted well to television. He was the first prime minister to allow himself to be questioned at length in a television interview. He also made a captivating party political broadcast which successfully conveyed Macmillan's showmanship as a relaxed and authoritative world leader justifiably at ease with power. His exposure on television made him better known than any previous prime minister and this helped to boost his popularity. His conspicuously public connection with President Kennedy helped to increase speculation over the comparability of presidential and prime ministerial power.

It is equally true, however, that Macmillan evidently belonged to a pre-television and even pre-modern age. His 'Supermac' cartoon image captured the anachronism of an elderly Edwardian defying not merely the laws of gravity but also his own age and epoch. It was an irreverent and totally incongruous image, but nonetheless a revealing one. Macmillan had become a television personality whilst in office. He had not been dependent on television and the influence of popular leadership for his rise to power. He recognised their importance and their relationship to each other, but such considerations were not second nature to him. In retrospect it may be clear that Macmillan was the first to grasp

> that television was neither a meretricious toy nor the instrument of torture he once termed it, but the means by which political leaders must henceforth reach

the electorate, and through which they must now as a matter of course account for themselves.[43]

But at the time, both Macmillan and the television organisations were in a highly fluid situation. Television journalists and producers were ambitious, yet unsure of their role or their future status. Macmillan played the part but he was neither a product of the electronic media, nor a dedicated disciple of it. He handled it, coped with it, even mastered it at times, but it was neither central to his conception of politics, nor integral to his political background and instincts.

Harold Wilson was different. His interest in television, and in the popular interest it could engender, characterised his whole programme of a modern Britain brought into being by modern leadership. Wilson was the first British political figure to realise the full potential of going public as a political strategy and to seize the opportunity of using the mass media in a coordinated manner to take his case to the people. Wilson made conscious efforts to radiate a popular image of a gifted progressive from a modest background, exuding pipe-smoking common sense and the integrity of a retained regional accent. This imagery was designed to throw into sharp relief the Tory government's contemporary reputation as a tired administration characterised by Edwardian privilege and damaging social backwardness. Marcia Williams is convinced that 'television and the visual first hand assessment that each individual could make of him'[44] allowed Wilson to become a populist figure and, in doing so, to cast the Conservative party in a most unfavourable light of grouse-moor complacency.

Wilson knew that for this strategy to succeed, it was necessary to take *himself* to the people and to plan an election campaign that took account of the needs of both the broadcast media and the party leadership. As a consequence, Wilson centralised control of his election campaign in the 1960s so that he could maximise the appeal of his leadership and thereby enhance the electability of his party. Even though the active encouragement of media attention, and his open accommodation of their requirements, provoked resistance from the party organisation, Wilson dominated Labour's election campaign. In doing so, he turned from being the party spokesman to being the party's supreme public figure.

Wilson's performance drew parallels with presidential politics. Peter Shore, for example, believes that because television was primarily an American medium in those days, the British public was becoming increasingly accustomed to American style politics. 'It was in many ways a presidential campaign but of course we were becoming familiar with the idea of presidential campaigns from really the time television became the mass media.'[45]

Marcia Williams recalls that the comparisons made between Wilson's leadership style and American presidential politics were not entirely coincidental. On the contrary, they were prompted by a deliberate attempt by Wilson and his administrations to introduce an American dimension into their election campaigns.

> We had watched absolutely mesmerised and terribly excited by what had happened in America during the Kennedy campaign and then his victory and in the Kennedy years afterwards. We looked at their methods of campaigning. The Tories in Britain had modernised themselves because they had the money to do it. We didn't. We could only do it by studying and copying.[46]

Wilson and his advisors examined Kennedy's style and his use of television very carefully. They even found some of his key messages, like the need to get the country moving again and the importance of leadership to national movement, to be directly applicable to Wilson's campaign. Wilson himself was keenly aware that for the Labour campaign to succeed, it was necessary to demonstrate the sort of leadership that could wrest the initiative of campaign management away from party headquarters. This in turn would allow him the licence to make leadership into an election issue, and also to characterise the election itself as a contest between leaders. Wilson largely succeeded in reaching these objectives. He took Labour's electoral challenge 'into his own hands and made it into much more of a leader's campaign rather than a party campaign'.[47]

Ever since Harold Wilson's successes in the 1960s, references to the presidentialisation of British political leadership have risen in number and intensity. As the number of television sets mushroomed and as the British people became increasingly dependent upon television for news and political information, party leaders were increasingly forced to come to terms with the medium, or face the consequences of a loss of public regard on grounds of personality and appearance. Gone were the days when Clement Attlee could express total astonishment at being recognised in a hotel by a member of the public. After the 1960s, it was tantamount to a failure in leadership *not* to be recognised constantly, universally and approvingly. Prime ministers and potential prime ministers could no longer afford a private life.

Assessments and appraisals of political leaders became increasingly subject to questions of personal characteristics. Leaders were evaluated according to their ability to project themselves to the public. They were now expected to arouse popular enthusiasm or, at the very least, to avoid any adverse public reaction. To a greater and greater extent, leaders had to lead in public and had to prove their leadership by working successfully in a political environment that was becoming increasingly saturated with media attention.

With these developments in mind, the Conservatives chose Edward Heath as their leader in an effort to broaden the party's public approval. The party hoped that a grammar school boy promoted to the leadership on grounds of professional merit would help to modernise the party's image. His subsequent failures were widely attributed to a congenital inability firstly to project his personality on television and secondly to mobilise public opinion behind him on a basis of affection and respect. Heath was not regarded as proficient in the new presidential arts of public leadership. In a televised post-mortem on his party's defeat in the 1966 general election, Heath was questioned on the alleged link between his lack of television skills, his low political popularity and his party's failure in the election. Heath snapped back

> Well popularity isn't everything. In fact, it isn't the most important thing. What matters is doing what you believe to be right . . . The question doesn't arise.[48]

While this may have been a morally defensible proposition, it was a damaging admission to make through such a popular medium. It revealed Heath's discomfort with popular politics and his mistaken belief they were not of central significance. To his detractors, Heath had a near fatal lack of appreciation of the need for self-promotion through publicisation. Many, even in his own party, believed that he had personally lost the 1966 election.[49]

Heath's media advisors helped to soften his image for the 1970 election. The change appeared to be successful, as the Labour government went down to a surprising defeat. Since 1966, Heath's 'supporters and colleagues were worried by his failure to "break through", and the public appeared to find him cold and boring. But his doggedness and seriousness were vindicated by the election outcome.'[50] Once in Number 10, however, Heath reverted to his original public posture. He shunned the press, avoided television and distanced himself in general from media attention. Heath's concern was for policy not public standing, which he regarded as a consideration confined largely to the vulgarities of the electoral process. He wished to distance himself from Harold Wilson's preoccupation with public appeals and media manipulation. Heath's abrasive personality, his distaste for publicity and his unease with his own party's grass roots and back-benchers gave him a reputation for aloofness and arrogance that dogged him throughout his administration (1970-74). These deadly vices and the public's reaction to them were instrumental in his final dramatic downfall in 1975.

Instead of revealing himself to be a modern leader adapted to the popular pressures and expectations of contemporary politics, Heath's failures and miscalculations seemed to underline the existence of a new set of protocols that linked leadership to personal worth and public esteem. Heath refused to acknowledge that his personality was anything more than a private matter. He contested the proposition that leadership had anything to do with personal characteristics that could be communicated by television. And he could not see how character traits might foster a relationship with the public that could lead to an appearance of prominence being transformed into the substance of political leadership. Heath's reliance upon the formalistic nature of institutional leadership seemed out of place and quite inadequate in the 1970s. Indeed, his excruciating discomfort with the politics of personal projection and popular appeal, together with his political reversals and loss of leadership, seemed to affirm the existence of an emergent presidential dimension to British politics, which Heath could not and would not reconcile himself to.

Michael Foot was another leader whose failure was thought to speak volumes. He was damned for his apparent lack of presidentialism. To Foot, such a deficiency was a mark of distinction and a sign of his allegiance to political principle. He made a point of refusing to compromise either his convictions, or the political style that emanated spontaneously from them, for the convenience of television campaign coverage. One of Foot's principles was that personal appearance had nothing whatever to do with the substance of ideological analysis and political reform. As a result, he neglected both himself and the possible benefits to be accrued from a successful exercise in personal projection and political imagery.

In the 1983 election, Foot pressed home his attack on Thatcherism with an integrity fostered by a lifetime in the world of ideas. At the same time as his opponent, Margaret Thatcher, was deploying the latest American techniques in image projection, Foot was seen limping through crowds with a walking stick, addressing audiences with rambling speeches and making public appearances in ill-fitting clothes. His hair was often unkempt and his sometimes thick glasses had the effect of reflecting the glare of the television lights. On one occasion, he appeared with his spectacles held together with sticking plaster. The effects of Mr Foot's dress sense and personal deportment was described in the *Observer* as giving him the appearance of 'a floppy toy on benzedrine'.[51] To Foot,

> the issues needed only to be allowed to speak for themselves. The messages on unemployment and on the dangers of nuclear war were so vital that the fripperies of the medium by which it was to be conveyed scarcely merited a thought.[52]

As it was,

> his enormously lengthy perorations made it virtually impossible to use extracts of his longer discourses on radio and television, the two media which he seemed least sure in handling.[53]

Foot's disabilities as a public leader were ruthlessly exposed during the campaign. He led his party to one of its worst defeats this century.[54] Foot, like Heath, was accused of not having adapted his leadership to the television age. Accordingly, they were both condemned for being insufficiently presidential in manner and style – i.e. for being unable to compete effectively in a political environment that seemed to be increasingly presidential in nature.

If the public discomfort of Edward Heath and Michael Foot *implied* the existence of a presidential dimension in British politics, Margaret Thatcher's election campaigns of 1979, 1983 and 1987 seemed to provide positive proof of its presence. It was Thatcher who saw the full potential of a public presentation of personal leadership. She regarded the effective portrayal of leadership not merely as a minimal requirement of a party leader, but as fundamental to a leader's modern role in publicising the party and its policies. Mrs Thatcher took it a stage further and made leadership central to the spirit of her party's programme. She proceeded on the basis of personal obligation to provide a sense of renewed direction and purpose to British public life. To this end, she exploited a prodigious array of advanced techniques to ensure that she should receive the maximum amount of public recognition for the leadership that was deemed necessary, and incessantly suggested, by Mrs Thatcher's own brand of politics. It was essentially Mrs Thatcher's success in cultivating and extending these methods of personal presentation that made leadership into a political issue and into a distinct category of political evaluation in the 1980s.

Margaret Thatcher set the pace and established the standards for leadership projection. It was she who prompted the unfavourable assessments of Edward Heath and Michael Foot. She even upstaged James Callaghan who was remarkably adept at populist and television politics in his own right, but who had mismanaged his media relations and damaged his public standing in the 'winter of discontent' (1978-79). Thatcher's campaign in the 1979 general election 'moved closer to American techniques of packaging a presidential candidate and projecting an image than had ever been seen before in Britain'.[55] Very little was left to chance: her clothes, her hair and even her voice and facial expression were honed to produce the appropriate visual effect of suggesting those personal characteristics of leadership that could be effectively conveyed by television. While the advertising agency Saatchi and Saatchi produced a highly sophisticated publicity campaign for the party, Gordon Reece groomed Mrs Thatcher for her television performances. He also organised the correct staging, lighting and camera angles to ensure that the desired effect was achieved. Mrs Thatcher's electoral success in 1979, therefore, was seen as an organisational triumph in presidential-style techniques. In particular, the mass media had been used not merely to neutralise the issue of her political inexperience, but to project her personal credentials as a prospective prime minister.[56]

By the time of her re-election campaign in 1983, Mrs Thatcher had had four years' experience of 'sound bites', 'photo opportunities', colour-coded backdrops, theme-matching wardrobes, and the manufacture of suggestive visual impressions. She led the way in publicising the government by publicising herself. She appeared on programmes like the *Jimmy Young Show*, *Wogan* and *Aspel and Company*. She also gave interviews to down-market but popular newspapers like the *Sun*. In the process, she appeared to break down barriers and make the premiership more familiar and more accessible and, thereby, better placed to engage in techniques of personal persuasion. Her confidence in having mastered the new personal dimension of political conflict was such that she approved and participated in an extraordinary party rally at Wembley.

The rally represented the climax of the campaign to market Mrs Thatcher herself as the embodiment of the government and the symbol of its achievements. An array of sporting and show business celebrities gave their personal endorsements to the prime minister before her triumphant entry into the arena. At that point, five thousand Young Conservatives with 'Maggie In' badges and hats and 'I Love Maggie' T-shirts yelled their delight amidst a blizzard of balloons and streamers. Michael Cockerell described the scene.

> The Prime Minister addressed the faithful, gazing directly into their eyes. She never had to look down at notes. The text of her speech was projected on to a pair of screens in front of her that only she could see. The so-called 'head-up device', or 'sincerity machine', was first used in Britain by President Reagan in his Westminster Hall speech last year. Mrs Thatcher took eagerly to the device, which enables her to turn her head from side to side to look at the whole of her audience.[57]

The event had been arranged and stage-managed by Christopher Lawson, the Conservative Party's first ever Director of Marketing. Before taking on the post, Lawson had had a successful career at marketing the product range at Mars. He spent some time in America, where he made a close study of Ronald Reagan's methods of political persuasion. At Central Office, Lawson made every effort to use these techniques in a British election campaign. It was Lawson who provided the Conservative Party with its special logo of a flaming torch, which was intended to give the party an enhanced corporate identity and a new visual symbol for its many media events. As well as being responsible for a whole host of new techniques for tracking public opinion and for identifying target groups of voters, Lawson ensured that 'like every presidential candidate in America, Margaret Thatcher had her own campaign song'.[58] His various efforts were motivated by the belief that commercial marketing could be directly applied to selling a political party. He believed that there was

only 'a slight difference from marketing a consumer product like a Mars bar
... It's more or less the same. It's communication. It's getting the message
across.'[59]

It was these convictions, channelled as they were into a strategy to sell
the party by selling the leader as a penetratingly incessant public image, that
led to the audacity of the Wembley confection. It had often been remarked in
the past that the 1963 Conservative Party conference resembled an American
political convention because of the utterly spontaneous conditions of Harold
Macmillan's sudden resignation from Number 10 and the party's urgent need
to find a successor. The Wembley rally by contrast was a consciously planned
attempt to imitate an American party convention, in order to project the
prime minister as a directly marketable political commodity. It is revealing
that the Conservative Party felt that it had both the physical resources and the
sense of political licence to engage in such a blatant attempt at political
packaging. The party's campaign in 1983 revealed the extent to which such a
strategy had become a viable form of electioneering.

If Margaret Thatcher represented a delayed reaction to Harold Wilson,
then Neil Kinnock's campaign in 1987 was in its turn a delayed reaction to
Mrs Thatcher. Like Thatcher in 1983, Kinnock seemed to push the nature of
electoral politics even further towards a presidential model. The Labour party
arrested its decline and revived its prospects as a future party of government
by what was generally agreed to have been a highly sophisticated campaign
centring upon the party leader. Under the directorship of Peter Mandelson,
the Labour party had planned for an election that it knew would be even more
intensively dominated by the electronic news-gathering organisations than
the previous elections. Mandelson and his team realised that the main challenge would be coping with, and exploiting, the inevitability of continuous
television coverage. Careful preparations were made to coordinate photo-
opportunities to chosen themes and to match the issues of the day to news
pictures. Considerable efforts were made to ensure that senior party figures
would not compete with each other for airtime and, above all, not conflict with
one another over the nuances of party policy. Partly to ease the problem of
central management in such a pluralist environment of multiple media organisations, and partly to respond to the mass media's native disposition to
make the leaders the prime source of news value, the Labour party not only
allowed but encouraged the campaign to be as leader-centred as possible. As a
consequence, Labour became as adept as the Conservatives in disseminating
imagery, symbolism and personality as the food for electoral choice.[60]

It was clear to Martin Harrison that the media battle had been joined by
Labour's strategy of mass marketing. The consequences were dramatic.

Never before had the parties tailored their efforts so single-mindedly to capturing the cameras' attention. This was the year of the designer campaigns, with their blue flags, red roses and yellow umbrellas, their theatrically spectacular rallies for a generation which had never known Nuremburg, their theme tunes lifted from Brahms, Purcell and Holst and reprocessed for easy listening, and above all their endless photo opportunities. Every party, from the largest to the Greens and the nationalists made television their first priority, and the broadcasters responded to scale.[61]

To Nicholas O'Shaughnessy, the 'election marked the full migration of American political packaging techniques to Britain'; so much so that 'throughout the land public bars murmured with the commonplace that politicians were being sold like a new brand of detergent'.[62] The two major parties were determined to promote their leaders, but none more so than Labour 'whose campaign focused as never before on the personal qualities of its leader'.[63]

Foremost in this regard was the astonishing party election broadcast that launched Labour's campaign on 21 May. The broadcast was in essence a cinematic cameo portrait of Neil Kinnock. It was also 'undoubtedly the major communications event of the campaign'.[64] Written by Colin Welland and directed by Hugh Hudson, the film combined a visual record of Kinnock's family and background with a statement of his personal beliefs and hopes for the country. Against a background of surging music, it was a moving tableau intended to be evocative of Kinnock's worth as a man and therefore as a leader. To this effect, the film included endorsements not only from party figures, but also from members of his own family. To drive the point home that here was a genuinely natural leader, the piece featured upward shot footage of Kinnock in full oratorical flight linking contemporary political issues with his own personal experience (e.g. education cuts with his parents' lack of education opportunities). The broadcast ended with the image of Kinnock and his wife, Glenys, looking out to sea – evoking a sense of personal and national destiny. In the final shot they were replaced with a single caption, not of Labour, but of 'KINNOCK'. In Michael Cockerell's view, 'the programme was nearer to an American presidential commercial than any previous election broadcast in Britain'.[65]

The film was well received by the public. It was also welcomed by the media organisations. Before Labour's offering of a 'new presidential-style prime minister', the media had been presented with the prospect of a dull election campaign, the outcome of which appeared certain.

Kinnock had just returned from a disastrous visit to the States, his party's morale and standing was low, almost as low as the Alliance. That opening position was not one that the media could hope to whip up into a cliff-hanger that would sell newspapers and glue people to *News at Ten*. Then, on the

Thursday evening, the film, 'Kinnock' burst onto the screens. This gave the media what they wanted. If not a party, at least a candidate who could make the election interesting. The media hype did for Kinnock what it had done for the Alliance the election before.[66]

The Kinnock broadcast was widely reported to have wrested the initiative from the government so emphatically that it induced a state of near panic in Central Office at the end of the first week of campaigning. The effect of the Tories' own broadcast was, according to Rodney Tyler,

wiped out by Hugh Hudson's brilliant and highly emotional portrayal of Neil Kinnock as a presidential figure. It was shrugged off as rubbish by most of Tory Central Office. . . . But its effect, along with other Labour successes that first week was startling. Kinnock's rating as a potential prime minister went up by 16 points in the space of seven days.[67]

The sheer professionalism of Labour's campaign management and especially its sophisticated use of image projection (e.g. the red rose logo, the smart visual appearance of its spokespeople, the use of the leader's statements and photo opportunities to set the agenda of issues on Labour's terms), initially reduced the Conservatives to a state of disarray. The anxiety induced by Labour led to a near public wrangle over Tory strategy between Number 10 in the shape of Lord Young and Central Office's campaign management team led by the party chairman, Norman Tebbit.

What made this extraordinary was that the rivals, including Lord Young, Lord Whitelaw and John Wakeham fought not by means of alliances within cabinet but with outside mercenaries in the form of private advertising agencies.[68]

The dispute was ultimately resolved in favour of Mrs Thatcher's private group of media and marketing advisors who were known as 'the exiles' and led by Tim Bell. Saatchi and Saatchi who held the Central Office's advertising account were prevailed upon by Lord Young to defer to what Mrs Thatcher and her exiles wanted – i.e. what Mrs Thatcher felt happy with. Lord Young made it clear to Maurice Saatchi that in modern British elections it was now the leader and the leader's feelings and morale that were all important. The image and therefore the welfare of the party lay in her hands.

We are here for one person – for her. If these ads are what she wants, then these are what she gets. . . . She's the one thing that is going to win this election. But she has to really do it in the next five days. We've always planned to end up with a bang. Now she thinks these ads will give her that. They give her confidence.[69]

The Conservative party duly changed its advertisements in the light of Mrs Thatcher's sentiments. It also ended the campaign with a much higher media profile for Mrs Thatcher. While Labour reacted to public demand and repeated the Kinnock video for its final broadcast, the Conservatives responded in kind. The party which had earlier condemned the Opposition for its glossy packaging, hit back on the leadership theme with the 'longest non-verbal sequence in the history of party broadcasting'.[70] For two and a half minutes, the audience witnessed a celebration of Mrs Thatcher as a world leader accompanied by an anthem composed for the occasion by Andrew Lloyd Webber.

Two days later, the Conservative party inflicted its third successive defeat on Labour. It was widely seen as a personal victory for Mrs Thatcher. Rodney Tyler typified the party's adulation.

> Above all it was Her Victory. It had been her date, her choice of people to fight it, her grounds of battle and, in the end, her personality which came to dominate it.[71]

It was seen as a presidential performance. Thatcher had competed with, and finally prevailed over, Kinnock's attempt to displace her popular claims to public leadership. She had also directed the party's advertising and media presentation to reflect what was acceptable to her and what was favourable to her. Thatcher's efforts left the impression of a victory that vindicated the marketing power of image projection and personal promotion. This impression of presidential politics was captured by the serialisation of Rodney Tyler's book *Campaign: The Selling of the Prime Minister* (1987).[72] The analysis of the Conservative Party's internal divisions over the 1987 advertising campaign was promoted by the *Sunday Times* as 'How Mrs Thatcher Really Won the Election'.[73]

The modern style of leadership-centred elections has spawned an easygoing inclination to compare British politics with all things American and especially with the thing which is most American of all in British eyes – the presidency. The prima facie case for comparison has been routinely leapt upon to generate a range of fevered allusions to presidential politics in Britain. It is 'argued that a general election is little more than a presidential contest, people voting mainly on the basis of their feelings towards the party leaders'.[74] 'Given the presidential nature of modern British elections',[75] it is to be expected that party leaders have become more concerned with personal promotions and public recognition than with policy statements and issue positions.

> Presidentialisation comes from the concern shown for the public image or charisma of leaders . . . A measure of this is shown at annual party conferences, where the leaders are unashamedly lionized, with stage-managed displays of mass adulation.[76]

Such conferences used to be occasions when the leaders met the party. Now they are devices by which leaders speak over the heads of the party faithful directly to the public by way of television.[77] This change, it is commonly asserted, makes every party conference into a preparation for an election campaign and, as such, turns them into American-style presidential conventions.

On occasions it can seem as if British politics is awash with references to American presidential politics and that every trend reveals nothing other than the 'sweeping presidentialisation of British political life'.[78] The uninhibited populism and personal image building of leaders in general elections has ramified into many other areas of political endeavour. For example, the new rules adopted by the Labour party in 1981 for the selection of the leader and deputy leader widened the franchise from the Parliamentary Labour Party to one that would include the trade union and constituency party organisations. Tony Benn challenged for the deputy leadership in 1987. Michael Cockerell described the manner of his electioneering in the following terms.

> In Benn's campaign, the big trade union conferences became like the American primaries; USDAW, ASTMS and the T. & G. equalled New Hampshire, Alabama and California. Benn's aim was to appeal directly to the conference delegates and to go beneath the head of the union general secretaries.[79]

When Neil Kinnock ran for the leadership in 1983, he had already prepared the ground. R.W. Johnson observed that he

> had tirelessly criss-crossed the country, addressing every constituency party that would have him – hardly unaware that the broadened franchise of Labour's election system had given a wholly new importance to such protracted cultivation of the grass roots. Kinnock's landmark presidential marathon – for that is what it was – bears comparison with the way Kennedy changed American presidential elections for ever, by his systematic crusade through the primaries.[80]

Johnson concluded that it was possible that the manner of his rise would represent 'Kinnock's chief mark on our political history'.[81] In 1990, Michael Heseltine attempted to emulate Kinnock's achievement. The franchise for leadership election in the Conservative party was still confined to its members of Parliament. Even so, Heseltine sought to generate support for his future candidacy by a concerted strategy of visits to constituency associations and personal appearances at local party events. He toured the country, often flying in and out of functions in his personal helicopter.

With these examples in mind, it can often seem as if the pathways to leadership, and the preparation and execution of election campaigns, have already given a presidential character to political competition in Britain. As a consequence, it becomes all to easy to concur with Nicholas O'Shaughnessy that the 'conditions are maturing for the emergence of an American-style prime minister'.[82]

The numerous references to this alleged process of presidentialism have led in their turn to an equally robust and characteristic set of reactions denying its presence. 'Presidential denial' comes in two main forms. *First* are the denials that come from politicians – very often the self-same politicians who are accused of being in some way presidential. It is politically prudent to deny any intention of acting presidentially, or to give even tacit approval to being described in presidential terms.

This 'attitude' is primarily based upon the link between Britain's governing institutions and its national identity. It can be seen to be un-British and mildly subversive to condone the intrusion of an outside political feature into the British constitution. This attitude is of course also connected to the British ambivalence towards American culture. Private admiration is often combined with a public disdain for its political vulgarities and a ready insistence that 'nearly all attempts to graft American politics on to British institutions are misguided'.[83]

Being characterised as presidential therefore may be titillating, but there is also a hint of abuse in the approbation. It can be turned into derogatory comment to demean the recipient by associating him with the stereotypical view of American politics as a mass of vacuous hype and fluffy egotism that substitutes platitudes and television 'events' for serious debate. As a consequence, having 'presidential qualities' in Britain can be equated with conceit and arrogance. It can also be associated with trivia and deception because it is widely held that in the United States, it is not politicians who are marketed so much as their manufactured images. Critics recall Joe McGinniss's celebrated proposition in *The Selling of the President* (1970) that

> the response is to the image, not to the man . . . It's not what's there that counts, it's what's projected – and carrying it one step further, it's not what he projects but rather what the voter receives.[84]

It is good politics in Britain to deny presidentialism and especially so for politicians, who in every other respect are seeking to cultivate presidential-style leadership in the British system. Apart from protecting oneself from unnecessary criticism, it is often a good way of keeping political opponents in their place. For example, when Ted Heath was desperate to make an impression upon Harold Wilson's leadership in the 1970 general election, he challenged Wilson to a television debate. Not wishing to give Heath the appearance of equal status and the image of an alternative prime minister, Wilson refused, stating that he did not wish to compromise the integrity of a British election with an American style presidential debate. The tables were turned in 1979. Mrs Thatcher as Leader of the Opposition had such a marked lead in the polls that it was Prime Minister James Callaghan who demanded a television debate. Mrs Thatcher refused, declaring,

We should continue with the traditional broadcasting arrangements. Personally I believe that issues and policies, not personalities, decide an election. We are not electing a President.[85]

In 1983, she turned down Michael Foot for the same reason. At a time when she was fully engaged in making the election more personalised and presidential than any previous election, Mrs Thatcher objected to a televised debate because in her terms she did not wish to turn the election into a presidential contest. The same pattern was repeated in 1987 when Kinnock was rebuffed. The only difference in that year was that Labour had the better campaign which led to Conservative complaints that the Opposition was trying to Americanise the election. After the result had been declared, it was left to Norman Tebbit, the Conservative party chairman, to turn the presidential critique on its head. Presidentialism, which had been cited as the cause of Labour's early and allegedly unfair success, was now given as the reason for its defeat. 'People are interested in issues and any advertising has to be linked to that', Tebbit intoned. 'The British public is not ready for the presidential style of campaigning.'[86]

The *second* and far more seriously argued form of presidential denial comes from political scientists who believe that the allegations of presidentialism confuse appearances with reality, manner with content and intentions with achievement. Richard Rose, for example, is scornful of the presidential analogy and goes to considerable lengths to demolish it. He points out that party politics in Britain is still first and foremost parliamentary politics. Leaders rise and fall in Parliament as a result of parliamentary judgement. A 'prime minister's presentation of self to Parliament reflects personal priorities and constraints, not the work of the government'.[87] While it is true that the media 'intensify the personalisation of government',[88] individual prominence has no discernible effect on government popularity or party features. In other words, a popular leader has no 'coat-tails' effect for his or her party. It is a self-contained prominence confined to the leader's own stature. To the party, 'political circumstances are more important than personality'[89] in determining the prospects for winning and retaining power.

Rose goes on to remind his readers that owing to the nature of executive power in Britain, a prime minister is not even required to be a popular political figure. 'Because prime ministers are not directly elected by the public, they have less need to cultivate popularity for its own sake. Success in government is considered the best guarantee of popular success.'[90] Furthermore, because 'parliamentary party support is virtually certain, independent of the leader's standing in the opinion polls' and because 'the authority of a prime minister is not diminished by lacking the approval of a majority of the voters',[91] it is

117

simply not necessary for a prime minister to seek a continuous affirmation of public support. 'The critical point is not the leader's popularity but the governing party's popularity.'[92] According to this basic tenet of the British constitution, the effects of the media and of marketing techniques in promoting the public standing of party leaders should be minimal. In Rose's view, this theoretical assumption is borne out in hard political experience:

> From the evidence of public opinion it would be difficult to argue that changes in the media have made a Prime Minister more or less successful in the presentation of self. New media techniques are best seen as neutral. In the absence of direct election of a Prime Minister, they are not crucial to the incumbent's fate, which is immediately decided in Westminster, not in television studios.[93]

Richard Rose's appeals to realism fall like an icy shower on the feverish claims of market analysts and image consultants. 'A vast amount of research on media effects . . . normally shows how *little* effect political marketing has.'[94]

> Studies of audience reaction to politics on television emphasize how little effect programmes have on political outlooks. People principally judge programmes by their *prior* party loyalty; they do not choose a party simply in response to a particular television programme.[95]

According to Rose, Kinnock's election defeat in 1987 provides graphic proof of the inadmissibility of American techniques of electioneering in Britain and, thereby, the inappropriateness of the presidential analogy in British politics.

> An opposition leader who concentrates on boosting his personal popularity – running a presidential-style campaign, as it is called in Britain – can expect little reward. In 1987 Labour leader Neil Kinnock ran a personal campaign with American-style media sophistication and evasion of difficult policy questions. The Labour party received less than one-third of the popular vote.[96]

The implication is clear. Labour may have had the better campaign measured in reference to American criteria but, in spite of it, the party had lost a British general election.

These trenchant observations provide a refreshing and important reminder that the alleged presidentialism of British politics is a contested feature of government in the UK. It would be difficult to describe it as a debate as there is no agreement on the terms of definition. Nevertheless, arguments asserting the growing presidentialism in Britain are confronted by claims that such propositions are misguided and misleading. It is the view of this study that the arguments on both sides have substance and are valid in differing respects. On the other hand, it is also true that each side overstates its case in such a way that together they almost invariably argue at cross-purposes. As a consequence, the claims and counterclaims generally obscure rather than clarify the nature of the developments that have given rise to such a controversy in the first place.

It is true for example that the usage of the presidential analogy is often made too readily without being properly thought through. There often seems to be an unseemly haste to jump enthusiastically from prima facie evidence to conclusive comparisons. On the other hand, political scientists who believe that 'much talk of the presidential trends in British politics is overdone',[97] can pursue the inexactitude of the presidential analogy so assiduously that they can miss the significance of those political conditions that can give rise to such comparisons. They can overstate their case by denying the presidential analogy in one respect, or even in several respects, solely on the ground that it is not a valid comparison in all possible respects. Such sophisticated appraisals of the various political, constitutional, historical and cultural differences between the two systems can obscure the significance of their similarities. Many of the references to presidentialism may be overstated and clumsy, but it is equally true that they are not wholly unjustified and the impulse to make such assertions should not be dismissed too lightly.

The irony of this dispute is that the contributions of the two sides are misleading in that they both tend to miss the central point. They are both in their separate and indirect ways responding to the same phenomenon which is largely unstated and usually concealed in the cross-fire, but which is nevertheless the most significant feature in the controversy. To enrich the irony still further, the feature in question is arguably more American in nature than any other aspect of the presidential comparison. It is the emergence in Britain of a highly advanced and self-conscious politics of leadership.

The British public has become increasingly exposed to, and conditioned by, a form of politics which is centred not only upon leaders, but on the sources, methods, uses, location and even meaning of leadership. The public expectations of leadership, together with the seductive appeal of the politics that surrounds it, not only radiates a leadership dimension throughout British politics, but draws ostensibly unrelated issues into its orbit. Leadership itself has become a political issue which accounts for those circumlocutions of party politicians who, as noted above, condemn the presidential pretensions of their opponents and deny their own presidential inclinations, whilst often earnestly seeking to cultivate a presidential stature for themselves.

The intensifying emphasis upon leaders and leadership is likely to have many unpredictable and possibly even quite arbitrary long-term consequences, but one thing is already quite clear. The politics of leadership in the British system has created an unprecedented public dimension to the perception of the political process and to the nature of political conduct.

CHAPTER 5

Leadership stretch in Britain

In March 1991, the *Independent on Sunday* ran a feature on a day in the life of Paddy Ashdown.[1] It dramatically revealed the prodigious lengths that a national politician now has to go to, in order to remain in the public arena of modern British politics. The 'day' begins with a series of radio interviews in the night. Lacking sleep, he arrives at his Westminster office for an 8.30 am policy meeting with his advisors. 'He sits down, opens a laptop computer, punches keys, barks instructions. Then the talk begins.'[2] By 9.40 am, Ashdown is giving a succession of television interviews to Sky, ITN, BBC *Points West*, BBC News, HTV, TV South Wales and Yorkshire Television. Before leaving for Preston to campaign in the Ribble Valley by-election, he

> goes to his office, talks to his speechwriter, answers several letters, bolts a cup of soup with crispy croutons and rushes across to Westminster Central Hall to make a long, passionate speech to 1,500 students.[3]

Next it is Prime Minister's Question Time in the House of Commons. After that comes a meeting with Sir David Steel. 'In the car on the way to the station Ashdown's voice is coming out of his mouth and the radio at the same time.'[4] On the train, he remains linked to his headquarters all the time by mobile phone and computer. He arrives in Preston ready for the next day's campaigning and walkabout before his scheduled return to London on the following afternoon and a major speech in Bournemouth planned for the evening.

The sheer scale of Ashdown's public activities and the energy and time he invests in them typifies the drives towards personal exposure and popular attention that have to come characterise so much of contemporary British politics. The self-conscious attempts by leaders to find the words, the style and the setting to claim air-time, in order to maintain the visibility of their respective leaderships has become an integral part of the public presentation of politics. Leaders struggle with one another on a continued basis to be the most effective expression of popular convictions and anxieties. What were once

120

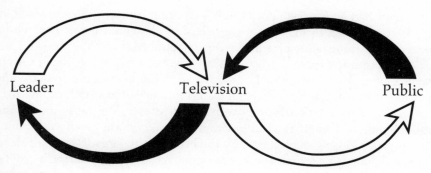

FIGURE 5.1

media opportunities to reach a wider audience have now been turned into overriding media obligations to publicise political positions through the effective projection of party leaders as national figures.

Much of the recent exposure and public attention given to leaders has come as a result of an underlying dynamic between the mass media and party politics. In short, television's inclination to personalise the treatment and presentation of politics has been matched by the willingness of parties to provide their leaders with the prominence and licence to fit the party product to its optimal form of communication. Just as 'the dominance of television helps to presidentialize the message of the parties',[5] so the messengers themselves have become increasingly presidentialised. Leaders are no longer merely party spokesmen, but the ostentatious flagships of their respective fleets. They have no choice. They are simply part of a self-generating and self-intensifying process that compels party leaders to achieve high levels of public attention and recognition by moulding themselves successfully to the medium that can best provide it. In doing so, leaders acquire further public prominence which enhances their television news value to an even greater extent than before (Figure 5.1). As a result of this process, a leader can improve the security of his or her position in the party and thereupon claim further executive discretion to exploit the visibility of that position for the party's interests and objectives.

An important qualification in leadership selection is now an individual's proven ability to attract publicity and media attention. For example, 'It was natural that the successor to Michael Foot as Labour leader in 1983 should be chosen with considerable care for TV skills.'[6] In fact, Neil Kinnock was said to have 'owed almost everything to television'.[7] He used it to compensate for his lack of political and governmental experience. As he himself said: 'I got to be Leader of the Labour Party by being good on television.'[8] David Owen was chosen as the SDP leader for much the same reasons. Roy Jenkins, the party's first leader, had performed poorly on television in the 1983 general election. He felt constrained to make way for a leader who could better exploit the modern opportunities for personal and party publicisation. Shirley Williams explained the main reasons why Jenkins' successor had to be David Owen. 'David Owen had a remarkable capacity . . . for being able to seize the attention of the media, capture it and turn it into headline after headline after headline.'⁹ This relationship between party leaders, the mass media and public opinion is strengthened still further by the emphasis given to elections, and especially to general elections, by the broadcasting organisations. Television and radio news services devote enormous resources to covering a general election. It is regarded by them as the centrepiece of their political reporting efforts and as their main claim to being a public service. Coverage of an election, right through to the authoritative predictions before the official announcements, is the forte of the electronic news gathering organisations. Elections are now not only conducted *through* the mass media, but to a large extent by them as well.

Given this special relationship between the mass media and elections, it is only to be expected that television and radio news programmes should reflect their interest in the electoral dimension of political events and disputes. This takes various forms but the most conspicuous effect is the way that political news is often presented and analysed in reference to its significance for a forthcoming election – even if that election is some years away. As a result, the handling of domestic news is riddled with allusions to electoral timing and voting projections, and to American-style calculations as to who is ahead, who is falling behind and who might not reach the start line. By-elections, for example, are now seen and treated as being prototypical of general elections. Accordingly, they are subjected to a blaze of publicity in which the party heavyweights spar with one another in preparation for the big contest. Such elections provide not only a testing ground for the parties' campaigning techniques, but also a proving ground for the media's own capacity to impose general election categories of analysis and evaluation upon a local voting exercise.

The next election is in many respects the central framework that is employed to make sense of events, to explain developments, and to justify the content and priority given to political news. One of the consequences of this fixation with elections is the way that the coverage of the news during the extraordinary period of a general election radiates outwards into the more normal periods, when the ballot boxes have been locked away. The most evident feature of this seepage is the media's concentration upon the party leaders. Partly to prepare the ground for the climatic election period of leadership clashes, and also partly to justify the media's own inclination towards the

TABLE 5.1 *Number of references to senior politicians in* The Times *(London)*

Year[a]	Prime Minister (1)	Leader of Opposition (2)	(1) as % of (2)	Chancellor of Exchequer (3)	Foreign Secretary (4)	Leader of House of Commons (5)	(1) as % of Total of (3-5)
1949	94 Attlee	62 Churchill	152	110 Cripps	96 Bevin	56 Morrison	36
1952	302 Churchill	64 Attlee	472	136 Butler	197 Eden	38 Crookshank	81
1956	193 Eden	70 Gaitskell	276	93 Macmillan	111 Lloyd	50 Butler	76
1960	303 Macmillan	88 Gaitskell	344	44 Amory	76 Lloyd	109 Butler	132
1964	278 Douglas-Home	169 Wilson	164	47 Maudling	106 Butler	23 Lloyd	158
1968	147 Wilson	50 Heath	294	46[b] Jenkins	45 Brown	14 Crossman	140
1972	141 Heath	82 Wilson	172	18 Barber	74 Douglas-Home	24 Whitelaw	122
1977	170 Callaghan	78 Thatcher	218	37 Healey	39[c] Crosland/Owen	59 Foot	126

[a]The January-March quarter.
[b]Stories concerning the March budget.
[c]Stories on the death of Crosland and the appointment of Owen are omitted.
SOURCE The quarterly *Index to The Times* (London).

personalisation of politics, the portrayal of everyday political events tends to be reduced to two main controlling themes. First are the implications for the possible timing and outcome of an election, and second are the electoral credentials of the parties' respective leaders. Given the central role of a general election in a parliamentary democracy, and given the party leaders' contemporary significance in such an exercise of popular choice, the mass media have been impelled to intensify the trend towards the condition of a permanent election. They have done so by keeping the leaders, and their ultimate electoral objectives, firmly and constantly in the public eye. The leaders, for their part, now find their *raison d'être* and daily agendas to be dominated by incessant electoral calculations. As a consequence, they strive for the kind of public attention and political prominence that attracts even more media interest over an even longer time scale.

In modern British politics, the possession of a public identity is a political resource in its own right. Party leaders have to be able to command public

TABLE 5.2 *Volume[a] of references to senior politicians in* Times *Publications[b]*

Year	Prime Minister (1)	Leader of Opposition (2)	(1) as % of (2)	Chancellor of Exchequer (3)	Foreign Secretary (4)	Leader of House of Commons (5)	(1) as % of Total of (3-5)
1980	Thatcher	Foot		Howe	Carrington	St. John Stevas	
	302.8	77.3	392	90.5	101.5	47.9	126.2
1984	Thatcher	Kinnock		Lawson	Howe	Biffen	
	342.5	185.1	185	73.8	109.3	17.0	171.2
1988	Thatcher	Kinnock		Lawson	Howe	Wakeham	
	383.8	145.6	264	59.0	59.1	21.1	275.7

[a]The volume is measured by the length (in centimetres) of the columns of entries for each politician printed in *The Times Index* in each of the years cited in the table.

[b]Publications in *The Times Index* include: *The Times, Sunday Times, Times Literary Supplement, Daily Telegraph, Sunday Telegraph Magazine, Times Educational Supplement, Times Educational Supplement Scotland, Times Higher Education Supplement*, and the *Sunday Telegraph*.

attention, in order to maintain the confidence of their parties. Leaders who are known to the public have access to the public domain. They can float ideas, discredit opponents, allay doubts, share concerns, sell policies and change the agenda of public debate. How well leaders perform these public functions, how effectively they use the public facilities of leadership to convey messages, and how proficient they are in commanding public confidence are themselves matters of public scrutiny and popular appraisal. The extent of the public's access to, and interest in, the words, images and behaviour of leaders – together with the scale of the media's leader-centred presentation of the news – produces an effect that can be called 'leadership stretch'. The term refers to the way that party leaders have increasingly stretched away from their senior colleagues in terms of media attention and popular awareness.

In a pioneer study of prime ministerial prominence published in 1980, Richard Rose showed that prime ministers regularly received more press coverage than that of the Foreign Secretary, the Chancellor of the Exchequer and Leader of the House of Commons put together.[10] It is also revealed that the coverage given to the Leader of the Opposition had grown in parallel with the increased publicity given to the prime minister (Table 5.1). In 1956, for example, Anthony Eden and Hugh Gaitskell together accounted for approximately the same number of references as the Chancellor, Foreign Secretary and Leader of the House of Commons combined.[11] By 1977, Callaghan and Thatcher were not far from having double the number of references given to the holders of the same three senior offices of state.[12] New tables covering the

Thatcher period demonstrate the intensification of leadership trends (see Table 5.2).

The pre-eminence of a modern prime minister is shown to even greater effect in a *Sunday Times* survey that measured the press coverage given to all public figures for a whole year.[13] Apart from drawing its data from fourteen publications[14] instead of relying on just *The Times Index*, the survey was not confined to politicians but included anyone whose name appeared in the press during the year in question. From this enormous pool of celebrities, John Major headed the 1991 poll with 10,814 'mentions'. He had an emphatic lead over second place Mikhail Gorbachev with 7,871 mentions and Saddam Hussein with 6,664. Neil Kinnock was sixth with 3,747 mentions, thereby giving the prime minister a preponderance over the leader of the opposition of 289%. Only two members of the cabinet reached the top ten. The Chancellor of the Exchequer, Norman Lamont, came fifth and the Foreign Secretary, Douglas Hurd, came tenth. In spite of these rankings, their total amounted to only 61% of that received by the premier. The nearest member of the shadow cabinet to Neil Kinnock's total was the deputy leader, Roy Hattersley. He was squeezed into 27th place by Gary Lineker (25th) and Madonna (26th). Hattersley's total number of mentions (1,048) revealed that the leader's prominence in the press was over three and a half times that given to his deputy.

Figures produced by Martin Harrison in the Nuffield studies of British general elections reveal the magnitude of leadership stretch where the broadcasting media are concerned. Working on the basis of the number of times that politicians had been quoted in radio and television news programmes during the election campaigns, Professor Harrison shows in graphic form the dominance of the party leaders over other senior political figures in respect to media coverage. The results of the 1987 election are given in Table 5.3.[15]

It is clear from these figures that even leading members of the cabinet or deputy leaders of parties cannot compete with party leaders where media attention is concerned. For example, the chairman of the Conservative Party, Norman Tebbit, had a very prominent role in his party's campaign, but he only managed to achieve 33% of the coverage given to the prime minister. Even the high-profile Chancellor of the Exchequer, Nigel Lawson, only received 18% of Mrs Thatcher's level of exposure. On the Labour side, Deputy Leader Roy Hattersley constituted one half of his party's 'dream ticket', but his appearances on the news amounted to barely 20% of the attention given over to Neil Kinnock. With two leaders attracting attention in the Alliance, the second string figures in the Liberal and Social Democrat Parties were engulfed by David Steel and David Owen. Roy Jenkins, for example, the first leader of the SDP, had just 4% of the news references given to the 'two Davids'.

TABLE 5.3 *Politicians quoted in radio and television news (number of times)*

Conservative	BBC1	ITV	C4	R4	Total
Thatcher	140	116	47	118	421
Tebbit	46	38	16	39	139
Lawson	26	23	7	22	78
Younger	12	8	7	8	35
Baker	10	12	7	6	35
Young	14	7	2	5	28
Hurd	7	9	3	5	24
Heseltine	8	4	3	4	19
Fowler	8	1	2	9	20
Howe	5	2	4	3	14
Clarke	6	3	3	1	13
Rifkind	7	-	-	3	10
McGregor	3	2	2	3	10
Parkinson	6	1	-	3	10
35 others	30	22	22	20	94
Labour					
Kinnock	147	144	59	131	481
Hattersley	26	30	10	29	95
Gould	27	19	9	17	72
Healey	12	9	6	13	40
Smith	9	4	5	8	26
Meacher	11	5	2	7	25
Kaufman	9	7	3	3	22
Prescott	7	6	2	3	18
Radice	3	3	2	4	12
47 others	38	20	22	18	98
Alliance					
Owen	127	115	49	93	384
Steel	102	82	37	66	287
Williams	9	10	5	10	34
Jenkins	9	8	5	6	28
Pardoe	8	3	5	4	20
Bruce	10	6	1	2	19
Ashdown	5	5	2	4	16
Hughes	3	5	3	2	13
Meadowcroft	2	6	1	1	10
34 others	34	9	20	13	76
Other parties					
Wilson (SNP)	16	7	2	6	31
Wigley (Plaid)	7	6	-	2	15
Powell (DUP)	2	1	1	3	7
Robins (Green)	-	4	1	-	5
30 others	28	5	5	11	49

SOURCE David Butler and Dennis Kavanagh, *The British General Election of 1987*

These figures do show that the news programmes attempted to diversify their coverage of politicians. Perhaps to counteract the dominance of the four main leaders and to enliven their treatment of the election, the news editors gave attention to a range of party notables. Nevertheless, by the end of the election all the attempts at diversification had merely underlined and exaggerated still further the leaders' prominence over their respective parties. By stretching the field of spokesmen, diversification also stretched the leaders' visible dominance over that field. It provided a larger number of individuals whose news coverage could be compared unfavourably with that of their party leaders.

In a separate study of television news programmes in the 1987 general election, Barrie Axford produces broadly similar results.[16] His findings are different insofar as they provide a more detailed classification of competing spokespersons and are presented in diagrammatic form, which gives dramatic emphasis to the leaders' domination of television news. Figure 5.2 shows the leaders' general preponderance over other types of political participant. Figure 5.3 displays the leadership's centrality to each party's television election campaign. This is especially marked with the opposition parties which were fighting not only the government, but their own lack of a widely recognised team on a par with senior cabinet members. Axford concludes that

> It is understandable that national television should report the national campaign. Perhaps more surprising, in a system which still applauds the virtues of collective leadership, is the extent of the coverage of the individual party leaders.[17]

Although there is evidence to suggest that the proportion of references given to the party leaders in election campaign television has increased since the 1960s and the advent of mass television ownership,[18] it can be claimed that even these measurements do not adequately convey the weight given to the leaders in news reports. Martin Harrison himself is swift to point out that his statistics, based as they are on quotations, ignore the visual sequences like the 'many photo-opportunities, containing no references to policy. The figures therefore understate the degree of "presidentialisation".'[19] Even the rate of leader 'mentions' in news broadcasts can prove to be deceptive. When such rates remain similar over time, for example, they can disguise the real nature of the leaders' penetration into the electoral process. What the figures based upon the percentage of 'mentions' overlook is the global increase in news reports, news analysis and news gathering services. While the proportion of references to party leaders may remain comparable between different periods, therefore, the net effect within an ever widening framework of news provision is significant because of the sheer scale of coverage given to the leaders. In the general election of October 1974, for example, the total number of leader

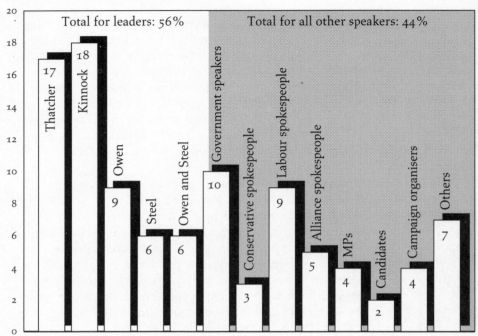

FIGURE 5.2   The dominance of the leaders in television coverage of political personalities during the 1987 general election.   SOURCE Barrie Axford, 'Leaders,
elections and television', *Politics Review* 1, No. 3 (February 1992).

mentions was 733.[20] By the 1983 election, the figure had reached 1,098[21] and
in the 1987 election, it had risen to 1,573.[22] If repetition is as central to
advertising as it is reputed to be, then the party leaders' *share* of the total
number of references does not need to rise for their prominence to be progressively enhanced in relation to what is an increasingly long tail of 'also rans'
who were 'also mentioned'.

Another element of 'leadership stretch' is provided by the resurgence of
a third force in British party politics. A buoyant and threatening third force
not only stretches the number of leaders but, in doing so, further intensifies
the process of leadership coverage. Third parties crowd the field with leaders
both in numbers and in proportion to the size of their organisations. In the
case of the Alliance, it doubled the number of major party leaders to be
covered, thereby concentrating available news time even further upon the
competition between leaders. The BBC and the IBA (now ITC) have rules on
the fair and balanced coverage of political news which the print media do not
possess. It is in the interests of the minor parties to exploit these rules, in order
to compensate for their relatively weak organisational base and to compete at

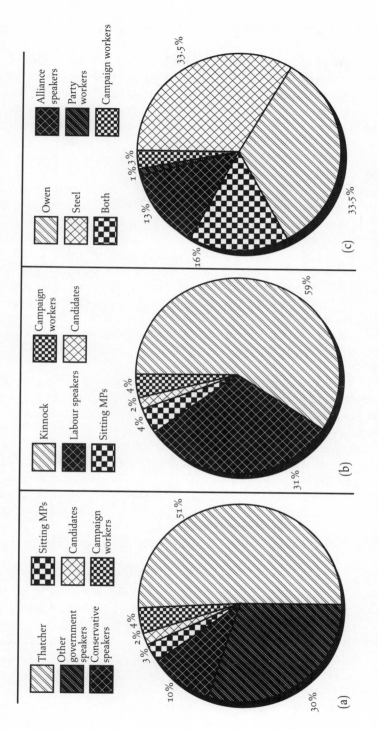

FIGURE 5.3   The dominance of the party leader in all mentions of the party in television coverage during the 1987 general election: (a) Conservative; (b) Labour; (c) Alliance.   SOURCE   Barrie Axford, 'Leaders, elections and television', *Politics Review* 1, No. 3 (February 1992).

the highest level of leadership politics in the hope of a 'top down' effect in the parties' electoral performance. As a consequence, the news organisations find themselves under pressure to respond to the third parties by simply extending the coverage given to the leaders of the two main parties to the leaders of the third force. This widens the ranks of leaders publicly engaged in leadership politics. It also raises the competitive edge between them as they increasingly draw attention towards themselves and reduce the priority afforded to other facets of political competition.

Imaginative, and arguably more substantive, ways of arriving at a 'balance' in news coverage are difficult enough to achieve with two parties. With the addition of another party, which if anything is even more disposed than the other two to set the pace on leadership exposure, agreements on alternative strategies of balance are especially more difficult to reach. Doubts and suspicions are raised with the net effect that the news programmes find it easier to work to the lowest common denominator of leadership coverage. This concern for equity reaffirms and reinforces the trend to what is becoming a fixed and increasingly stylised formula of saturated leadership attention. This satisfies all three parties and at the same time enhances the news value of the leaders, which the news organisations then have to defer to in the selection of stories.

The various pressures that orientate election coverage to an identifiable cadre of leaders are not peculiar to an election period. They may be particularly intense during a campaign, but they are symptomatic of a more general trend towards a permanent election, in which the effective leadership of a political party and the effective marketing of political issues are closely tied up with one another. There are no figures for non-election periods that are directly comparable figures to Martin Harrison's measurement of the broadcast media's fixation with the party leaders during the heat of the electoral battle. But bearing in mind the public's ability to recognise political figures during non-election periods, there seems little doubt that the level of media interest shown in the party leaders is very similar to that revealed in election periods.

In polls where members of the public are asked to recognise photographs of leading politicians, they have no difficulty in correctly naming the party leaders. The prime minister and the Leader of the Opposition can normally be assured of recognition by about 95% of the respondents. Such familiarity is in stark contrast, however, to the low levels of public recognition afforded to most members of the cabinet and shadow cabinet. According to a Gallup poll in October 1990,[23] the recognition rates of leading Conservative politicians were remarkably low. Apart from colourful characters outside the cabinet like Cecil Parkinson (62%), Norman Tebbit (67%) and prospective party leader

Michael Heseltine (61%), the public found it difficult to put a name to senior cabinet ministers like Douglas Hurd (47%), John Major (47%) and Sir Geoffrey Howe (48%). Tom King (35%), Kenneth Baker (37%) and Kenneth Clarke (27%) posed even more recognition problems, while the public found it practically impossible to identify John MacGregor (10%), Michael Howard (4%) and Peter Lilley (2%). Even after eleven years of Conservative government, the public could not be relied upon to recognise any member of the cabinet apart from the prime minister, whose aura of familiarity was overwhelming.

The same relationship between the public, the leader and the leader's team holds for the chief opposition party. The only difference is that the gulf between the Leader of the Opposition and his shadow cabinet is even greater than that between the prime minister and the cabinet. In another Gallup poll, published in May 1991,[24] Neil Kinnock was correctly recognised by 96%. The deputy leader, Roy Hattersley, only achieved a level of 53%, while most of his colleagues struggled to raise even a flicker of acknowledgement across the dark cave of the public's consciousness. The *Daily Telegraph*'s presentation of the poll gave visual emphasis to the differentials (Figure 5.4). In the accompanying commentary, Anthony King was prompted to come to the following conclusions.

> People desperately craving obscurity could do worse than consider becoming a Cabinet minister under Mr Major or a shadow minister under Mr Kinnock. The Gallup Poll's latest survey for the *Daily Telegraph* indicates that even in the television age, most voters stubbornly refuse to recognise the existence, or at least the faces, of most politicians. The survey suggests that most ministers and their shadows are so anonymous that they could become spies without serious fear of detection. Backbenchers thinking of achieving fame by becoming ministers should reconsider their position.[25]

According to some commentators, the massive growth in the televised exposure of leading politicians 'acts as a constraint on the prime minister'.[26] Far from enhancing the prime minister's position, it has been claimed that the televising of the House of Commons would

> provide opportunities for ministers to win reputations. A Prime Minister's stature may even be diminished as they are continually seen in the midst of unseemly rows and being browbeaten by the opposition instead of, as previously, being seen speaking in splendid isolation from a podium or in the company of world statesmen at international gatherings.[27]

This overlooks the fact that prime ministers benefit from increasing opportunities to speak from podia and to appear on international stages. It also overlooks the extent to which recent prime ministers seem either to be

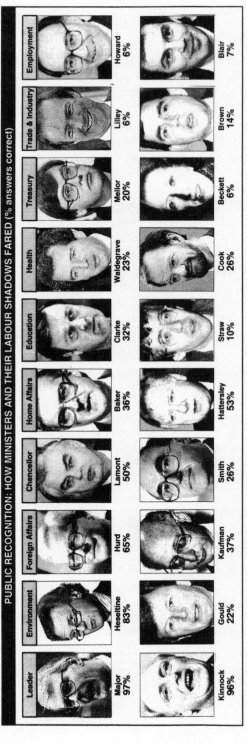

FIGURE 5.4 (SOURCE *Daily Telegraph*, 13 May 1991)

magisterially absent from the chamber, or else to be conspicuously disengaged from the debates. Mrs Thatcher, in particular, was 'far and away the least active prime minister in the Commons for the last one hundred and twenty years. Her abandonment of debating interventions and her very infrequent speeches set her strongly apart.'[28] Instead of needing to participate actively in the House of Commons to sustain her authority, Mrs Thatcher's prominence and influence appeared for many years to be inversely proportional to her parliamentary activity.

The only regular occasion when a prime minister's presence and participation are assured is during prime ministerial Question Time. This is when the premier is publicly engaged by the Leader of the Opposition in what has become a gladiatorial contest between two leaders on the implicit theme of leadership. This much exposed twice-weekly event, which is often the only occasion when the public observes the House of Commons in action, or sees it full, is dominated by the party leaders surrounded by their front-bench supporters. It is clear from the public recognition levels of politicians that most of these senior figures are merely faces in a crowd to most observers. The collective ranks of cabinet and shadow cabinet members merely provide the human stages upon which party leaders engage each other.

The leadership stretch of the premier is evident in Prime Minister's Questions, but it is also clear that the Leader of the Opposition has the opportunity, and arguably the need, to stretch away from his colleagues in what is now a public exhibition of leadership. Just as the occasion of Prime Minister's Questions assembles the governing party together for the main purpose of giving visual expression to the prime minister's pre-eminence, so it also provides the Leader of the Opposition with a comparable opportunity for political status. It offers him or her the chance to raise the profile of his party, to challenge the premier's access to national publicity, and to compete with the prime minister in looking and sounding like a statesman.

> Prime Ministers are rarely seen in a critical environment in which they cannot control the agenda. Question Time not only provides Leaders of the Opposition with guaranteed and frequent opportunities to demonstrate their prowess in face-to-face confrontation but is also one of the rare occasions upon which it is they who have the chance to set the agenda for that confrontation. The opportunity to play this leading part may be used to serve a number of purposes . . . It offers an Opposition leader who may be experiencing intra-party difficulties a means of strengthening his or her position not available to potential rivals or critics and thus edge over them.[29]

While critics of Prime Minister's Questions, like Enoch Powell, deplore the way it places 'an unhealthy spotlight on the chairman of the cabinet',[30] Opposition leaders have found that it can provide life-enhancing properties both to their leadership positions and to their efforts to challenge the prime minister on grounds of public leadership.

These encounters between leaders – and very much acting as leaders – have now become an institutionalised part of House of Commons business. With the advent of parliamentary broadcasting, and in particular the televising of the Commons, Prime Minister's Questions have likewise become an institutionalised feature of radio and television news. It is the one aspect of the Commons' business which is assured of live coverage and of extensive highlights during the day's news broadcasts.[31] While broadcasting has helped to provide an extensive array of material on all the members and their varied activities, nothing can match the focal intensity of Prime Minister's Questions for concentrating media attention on the House of Commons and on the issue of public leadership. It receives a disproportionate share of the media's coverage given to the work of parliament. One 1989-90 study for the Select Committee on the Televising of the Proceedings of the House found Prime Minister's Questions to be the largest single Commons event covered by ITN's *News at Ten* – amounting to 38% of the programme's House of Commons material. The figures for the other network news broadcasts were not so high but they were still considerable.[32] It was in these 'national news programmes (i.e. the newscasts with the largest audiences) where the emphasis on party leaders was most evident'.[33] Reports on Mrs Thatcher and Mr Kinnock accounted for 34% of the politicians covered by *Sky News*. The equivalent figures for ITN's *News at Ten* and BBC's *Nine O'Clock News* were 28% and 18% respectively[34] – a remarkable level of coverage for what represented only 0.3% of the House membership. It is the sheer scale of the coverage given to Prime Minister's Questions that has been instrumental in enlarging the leaders' media prominence and in stretching them away in popular perception from their ministerial and shadow colleagues (see Table 5.4).

The distinctive properties of 'leadership stretch', and the ramifying nature of its consequences upon leadership politics, are probably shown to their fullest effect in the content and treatment of public opinion polls. The polls are a product of the public's fascination with party leaders. They are also a stimulus to even greater public interest in the leaders' qualifications for leadership and in their performance as public figures. Opinion polls used to be primarily concerned with the level of public support for the various parties. But over recent years they have become progressively more orientated towards categories of leadership assessment. The polls commissioned by, and published in, the national press regularly feature questions not only on how well the party leaders are doing in leading their parties, but also on how well

TABLE 5.4   *Number of actuality contributions and occasions in national news programmes*

	Network news
Prime Minister	68(39)
Leader of Opposition	43(31)
Cabinet	39(32)
Shadow cabinet	20(13)
Junior ministers	24(21)
Shadow spokespeople	16(16)

NOTE Non-bracketed figures show the number of actuality contributions. Figures in brackets give the number of items in which such contributions were made.

SOURCE Adapted from Brian Tutt, 'Televising the House of Commons: A full, balanced and fair account of the work of the House', in Bob Franklin (ed.), *Televising Democracies* (London: Routledge, 1992).

the prime minister is doing in his or her job, together with how effective the other party leaders might be as premier.

These polls, along with their accompanying commentaries, follow an internal logic of their own that gives a self-perpetuating quality to the interest they show in leadership. To begin with, polls are expensive and the newspapers which commission them want to ensure that they will derive the maximum publicity from their investment. Large shifts of support between the parties will provide headlines, but as there are now so many polls it is unlikely that one poll will catch an attention-grabbing swing to one or other of the main parties. Levels of party support are no longer enough to command public attention. Questions on the leaders and on the requirements of leadership not only provide a colourful background to the party figures, they tap a different dimension of political interest and allegiance. It is a personal dimension that has an immediate popular appeal. It provides a subject area in which questions and opinions can freely proliferate by drawing upon different facets of the public's perception and judgement of the party leaders. Furthermore, the greater the number of questions, the higher will be the probability of newsworthy fluctuations in the categories of response. Indeed, it is this high volume of information generated by leadership polls which provides the raw materials, and to some extent the licence, for all manner of speculative inferences concerning the political significance of the leaders' personalities and behaviour.

These polls and the myriad conclusions drawn from them often give rise to eye-catching and highly suggestive headlines about leaders and the effect of leadership.

Prime Minister's image suffers a battering
(*Daily Telegraph*, 10 May 1991)

Major wins back the commanding heights
(*Independent*, 19 July 1991)

Labour close gap despite Kinnock
(*Observer*, 16 December 1990)

Major's popularity with voters is key to Tory fortunes
(*Daily Telegraph*, 5 July 1991)

Major's rating up as Labour lead is halved
(*Independent*, 19 July 1991)

It's Major for the good life: but 25 per cent might switch votes if Kinnock goes
(*Sunday Express*, 15 September 1991)

The net effect of such polls, and of the reviews and headlines generated by them, serves both to reaffirm and to enhance still further the news value of leaders. This in turn promotes even greater coverage of leaders, and increases their centrality in political interpretation and explanation. The commentaries and speculations prompted by such leadership polls feed back into the public domain by way of the newspapers themselves and through television and radio – thereby generating controversy and arousing further public interest in the significance of political leadership. This increases the momentum for more polls, more questions, more analysis and for the nature and location of leadership to become a rolling public issue.

What is clear from any examination of the way that present-day polls are publicly presented in the national press is the extensive coverage given to leadership and the importance attached to it as a component of public choice and an indication of prevailing public trends. The significance of leadership is registered in terms both of the priority given to leadership categories in the presentation of poll findings and the relative space reserved to the subject in proportion to other polling categories.

To begin with, the various polls now have a near standard set of priorities in the manner of their presentation. The customary format is to start with the levels of party support. This is almost invariably followed by the responses to questions concerning the personal leadership record of the prime minister either singly, or in comparison with the Leader of the Opposition, or alternatively with the leaders of both main opposition parties. It is only after dealing with the leaders that the polls move on to presenting the public's responses to current political issues. What makes the prominence given to the leaders and to the dimension of leadership even more marked is the column inches reserved for discussing the significance of the findings. The attention given to leadership and the accompanying analyses not only underlines the importance assigned to the leaders' rankings in the overall poll, but often has the effect of reversing the original priority given to parties over leaders. In a content analysis of a random sample of polls published during the first nine months of 1991, it is clear that the emphasis given to leadership in the commentaries can be quite considerable (Table 5.5). In some cases, it can be overwhelming.

This *de facto* elevation of leadership into a high profile consideration is exemplified, and further exaggerated, by the disposition of editors to use arresting graphics, diagrams and pictures in their page design to give maximum visual prominence to the leadership poll results. A representative example is given in Figures 5.5 to 5.9. These sorts of design draw particular attention to the information presented and in so doing, give their contents a much greater impact and sense of significance than they might otherwise have received if they had been left in plain print or kept to the main body of the commentary. The inclination to give leadership material a high priority through the use of visually appealing boxes and insets is often completed by the positioning of such features at the head of the articles involved.

The weight given to leadership in opinion poll findings and analyses in terms of space, design and positioning is considerable, but the emphasis on leaders and the significance afforded to them in the polls is not confined solely to such presentational techniques. More substantive constructions of leadership salience arise from the juxtaposition of questions and responses in the polls. The progression of findings, from party support to leader assessment and subsequently to issue identification and measurement, generates a system of autosuggestion within the polls themselves. The succession of findings on party, leadership and issues leads the analysis and commentary of each category to run into one another. If the result is not exactly a seamless web, the impulse to make connections, either implicitly or explicitly, seems quite irresistible. The presumption becomes one of interaction and interdependency as analysis follows the inertial properties of the polls' own progression from party to leadership and on to policy connotations. The varied assessments of party leaders become bound up with the current level of support for their parties and with the nature of contemporary issues in uninhibited, and often quite arbitrary, forms of conjecture. It is true that this frenetic confection of causal assumptions and attributed effects is greater in the more popular and openly partisan newspapers. Nevertheless, senior political correspondents, editors and respected political scientists, who are most aware of the problematic nature of drawing conclusions in this area, are not immune from the autosuggestiveness of the opinion polls.

The provision of the data, and the need to report upon the figures and relate them to recent developments in the news, prompt an exceptional interest in the party leaders. Leaders are not only seen as being instrumental in the

TABLE 5.5   *Space given to the assessment of party leaders in newspaper poll analyses*

Polling organisation	Newspaper (date)	Percentage of accompanying review devoted to party leaders
NOP	*Independent* 16/2/1991	58.2
MORI	*Sunday Times* 31/3/1991	12.0
Gallup	*Daily Telegraph* 5/4/1991	35.8
NOP	*Independent* 26/4/1991	25.0
Market Research	*Independent on Sunday* 28/4/1991	37.9
MORI	*Sunday Times* 2/6/1991	34.4
Harris	*Observer* 16/6/1991	69.3
Gallup	*Daily Telegraph* 5/7/1991	42.6
ICM	*Daily Express* 26/7/1991	100.0
ICM	*Sunday Express* 15/9/1991	21.1
	Average	43.6%

SOURCE Data acquired from a random selection of ten polls drawn from a nine month period (i.e. 1/1/1991 to 31/9/1991).

generation of news, but are regarded as encapsulations of it, especially in respect to the effects that recent developments have had upon their standing and reputations. The impulse to draw conclusions of political changes by reference to the state of respective party leaderships is fired by the need to comment upon and explain why one poll is different to its predecessor. An opinion poll is largely meaningless on its own. Its usefulness is drawn from what it can show in comparison to either one or a series of previous polls.

This means that analysts are often put in a position of trying to explain changes in the configuration of opinion by reference to events and developments that have occurred in the previous two or three weeks. The public prominence of leaders, the volatility in their support levels and the way that

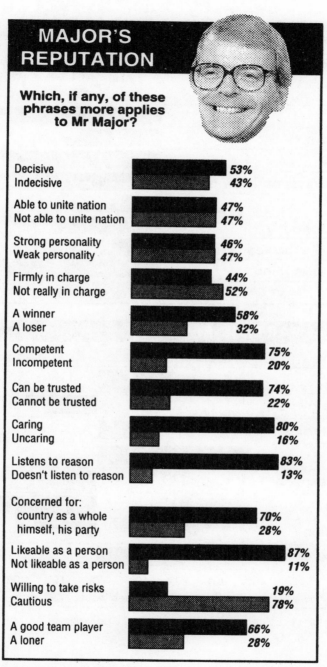

MAJOR'S REPUTATION

Which, if any, of these phrases more applies to Mr Major?

Decisive	53%
Indecisive	43%
Able to unite nation	47%
Not able to unite nation	47%
Strong personality	46%
Weak personality	47%
Firmly in charge	44%
Not really in charge	52%
A winner	58%
A loser	32%
Competent	75%
Incompetent	20%
Can be trusted	74%
Cannot be trusted	22%
Caring	80%
Uncaring	16%
Listens to reason	83%
Doesn't listen to reason	13%
Concerned for: country as a whole	70%
himself, his party	28%
Likeable as a person	87%
Not likeable as a person	11%
Willing to take risks	19%
Cautious	78%
A good team player	66%
A loner	28%

FIGURE 5.5 (SOURCE *Daily Telegraph*, 5 July 1991)

139

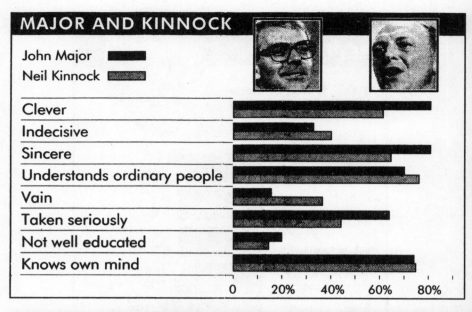

MAJOR AND KINNOCK

John Major ▬

Neil Kinnock ▬

Clever	
Indecisive	
Sincere	
Understands ordinary people	
Vain	
Taken seriously	
Not well educated	
Knows own mind	

0   20%   40%   60%   80%

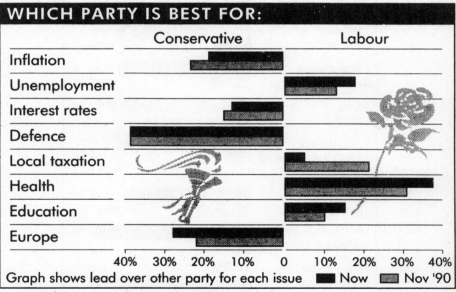

WHICH PARTY IS BEST FOR:

Conservative   Labour

Inflation	
Unemployment	
Interest rates	
Defence	
Local taxation	
Health	
Education	
Europe	

40%   30%   20%   10%   0   10%   20%   30%   40%

Graph shows lead over other party for each issue   ▬ Now   ▬ Nov '90

FIGURE 5.6 (SOURCE *Independent on Sunday*, 28 April 1991)

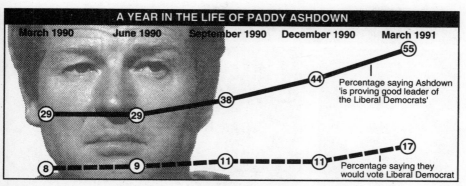

FIGURE 5.7 (SOURCE *Daily Telegraph*, 5 April 1991)

HOW WOULD YOU DESCRIBE THE PARTY LEADERS?

	Kinnock	Major	Ashdown
		%	
Tough	37 (+ 7)	31 (+ 7)	20 (+ 2)
Arrogant	50 (+ 6)	20 (- 6)	13 (- 1)
Understands people like me	31 (- 1)	32 (- 6)	24 (+ 4)
Down to earth	36	35 (- 1)	30 (+ 4)
Competent	28 (- 2)	49 (+ 1)	21 (- 1)
On my wavelength	28 (+ 2)	29 (+ 4)	20 (+ 4)
Sympathetic	32 (+ 1)	32 (- 5)	26 (+ 2)
Decisive	29	43 (+ 6)	19 (- 1)
Persuasive	35 (+ 2)	34 (+ 5)	21 (+ 1)
Friendly	37	46	31

(bracket shows comparison with April ICM findings)

WILL YOU BE BETTER OR WORSE OFF NEXT YEAR?

Better off	19%
Worse off	28%
Neither better nor worse	47%
Don't know	5%

WHO IS, OR WOULD MAKE, THE BEST PREMIER?

John Major	41%
Neil Kinnock	26%
Paddy Ashdown	16%
None/Don't know	16%

WHO WOULD YOU VOTE FOR IN A GENERAL ELECTION?

Conservatives	38%
Labour	44%
Liberal-Democrats	13%
Scottish National Party	2%
Greens	2%
Others	1%

FIGURE 5.8 (SOURCE *Daily Express*, 26 July 1991)

141

KINNOCK: Poor second

ASHDOWN: Good conference

MAJOR: Buoyant yesterday at his Huntingdonshire home

How would you vote if there was an election tomorrow (last poll figures in brackets)?

Conservative	41	(40)
Labour	37	(43)
Lib Dem/Lib	17	(12)
Scot Nat	1	(2)
Green Party	2	(1)
Others	1	(1)

Which party do you think will make you better off over the next five years?

Labour	30
Conservatives	41
Others	3
None	27

Who would make the best Prime Minister?

Neil Kinnock	23
John Major	43
Paddy Ashdown	20
None of these	7

In the event of a hung parliament after the next election, would you prefer to see...?

A coalition of Labour and the Lib-Dems	37
A coalition of the Conservatives and Lib-Dems	48
Neither	6
Don't know	8

FIGURE 5.9 (SOURCE *Sunday Express*, 15 September 1991)

issues are so often portrayed on news programmes as having a leadership dimension, draws commentators to leaders as one of the most conspicuous agents and objects of opinion variation.

This conspicuousness is often reflected in the priority given to the leadership issue in the poll commentaries. For example, Peter Kellner's monthly analysis of the *Independent*/BBC poll often begins with a discussion of the leaders' ratings. This is noteworthy because as it is a large poll regularly incorporating responses to eight or more areas of inquiry, the prominence given to leadership is quite extraordinary. Kellner's first sentence in the July 1991 poll read as follows:

> John Major has re-established a commanding lead over Neil Kinnock, according to the latest NOP survey for the *Independent* and BBC2's Newsnight.[35]

Discussion of the leaders' ratings had priority over such issues as the economy, the National Health Service, the Citizen's Charter and the situation in the Soviet Union. A similar format had been followed in the April 1991 poll when analysis of the leaders had a higher priority than the economy, the poll tax and the Gulf crisis.[36]

Such concentrated attention upon the party leaders carries the implication that they are not merely sensitive registers of news developments and opinion movements; they are also active agents of explanation in the varied fortunes of the government and opposition parties, and in their prospects for retaining or acquiring power. In many cases, the nature of this implication is not made clear. It depends for its effect upon techniques of inference. For example, in his analysis of *The Times* MORI poll in July 1991, Robin Oakley inferred a causal connection between Paddy Ashdown's rating as a leader of the Liberal Democrats and the increased public support for his party. This was the point that the readers of *The Times* were left to conclude by the juxtaposition of two sentences.

> During the same quarter the Liberal Democrats increased their support in virtually all categories, doing particularly well among white collar workers, mortgage holders, and voters in the South. Paddy Ashdown, the Liberal Democrat leader, has a better net popularity rating than either John Major or Neil Kinnock.[37]

A similar example of inference by juxtaposition is given in Anthony King's commentary on the July 1991 Gallup 9000 poll in the *Daily Telegraph*.

> The Labour party shows no signs of re-establishing the formidable position it held during the Thatcher era's twilight months. A year ago, the Labour lead was nearly 16 points. Mr Major maintains his firm grip on voters' affection and respect.[38]

In Peter Kellner's commentary on the *Independent*'s June 1991 poll, the implication was that John Major's popularity was a political *issue* on a par with the recession and the poll tax.

> John Major is more popular than his predecessor; the poll tax has disappeared from headlines; inflation and mortgage rates have fallen. But the economy is in recession, unemployment has risen and Labour's strongest issue – the health service – has climbed the political agenda. The two sets of issues seem to have cancelled each other out.[39]

The explanatory appeal of the leaders and the stimulus they provide to political conjecture are not limited, however, to such implicit assertions. Serious analyses of the polls are replete with remarkably explicit claims regarding the wider significance of the leaders' performances. A representative selection of examples are given below.

> Only two factors prevent Labour's lead from being even bigger. One is the Prime Minister himself . . . Labour would almost certainly be even further ahead but for the Prime Minister's personal standing. (*Daily Telegraph*, 7 June 1991)[40]

> The Tories' biggest asset remains the Prime Minister himself. The numbers saying he is doing well as Prime Minister are down a smidgeon, but at 71 per cent the figure remains impressive. Neil Kinnock still lags badly: only 32 per cent think he would do well as Prime Minister. (*Independent*, 15 March 1991)[41]

> John Major's personality is helping to turn around Conservative fortunes, according to the latest *Observer*/Harris poll . . . Mr Major's already commanding lead over his rival has been boosted by coverage of his chairing of the summit last week. . . . Mr Major scores highly across the board when voters were asked about his personal qualities. (*Observer*, 21 July 1991)[42]

> John Major flies to Moscow today on the next stage of his intensive global diplomatic round. . . . The first Western leader to visit Russia since the failed coup will be studying a new Market & Opinion Research International (Mori) poll for *The Sunday Times* showing that his recent high-profile role on the international stage has helped the government to a dramatic lead over Labour. (*Sunday Times*, 1 September 1991)[43]

> In one of the most bruising weeks since Mr Major became Prime Minister, Labour have opened up a 10 point lead over the Tories, registering their highest figure since the resignation of Margaret Thatcher. The poll also reveals a growing concern about whether Mr Major is 'fully up to the job of Prime Minister.' (*Observer*, 16 June 1991)[44]

> The importance of Mr Major in sustaining the Government's standing in voters' eyes would be hard to overstate. He is liked personally and seems to symbolise competence and decency. His presence almost certainly pervades voters' answers to other questions, not just questions relating to him as Prime Minister. For the time being at least, many voters give him the benefit of any doubts and

therefore give the Government as a whole the benefit of the same doubts. Mr
Major's lead over Mr Kinnock as the person who would make the best Prime
Minister is smaller than it was at the height of the Gulf crisis but is still
substantial. (*Daily Telegraph*, 5 July 1991)[45]

These statements accurately reflect the extent to which leadership has become
a medium of political discourse and explanation. For their part, the polls,
together with the increasing proliferation and elaboration of questions on
leadership, help to enhance the profile of leadership as an issue and to provoke
assertions, arguments and debates about the individual party leaders. When
the sheer volume of opinion-taking on leadership is taken into account, together with the tenor of the accompanying commentaries, it can seem as if we
are no longer living in a parliamentary system of government. Any strangers
to these shores confronted by the outcomes of such poll enquiries as 'Is he fit
to govern?',[46] and 'Is Britain safe in his hands?'[47] or 'Do you think that Mr
Major is doing a better job of running the country than Mrs Thatcher?'[48]
might be forgiven for thinking that Britain has already developed into a
presidential system.

The polls, together with the hinterland of inference and controversy that
they evoke, not only illustrate many of the properties of 'leadership stretch',
but also demonstrate the degree to which a new and highly advanced form of
leadership politics has developed in British public life. This dimension of
politics is qualitatively different to the normal or basic leadership politics that
revolves around a loose mixture of political issues and party leaders. The
presupposition of this new form of political competition hinges upon leadership itself. It is geared to the components, conditions and usages of leadership.
In effect, it casts leadership as a political issue in its own right – one which is
employed as an evaluative category of political judgement and one to which
substantive political effects can be convincingly attributed. The precise extent
of political leadership's autonomy as an issue will always be open to dispute.
What is clear is that this type of politics centres upon what the properties and
credentials of leadership are, who has the personal attributes to fulfil these
requirements, and how such considerations relate back to party politics, policy
programmes and government performances. While the more general form of
leadership politics tends to concentrate on the projection of political issues
though publicly prominent leaders, this more developed form of leadership
politics takes leadership itself as a primary political consideration and as a
basis for political analysis. It would be more accurate to call this not leadership
politics but the 'politics of leadership'. This is because leadership itself is the
subject of political controversy and the vehicle for a continuous form of
political appraisal. The presence of this distinction is a subtle but highly
significant one and denotes a radical change in the character of British politics.

The dynamics of opinion polls and their high-profile analyses both reflect and fuel the rising public consciousness of leadership as a separate entity of political motivation and choice. Whether or not the assertions made about individual leaders and their effect, for example, on the current support or electoral prospects of their parties are true, they do have an effect on how politics is perceived and argued in the media and by politicians themselves. Even if the various propositions which are floated in the polls are not verifiable, they do possess self-authenticating properties that alter the context within which the main battle between parties and over issues is fought. These authenticating characteristics are born out of what politicians, party workers, commentators and especially political leaders believe to be true, or likely to be true. The nature of politics is as obscure to working politicians as it is to political theorists. What practical politicians are aware of, however, is the importance of general beliefs and convictions about the composition and conduct of contemporary politics. Mrs Thatcher, for example, was convinced that a set of personal television interviews turned the 1987 general election in favour of the Conservative party. There is no evidence to support such a contention. Nevertheless, if she believed this to be true at the time, it is quite possible that the morale of the prime minister and her party may well have been raised at a decisive moment in the campaign. Irrespective of their content or their immediate effect, the interviews may well have helped to tip the balance.

The same point can be applied to polls and to the politics of leadership that they evoke so strikingly. Poll findings and the responses they generate amongst politicians prompt leaders to monitor their relationships with the public ever more closely. They become aware that they are being subjected to a form of continuous personal appraisal. They become intent upon improving their poll ratings or, at least, preventing any deterioration in their level of public approval. They will arrange public appearances and participate in media events solely in order to achieve an effect on their public estimation as a leader. This may well add further fuel to the flames of public exposure, but in contemporary politics there is little alternative other than to conform to such popular and professional expectations. No modern party leader can afford to ignore what the public image of leadership might provide to these individuals who are seen to have it.

It is no good when sober-minded analysts remind such leaders that past evidence suggests no substantial correlation between leader popularity and electoral success.[49] Politicians work prospectively. They fear for the future. Each leader competes furiously with other leaders on the basis of a shared conviction that public exposure and approval may be crucial *next* time. This concern for the future gives rise amongst the leaders to a daily preoccupation with the current state of public opinion and their own place within it. Each leader has to promote his own leadership and to defend it not only from partisan attacks, but also from those in his or her own party who might wish to place unfavourable constructions upon the leadership's relationship to the party's level of public support. These future concerns and current anxieties amount to a collective force which helps to politicise the location and provision of leadership. As leadership poll categories, results and speculations insinuate themselves into the vocabulary of political discourse and into the popular conception of political competition, the party leaders respond in kind. Through a process of media pull and party push, they are differentiated, individualised and stretched away from their parties to compete in what has become a highly advanced politics of leadership, where the ultimate prize, and the ultimate stretch, is the premiership itself.

CHAPTER 6

The presidency and the premiership: power, nation and constitution

The politics of leadership do not end with a general election and with the onset of a fresh, or refreshed, administration. It is true that the ultimate purpose behind the various individualising facets of contemporary political competition is the acquisition of the premiership. In order to capture Number 10, individual leaders are expected not merely to withstand but also to exploit the rigours of media attention, opinion polling, personal campaigning and public engagement. But once there, a prime minister quickly finds that holding the premiership is not an antidote to leadership politics, so much as a further stimulant to its varied dynamics. In the rise to power, a modern prime minister comes to embody the many factors that contribute to the development of competitive public engagement and leadership stretch. The prime minister's comparability with the American presidency in these particular respects has been acknowledged and appraised in previous chapters. Nevertheless, the analogies with the presidency do not stop there.

Having acquired a position of enhanced political status within the governing party and within the government as a whole, a prime minister has to convert that status into a form of workable authority. Like an American president, a British premier will often find that his or her position is more provisional and his power more contested than his formal status would at first suggest. The already contingent nature of such leadership is made worse by a system increasingly permeated with the strictures and strategies of leadership politics. In seeking to use their leadership position to acquire an approximate condition of leadership, modern prime ministers have to make considerable efforts to diversify their political resources and to augment their influence within government. It is these problems of life at the centre, and the solution pursued by prime ministers to correct them, together with the reactions they generate, which reveal a clear resonance between the present state of the premiership and the president's position inside Washington. Three areas of direct comparability are particularly significant in this respect. They are important because they demonstrate the extent to which American parallels can illuminate the nature and ramifications of current British developments.

The three areas in question are (i) the properties of executive power in an increasingly pluralist society; (ii) the relationship of national interests and nationalist attachments to the role of chief executive; and (iii) the conditioning effects of constitutional considerations and constraints upon the exercise of political leadership. These subjects will be considered individually in the succeeding three sections.

Power

If there is one thing that is quite clear about the American presidency, it is the fundamental ambiguity of its powers. In one respect, presidents benefit from a set of formal executive powers which are constitutionally guaranteed by virtue of the office's established status in a separation of powers system. In another respect, presidents have to operate in a scheme of government that is fragmented into multiple centres of power, whose divisiveness is supported and promoted by the constitution's checks and balances. A president cannot rely solely upon his formal executive powers to fulfil even his basic responsibilities – let alone the prodigious social, economic and military obligations that presidents have acquired since the Depression in the 1930s and World War II and its aftermath in the 1940s and 1950s. Given the unbridled force of American political competition amongst parties and groups, the American enthusiasm for legal dispute over the powers and demarcation of the separate branches of government, and the general American disposition to challenge political authority wherever it is most evident, the president does not even have assured access to his basic executive powers.

Richard Neustadt is the figure who has done most to point out that the chief executive's powers are not always available and that even when they are, they are not always workable. Neustadt suggested that, contrary to appearances, the presidency is continually confronted by a system which imposes severe limits on the exercise of executive command. In fact, 'the mere assertion of a formal power is rarely enough'[1] to assure its actual presence. In a study that relies upon aphorisms for its effect, Neustadt is at his most succinct in driving home this point about the provisional nature of presidential authority. 'Formal powers have no bearing upon influence' because in his view '"powers" are no guarantee of power'.[2] Neustadt emphasises that presidents do not inherit their power, but appropriate it through their own proficiency in persuasion and bargaining. A president needs to have a professional politician's sixth sense in locating and exploiting the possibilities of power. In a system where so many participants have political resources at their disposal and where executive authority is far from being intact, let alone complete, a president is required to maximise his position by working with and through the reciprocal nature of power relationships.

Neustadt's revision of presidential power, from a fixed corpus of executive authority to a highly mutable and unpredictable state of influence, has spawned a large literature on the ways and means of the presidency. Much of it is centred upon the central thrust of the chief executive's position being contingent upon a range of factors like the state of the economy, the incidence of international crises, the level of presidential popularity and the political skills and personal temperament of the president himself. The last has led to the creation of an entire genre of analysis based upon the working premise that because the nature of the presidency is one of personally acquired power, then the office can best be explained by reference to the person who holds the office. This entails studying not merely the individual president, but what lies beneath the person and determines his character, his behaviour and, ultimately, his decisions. According to James Barber who represents the vanguard of this form of study, a president's character is the critical factor in understanding the office – 'the connection between his character and his presidential actions emerges as paramount'.[3] The basic objective of this type of analysis is to trace a line of causation from childhood to adulthood, from personality to action, and from the subconscious to political decision. It has been claimed that such analysis can even provide a predictive capacity and that this could be, and moreover should be, used to assess the suitability of prospective Presidential candidates. Whether this type of analysis is or is not as fruitful as its defenders assert, it is a reflection in its own right of the abiding interest in presidents not merely as individuals, and not even as different individuals, but as significantly different individuals.

Even though Neustadt's scheme of analysis has been criticised on a number of grounds,[4] its basic conclusions remain central to an understanding of the modern presidency. Despite all the formal appearances of a solid executive hierarchy, the presidency is now comprehended far more as an active agent in the construction and maintenance of his own *de facto* hierarchy in an openly pluralistic system. A president may have certain bargaining advantages because of his position. Nevertheless, his strength has to be negotiated in relation to other centres of power. These have to be consulted and accommodated, in order for the president to exercise that authority which, to many outside observers, he seems to exert without effort.

The British prime minister has traditionally been thought of as a given unit of authority, functioning within a system of disciplined parties and collective government. 'The very high degree of institutionalisation in British government' is widely regarded as the 'most powerful determinant of what a prime minister can and cannot do'.⁵ A prime minister is thought to assume the office, and the functions and power attached to it. The centralisation of authority in the British system produces a chief executive figure, whose formal position is well established and who is generally secure from any open and direct competition for the influence at his or her disposal in Number 10.

According to this traditional view of the premiership, the personal characteristics of a prime minister are not really relevant to an understanding of either the position, or of an individual's conduct within it. For example, in the opinion of Richard Rose,

> Personal style influences how a Prime Minister carries out the demands of office, but it does not determine what is done. The first priority of a Prime Minister is to do what is expected of him or her. How a Prime Minister meets these role expectations reflects not only his or her basic personality, whatever that may be, but even more what the incumbent has learned in a quarter century of socialization in Westminster and Whitehall.⁶

As a result of this view of the office and of the orderly system that allegedly surrounds it, the role of personal leadership has often been dismissed as something of an aberration in British political life. Except for the most extreme conditions of wartime, leadership has been seen as unnecessary, unseemly, and largely non-existent. Accordingly, 'British political science has little or no literature on political leadership. In Britain we refer to the office of prime minister and his or her performance rather than national leadership or individual leaders.'⁷ The dearth of systematic studies on the individual characteristics of prime ministers and on the personal components of leadership still represents a highly conspicuous feature in an otherwise burgeoning field of British political analysis. It also betrays a basic cultural aversion to taking the role of personality in politics very seriously. This traditional disposition is superbly captured in the following passage written by Anthony King in 1977.

> Psychobiography as an art form if that is not too strong a term has never really arrived in Britain. Anthony Storr once wrote a perceptive essay on the origins and consequences of Churchill's 'black dog' moods, but otherwise we have not been treated to accounts of how the repressions inflicted upon Lord Home by his nanny caused him to develop a phallic fixation on matchsticks, or of how the rigours of Harold Wilson's toilet training wrought such havoc on his cognitive structures that he came to imagine that a week was a long time.⁸

In reality, this phlegmatic indifference towards the personal properties of prime ministerial leadership was always slightly misplaced. Prime ministers needed to have an awareness of the sources of power and an ability to cultivate and protect their own access to these sources, in order to remain prime ministers. A premier and the properties of his or her position could never be satisfactorily reduced to the exterior status of a servant to the crown. The true position was always more akin to the analysis of the nature of organisational power and the conditions of usage, which Richard Neustadt pioneered in his study of the presidency. If the British premiership always had something in common with the American presidency on the basis of them both being similarly influenced by the contingent and provisional nature of power relationships, then this comparison became far more direct and immediate after the events of the 1970s.

It was noted earlier that during this period, the British system of government and especially the conventions that guide its operation and outlook, were subjected to the severest of challenges. One of the most significant effects of this period of corrosive political controversy was the stripping away of much of the veneer that used to cover the tacit understanding and discreet arrangements of the British system. It not only exposed how deeply contested political disputes could be at the highest levels of government, but revealed the true extent to which political authority is dependent upon a range of political, economic and social factors. The period even demonstrated that such authority in such an ostensibly stable system could be highly unstable and precarious. In some respects, these revelations were prompted by the unusually divisive conditions which prevailed in the 1970s. But in many other respects, the improved general perception of the constituent components and working arrangements of the wider political process was a product of sheer publicity. Whether it was more a case of political divisions becoming increasingly explicit because of the nature of their severity, or more a matter of the media's improved coverage and penetration of politics, the 1970s literally witnessed the multiplicity and complexity of political forces at work within society and government.

Set against a highly charged atmosphere of industrial unrest, economic disarray, social dissent and civil strife, successive governments sought to mobilise their reserves of institutional power, but succeeded only in exposing the fragility of their own legitimacy. Strikes, inflation, stagnation and often open and violent defiance of the law threatened to degenerate into social disintegration. The electorate grew more volatile, third parties became more assertive, and nationalist demands for Welsh and Scottish devolution reflected a growing disillusionment with traditional forms of central government. The old collective certainties of cabinet government and the two party system began to evaporate in the face of claims that Britain and its corporate state were becoming ungovernable and that the Northern Ireland problem was a sign of a deeper malaise spreading throughout the United Kingdom. The claims made upon government were too many, too strident and too contradictory to be satisfactorily accommodated. As a result, government was often seen to be helpless in the face of intransigent demands from such powerful participants as trade unions and producer groups.[9]

The stark realism of the 1970s disrupted the conventions of governmental propriety that had prevailed in the 1950s and 1960s. It laid bare the problematic status of the many changes which the British system had accepted, but had hardly assimilated, over the period of its modern development. The British constitution suddenly appeared to have stopped working and to be in a state of terminal decline. Whereas in the 1960s, 'there was almost a concern to avoid the problem of the British state', by the 1970s 'there was agreement that British politics had slipped beyond the explanatory grasp, and the control, of the established constitutional theory'.[10] The enhanced public awareness of the British system, and the anxiety induced by its condition, prompted widespread calls for its immediate reform. It was as if what had passed as the machinery of state in the 1950s and 1960s had suddenly been shown, by virtue of a cutaway display, to be a primitive device full of friction, flash points, vibrations, and breakdowns. Political influence was seen to be widely diffused. Its mobilisation was now visibly dependent upon a process of consultation, accommodation and persuasion. In the 1950s, government and its facility for containing political forces was largely a private matter, conducted for the most quite anonymously. The 1970s showered the structures, personnel, conduct and functions of the government's interior into the public's gaze. Whether it was strikes, IRA bombs, cabinet leaks, back-bench revolts, street protests, civil service power or the disputed membership of the EEC, the effect was to illuminate the scale and severity of conflict, to identify the individuals and organisations involved, and to reveal the need for political authority to be skilfully assembled and prudently used.

Mrs Thatcher entered office in 1979 after her predecessor had suffered the humiliation of the 'winter of discontent'. During this period private groups had undermined governmental authority by openly defying the Labour administration's pay agreement negotiated with the trade unions. In some respects, Margaret Thatcher represented a reaction against this form of governing. In many other respects, however, she inherited its infrastructure and its characteristics. Despite her advocacy of conviction politics and her reputation for intransigence, Margaret Thatcher had to conduct her premiership in the now customary glare of the public arena, where political forces were far more uninhibited and insistent in their demands than they had been in the recent past. It was a system where the veto powers of its component parts were conspicuously evident. The Labour party, for example, was in opposition, but it was quite clear that it held an effective veto power over any serious attempt to dismantle the welfare state.

Mrs Thatcher, in effect, had to optimise her chances of governing in a system now recognised as one of internal conflict and dissent, and in a context of increasing public information where there was a growing insistence on the 'right to know'. These conditions compounded the already prodigious problems facing the government (e.g. recession, growth of public expenditure, inner city disorder). Contrary to her public reputation for strident inflexibility, her private conduct was much more measured – much more akin to Neustadt's description of presidential power. In the words of Anthony King,

> Thatcher is in fact a remarkably cautious politician. Not only is she cautious, but she respects power and has an unusually well-developed capacity for weighing it, for seeing who has it and who has not, for calculating who can damage her and who cannot. She is often described as an emotional person; in her ability to weigh power, she is more like a precision instrument.[11]

She realised the limitations of her position but she also had an ability to work within those constraints to maximise the potential for power that was available in the office. Her professional reputation in Whitehall and Westminster as a leader who could and would exploit all the bargaining advantages of the office increased her leverage. It also enhanced her public prestige as a leader, which as Neustadt recognised in the presidency, was essential to preserving her status as a leader inside the government machinery.

All this is not to say that Margaret Thatcher's pre-eminence was achieved without a struggle. On the contrary, there was almost continual hand to hand in-fighting within the cabinet, which often turned into public trials of strength. To Mrs Thatcher, these conflicts both confirmed the existence of a system of burgeoning checks and balances and affirmed her licence to operate competitively in such a system. Like many an American president, Thatcher's attempts to maintain her effectiveness by seeking to maximise her fragments of power in an unequal struggle against other power holders led to charges of imperiousness. The consequences of her private convictions of weakness led to public complaints of her alleged power and control over government.

Whether Margaret Thatcher is seen as either strong or weak, what is clear is that she always remained firmly in the centre of the stage during her administrations. The position of the premier, the political skills needed to be a prime minister and the extent to which the government's outlook reflected her own temperament became subjects of public interest and debate. Being a prime minister was no longer seen as simply being an occupant of a position. The office itself was now interpreted as being far *less* institutionalised than it used to be and far *more* dependent upon the individual incumbent for its meaning and effect. This being so, there arose a much greater British interest in the psychological analysis of leadership, and in the wider explanatory significance of such revelations as Mrs Thatcher's strained relationship with her mother and John Major's loss of memory over the number of O levels he acquired at school.[12]

Nation

The second area of comparability between the modern presidency and the contemporary premiership in Britain concerns the theme of nationalism. The presidency has always had a close association with the American nation. 'The presidency has grown and expanded as the nation has grown and expanded.'[13] This dual growth has not been coincidental. Great presidents of the past contributed not only to the development of their own office, but, in doing so, they were instrumental in the rise of the American nation. The office and the nation grew up together and progressed very much in terms of one another. The integration and progress of the nation are habitually portrayed through the lives of American presidents, as if personal leadership was the main causal agency of a nation being born and advancing in development. Likewise, the nation's ideals are commonly embodied in the form of national archetypes who have achieved the ideal of becoming president.

In the modern era, the presidency and the nation have achieved an even closer identity. The 'redeemer nation' is expressed through the power, centrality and singularity of a redeemer president who in national emergencies can, for all practical purposes, reformulate government to respond to national needs. At the same time that America's nationhood finds expression in the presidency's foreign policy and national security powers, the presidency itself can stimulate, focus and enhance the level of national consciousness. It is not merely that 'the power of the nation is identified with the power of the president',[14] it is that, to all intents and purposes, 'the president can symbolise the nation and [its] government'[15] to the American people. Studies show that a president enduring low levels of public approval and suffering from the myriad restrictions of a pluralist society and of a constitutional framework of checks and balances, can suddenly be given a prodigious freedom of action and a high level of popular support whenever America finds itself implicated in an international crisis.[16] This 'rally round the flag' effect is even evident when the president himself is seen as being responsible for the crisis. Events like military interventions, major diplomatic initiatives and actions leading to international tension confront the nation as a whole through the person of the president. As such, they generate an intense national loyalty that devolves upon the presidential office as the only entity capable of giving symbolic and material substance to the idea of the nation. Nationalism has proved to be such a palpable and potent political resource that it is not uncommon for presidents to try and establish international affairs as the centrepiece of their administrations. Foreign policy can provide a refuge from domestic factionalism and a way of rising above politics by exploiting the disjunction in the American constitution that limits a president at home, while providing him with generous emergency powers and executive prerogatives in the hazardous area of international relations.

The nationalist card, however, has by no means been confined to the field of foreign policy. The compulsive forces attached to American nationalism are strongly rooted in American ideals and principles. Indeed, it is often observed that America's unanimity on the precepts of liberty, democracy, equality, human rights and the role of law provide the fundamental cohesion to a highly heterogeneous culture that would otherwise be incapable of generating a national community.

> The United States indeed, virtually alone among nations, found and to some extent still finds its identity not so much in ethnic community or shared historical experience as in dedication to a value system; and the reiteration of these values, the repeated proclamation of and dedication to the liberal creed has always been a fundamental element in the cohesion of American society.[17]

While this dedication can be seen as 'an absolute national morality',[18] it does contain within it an extraordinary scope for conflicting interpretations and varying applications. Presidents are normally adept at characterising American foreign policy decisions in terms of America's obligations to its own principles and to its destiny to propagate these principles in the outside world. But presidents have also attempted to exploit the mobilising properties of national ideals to arouse public support for their domestic policies and programmes.

The colouring of domestic issues in nationalist tones can take the form of an association of a domestic policy either with military terminology (e.g. 'war on poverty', 'war on drugs') or with an ultimate pay-off for national security. Occasionally, presidents have used their national and public prominence to instil a direct linkage between national instinct and social policy. No recent president was more proficient at channelling the nationalist potential for political mobilisation into internal affairs than Ronald Reagan. Reagan sought to fuse together what was a conventional technique of using national security anxieties to expand America's military capability, with a radical strategy of using these same nationalist drives to reduce the level of central government inside the United States. Reagan attempted to generate a national revival, in which America's armed forces would be built up by central government, at the same time that Reagan would be leading a crusade against the government's domestic presence. Reagan used his position at the centre of the state to evoke a traditionally American and libertarian response to the state. He encouraged his countrymen to give maximum expression to their ancient anti-statist impulses. Reagan hoped that America could recover its lost sense of national confidence by returning to that laissez-faire posture which had coincided with America's rise as a world power.[19]

Reagan's attempt to fuse his own programme of tax and expenditure cuts with a nationalist fervour, that might best express itself through an insurgency against the abstraction of government, was remarkably successful during the early part of his presidency. It was also a strategy that was thoroughly consistent with the maintenance of media attention upon the president and with Reagan's own brand of spatial leadership. In fact, it was often difficult to discern whether national sentiment was being used to service a campaign against the state, or whether Reagan's antipathy towards 'government' was a device to fuel his national revival; or indeed whether both were being used as the best available means by which to sustain a position of 'spatial leadership' in the modern system of American government. Whatever the true position, the mass media gave him the opportunity and the tools to engage in a dual appeal to mass temperament.

In the past, modern presidents had generally sought to depress the raw anti-statist prejudices of American nationalism, in favour of a national democracy and a positive state. Ronald Reagan set out to use his considerable skills in popular communication to unleash America's primal drives against the state in a sustained display of patriotic emotion and national self-assertion. Reagan was able to combine the portrayal of himself as a national archetype with the unique national symbolism of his office, and, thereupon, to equate the display of his own convictions with that of an authentic national spirit. He urged his audience to recognise that it was his ideals that had made America into a nation. Americans are not averse to their presidents taking upon themselves the task of revealing the inner light of their national idealism. Reagan was not averse to using this licence to define America's moral self-image along the lines of a public philosophy of national liberation – even from its own government.

Even after Reagan had reached the limits of public consent on the issue of the positive state's diminishment, he was still able to marshal popular support for his presidency by virtue of his appeal to national sentiment. His successor George Bush continued with the same tactic. He came under attack for the drift in domestic policy and for his opposition to the growth in government expenditure. And yet at the same time, he also successfully appealed to America's sense of patriotism, first over the Panamanian invasion and then in the Gulf war. The spectacular victory against Iraq was not just a vindication of Bush's leadership. As Bush himself was swift to point out, it represented nothing less than a national revival that would finally allow America to recover from the trauma it had suffered in South-east Asia during the late 1960s and early 1970s. 'By God, we've kicked the Vietnam syndrome once and for all',[20] declared a jubilant President Bush after the liberation of Kuwait. As the president's public approval rating soared to unprecedented levels,[21] Bush was made acutely conscious of the political force of American nationalism when it is uninhibited and fixed upon a particular success. As president, he had sound political reasons to ruminate publicly about national pride. In the afterglow of Operation Desert Storm against Iraq, Bush said, 'I sense there is something noble and majestic about patriotism in this country now'.[22] Given this groundswell of American national fervour and the president's capacity to express and symbolise the nation's spirit, Bush emerged from the war with his position so enhanced that even his Democratic opponents conceded that his re-election in two years' time was practically assured.

There is no sense in which British nationalism is comparable to the legendary patriotic fervour of the United States. This being so, a British prime minister does not have the same potential for eliciting nationalist drives, or for embodying the spirit of the nation.

> A President is such a constant presence in the nation's consciousness, the nation is subject to mood swings as a result of the ups and downs of his performance.[23]

Apart from such extreme conditions like World War II, prime ministers normally cannot hope to emulate the symbolic and emotive properties of America's nationally elected office. In British politics, it has always been dangerously unconventional to risk the presumption of identifying political leadership and the allegiance to it directly with the nation's interest and purpose. According to the British political tradition, prime ministers are expected to be the main representatives of the national government, not to be the personification of the nation itself. Any effort by a party leader to unite the nation by claiming it for his own had always risked dividing the nation and undermining his own position of leadership.

Mrs Thatcher's premiership represented a departure from this tradition. She attempted to use her position in a way very similar to President Reagan's usage of the presidency. She sought to project herself and her office as an embodiment of national principles and values. This extended a lot further than rousing appeals to British industry to improve its international performance, or to a loose symbolic usage of the Union Jack. It was a concerted policy to identify the Thatcher programme with the essence of Britain itself. Thatcher consistently sought to identify her values of individual freedom, hard work and courage as native British qualities and to denote her opponent's values as alien, false and divisive.

In this guise, Mrs Thatcher tried to make her economic reforms into the equivalent of a national revival, in which Britain could be construed as returning to that authentic state which had once given rise to an empire. The prime minister promoted her radical programme on the radical ground that Thatcherism would integrate the people into a nation at one with its origins. To Mrs Thatcher, the Falklands War had evident connotations with the state of British society and the economic challenges of the 1980s. In her eyes, Britain's victory demonstrated the fact that modern Britain could still emulate the achievements of its forebears. The same determination and willpower could release the same inspiring national spirit of the original empire builders. The war characterised the possibilities and promise of national will, both in the South Atlantic and at home where Mrs Thatcher was engaged in another war of liberation. The spirit of the South Atlantic was regularly invoked by the prime minister to lend inspiration and legitimacy to her economic vision through which Britain would reclaim itself.

> The battle of the South Atlantic was not won by ignoring the dangers or denying the risks. It was achieved by men and woman who had no illusions about the difficulties. They faced them squarely and were determined to overcome. That is increasingly the mood of Britain. And that's why the rail strike won't do. What has indeed happened is that now, once again, Britain is not prepared to be pushed around. We have ceased to be a nation in retreat. We have instead a new-found confidence – born in the economic battles at home and tested and found true 8,000 miles away. That confidence comes from the rediscovery of ourselves, and grows with the recovery of our self-respect.[24]

Mrs Thatcher's attempts to mobilise the public around the idea of the nation was particularly reflected in her habitual use of national history to validate her positions. Like Ronald Reagan, Mrs Thatcher's deployment of history was erratic and eclectic, but it was used with the same purpose in mind – to convey a sense that Thatcherism offered a process of revitalisation upon which Britain depended for its continuity as a nation. The prime minister promoted her radical programme on the radical ground that Thatcherism would integrate the people into a nation at one again with its own rediscovered nature. In this context, socialism and collectivism were denounced not just for being wrong or misguided, but as national aberrations that had made Britain deviate from its true course. Mrs Thatcher's numerous and varied references to Britain's Saxon origins and Norman ancestry, to Magna Carta and the Glorious Revolution, and to common law, Protestant individualism and the empire of free-born Englishmen were all geared to the same end of proving that Britain has one all-embracing national tradition.

According to Sarah Benton's study of Mrs Thatcher's speeches, the prime minister sought to appeal 'over the conflict to the "spirit of Britain"',[25] which she always presupposed to be unified in nature.

> Her resolution of all conflict was to deny that it existed. Her history of democracy in Britain admitted of no fights, no opposition ... History in fact abolished politics. There is only one truth, and we have access to it through our 'hearts' and 'instincts'.[26]

The alleged unity of British history and national life afforded Mrs Thatcher the prospect of acquiring a status that is more commonly associated with the American presidency. In the United States, the president is not merely in a good position to present a public philosophy.[27] It is that the very centrality and enriched national symbolism of the office arouses a historical consciousness of American society and evokes a belief in the existence of a public philosophy.

It is of course harder for a prime minister to establish both the office and the policies of the chief executive at the centre of some mainstream national consciousness. While 'Americanness' has always been closely tied to the theme of national principles and ideals, Britain has not generally been regarded as a moral concept in its own right, or as a solid entity of timeless and unifying values. Indeed, 'the notion of a public purpose is alien to ... [Britain's] political class'.[28] The Whig tradition of historiography has certainly encouraged the British to value their political institutions of constitutional monarchy and parliamentary government as the culmination of a particular historical process. But the tradition has also encouraged the British to take their political institutions for granted. They are seen as being so self-evident and beyond reproach that they have become a silent substitute for the self-conscious doctrines associated with the rise of European nationalism. Political leaders have generally not sought to claim proprietorship of British nationalism for party gain. This is partly because of the traditional idea that Britain has no need of continental nationalist stimulants, bearing in mind that its unwritten constitution presupposed a fundamental unity. It was also partly because of the intuitive deterrent against using Britain and its history for explicitly political purposes for fear of opening up its course and development to damaging dispute. Notwithstanding these customary inhibitions, Mrs Thatcher immersed herself in national stories and symbols in an effort to project her programme and her office, above party politics and doctrinaire divisions, into the transcendent realm of the national spirit. She tried to reawaken the national dimension to British liberty; she tried to root it explicitly in a national epic and she tried to raise the public's consciousness over Britain's political institutions and traditions by engaging in an uninhibited celebration of them as the touchstone of British exceptionalism.

It is entirely consistent with this nationalistic style of leadership that

Mrs Thatcher should have appreciated the advantages of resisting European integration. She had projected British nationalism as the spirit and content of her programme, and as the basis of her authority to move beyond party towards a national philosophy. As a consequence, Mrs Thatcher reacted to the prospect of enforced European integration as any professional politician would be expected to respond to such a challenge to her political resources. Mrs Thatcher was fortunate in that she was able to respond exactly in the manner that suited her leadership style. She was combative, solitary, righteous and outnumbered – a symbolic recollection of the nation's greatest modern myth of standing alone and at bay in 1940. In defending British sovereignty, she made it clear that 'you have to identify with something which has been part of your life, part of your experience, your memory, your ceremony, your culture'.[29] This defiant position not only matched her temperament, but was consistent with her crusade against socialism. This time the threat of state collectivism came from without. It was fuelled by Europeans who, in Mrs Thatcher's view, were seeking to reduce British sovereignty and compromise Britain's newly reclaimed national integrity by what, she regarded, as backdoor attempts to impose a European agenda of state-centred social and economic development. In the face of such provocation, she adopted her preferred role of outsider set, on this occasion, against foreign governments and Euro-bureaucracy. In her celebrated address to the College of Europe at Bruges on 20 September 1988, she openly distanced herself from the developing consensus on the subject of European integration. She warned that Europe must not become 'ossified by endless regulation'.[30] She went on:

> We have not successfully rolled back the frontiers of the state in Britain only to see them reimposed at a European level, with a European super-state exercising a new dominance from Brussels.[31]

For a leader with Mrs Thatcher's grasp of populist politics, she was well aware that what she might lose in party unity with such views, she would gain in personal stature as an expression of Britain's widespread anxiety over European integration. She knew how to tap the largely silent groundswell against the EEC in a country of largely reluctant Europeans. Although 'the nature ... and the ultimate sources of British national awareness remain obscure',[32] the British do know enough about themselves to be sensitive over the idea of Britain being progressively diminished by a distant and anonymous supranational entity.[33]

Mrs Thatcher, who aspired to the presidential posture as of the voice of the nation, was even prepared to jeopardise her entire administration to preserve her access to the public prejudices aroused by this issue. Her heightened sense of nation and her willingness and capacity to project it was central not just to her own self-image, and to the spirit of her political programme, but to her whole conception of the prime minister's role.

Ronald Reagan's appeal to Americans has often been attributed to his ability to tell stories. According to Ellen Reid Gold,

> What he developed over the years was a great cultural narrative incorporating fundamental American myths, orally transmitting the Horatio Alger vision of striving and succeeding, the Frederick Jackson Turner notion of the western frontier as the birthplace of individualism and democratic ideals, George Bancroft's version of American history, and 'epic of liberty', and Mark Twain's depiction of Americans as sturdy originals ... Reagan's genius lay in his ability to establish a close relationship with his audiences and his ability to select vivid and compelling themes which spoke clearly to the deep-felt feelings of contemporary Americans.... Like the old epics, Reagan's discourse is enriched with narratives, an easy-to-remember form which incorporates abstract ideals into a concrete form.[34]

Margaret Thatcher's style of leadership was very similar. She also 'made up stories ... to tell the people their history' implying that she herself represented 'the essence of British values'[35] and was, therefore, uniquely positioned to tell the truth about Britain to the British. Both their successors have been neither willing nor able to conjure up the same sense of national identity in their own persons. Nevertheless, both George Bush and John Major have been highly conscious of the extent to which the cultural identities of their respective countries are dependent upon the integrity of their nation's political principles and governing arrangements. Both of them have been aware that the leadership appeal of their predecessors was rooted in a form of nationalist reaction against the onset of a world of increasing economic interdependence, international mass culture and diminishing national sovereignty.[36] Thatcher's and Reagan's nationalism was a form of cultural defiance. It acknowledged the progressive development of the international economy and the globalisation of political issues, but it also gave expression to the impulsive drives of national sentiment and communal resentment against the prospect of economic decline and limited national autonomy. To a large extent, George Bush was able to replace Reagan's oral tradition of national celebration with an actual military victory in the Gulf war. John Major was also able to enjoy what was called at the time the British army's last adventure. But in contrast to Bush, Major is part of a political culture which is much more ambivalent over the political uses of nationalism. Even though the prime minister's personal reputation was enormously enhanced by the Gulf war, he had to give every impression of not exploiting the war for political gain. The prime minister has also had to confront the perennial problem of Britain's role in the process of European integration. This remains an issue which explicitly presents the dilemma of the idea of national identity and sovereignty set against the practicalities of international interdependency and progressive cooperation.

It is an issue which any prime minister is now obliged to straddle. The national interest has to be served by being part of a developing EEC, but a British prime minister still has to be extremely cautious about submerging the nation's identity, especially so in an era of revived nationalism outside the EEC. To this extent any British prime minister will have to emulate, in one form or another, Mrs Thatcher's leadership politics of making appeals to national sentiment and distancing the nation's objectives from the allegedly unwarranted and capricious proposals for European federalism.

Constitution

The third area in which a justifiable case can now be made for comparing the prime minister with the presidency is that of constitutionalism. The United States possesses not only a written and entrenched constitution, but also a highly developed constitutional culture that accepts the constitution as the ultimate source of sovereignty and, therefore, as the ultimate reference point of society. The constitution is seen as exemplifying the form and ideal of a government under law. Political institutions are defined, their powers enumerated, their relationships specified, and the rights and liberties of the citizenry are specified. The underlying objective is one of ensuring that the exercise of power is conducted according to legal criteria with the object of preventing the occurrence of arbitrary and unlimited government. The central principle of American constitutionalism, therefore, has been one of determinable powers, ascertainable rights and government restricted under the higher law doctrine of constitutional sanction.

Alongside this characteristic feature of constitutionalism lies the concomitant constitutional objective of sustaining a political community and providing it with a structure of government commensurate with the needs of that community. This was always as important a purpose to the Founders as the objective of self-restraint. The two features were aggregated together, rather than fused into an organic conception of community interest and individual rights being served by a government integral to both. The danger of the state was identified quantitatively as being the physical bulk of government entrusted with the power of coercive force. This was confined to a separate department demarcated as the executive and designated as a co-equal branch of government.

As the republic grew in size and power it became increasingly evident that the executive could not be reduced to a defined condition. The executive was increasingly expected to use the instruments of state to provide central direction, forceful energy and initiating drive on behalf of society's welfare and the nation's interest. While the executive's authority had constantly to be legitimised by recourse to constitutional validation, it also became evident that the executive possessed inherent prerogative powers that were not based upon the procedures of consent, or upon any general understanding of the rule of law. Executive prerogative sat very uneasily in such an explicitly constitutional system. As Harvey Mansfield has pointed out, 'for a constitutional people, nothing is more difficult, nor more necessary, than to define what executive power is'. But in having said that, Mansfield recognises that executive power is 'the power that most resists definition'.[37] During the era of the modern presidency, the problematic position of the executive's discretionary power was thought to have been resolved by steady recognition and assimilation of the need for a strong and active president. Implicit in the modern presidency was the idea that it was both the agent and the outward evidence of the political system's necessary evolution into a form and function necessary for modern conditions. The modern presidency was presented as a rising and irreversible curve of accumulated power, delegated authority and assimilated prerogative.

The 'imperial presidency' episode of the late 1960s and early 1970s, however, dramatically revealed the extent to which the nature and scale of presidential power had not been settled by convention and precedent. What had seemed an irreversible fact of modern governing conditions was suddenly challenged by a popular front of constitutional fundamentalism. Critics of the Nixon administration reasserted another key feature of the American constitution – namely the ethos of check and balances. The use of executive power, especially in foreign policy and national security, had in many respects superseded the formal arrangement of separated power held in competitive tension by the interplay of reciprocal checks. In this field, the adversarial claims and counterclaims to contested constitutional authority, that normally permeate American political debate, were largely suspended. They were replaced by a general acquiescence in the overriding need for executive power in a world dangerously polarised into competing ideologies, military alliances and nuclear arsenals. It was when presidents began to project their international prerogatives into domestic affairs that the public renewed its interest in the old principles of constitutional dispute, legal challenge and institutional friction.

The Watergate scandal represented the climax to this revival in the constitution's checks and balances. Watergate's 'importance was in the way it brought to the surface, symbolized and made politically accessible the great question posed by the Nixon administration ... the question of the unwarranted and unprecedented expansion of presidential power'.[38] The executive power of the chief executive had been politically accommodated, and selectively sanctioned by the courts, but the issue had never been fully resolved. This was because the executive's access to, and its cultivation of, the coercive powers of the state ran against the constitutional grain of dispersed powers and delimited government. The Watergate crisis opened up the fundamental question of executive power to intensive analysis and critical evaluation. It subjected the executive to a form of scrutiny which it was unaccustomed to receiving and unable to withstand. The insurgents demanded precision in the definition and demarcation of executive force. Such a demand was quite alien to the conventional negligence by which the presidency was normally accommodated within the constitution's sphere of legitimacy. The end result was a presidency broken on the wheels and cogs of a refurbished constitutional machine, that drew its strength from a heightened public interest in the potential abuse of power and in the value of checks and balances to prevent it. Progressive evolution was no longer interpreted as a form of advance but as the sign of constitutional subversion and degeneration. The legitimacy of executive power was suddenly brought into question. The problematic nature of the executives's constitutional position was exposed. Critics and reformers became constitutional zealots, insisting that executive power was reversible and that the presidential office should be reduced to a definable position.

The same zeal for textual analysis and for debate over final authority was shown during the Iran–*contra* scandal. This incident also led to calls for balanced government and, in particular, to a restoration of 'the constitutional roles of both Congress and the courts as active players in a system of balanced institutional participation'.[39] In both the Watergate and the Iran–*contra* cases, presidents had provided the stimulus to a full scale constitutional debate. They did so by their actions, but more importantly by their status as chief executives, which not only attracted critical concern over the demarcation and rightful use of executive power, but made discussion of the whole system that much more accessible because of the presidency's central role within it. It is the presidency's very conspicuousness as the 'state personified'[40] which can accentuate any public dismay over government into charges of an executive blight upon the whole of America's constitutional democracy.

Until recently, Britain did not have the sort of constitutional awareness to foster concerns like the distribution of political power and the legitimacy of government action. The British had no modern tradition of challenging, on constitutional grounds, the performance and authority of any part of the political system. As for contesting the rights and prerogatives of the state's executive heartland, with its heavy responsibilities for national security and its high status as the epitome of parliamentary development, such effrontery was unthinkable. Apart from being inconceivable, it was also regarded as unnecessary. The British constitution was distinguished by its spontaneous flair for absorbing stress and assimilating change without disturbing the continuity of British society. It had been able to adapt to the demands for popular participation whilst retaining the heritage of established structures of traditional authority.

The British constitution's reputation for stability and equilibrium was based upon three main factors. First was the widespread conviction that British political development was evolutionary in form and, as a consequence, progressive and benevolent in outcome. Second was the way in which 'parliamentary sovereignty' provided a controlling principle that could explain the organisation of the state. The principle foreclosed damaging discussion about the location of final authority and invested the entire system with a prevailing legitimacy rooted, ultimately, in parliament's democratic credentials. And third was the central importance given to the spirit of custom and tradition both in the constitution's essentials and in its usage.

As a result of these factors, the British constitution has generally been noted for its dependence upon conventions and unwritten understandings in the task of managing government, and for the necessary dependability of government's participants to abide by such informal arrangements. The constitution's silences were thought to be not only the sign of its viability, but also its chief means of maintaining life. Social outlook, political manners and self-restraint became the substitute for any consciously conceived constitutional doctrine. What was in effect an improvised bundle of laws, customs and institutions defying collective definition, nevertheless assumed an 'irrefutable authority as an embodiment of historical progression and social obligation'.[41] Habits and sentiments were the 'works managers'[42] of the constitution. They obscured its anomalies and contradictions and made its arrangements workable to the general satisfaction of those whose mutual trust sustained its integrity.

Liberties were protected by public authorities being confined to their statutory powers by the courts. Democratic accountability was assured by parliamentary checks and the ministerial system. The British constitution, therefore, had a tradition of stability based upon the intuitive capabilities of its participants to conform to the spirit of its understandings. The constitution operated on the basis of a public trust that its anomalies and areas of unsettlement would not be exploited for political gain. The constitution, therefore, was dependent upon a strong sense of political and public propriety. Reciprocity and manners at the top were complemented by a common core of liberal beliefs concerning the importance of individual rights and the permanent need to limit the sphere of the state's coercive powers.

When this collegiate style of government began to corrode is not clear, but what is certain is that by the 1970s its internal points of conflict and the political attitudes supporting the structure and style of its operation were coming under severe pressure. The economic and social turmoil of the period was translated into a form of constitutional irreverence that led to a series of public critiques and a range of proposed reforms. The stark realism of the 1970s stripped away the comfortable securities of the 1950s and laid bare the problematic nature of many of the British constitution's governing arrangements. As the British constitution seemed suddenly to have stopped working and to be in a state of terminal decline, the British were placed in the unaccustomed position of having seriously to question their constitution.

In many respects, Mrs Thatcher's accession to power curtailed the crisis of the constitution. Her administration was committed to reducing the powers of the state and, in particular, to scaling back the heavy accoutrements of corporate government. The effort to return responsibilities and liberties to the individual, however, led to the widely recognised 'Thatcher paradox'. In order to release personal energies and to emancipate the productive potential of the market, the Thatcher governments had to draw increasingly upon their central powers. They found that their libertarian crusade had to be a government-directed campaign for less government. Instead of defusing the controversies over centrism and 'elective dictatorship' which had afflicted the 1970s, the Thatcher governments had the opposite effect. The earlier constitutional disarray of 'ungovernability' and the colonised state was replaced by a new constitutional disarray of 'overgovernability' and the spectre of coercive statism. This prompted an enriched form of new constitutional debate which was able to focus on the natural object of constitution – namely the nature and scale of executive power.

A host of factors were at work in the ignition of the constitution as a political issue in the Thatcher era. In part it was a continuation of the constitutional criticism of the 1970s. In part, it was a response to the radicalism of Mrs Thatcher's programme during a period when the political opposition was impoverished and critically divided. Another factor was the abrasive and uncompromising nature of Mrs Thatcher's style of government. The growing scale and remoteness of the state was also a source of general concern particularly in the outlying areas of Britain, where Mrs Thatcher seemed to embody the idea of government as a foreign land. To others, the constitution was more a case of using any available stick to beat back the Tory government and to maintain the party battle of accusation and condemnation.

Whatever the exact mix of these sorts of factors may have been, the net effect of Mrs Thatcher's governments was to generate a much greater awareness of the forms and organisation of public power, and to arouse a stronger inclination to question their legitimacy. The critical reflection of governmental power, and of Mrs Thatcher's relationship to it, was rooted in the public's impression of her conduct in, and usage of, the cabinet. The Thatcher years were replete with stories of the prime minister's personal domination of the cabinet. A number of insider accounts disputed this view,[43] but they were never able to dislodge the overriding impression that Mrs Thatcher openly defied the ethos of cabinet government. What made matters worse for Thatcher was that her public persona made the stories of her cabinet behaviour immediately credible. Moreover, the palpable evidence of her cabinet style in the form of sackings and resignations all seemed to point in one direction.

The record shows that she did intervene in her ministers' departmental affairs, she did remove ministers who were in her view not 'one of us', and she did engage in the tactical use of cabinet committees and informal groups to achieve objectives. Writing in 1986, Peter Hennessy concluded that the

> Cabinet does meet less frequently, it discusses fewer formal papers, it is pre-sented with more virtual *faits accomplis* at the last moment, and she does prefer to work in ad hoc groups – many of the most important ones remaining outside the Cabinet-committee structure. She has certainly flouted the spirit of tradi-tional cabinet government.[44]

It is likely that Mrs Thatcher believed herself to be confronted by a multiplic-ity of constraints and that, in the political style celebrated in Richard Neustadt's study of the presidency, she was necessarily exploiting her limited political resources to the fullest effect. In the public domain, however, Mrs Thatcher's attempts to maximise her executive influence created doubts that provided the basis for a deeper scepticism about the state of the British constitution. Her detractors used the outward impression of her style of cabinet management to popularise the view that she was the source of the 'predatory, authoritarian and dishonest trends in government'.[45] When Michael Heseltine resigned from the cabinet during the Westland crisis, he made explicit allusions to the constitutional irregularities in Mrs Thatcher's management of cabinet government.[46] This was not just a case of a senior minister justifying his withdrawal from government on spurious grounds. He deliberately invoked constitutional impropriety because it had become such a potent term of political dissent. In doing so and in withdrawing so dramati-cally from the cabinet room, he strengthened the public's impression that there were constitutional issues at stake; that they were worth resigning for; and that the ethos of cabinet government was not a private value system restricted to the interior of government, but was a subject of genuine concern.

Heseltine's resignation may not have been central to the creation of a constitutional dimension to British politics, but it was a significant contribu-tion to a pattern of discourse that had come to surround the Thatcher governments. This, and other equally controversial episodes, raised the question of whether Mrs Thatcher's radical style and radical programme were proof that she must in some way be breaking the rules of government. This led not just to a heightened sensitivity over such transgressions, but to an increased interest in what the rules might be, what consequences flowed from them being breached, and whether they needed to be reformed.

The Labour opposition fell upon the issue and exploited it to the full. In the 1989 general election, Neil Kinnock spoke of 'Thatcher totalitarianism'.[47] He charged the prime minister with having inaugurated a 'long process of removing all opposition in the great institutions of Britain'.[48] The working assumption which gained popular credence was that Mrs Thatcher's departure from the post-war consensus was synonymous with a deviation in constitutional practice. Mrs Thatcher and the British constitution had in effect become mutually deranged. This claim was repeated so many times that the following editorial became quite commonplace. It is representative of what became a genre of political comment.

> When will some members of the cabinet – any member – have the guts to stand up to that woman? She rides roughshod over them, humiliates them and treats them with contempt. Powerful men, men of dignity, experience and authority, men who might themselves have been prime minister if she hadn't existed, are forced to kow-tow and grovel before her. Politicians of principle have become jelly babies without backbone. Mrs Thatcher has no regard for our history, our constitution or our democracy. She has surrounded herself with unelected toadies. Her behaviour veers between the irrational and the bizarre. Abroad, she insults our friends and breaks our agreements. At home, she does what she pleases.[49]

This type of criticism was not confined to the opposition parties, or to the realms of simple partisanship. Concern over the constitution and over what was widely seen as Mrs Thatcher's cavalier disregard of constitutional proprieties was expressed by legal scholars, political analysts and elder statesmen. The tone and subject of their criticisms varied, but they shared a sense of disquiet over the aggressive way that power was being exercised and over the increasingly casual manner in which legal and customary controls on the use of government power were being set aside. Enoch Powell, for example, commented on the 'atmosphere of near-hysteria in which … parliament gets to trample upon the rights and freedoms which it has nurtured and protected through its long history'.[50] David Marquand pointed out that it had always been a supposition of Britain's traditional 'club government' that

> no one would push his formal constitutional rights to the limit: that governments would use the huge battery of powers available to them.[51]

After the Thatcher era, Marquand noted 'no such assumption could be made today'.[52] The absence of self-restraint and consequent lack of collective re-straint had led to the suspension of rights, to the restriction of freedoms and to a further increase in central power. As part of the same pattern, she was seen to challenge the influence of other centres of political authority that had traditionally constituted a form of corporate countervailing power in the British system. The trade unions, the civil service, the universities, profes-sions and the church all received critical attention from the government. In particular, the Thatcher governments were accused of attempting

> to whittle down, reduce or eliminate the role of local electoral institutions; local participation in the administration of services affecting local areas; and local opposition, lawfully expressed, to central government policies.[53]

In sum, the strident style of Thatcher's conviction politics raised the issue of the government's own legitimacy. Its 'arrogance in the use of power', its 'general pattern of contempt for ... the constraints on power' and 'its belief that the rightness of the policies to be executed, excused or justified the methods whereby they were executed'[54] all added weight to the change that the government was acting improperly. To many, even raising the question of the government's legitimacy was demonstrable proof of its damnable proper-ties. The question suggested its own answer. It betrayed the existence of a 'concentration of power in the hands of the executive – and the prime minister in particular – and the absence of any effective checks and balances'.[55] The necessary consequence was that 'civil liberties in Britain were in a state of crisis'.[56]

The thrust of these critiques was strongly suggestive of the sort of challenges that American presidents have often been subjected to in the past. *First*, there was a strong sense that Mrs Thatcher's success in rearranging the priorities of the political agenda was achieved by her willingness and her ability to 'use the vagueness and flexibility of the constitution to her own ends'.[57] She revealed herself to be 'increasingly unimpressed by the conven-tional notions of what was politically possible'.[58] As a consequence, she was said to have 'utilised to the full the scope for untrammelled power latent in the British constitution but obscured by the hesitancy and scruples of previous, consensus-based, political leaders'.[59] Her actions, therefore, exposed the con-stitution's weaknesses and led to accusations that she and her policies were motivated by the desire for self-aggrandisement.

Second, her reputation for dominance and intervention increased the susceptibility of the public to see the hand of Thatcher in practically every area of government action. Her conspicuous presence in government and her central position of leadership lent weight to the popular notion that the government's performance could be convincingly attributed to Thatcher's ubiquitous influence. This association of the person with the administration was given credence even when there was explicit evidence to the contrary. This common perspective increased her public prominence to an ever greater degree and intensified the concern not just over whether the constitution was being subverted, but over whether Margaret Thatcher's hegemony could only be explained in terms of such subversion.

Third, her tendency to see British government transmuted into prime ministerial government increased the tendency to view the state of the nation, as a whole, in the light of Margaret Thatcher and her programme. In some circles, the totality of society's ills was reducible to Thatcher's radical politics. The term Thatcherism was especially important in this respect for, like the programmes of American presidents in the past, Thatcherism among other things gave Thatcher herself the appearance of a universal presence in society. Hers was a broad challenging programme of national renewal. It possessed universal pretensions. It aroused fierce debate concerning national values and the social fabric. Ultimately, it came to characterise the political condition of the country.

As Thatcher's Britain, Thatcher's society and Thatcher's children passed into the currency of popular political conception, Thatcherism became a double-edged sword for Margaret Thatcher herself. It provided her with considerable influence at the centre of government, but it also rendered her personally accountable for nearly every point of stress and maladjustment in society. It increased, rather than decreased, the tendency to hold government culpable for the state of civil society. It might even be said that because Thatcherism was widely characterised as the consequence of one person's idiosyncrasies, it was interpreted as an aberration at the centre of government that in its turn multiplied social complaints and laid them directly at the door of Number 10. Thatcherism, in other words, entailed the idea of personal government in which Mrs Thatcher was held to be individually blameworthy for the state of society. This may have been an implausible and an unjustified assumption but it became integral to the circular way that Thatcher and Thatcherism were subjected to critical review. As Thatcher's reputation for power was enhanced, it made the alleged totality of Thatcherism more credible. And as the latter became more convincing, it substantiated the proposition that Thatcher was necessarily predominant in government. Thatcher's government was already a political issue, but under pressure from this form of reasoning Thatcher's position in government became just as pressing a point of political controversy.

The linkage made between Mrs Thatcher's programme, her success in pushing it through, together with its social and economic consequences, and the scale – real or imagined – of her power as prime minister, led to an increase in the use of constitutional principles to analyse and evaluate her government. This *fourth* element in Mrs Thatcher's arousal of constitutional consciousness produced an American-style fusion of policy criticism and constitutional dispute. Poor policy decisions by American presidents have traditionally been attributed to an excess of executive power, and thereby to a chronic imbalance in government. Bad policies are directly inferred from bad government where powers are incorrectly located and distributed. In the United States, the means and mechanics of government are a valued source of political ethics in their own right. It is possible to challenge policy by directly challenging the way in which it is made and the authority under which decisions are taken.

Britain lacks the entrenched constitutional and textual basis that would allow such appeals to an authoritative frame of reference. Nevertheless, during the Thatcher period many attempts were made to link Thatcherism to a fundamental breach of governmental protocol and political ethics. It was common for her opponents to challenge the legitimacy of her policies by attempting to challenge the legitimacy of her government and its form of operation. In particular, they made use of the American inference that concentrated executive power was deleterious not just because of how it *might* be used, but because it was inherently dangerous as it would *always* be used to ill effect. It was simply a question of mechanical cause and effect. Margaret Thatcher's alleged authoritarianism, therefore, was deduced both from her proposed abridgements of rights and liberties, and, far more significantly, from her apparent ability to secure their passage. The end result on both counts was assumed to be evidence of a subverted constitution. The breadth of such criticism fostered the rise of a more explicit constitutional dimension in British politics, in which powers were questioned and authority contested. While Thatcher's position and her behaviour were often taken as a barometer of the state of the constitution, the idea of a constitution was increasingly employed as an evaluative point of reference and as an instrument of dissent.

The *fifth* and final element was the search for a solution to what had been defined in many quarters as a constitutional problem. In this way, Mrs Thatcher and the 'extent of her unchallenged success, signalled the need for new forms and structures'.[60] Her use of, and effect on, government were cited as evidence of a systemic condition of imbalance and disharmony, requiring equally systemic solutions. It was significant that the radicalism of the Thatcherite programme required no constitutional reform to accommodate it. It entailed 'no proposals reflecting a conscious and thought-out plan to redraw the constitutional map in Thatcherism's own image'.[61] This revelation brought to the surface the need not merely to examine ways of curtailing executive power, but to restructure the constitution into an integrated framework of powers and rights. By the end of the Thatcher period, the constitution and the many proposals for its reform had become the subject of widespread public debate.

The most notable example of such constitutional concern was the Charter 88 organisation which called for a new constitutional settlement. According to Charter 88, political rights were being curtailed while the powers of the executive were increasing. This 'identification of authoritarian rule had only recently begun' through the government's exploitation of the 'dark side of a constitutional settlement which was deficient in democracy'.[62] Because freedoms were not encoded and powers were not defined, the old constitutional order had 'enabled the government to discipline British society to its ends'.[63] What was required to reverse this process was a comprehensive restructuring of British government in a written constitution embracing such measures as a bill of rights, a freedom of information act, proportional representation and the subjection of executive powers, prerogatives and agencies to the rule of law and to the control of a democratically renewed parliament.

It would be no exaggeration to say that Mrs Thatcher's premiership provided the catalyst to this revival in constitutional fundamentalism. Whether prime ministerial power is seen as having been the general spur to a number of specific constitutional proposals, or a specific spur to a search for a new constitutional settlement, there is no doubt that Mrs Thatcher's conduct in office directed attention to constitutional constraint. Her premiership dramatised the problem of centralised power inside British government and fostered a much greater interest in looking at government not from the traditional outlook of *ad hoc* improvisations and discrete issues, but from the point of view of general principles of political authority and citizenship.

Even after her demise, which under normal conditions would have amounted to a political solution to a constitutional problem, the vocabulary of constitutional dispute and the momentum for constitutional reform have not abated. Charter 88 continues to publicise its programme through rallies, conferences, publications and an ingenious use of opinion polling.[64] The Liberal Democrats have produced a comprehensive proposal for a written and fully integrated constitution, in preparation for a new constitutional settlement.[65] The Labour party has been pressured into endorsing a series of measures on electoral reform, on freedom of information, on a new second chamber and on a charter of rights. Even John Major, leading the post-Thatcher Conservative government, has made the Citizen's Charter his top priority domestic measure and the one reform he has assiduously sought to attach his name and political reputation to in the period before his first general election campaign as prime minister. Following his re-election in 1992, he felt constrained to go even further. He launched a series of measures (e.g. the publication of cabinet committee memberships and the removal of the blanket exemption of Joint Intelligence Committee papers from the normal 30 year rule for cabinet records) designed to reduce executive secrecy in favour of more open government.

Although the debate on the constitution and on prime ministerial power did not begin with Mrs Thatcher's premiership, her period in office did act as the catalyst to a process of constitutional inquiry, which propelled the flaws of the British constitution, and their remedies, into the forefront of normal political activity. Mrs Thatcher's performance as prime minister was instrumental in conditioning the British public to a political debate and a political language very similar to that which American presidents have long been accustomed to living with. This pertains to an unremitting interest in the origins, location and legitimacy of power; an intense concern over the principles and conditions of its usage; a deep conviction that power must be limited by legally enforceable restraints and by the existence of entrenched liberties; and lastly a belief in the central idea that government possesses an ethos of its own. Presidents are often accused of usurping powers and creating a constitutional imbalance that requires action on the part of the other agencies to correct. During the Thatcher years, British commentators began to interpret her premiership in the same specific terms of mechanical equilibrium. 'On this view, the subtle balance of powers in the constitution was totally thrown out by her imperious premiership'.[66] By the same token, it was up to forces within the constitutional structure 'to bring about reductions in prime ministerial authority and to redress the balance towards more traditional forms of cabinet government'.[67]

It is true that Mrs Thatcher's tenure as prime minister was exceptional in inciting intense interest in the constitution. Nevertheless, it is also true that such fixations will not be confined to the Thatcher era. The constitutional conception of politics, and the style of dispute associated with it, appears certain to continue even in the absence of Mrs Thatcher. The debate over the need for a new constitutional settlement and over what it might contain now seem set – especially with Europe's assistance – to become a permanent issue in British political life. As a consequence, any prime minister will be expected to use his or her available powers to the full in an increasingly pluralist system. But he or she will also be required to justify them in an increasingly constitutional context of critical watchfulness, of principled arguments supporting demarcation and constraint, and of openly contested criteria of political evaluation and authority.

CHAPTER 7

Thatcher, Heseltine, Hurd and Major: presidential politics in the 1990 leadership contest

In November 1990, Mrs Thatcher was challenged for the leadership of the Conservative party. It precipitated an extensive debate into the past performance and future prospects of her government. What it also revealed was the extraordinary extent to which leadership politics had penetrated British public life. It demonstrated how far leadership had become a category of political evaluation and an instrument with which to mobilise dissent and arouse public opinion. The events of that month amounted to a paroxysm of speculation and dispute over personal leadership. The struggle for Number 10 gave graphic illustration to those underlying presidential forces in British politics, which had up to then only been sensed rather than fully recognised. The significance and implications of public engagement, 'spatial leadership', outsider politics, 'designer populism', media image-making, 'leadership stretch', executive-centred nationalism and constitutional fundamentalism were all explicitly revealed in Margaret Thatcher's discomfiture and in her ultimate defeat as party leader and prime minister.

Mrs Thatcher's decline was a product both of general conditions of debilitation and of immediate triggers to dissent and defiance. The general causes were not difficult to discern. First, the economy was entering a recession. While inflation exceeded 10% (its highest level for eight and a half years), unemployment had risen by half a million in six months to 1.7 million. During the previous year, the trade deficit had reached the record level of £19 billion and there were few signs that the position would improve in 1990. At the same time, the government's policy of high interest rates, to correct an overheated economy, threatened to deepen the recession still further as the rate of bankruptcies and mortgage repossessions rose sharply. What made these affronts to the Conservatives' reputation for economic competence more damaging was the allegation that they had been self-inflicted by the prime minister's obstinate refusal to join the Exchange Rate Mechanism in the mid-1980s. Britain eventually joined the ERM in 1990, but according to Nigel

Lawson (Chancellor of the Exchequer from 1983 to 1989) much of the Thatcher economic miracle would have been saved if his and the Treasury's advice had been accepted by the prime minister, and Britain had entered the mechanism at an earlier stage.

Second was the persistent and damaging opposition to the poll tax on grounds of equity and justice. The measure came to embody the methods and objectives of Mrs Thatcher's governmental mission. It was essentially a device to sting local electorates out of their lethargy and into a greater awareness not merely of the costs of local government, but also of the level of mismanagement and wastage present within it. The reform was an assault upon what Mrs Thatcher regarded as enclaves of municipal socialism which were dominated by public sector unions to the detriment of local economies. To Mrs Thatcher, the old domestic rating system amounted to a restrictive practice that compelled a minority of property-owners to finance local government in a way that made it unaccountable and immune to pressures for improved management, or to any reordering of priorities. The intention was to increase democratic participation by adopting the principle that everyone should make a flat rate financial contribution to their local government. The effect was the provocation of an immense campaign of opposition fuelled in particular by the introduction of a new sector of local unpropertied tax-payers, who were already being squeezed by the recession. In spite of the huge administrative problems posed by such a reform, Mrs Thatcher had been adamant over its passage and application. Even in the face of the considerable political difficulties of educating the public over a new tax that gave insufficient recognition to the individual's ability to pay, Mrs Thatcher remained intransigent. It seemed to typify her approach to government.

> That the poll tax continued to be driven through the ranks of every opposing judgement, not least in her own party, was an illustration of a central (and self-destructive) paradox in Mrs Thatcher's political actions: that she pursued libertarian and democratic ends by often authoritarian means and tried to create a new Tory Jerusalem by banging people's heads together.[1]

Even with the government's attempts to cushion the tax's impact, the community charge continued to give rise to street demonstrations, to non-payment campaigns and to a high level of political opposition that drew support away from the government and from Mrs Thatcher in particular.

The third reason for Margaret Thatcher's vulnerability to a leadership challenge was her position on Europe. In many respects, Mrs Thatcher's vigorous defence of British interests in Europe and her scepticism of the more speculative ideas on future European integration were consistent with the contemporary state of public opinion. Mrs Thatcher certainly believed that

176

her reservations over further European economic and political union were widely supported in the country and represented a point of unity for the Conservative party. Some sectors of the party, however, believed that the aggressive and fundamentalist manner of her attitude to Europe was not only counterproductive to the spirit of European cooperation, but also detrimental to the unity of the party. The general public was not greatly animated by the theme of European partnership. Nevertheless, the divisive nature of Mrs Thatcher's leadership threatened to put the delicate issue of Europe into the hazardous position of being a source of open political controversy. Some elements of the Conservative party believed that Mrs Thatcher's obduracy over Europe, and her habit of implying that the mere presence of European options were synonymous with the prospect of their forcible imposition upon Britain, were detrimental to the national interest. They pointed to the wrangle over ERM in particular when Nigel Lawson and Sir Geoffrey Howe – Mrs Thatcher's two most senior ministers – managed to secure agreement in 1985 to join the ERM. The problem was that they had only gained her consent in principle. Mrs Thatcher thereupon embarked upon a strategy of procrastination in which she agreed to enter the ERM but only 'when the time was right'. It became clear that Mrs Thatcher had no intention of joining the ERM. At the 1989 European Community meeting in Madrid, Howe and Lawson privately threatened to resign if she did not suspend her anti-European prejudice enough to gain access to the mechanism. Britain duly joined only to be confronted with the fact that European proposals for future integration had moved on to areas of monetary and political union. By 1990, it had become clear to a number of senior Conservatives that Mrs Thatcher's brand of negative populism risked Britain's isolation in the new process of integration.

The final element in Margaret Thatcher's encroaching weakness was the increasing precariousness of her electoral position. Much of Mrs Thatcher's political standing had come from her record of three successive general election victories. By 1990, a further victory had come to look like a remote contingency. The Labour party had recovered from the divisions which had favoured Mrs Thatcher in the 1980s. Under Neil Kinnock's leadership, the party had regrouped into a more disciplined electoral organisation which had seen off the SDP and established itself once again as an alternative governing force. In March 1990, the Labour party had a 20% lead over the Conservatives. In the same month, Labour won the 'safe' Conservative seat of Mid-Staffordshire with a swing of 21.4%. This was the largest swing from Conservative to Labour since 1935. By the end of the month, Labour had amassed an opinion poll lead of 28 points. While polling organisations were claiming that no government had ever recovered from such a deficit to win a general election, Mrs Thatcher was confident that the lack of support was nothing other than a mid-term hiatus. She was 'convinced that despite opinion polls that condemned her as an electoral liability – she understood better than any of those around her the fears, hopes and preoccupations of the British people'.[2] Mrs Thatcher recalled that she had come back from the dead in 1983 and insisted that she would do so again in 1991 or 1992. Others were less certain. There was a strong body of opinion which believed that Mrs Thatcher should have resigned shortly after her victory in 1987. This would have given her successor a chance to establish himself in the party and in the country before the next election against a revitalised opposition. Mrs Thatcher not only showed no indication of stepping down, but had no prospective successor in mind. As the Labour lead stabilised for month after month of opinion polls, and as the government suffered further by-election reversals, Mrs Thatcher began to look like a lame duck premier who was insisting upon running in the next election. She would either lose and stand down, or try to win by persuading the electorate to place its trust in a leader who, in all likelihood, would stand down after the election in favour of an unknown successor.

The government's bleak electoral prospects, in conjunction with its poor economic performance and the divisive effects of its policies on Europe, local government, the National Health Service and the education system generated an environment of speculation on the subject of political leadership. The environment was enriched on a personal level by those MPs whose political careers had not fared well during the Thatcher years. By November 1990, 68 MPs had lost their front-bench positions, while 97 Conservative members had served 11 years on the back benches without being considered for promotion. The presence of such injured ambition, together with the brooding dissent of those who had never been supporters of the Thatcherite persuasion, had until late 1990 not counted for very much.

It is true that in 1989 one of their number, Sir Anthony Meyer, had made the supreme sacrifice of putting himself forward as a challenger for the leadership. The result was never in doubt, but Meyer's purpose was to test the *potential* for dissent against Mrs Thatcher. To this end, he succeeded. Sixty members denied their support for the prime minister in one form or another.[3] Although 60 was only a fraction of the parliamentary party, and even though their influence was dismissed by Mrs Thatcher, the Meyer challenge did 'destroy the aura of invincibility, it made it less of a daunting leap into the unknown for someone to try again'.[4]

A year later, such dissidence no longer seemed so foolhardy. The disaffection of the 'wets' and of the Thatcherite sceptics was now shared by many who had previously supported the prime minister. The large number of Conservative MPs who were not inclined to ideological dispute and who could normally be relied upon for their instinctive allegiance to the party hierarchy were showing signs of dismay. They were growing alarmed over the deterioration in the government's position and over the prospect of a quarter of the party's seats becoming marginal at the next general election.

This background of political and electoral deterioration would not have been transformed into the open turmoil that erupted in November 1990, had it not been for a number of specific incidents that precipitated a full-blown crisis. The first came when Mrs Thatcher was outmanoeuvred and left isolated at the European Council meeting in Rome at the end of October. After refusing to participate in any attempt to set a timetable for the next stage of economic and monetary union, she left Rome accusing other European leaders of living in 'cloud cuckoo land'.[5]

In her report to the House of Commons, Mrs Thatcher engaged in a splenetic condemnation of creeping European federalism that would diminish British sovereignty. What made her outburst all the more remarkable was that it not only deviated from the prepared statement but completely undermined it. She had agreed to a brief prepared by the Treasury and the Foreign Office which incorporated John Major's compromise position accepting a 'hard ecu' common European currency alongside existing national currencies. This device retained the pound in its central position, but held out the option of a single currency in the future, should Britain and the rest of Europe wish to make such a choice. Although the Chancellor had made considerable efforts to arouse European interest in the hard ecu idea, Mrs Thatcher undid much of his work by her unguarded remark that it was likely the ecu would not become widely used throughout the Community. Worse still for many observers in the House of Commons, who were hoping that Britain might one day adopt a more positive and creative role in the swiftly moving timetable for European integration, was Mrs Thatcher's intransigent posture of no further surrender of British sovereignty. Her lack of self-restraint in denigrating the whole process of European union was thoroughly characteristic, but it was also alarming in its ferocious negativism.

One of those who was most disappointed was Sir Geoffrey Howe, the deputy prime minister. He was so appalled by the tone of the prime minister's remarks that he felt he had no alternative but to resign from the government. This provided the second trigger to the crisis. Whether it was Mrs Thatcher's performance in the House of Commons on 30 October, or her treatment of Sir Geoffrey over an extended period of time, the deputy prime minister decided to use the issue of Europe to make his stand. He made it quite clear in his letter of resignation that:

> We should be in the business, not of isolating ourselves unduly, but of offering possible alternatives that can enable us to be seriously engaged....The need to

find and maintain common ground on the European issue within our own party will be crucial to our electoral success and the future of the nation.[6]

Howe's resignation was significant for a number of reasons. For example, he was deputy prime minister and, apart from Mrs Thatcher herself, the last remaining member of the prime minister's original cabinet in 1979. He had been her most loyal supporter in the Thatcherite revolution. As Chancellor from 1979 to 1983, Howe believed he was the chief architect of Mrs Thatcher's programme of curbing public expenditure and reducing taxation. He was made Foreign Secretary in 1983, but was summarily removed from the post he loved in July 1989 – reputedly because he and Nigel Lawson had forced the prime minister's hand on the ERM a month before. His departure from the Foreign Office was widely seen as a shabby form of revenge by Mrs Thatcher. It was felt at Westminster that Howe had been badly treated and that it was a tribute to his loyalty to Mrs Thatcher when he stayed in the cabinet as Leader of the House of Commons and as deputy prime minister – especially after Bernard Ingham had disclosed that the latter was merely a courtesy title.

It was later reported that Mrs Thatcher was irritated with his stodgy self-effacement and soporific style of delivery. She likened him to 'blanc-mange' and to 'a comfortable slipper turned into an old boot'.[7] For Howe to have had the temerity to resign, therefore, was deeply damaging. The fact that none of the original cabinet was left dramatised the charge that Mrs Thatcher could not work with her ministers for any sustained period. Coming only a year after Nigel Lawson's equally controversial resignation from the cabinet, Howe's withdrawal lent considerable weight to the proposition of a pattern of political and personal mismanagement at the centre of British government. It suggested 'that policy and personal differences worked together to undermine collective cabinet agreement and that Mrs Thatcher would act unilaterally and not bow to what she disliked'[8] even if it meant losing senior members of her own government in the process.

The last trigger came with Howe's resignation speech in the House of Commons on November 13. Instead of a subtly coded set of oblique criticisms which was expected of an individual like Howe, he used the occasion of a packed chamber to deliver what Peter Jenkins described as a 'bill of impeachment'[9] against the policies and style of the prime minister. Howe satirised Mrs Thatcher's view of Europe as

> positively teeming with ill intentioned people scheming in her words, to extinguish democracy, to dissolve our national identity, to lead us through the back door into a federal Europe.[10]

He reminded his gasping audience of the way that the prime minister had casually remarked to the House that she could not believe that people would use the hard ecu 'even as a common currency let alone as a single one.' He went on

> How on earth are the chancellor and the governor of the Bank of England, commending the hard ecu as they strive to do, to be taken as serious participants in the debate against that kind of background noise? ... It is rather like sending your opening batsman to the crease only for them to find the moment that the first balls are bowled that their bats have been broken before the game by the team captain.[11]

Howe concluded that Mrs Thatcher's attitude to Europe was posing a serious risk to the future of the country. It amounted to a 'very real tragedy' not least to the prime minister herself. He believed that the conflict of loyalties he had experienced could only be resolved by leaving the government. He fulfilled his indictment by calling on 'others to consider their response to the tragic conflict of loyalty with which I have myself wrestled for perhaps too long'.[12] The content of the speech was devastating enough but the fact that it came from the normally inhibited and totally loyal Howe made its impact all the more damaging. If a figure like Howe had been prompted to act so completely out of character, then it seemed reasonable to make all manner of critical suppositions about the severity of the conditions that had motivated such a *cri de coeur*. The speech brought to the surface all the anxieties and grievances that had up to then been mostly concealed. After the speech, the whole issue of Thatcher's leadership became more accessible to critical enquiry and to direct challenge. For Michael Heseltine, 'it was the catalyst'[13] which led to the announcement of his candidacy for the leadership. This in turn set in motion the two weeks of turmoil within the Conservative party which led to Mrs Thatcher's spectacular resignation and to the emergence of John Major as her replacement.

The rules of leadership politics, the currency of its terms and codes and the nature of its public and private strategies were all particularly well illustrated in the contender's stated intention to preserve, protect and defend the British cabinet. In his resignation letter and in his address to the House of Commons, Howe referred to the cabinet and to its principle of collective persuasion.

> cabinet government is about trying to persuade one another from within.... I realise now that the task has become futile of trying to stretch the meaning of words beyond what was credible, of trying to pretend there was a common policy when every step forward risked being subverted by some casual comment or impulsive answer.[14]

Sir Geoffrey was invoking what had almost become a constitutional complaint in Mrs Thatcher's policies by criticising her leadership and, by implication, the prime minister herself. He did so on the grounds that she had transgressed the constitutional frame of reference known as cabinet government.

Mrs Thatcher's dynamic presence in government had led to the objectives, policies and consequences of her government becoming synonymous with her leadership position and with her own personality. This had led to a triangular interrelationship between person, policy and position. In the past she had cultivated this arrangement to her advantage, but now it was her opponents who exploited the many permutations for criticisms offered by such a device. It was possible to attack Thatcher's policies by attacking her and, therefore, her leadership. It was just as possible to criticise her policies, in order to condemn Mrs Thatcher and the personalised style of her leadership. In answer to the charge that he had resigned only on grounds of the prime minister's style rather than on policy substance, Sir Geoffrey insisted that 'in many aspects of politics, style and substance complement each other; very often they are two sides of the same coin'.[15] Howe did not want the triangular nexus broken up. He had not resigned purely on personal grounds, or simply on policy grounds, but because of the lethal mixture of the two located in her leadership. Whatever else cabinet government might offer, it provided an alternative conception of government that highlighted the alleged iniquities of the Thatcher triangle and presented a form of critical leverage to any dissident.

Michael Heseltine was one dissident who wanted to maximise the idea of the cabinet alternative to the point of toppling a prime minister. He had already justified his departure from government in 1986 on the grounds that Mrs Thatcher had mismanaged the cabinet during the Westland affair. He had accused her of restricting the cabinet's discussion of issues, of manipulating the cabinet to suit her own policy purposes, and of using the Cabinet Office as an instrument of political censorship upon the views of a senior member of the cabinet. Heseltine resigned because in his view, the trust between himself and the prime minister no longer existed. He could only look back as a treasured memory to the time when he was a member of the 'cabinet within the constitutional understandings and practices of a system under which the prime minister is primus inter pares'.[16]

In 1990, Heseltine wished to force the issue of unconstitutionality to a conclusion by casting himself as a remedy for revived cabinet government. In his reasons for challenging Mrs Thatcher, he gave particular emphasis to the decline of the cabinet during her premiership. The evidence of Howe's departure, together with that of Lawson's resignation and his own, led Heseltine to conclude that the prime minister 'held views on Europe behind which she has not been able to maintain a united cabinet'.[17] The implication was that Mrs

Thatcher could only prevail in isolation. The disruption to cabinet government that this entailed was necessarily detrimental to public policy and in particular to the 'Proper pursuit of British self-interest in Europe'.[18]

Heseltine had to tread very carefully on this issue. He had generated a good deal of cabinet disunity in his time, culminating in his own dramatic exit from the cabinet over the Westland incident. Furthermore he was placing the party's already fragile unity in even greater jeopardy by attempting a decapitation strike upon the present cabinet. His declaration of personal perspective and sense of purpose carried with them the implication of criticism of the cabinet's membership at the time. He had to act because they could not or would not. To his critics, Heseltine's challenge would produce the sort of disunity in the governing party that would make any form of cabinet government impossible. Aware that the leading members of the cabinet (i.e. Douglas Hurd and John Major) would be potential rivals for Thatcher's crown, Heseltine had to proceed with caution. He continued to criticise the unconstitutional and outmoded content of Mrs Thatcher's leadership through coded references to cabinet government, while at the same time making it clear that he would keep Hurd on as Foreign Secretary and Major as Chancellor in a Heseltine cabinet.

The emphasis upon power distribution and constitutionality was effective in evoking the required response in a range of editorials and feature articles. The *Guardian*, for example, defended Mr Heseltine's challenge against claims of fostering disunity.

> He's not the problem: she is. He didn't drive Nigel Lawson out: she did. He didn't so utterly provoke Sir Geoffrey to sudden eloquence: she did. He isn't the only cabinet minister who has remained in office for 11 years: she is. Her re-election tomorrow cannot bring a semblance of unity. She is incapable of it.[19]

The *Sunday Correspondent* believed that whoever won would have to show that he or she could unite the party on one of the great issues that had divided it: 'the role of the prime minister and cabinet government, where there needed to be a proper balance'.[20] A cabinet required a 'fearless captain ... but also a sense that all the members have a say in shaping policy'[21] and that the Foreign Secretary and Chancellor in particular are not 'undercut by prime ministerial diktat'.[22] The question of power and the 'often overbearing and secretive ... way she ran her government'[23] was not limited to the more independently disposed publications. It spread to papers that might have been expected to support her.

> The Prime Minister has a number of faults, some of which have become more exaggerated with the passing of the years. She cannot brook opposition, she misses opportunities in negotiations which a subtler mind might perceive, she is

not a team player, in particular she allows Mr Bernard Ingham to rubbish Cabinet colleagues in a way that can be described at best as divisive and at worst as grossly disloyal. (*Spectator*)[24]

It was thought right up to and beyond the last cabinet reshuffle that she was so powerful she could, in effect, nominate her own successor. No longer. This most powerful piece of patronage of all she has lost for ever ... The era of one woman rule is over. (*Mail on Sunday*)[25]

The crisis is entirely the responsibility of the prime minister, of her arrogance, of the contempt with which she treats her colleagues ... she will destroy any minister who crosses her, she lacks the common sense and even, dare one say it, the common decency to preside over a talented cabinet; she has become a menace to our system of government and to our national interest; that she is, in sum, unfit to rule. (*Sunday Times*)[26]

Her heavy-handed management of government and her casual treatment of constitutional convention had been overlooked in many quarters during her ascendancy. With a leadership challenge focusing attention on the constitutional dimension of her power, it became much more difficult to dismiss the indictments as irrelevant to the basic nature and configuration of British government.

After Major and Hurd had entered the leadership contest themselves, they were both able to argue that they had superior claims to Michael Heseltine as agents of party unity and cabinet government. They were not tainted by assassination. They could offer change with continuity. As Heseltine's support was eroded from two sides, he reaffirmed his commitment to cabinet government even to the point of suggesting that Major and Hurd could occupy the central position in the cabinet while he went out and won the election for the Conservative party. This was an astonishing proposition for a prospective prime minister to make because in it he appeared to be diminishing either his own role within the cabinet, or the position of the cabinet as a whole within his political priorities. Either way he would seem intent upon distancing himself from the cabinet. Whether a prime minister acting explicitly as an electoral manager, responsible for the national campaign, and presumably the chief beneficiary of any popular mandate, was a plausible position is open to question. It is difficult to imagine such a division of responsibility and authority between the prime minister and the cabinet being sustainable. In the event, the implications and contradictions of such an arrangement were never followed through because John Major's credentials for party and cabinet unity were in the end stronger than those of Michael Heseltine.

Major's victory in the second ballot, however, was not a foregone conclusion. Major had had to confront the full force of Heseltine's leadership challenge. He had to learn from it and adapt to it because it embodied those forces central to modern political leadership in the British system. Major very quickly had to come to terms with these forces for it had been Heseltine who set the pace, the tone and the style of the leadership bid. It was Heseltine who exploited to the full the opportunities available for leadership projection. It was Heseltine who demonstrated the potential for harnessing the energies that supported an increasingly intense and public politics of leadership provision. And it was his skill in mastering the strategies and disciplines required to market himself within such an ostensibly collegiate environment that made Heseltine not only a formidable challenger to a sitting prime minister, but a showpiece of modern campaigning techniques that others could only seek to emulate.

Long before November 1990, Michael Heseltine had already assembled the components of a campaign for the leadership of his party. In an organisation that placed a high value on loyalty and hierarchy, his strategy was to test himself in the position of an heir apparent without ever having to challenge the prime minister directly. He would never strike out at his quarry. He would merely wait for her to fall and hope to claim the leadership when the opportunity arose. With this objective in mind, Heseltine worked tirelessly for the party, visiting constituencies, making speeches supporting local MPs and offering any form of assistance he could provide. This prodigious activity protected his flanks from accusations of party disloyalty. At the same time, it allowed Heseltine the opportunity to cultivate support in the party's grass roots. For over four years, Heseltine was a persistent visitor to Conservative constituency associations plying 'the rubber chicken circuit' of barbecues, fund raisers and socials. He would endear himself to party workers and often stay overnight with the local chairman or agent, building up alliances of the future. It is estimated that he spent over £100,000 every year on what was in effect an American-style attempt to construct a coalition of support in favour of an individual candidacy for national leadership.

There were other American parallels. In the view of Robert Harris, Heseltine used his years in the wilderness 'like an American presidential candidate'.[27] Apart from the countless visits and speeches, Heseltine had produced a flurry of articles and had written two books in which 'he had constructed a platform of policies in preparation for a Tory leadership election. It was a philosophy that was distinctive, well thought-out, and craftily designed to appeal to all sections of the party.'[28] For the left wing of the party he advocated a 'caring capitalism', a greater degree of cooperation between government and industry, and a concern for the social issues of the inner cities. He tried to protect himself from right-wing criticism by recalling his tough record in government on monetary discipline, unemployment and defence.

185

He also made it known that he was an advocate of 'workfare' whereby the unemployed would be obliged to undertake some form of community service as a condition of being supported by social security. Although his positive attitude on European integration would always give rise to anxiety on the right, Heseltine hoped that his centrism, his openness to persuasion and his ideas for a balanced and collegiate cabinet would make him an object of consensus.

Heseltine had one other characteristic to offer the party. It was a property that any challenger to the presidency in the United States would recognise as a very valuable commodity. Heseltine was in a superb position to undermine the prime minister's populist authority as an 'outsider' and her capacity to engage in spatial leadership. Heseltine was something of an 'outsider' himself and he made every effort to build upon this reputation and convey it to a public audience. Apart from being rather an unclubbable individual not given to the sociable dimension of life in the House of Commons, Heseltine was considered too brash and attention-seeking for the Tory establishment. His theatrical departure from Number 10 during the Westland affair may have established him as 'unsound' in the eyes of the party grandees, but to a national audience it established him as a literal 'outsider'. His entry into the wilderness, therefore, was a highly visual and public affair, made all the more compelling for being made on grounds of personal and constitutional principle. Once there, he turned necessity into a virtue. He used the available time and the political licence of an outsider to undo Mrs Thatcher's own formidable status as the consummate 'outsider'.

In some respects, Heseltine's 'outsider' credentials for leadership were enhanced simply by his being out of the cabinet during the down years of 1988-90 when inflation, declining growth, record interest rates and the disarray over the poll tax and Europe corroded the renewed sense of confidence that the government had acquired in the 1987 general election. As Mrs Thatcher lost more senior members of her cabinet, she became more identified with the government in general and with the government's failures in particular. With the demise of Howe, the process was complete. She was the only survivor from her original cabinet. Apart from reinforcing the already current impression that it was time for a change at the top, Mrs Thatcher's conspicuous longevity made it increasingly more difficult for her to dissociate herself from government. She had not only become synonymous with government, she had become enveloped by it and its controversies. As Michael Heseltine increased his own distance from the Conservative government, Mrs Thatcher's own once revered aura of detachment from her own administration became blighted by her evident proximity to its miscalculations and failures.

While Mrs Thatcher became increasingly isolated as the supreme symbolic representation of her own government, her predominance became massively counterproductive. The growing disarray of her administration was blamed not merely upon her stewardship of government, but upon her apparent possession of it. This was always an exaggerated perspective, but by 1990 it was becoming ever less implausible. Whether it was Margaret Thatcher's actual behaviour, or the damaging public reputation of her behaviour, the net effect was that she was seen to be losing touch with her party at Westminster and with many of her supporters at the constituency level. Even to those on her own side, the faults of the Conservative government were now being attributed to the personal faults of her leadership and, in particular, to those character failings that generated Mrs Thatcher's impulse for dominance. With the basis of her old populist appeal being visibly undermined, she even had to suffer the indignity of Sir Geoffrey Howe spelling out to the British people that her nationalist instincts placed the long-term interests of the country in jeopardy.

Michael Heseltine was in the perfect strategic position to exploit these disabilities. He had not only proved himself to be an 'outsider' whose departure from government looked more prescient and principled with each passing day, he could convincingly assert that only an 'outsider' could recognise the need for new leadership and provide that refreshment at the top. Heseltine gave the appearance of an individual whose convictions and integrity had led him into the wilderness. That vantage point had given him the perspective and authority from outside government to see the need for a new leader with 'a new style and new personality, different phrases and a different way of presenting arguments'.[29] Heseltine used his evident and much adorned 'outsider' status to suggest that he was nothing less than the incarnation of novelty. He was untainted by past policies and uncluttered by connections with the government's present disarray. As an 'outsider', he was offering what an 'outsider' can only ever offer – namely himself, his individual leadership, his private licence for political vision and his own personal popularity with a public encouraged to want and to expect change.

Heseltine's campaign was suggestive of an American presidential challenge in a number of other significant respects. For example, he was acutely aware of the need not to criticise the prime minister directly or personally, as this sort of irreverence would have counted heavily against him. He was also conscious that challenging the prime minister on policy was potentially fatal to his prospects. This was not only because most major policies had the prime minister's personal imprimatur upon them, but because it would risk jeopardising his own coalition and his claims for inducing unity in the party and the country. Heseltine, therefore, adopted the American campaigning device of offering new leadership. Apart from being the best commodity upon which to base an individual challenge to be prime minister, it also carried with it the implication that the current leadership was the main systemic problem and that the only conceivable solution was its replacement. Since Margaret Thatcher's 'style' was seen as being synonymous with 'substance', there were substantive policy implications to a new leader. But for the most part these could be left as inferences and assumptions, while the main battle could be limited to the medium of personal leadership and its disputed meanings and consequences. While Heseltine's own outsiderdom pushed Mrs Thatcher further into the maelstrom of her own government's problems, the challenger was left free to offer a populist replenishment of the government's appeal and electoral prospects through the fast-track device of the leader's replacement.

Heseltine's careful strategy of oblique criticism and suggested remedies, placed the prime minister in a position that many American presidents have experienced in similar circumstances. If she did not respond, she would appear to be the unresponsive prisoner of her own government which was precisely the impression the challenger was seeking to foster. If she reacted and tried to defend herself, she would be acknowledging the challenger's criticisms, giving him the initiative and enhancing his political status. In the event, Mrs Thatcher made the mistake firstly of ignoring both the challenger and the grounds of the challenge, and then suddenly changing tactics by engaging in a direct and personal condemnation of Mr Heseltine. She had already alluded in general terms to the 'personal ambitions and private rancour'[30] that had afflicted the party. Now her animosity towards Heseltine led her to claim that he would 'jeopardise all I have struggled to achieve'. He would take the country back to the bad old days of consensus, compromise and corporatism.

> If you read Michael Heseltine's book, you will find it more akin to some of the Labour party policies: intervention, corporatism, everything that pulled us down. There is a fundamental difference on economics and there's no point in trying to hide it.[31]

In her view, Heseltine's plans sounded 'just like the Labour party. We would end up with more community charge and more tax. We cannot go that way. We cannot go that way!'[32] Senior cabinet colleagues like Douglas Hurd were appalled at the personal and divisive nature of such remarks. By not responding in kind, the challenger by contrast looked conciliatory and statesmanlike even from a position outside the cabinet.

In no sector was Heseltine's challenge more evocative of presidential politics and more revealing of modern leadership politics in Britain than in his use of the media to project himself and to substantiate his claims of popular leadership. At the same time that he was impugning her natural and necessary connection to the national interest and fostering disaffection in her grass roots support, he also sought to displace the prime minister from her central position in the mass media as the party's central spokesperson and most newsworthy individual. Once it was clear that a leadership challenge was in prospect, Heseltine made sure that he was hugely available to the media's attentive approaches. A trip to the Middle East brought with it a profusion of photographers and journalists who duly reported on his prime ministerial style in one of the world's flashpoint areas. Days later, he was in Hamburg in a setting fit for a prospective European statesman. Back in Britain, he was keeping his word to campaign for the party in two Scottish by-elections. In between time, Heseltine was seen in Westminster, outside his town house and in the grounds of his country mansion. With a blitz of interviews, articles and photo-opportunities, the face and figure of the challenger had become almost unavoidable to anyone reading a newspaper or watching television.

Heseltine was well aware that such intensive media attention could become a two-edged sword. While the momentum of his news value and his candidacy gathered the sort of pace where it was becoming possible to appeal quite openly over the party to the voters, Heseltine sought to safeguard his media position. He began to cultivate the image of a public person who was the equal of any prime minister. He did as much as he could to control not merely the media's access to him, but what they could elicit from their contact with him. This meant cutting down on impromptu comments, on spontaneous responses and on unprepared appearances. What the media could show or interpret was confined as much as possible to what the candidate intended them to convey. In the view of Charles Laurence, Heseltine 'took the American presidential techniques of the campaign trail to a new level in British politics'.[33] In the process, he

> provided his colleagues with a free lesson in the latest techniques for handling the media, techniques pioneered by no less a master than Ronald Reagan. Press conferences and off-the-cuff remarks are unreliable and should be avoided. The trick is to divide the coverage into two: words and images.[34]

Heseltine's public appearances were carefully controlled to emphasise pictures rather than words which were reserved for setpiece interviews or statements.

> The cameras uninvited but eager for footage, have dutifully followed him everywhere. The key is to play the media on your own turf, and stick to the script. By the end of the week, the collective Heseltine image was of the all-round politician fit for high office.[35]

Heseltine's efforts to arouse public interest and to exert influence and even pressure upon his parliamentary colleagues and the government was remarkably successful. His flamboyant exercises in attracting public attention helped to substantiate his claims that new leadership was available, viable and necessary. Heseltine's use of the media had not only demolished the 'leadership stretch' of the prime minister, but provided an arena of elevation for the aspiring premier. The sitting prime minister, by contrast, was afforded the same coverage that had always been reserved to her position. This was spectacular but static in relation to the pyrotechnics of a rising prime ministerial contender. Once the leadership contest was formally underway, Heseltine and Thatcher received equal air-time much to the benefit of the former and to the detriment of the latter.

The way in which the public dimension of the contest played into the hands of the challenger was demonstrated to the fullest extent in the opinion polls. News organisations commissioned a very large number of polls during the contest. On the Sunday before the first ballot, for example, six newspapers carried their own opinion polls on the contenders. The news coverage given to the polls was comparable to that of a general election. This helped to intensify public interest in the contest as each candidate's progress could be plotted on a day to day basis. Another effect of the polls was to present the issues of the contest in precisely the terms that the challenger had defined them. The whole point in asking opinion poll questions on leadership was because Heseltine was challenging the prime minister's competence to lead. The physical existence of the contest was in itself a standing indictment on one individual's leadership and an invitation to think critically about leadership in general terms. Given such conditions, the questions posed and the answers given were almost inevitably going to favour the seductively unknown and untested characteristics of the potential leader.

Heseltine had in many respects demonstrated leadership in publicly campaigning against a formidable prime minister.

> It takes guts to voluntarily move into the political wilderness. It takes guts to challenge a Prime Minister for the leadership of the Party.[36]

He had taken on Mrs Thatcher in a head to head fight that was bound to hinge upon the way personal differences would be related to the capacity to provide leadership. It is true to say the favourable nature of the public's response to Heseltine was in part a consequence of the decline in Mrs Thatcher's personal standing. But this was far from being the whole picture. Heseltine himself was highly adept at presenting the personal qualities of Michael Heseltine as a positive programme in itself. He succeeded in effectively incorporating the policy components of the contest into the individualised characteristics of personal leadership. This had the effect not only of making the contest even more engaging to the public, but of encouraging the public itself to believe that it could judge the contenders in what was ostensibly a private election. By being presented as a clash of personal credentials, the contest was made highly accessible to the categories of popular appraisal.

Conservative MPs might complain that the public could not possibly know the candidates well enough to assess their characters. They might argue that other more private criteria ought to be more decisive. But Heseltine's outsider campaign had made it a public contest. Leader and prospective leader presented themselves as public commodities. It was only to be expected that they would be assessed accordingly both by the public and, ultimately, by the Conservative MPs who had no alternative but to take account of such animated public opinion.

Shortly after his declaration as a candidate for the leadership, opinion polls provided independent evidence supporting Michael Heseltine's claim that he could lead the Conservatives to a general election victory. The polls agreed that Heseltine 'would transform the Tories' electoral prospects overnight'.[37] According to MORI in the *Sunday Times*, Heseltine would turn an 11 point lead for Labour into a 1 point lead for the Conservatives.[38] The swing was even greater in a Harris poll for the *Observer* suggesting that Heseltine would shift a 15 point deficit into a 1 point Conservative lead.[39] The Labour lead appeared to evaporate day by day. The research for the NMR poll in the *Independent on Sunday*[40] and for NOP in the *Mail on Sunday*,[41] for example, was conducted a day later than the MORI and Harris polls. While NOP had the Conservatives under Heseltine with a lead of 7 points, NMR registered a 10 point lead.

Under closer inspection, the polls revealed just how formidable a candidate Heseltine had become in the eyes of the public. He was shown to be considerably more popular amongst women, the young and the key C2 sector of skilled manual workers. He was also seen to be more able to win back those Conservative voters who had defected since the 1987 general election. Because Heseltine did not arouse the same level of antipathy in the electorate that Mrs Thatcher did, he was better placed to draw the uncommitted and centre party voters towards the Conservative party. Only days after his declaration, the polls revealed that the 'Heseltine factor' reached as far as the public's perception of the economy. With Heseltine as leader, the public would feel altogether more confident about the nation's economic prospects.[42] Under Heseltine, 23% of all voters would, according to Gallup, be more inclined to vote Conservative. This included 28% of Labour voters, 41% of Liberal Democrat supporters and 46% of Conservative defectors all of whom would be more disposed to vote Conservative with Heseltine as leader.[43]

All these figures were immensely advantageous to the Heseltine campaign. The candidate was quick to draw attention to them in order to maintain the initiative. In his appearance on *Walden*, he sought to validate his challenge by reference to opinion poll evidence. 'The Tory party is determined to win and I think I have created the opportunity for them. Patently it is in the opinion polls where they now can win.'[44] What was more, the profusion of polls afforded increasingly favourable publicity to the challenger and to the party. For example, the polls generated a host of flattering and valuable headlines.

> Public Favours Heseltine for General Election Win (*Sunday Times*, 18 November 1990)
>
> People's Favourite 'Tarzan' would swing general election for the Conservatives (*Observer*, 18 November 1990)
>
> Marginals Say No to Thatcher (*Mail on Sunday*, 18 November 1990)
>
> PM no longer Tory favourite says poll (*Sunday Telegraph*, 18 November 1990)
>
> Polls back the challenger (*Guardian*, 19 November 1990)
>
> Heseltine attracts wavering voters (*Sunday Telegraph*, 18 November 1990)
>
> Poll Predicts that Tories on the Heseltine ticket would beat Labour (*Sunday Correspondent*, 18 November 1990)
>
> Voters' Choice is Heseltine says Gallup (*Daily Telegraph*, 20 November 1990)
>
> Voters Back Heseltine in Gallup Poll (*Daily Telegraph*, 22 November 1990)

In addition to the headlines, Heseltine could show that in what was the equivalent of a primary election question, on who the public would like to see as leader of the party, he had a commanding lead (38%) not only over Mrs Thatcher (19%) but over his potential rivals such as Tebbit (10%), Hurd (9%), and Major (5%).[45] Heseltine could also show that nearly two-thirds of Conservatives believed that, with Heseltine as leader, the party would have the best chance of winning the election.[46] Furthermore he could absolve himself from splitting the party by referring to Ivor Crewe's conclusion in the *Independent on Sunday* that 'against all expectations, voters had swung heavily to the Conservatives in response to the leadership contest' as a whole. The Conservatives had benefited precisely because the contest 'focused voters' attention on the question of whom they would prefer as prime minister'.[47]

In some respects, the opinion polls were quite misleading. It can be suggested that many of their findings were based on the by-election premise of 'sending a message' to the government, rather than giving an accurate impression of true voting intentions in a general election. The sheer number of polls and the intense publicity given to them and the leadership contest generated enormous interest in the Conservative party. It could be construed that it was this publicity that helped to raise the Conservative's level of public support, irrespective of the merits of either the party or its leadership candidates. On occasions, poll findings were interpreted in misleading ways. For example, the percentage of respondents who said that they would be 'more likely' to support the Conservatives if Michael Heseltine were leader of the party was often interpreted as proof of a commensurate Conservative lead over other parties. This overlooked the fact that respondents were not asked which party they would actually vote for in a general election. Nevertheless these 'quite erroneous interpretations of poll findings were common amongst television and newspapers'.[48]

The use and misuse of such polls exemplified the whole leadership contest. They both reflected and reinforced the sense of public spectacle and popular appraisal in the campaign. As the candidates played *to* the public, they were also playing *for* the public. They were seeking to engage the public's interest and to mobilise popular support through the candidates' own accessibility and through the currency of easily understood ideas on personal leadership. The influence generated by such an open appeal to public appraisal and recorded in the profusion of opinion polls, was used to exert pressure upon Conservative MPs. The polls not only provided the public with a form of surrogate participation, they complemented the other forms of public engagement to make the battle for the leadership into an explicitly populist form of political competition. The Thatcher camp might complain that Heseltine was 'all glamour and no substance'[49] and that he was giving the election a sense of public immediacy that threatened to eclipse the professional and long-term consideration of MPs' judgements at Westminster. But in the end, Michael Heseltine was simply challenging Mrs Thatcher on the same 'outsider' and populist grounds that the prime minister had based her own leadership upon over the previous eleven years.

Herein lay the central and most significant irony of Heseltine's claim to the leadership. The challenge was made possible by Mrs Thatcher herself. She it was who had fostered the presidential centrality of leadership that Heseltine was attempting to assume for himself. The Conservative party had won three general elections with a high-profile leader who was differentiated from the party. That leader was now thought by many to be an electoral liability. But even to these sceptics, many of whom had criticised her style of leadership, in the past, the solution lay not in the abandonment of such leadership but in its replacement – in a new leader with personal drive, ideological vision and an overriding sense of purpose.

To this extent, Heseltine was a comparable substitute for Mrs Thatcher. He even claimed that they were both 'very large personalities'[50] who were significantly similar to one another.

> It has been most gratifying the numbers of former supporters of Mrs Thatcher who have come straight over to me. In a way they see in me some of the characteristics which have made Mrs Thatcher's premiership an exciting one.[51]

> The fact is that I am perhaps too similar to Mrs Thatcher; that in the end we are people you can trust, who stand up and say what we think and stick to it.[52]

It was clear to Robert Harris that a 'Heseltine premiership would be all shirt sleeves, dramatic initiatives and action-this-day memorandums'.[53] One paper described him as 'another strong character of vibrant views' which was a disadvantage in a 'country weary of vibrations'.[54] *The Times* even regarded the comparability factor as a sound reason to deny its support for Heseltine:

> Ironically, he comes closest to his antagonist, Mrs Thatcher, in radical icono- clasm and possibly even as a free-market buccaneer. Those who want a repeat of Mrs Thatcher's temperamental idiosyncrasy may choose to go with him.[55]

It was always difficult to imagine how Michael Heseltine's self-effacing proposals for cabinet government would square with his programme of vigor- ous personal leadership. For example, his initiatives for a review of the com- munity charge was an impulsive move made familiar by Mrs Thatcher herself during her premiership. Policy-making 'on the hoof' had been criticised by Michael Heseltine in the past. Now they were both at it in a head to head encounter. Mrs Thatcher hit back with a wholly unexpected proposal for a referendum on European monetary union. This undisguised venture into populist solutions caused considerable dismay amongst members of the cabi- net. As Heseltine was justifying his own leadership bid by reference to cabinet government, he knew how to derogate such a bold prime ministerial initiative. He assumed a statesmanlike disdain for the 'impossibility of designing a question on an issue of that sort to the people'. More significantly, he dis- missed the proposal as not 'in keeping with the constitutional arrangements in this country'.[56] Heseltine alleged that his challenge was prompted by a desire to secure the changes of the 1980s and to continue and develop Mrs Thatcher's legacy in the 1990s. In many ways these were emollient words covering a bitter clash, but in one important, and largely inadvertent, respect Heseltine was accurate in his description. The underlying premise of his challenge was to displace Mrs Thatcher firstly by emulating the forcefulness of her personal leadership and secondly by running a campaign that would be appraised on the presidential criteria for leadership that Mrs Thatcher herself had sought to make her own.

The result of the Thatcher–Heseltine contest was that the prime minis- ter won more votes than her challenger but not enough to secure victory. In fact, because Heseltine acquired the support of over 40% of the parliamentary party he had in effect destroyed the prestige and hold of her personal leader- ship. For such leadership to be effective, it must not be compromised by being seen to be less than predominant. The result doomed the prime minister because it showed the extent to which her personality had become a major issue in its own right. Hugo Young concluded that,

> Her personality, her very being, shows up time and again as the biggest loser with the people, just as it has been the principal reason behind the unprecedented quantity of Thatcherite friends who have left the Thatcher government. Pity – or perhaps, better, scorn – the prime minister who has become the helpless architect of an irresolvable personal crisis.[57]

After a brief hiatus, Mrs Thatcher resigned. This allowed the Foreign Secretary, Douglas Hurd, and the Chancellor of the Exchequer, John Major, to enter the field for the second ballot. Their appearance dramatically altered the configuration of the leadership battle. They had remained loyal to the prime minister and had only put themselves forward for elevation after she had stood down (i.e. exactly what Heseltine had always planned to do during his wilderness years). They also had a far superior claim to building party unity at a time of potentially chronic disunity. Both Major and Hurd had powerful backing from different sectors of the cabinet. Heseltine by contrast had virtually no support from the cabinet. Moreover, he was now tainted with the responsibility both for having assassinated Mrs Thatcher and for having brought a leadership crisis upon the party. The discomfort and embarrassment even on the part of those who had opposed her, but who had perhaps willed the end rather more than the means, led to something of a backlash against Michael Heseltine. It was always going to be difficult for the challenger to unite the party in such circumstances. He had tried to steer away from policy differences and to concentrate upon the issue of leadership but, in doing so, he had given the impression of a personal assault upon the prime minister which had in the end destroyed her leadership. Heseltine was now confronted with the prospect not only of having aroused a sector of intransigent opposition to his 'act of betrayal', but of being squeezed by two highly influential members of the cabinet who were rising rather than falling in political status.

Although Heseltine had become merely one of three challengers, he had maintained the initiative in one important respect. Hurd and Major insisted that no policy differences existed either between themselves, or between the two of them and Mr Heseltine. As a result, Hurd and Major had no alternative but to campaign on Heseltine's chosen ground of personal leadership. Far from reducing the presidential characteristics of the struggle, therefore, the onset of two new candidates merely intensified the effect of personalisation. It propelled all three contenders into a form of saturated media attention, in which each had to distinguish himself from the others on the basis of public appeal, electoral potential and individual leadership qualities. It was necessary for each to engage the public's already aroused interest in the contest and to channel it by force of personal merit to enhance each of their prospects for selection at Westminster. Having three equally favoured candidates not only generated all manner of speculation on tactical voting. It also concentrated minds upon the appraisal of political character, the components of leadership, the prime ministerial timber of the candidates and the extent to which the modern premiership implied a set of specific requirements from its incumbents.

The contest for the second ballot raised the exposure and significance of political personality to new heights. Hurd and Major quickly learnt how important presentation and symbolism could be in radiating impressions and giving a sense of their inner worth. They found how nuances of policy could be inferred from personal background and contemporary style. They also discovered the significance of the public's reaction to them, and of the public's categories of personal estimation, in appealing to their parliamentary colleagues. As a consequence, they felt compelled to pose for photo-opportunities, to give in-depth interviews and to encourage public interest in their domestic arrangements even to the point of inviting television crews into their homes.

Unprecedented prominence was given to the candidates' wives. It never reached the American level, where a candidate's wife is seen as the equivalent of a prospective vice-president. Nevertheless, it did amount to a considerable advance in the weight given to the individuality of leadership. Anne Heseltine, Judy Hurd and Norma Major were all featured in the national press[58] and were all made the subject of an individual profile by ITN. The impression left was that wives were being deployed in this way not only in order to appeal on behalf of their husbands for the support of women, but to enhance the personal accessibility of each candidate. The wife reflected the candidate as an individual – the real man at home and verified by sources sufficiently intimate to disclose the inner worth and personal integrity of the candidate. The contender's wife conveyed the idea that there was a private person behind the public face, and that this normally concealed dimension was just as important to a position like the premiership as a politician's exterior form. The public attention given to wives reaffirmed the suggestion that each candidate's political credentials for high office were being actively based upon his character and personal background. This was inferred both from his choice of wife and from what she had to say about her husband's personal experience and attributes. The net effect was to inflate the significance assigned to the individual still further; to reinforce the notion that the office of prime minister was a uniquely individual office for unique individuals; and to evoke the idea that leaders have a personal destiny to fulfil which makes sense of, and represents a culmination of, an individual's formative background.

Perhaps the most bizarre example of this competitiveness between candidates to personalise their political appeal came when all three agreed to

discuss matters of religion and morality on BBC Radio 4's *Sunday* programme. Each candidate had to respond to a series of searching questions on
such subjects as the established status of the Church of England, the relationship between church and state, the concept of a 'just war', the plight of the
poor, the contribution of charities to social welfare provision, and the place of
minority religions in contemporary British society. In some ways, the interviews were an opportunity for the candidates to display their nimble footwork
over difficult terrain. They also provided an occasion for the candidates to
distinguish themselves from each other in a contest where there were very
few criteria to differentiate one contender from another. More significantly,
the candidates' agreement to submit themselves to such questions was
symptomatic of the general conception underlying the contest – namely that
individual beliefs and convictions were central to the credentials for leadership. Religious enquiry, therefore, was a doorway to the inner core not only of
the contenders' private faith, but also of their personal principles, motivations
and objectives. The assumption that candidates should possess a sensitivity
towards religious and moral questions also strengthened the suggestion that
the position of prime minister had become a highly individualised office, in
which personal drives and ethics would necessarily be pivotal in the high
decisions of state.

As the furious campaigning for the second ballot came to an end, it was
clear that the intense exposure of the candidates had had an effect on all three
contenders. The chief victim was Douglas Hurd, whose campaign had not
fulfilled its early potential. Despite Hurd's prodigious experience of government and his considerable ability as a pragmatic conciliator, his campaign
could not disguise the fact that he looked and sounded like an old-style Tory
given to one-nation paternalism. His high standing in the party counted for
little once he had acquired an unfavourable public image as an old Etonian
classics scholar, and a Foreign Office mandarin and a fastidious patrician. The
campaign left Hurd insisting that he was the 'iron fist in the velvet glove'[59]
and complaining that 'a blunderbuss and a loud-hailer were not always the
best weapons'.[60] It also left him complaining that he had been misrepresented.

> I think there's too much image-making in politics at the moment. It's an
> American transplant: advertising gentlemen telling us who's going to win elec-
> tions. It's not what politics are really about. I don't think Conservative MPs
> when they coolly consider the matter will do other than choose the person they
> think's going to be the best Prime Minister. Because that's what's needed, and
> that's actually what wins elections.[61]

Hurd still believed that a prime minister was essentially a collegiate position.
He looked with disdain upon what he called 'the vision thing' and felt that

being a premier was nothing to do with preaching. This view was reflected in his wholly inadequate answer to the question why he wished to be prime minister.

> Everyone who stands for parliament wants to be prime minister but not everyone gets the chance. It's an amazing job … [a] mountain presents itself, and I'm going to climb it.[62]

Michael Heseltine did have the 'vision thing' but his support was being pressured both by the other two candidates and by a backlash in the constituencies over Mrs Thatcher's departure. *The Times* called him a 'political exotic'[63] who was temperamentally unsound. Feeling the erosion of his support, Heseltine complained that it was he who had shown leadership and that this ought to be recognised in what was a leadership election. 'The real matter is one of leadership,' he said, 'that is the heart of the matter. My colleagues will have to decide whether I have displayed the self-control and the discipline and, in the end, the will to stand up and be counted that is the essential ingredient of leadership.'[64] Heseltine clearly believed that where personal leadership was concerned, there was no contest.

> I responded to the wishes of colleagues to give them an opportunity to unite for the 1990s. I said we had to grip the issue of the community charge and deal with it. Until that moment we were drifting on, with the odd patch of Elastoplast, to what most of my colleagues felt was an electoral disaster. I led. Others followed.[65]

He concluded by repeating his claim that as prime minister he 'could go out and secure the popular assent to the policies that they [i.e. Hurd and Major] were now promising'.[66]

It was all to no avail, for the candidate who had benefited most from the campaigning was John Major who had come through the field to secure 185 votes to Heseltine's 131 and Hurd's 56. This was not quite enough for outright victory but as Hurd and Heseltine withdrew their candidacies for the sake of party unity soon after the declaration, John Major became Conservative party leader and prime minister. He it was who had profited from Heseltine's challenge, who had adapted successfully to the controlling characteristics of the contest and who had maximised his resources to take full advantage of the opportunity provided. In what was a meteoric rise to prominence, Major used the political conditions he encountered to his own advantage and, in doing so, revealed in graphic form the new strategies of leadership that were now open to exploitation.

Major's accession to Number 10 was secured in the face of several severe handicaps. He was young (47 years) to the point where his inexperience was thought by many to be a bar to the premiership this time round. He had only been in Parliament for eleven years. He had held two prestigious posts (i.e. Foreign Secretary and Chancellor of the Exchequer), but had only done so for short periods of time. He was also seen as a cabinet 'insider' who was Mrs Thatcher's favourite and was being groomed by her as a long-term prospect for the succession. To make matters worse, he was Chancellor during a deepening recession and was, as a consequence, the government's chief spokesman for an economy in decline. Finally, he had to contend with a personal image that was grey and technocratic in nature, and implied the presence of a vacuous individual who had no ideas or sense of purpose.

Given the way that Michael Heseltine had popularised the connection between leadership and vision, John Major's apparent lack of guiding philosophical principles was considered to be a significant disadvantage. To Ian Aitken, it was 'this difficulty in categorising Mr Major's political character which made one wonder whether the hundred plus Tory MPs expected to vote for him ... had any real idea what they would be getting if he emerged as the eventual winner.'[67] Others agreed and thought that the 'job of premier' required 'policy vision, an ability to lead the government, Parliament and the country as well as political judgement'. Major's record, however, seemed to suggest 'a politician without an ideology of his own who would rather be led, by a strong prime minister and well informed officials, than lead himself'.[68]

In spite of these handicaps, Major's capacity to listen and to conciliate was widely recognised and much valued in a time of turmoil for the party. He had a reputation for being disarmingly honest, and courteous to his colleagues and opponents alike. At Westminster, Major was universally liked as a person. He was also enough of a politician to know how to cultivate and to deploy such personal resources to the maximum effect. Major's style was built on caution, persuasion and accommodation. While this led some to question his ability to resist pressure, it appealed to many in the party looking for a leader that could assimilate the party's vociferous factions into a common purpose. Major was highly adept at providing signs and hints to different groups. He stressed continuity and the defence of the Thatcherite legacy, while implying that adjustments in areas like local government finance and European integration were necessary. He could claim with conviction that he was of Mrs Thatcher's persuasion but was not the lady herself. This was in itself a very effective form of balanced appeal.

But there was something more to John Major than quiet accommodation. He had a spectacularly usable past. Once he became a leadership contender, stories began to circulate concerning his colourful father who had been a vaudeville artist, circus performer and a one-time baseball player in the United States. Upon returning to Britain, his father had been a farmer and

then a businessman manufacturing garden gnomes. When the business collapsed, the family had to move to a top floor flat in Brixton. John Major felt
obliged to leave school early to help the family finances. The son's adventures
in casual and labouring jobs and his weakness for transport cafe meals quickly
acquired a notoriety equal to his father's exploits. From this very meagre
background in Coldharbour Lane, John Major had risen through a career at
the Standard Chartered Bank and through local politics in Lambeth Council to
be Chancellor of the Exchequer. It was a rags to riches story that made him
into the living embodiment of the social mobility associated with the
Thatcherite revolution. Nicholas Wapshott described him as 'more the sort of
meritocratic leader that the Labour party might have produced'.[69] His background made Major fiercely sensitive to the possibilities of individual advancement, irrespective of social background and position. It also made him
much more difficult to classify as a right winger or left winger, or as a 'wet' or
'dry'. He could be tough on public expenditure, but it was felt that his
formative background made him far less doctrinaire than Mrs Thatcher and
more sympathetic to the plight of the socially disadvantaged.

John Major's political astuteness led him to recognise how his background could be used to broaden his appeal to the party. He already had a
reputation of being devoid of guile. It was natural that John Major's honesty,
which his colleagues found so engaging, should extend to the revelation of his
background. It was a matter of personal frankness but it was also a source of
pride. Joe Rogaly noted that Major's 'reflections on his career to date amount
to a fiercely proud assertion of his distinct individuality'.[70] Major was quite
aware that his past was to his advantage and he allowed supporters like David
Mellor to use it as a campaigning device. Major himself knew the importance
of personal image and public opinion and was not averse to helping the process
along by making a 'classless society' his chief objective. He also knew how his
background could provide not only a model for what individual opportunity
could achieve, but also the colour and personal depth in a campaign that would
otherwise lack these characteristics.

It was Douglas Hurd who was the first to feel his leadership chances slip
in the face of Major's suggestive personal history. He was clearly irritated at
being sidelined into a declining establishment by Major's theme of
classlessness. At first, he tried to dismiss Major's categories altogether: 'I am
standing to be leader of the Conservative party, not a curious Marxist outfit that
is obsessed by class'.[71] Then he felt compelled to meet the problem head on.

> Nothing in my family is remotely patrician, neither my family, nor my scholar-
> ships, nor anything in my attitude is remotely patrician. It's a misuse of words
> and a very old-fashioned line of thought.[72]

> There ain't no grandees, I mean there are, but they're distinguished, elderly and
> no longer central. I'm certainly no grandee.[73]

Hurd claimed that where his family was concerned 'none of them had any
capital'.[74] His ennobled father had had to make his money as a tenant farmer
and as an agricultural journalist for *The Times*. Friends disclosed that the
Hurds were far from being financially well-positioned. The disclaimers fell on
deaf ears. Hurd could never hope to aspire to Major's two O Levels. He just
could not live down his background in the fevered symbolism of modern
populist polls.

Major's political status as a social 'outsider' also cut into Heseltine's
reputation as a political 'outsider'. In comparison to Major's modest house and
life-style in Huntingdon, Heseltine's private estate in Oxfordshire began to
look pretentious and a product of an overweening ambition. The fact that his
initials were woven into the wrought iron gates did not help to dispel such an
impression. Major's self-effacement threw Heseltine's self-promotion into
stark relief. Heseltine the 'outsider' began to be seen as an 'outsider' who was
also condescending and manipulative – a glitzy schemer who had pursued Mrs
Thatcher a little too assiduously for doubts not to be raised about his integrity.
To Edward Pearce, Heseltine's 'outsider' politics were not born out of a
genuine regard for the public but out of his distaste for its vulgarity.

> He is almost excessively aloof from and sardonic about his own party. That is
> closer to an older Tory tradition by which at conference the little people – noted
> for their wrong accents, inadvisable hats, barbarous opinions and general bone-
> headed staunchness to use a Thatcher word – were left rattling their playpen
> until the afternoon of the last day. Then, the Leader, an educated man from the
> governing classes, would condescend to endure rapture and make some ringing,
> if minimal, communication.[75]

In Pearce's view, Heseltine could best be understood in the light of this
manipulative tradition. 'The highest flights of rapture are flecked with an
ironical knowledge that if this is what the masses want they had better have
it.'[76] That is probably too severe a judgement. What is certain is that even
from within the cabinet, Major managed to establish himself as an 'outsider'
in terms of his youth, background, achievement and sense of purpose. This
placed Heseltine's own 'outsider' credentials under severe strain and his
campaign faltered accordingly.

What finally undermined Heseltine's precious gift of intimacy with the
public and effectively reversed the momentum of his challenge was the opinion polls. Heseltine's challenge had been built around the proposition that he,
and only he, could rescue the Conservative party from public opprobrium and
win the next general election. The early opinion polls gave emphatic support

to such a contention. A week later the polls revealed that there was more than one saviour at hand. From a position where he had only a 3-5% level of support in the leadership polls when Heseltine had first challenged Mrs Thatcher,[77] Major had surged into contention within a matter of days. By 24 November, two days after Thatcher's withdrawal, Major was attracting a 43% level of potential support for his party.[78] Heseltine appealed strongly to a wide sector outside the party and to those who had defected from the Conservatives since the 1987 general election. Major appealed more to the Conservative voters and was seen by them as a source of unity. Heseltine not only had more widespread popularity, he was still seen as being better than either Hurd or Major at handling most of the important issues confronting the country (e.g. the Gulf crisis, the National Health Service, poll tax, education, law and order, unemployment, industrial problems and the inner cities).[79] John Major did outscore Heseltine in public confidence on the issue of the economy and inflation. It had been one of Major's campaign themes that his strengths lay in the areas that always determined elections – namely the economy, interest rates, inflation, mortgages and social security. This ploy appeared to be bearing fruit in the polls and offered the prospect of a foundation upon which to develop his claim to national leadership.

On 25 November, the Sunday papers produced a flurry of polls. They confirmed the advances made by Major. Some polls still showed Heseltine with a comfortable lead over Major on the question of who would attract most support for the party. The *Observer*'s Harris poll had Conservative support at 48% with Heseltine and 39% with Major.[80] In the *Sunday Telegraph*'s Gallup poll the levels were 47% for the Conservatives with Heseltine and 42% with Major.[81] The ICM poll for the *Sunday Correspondent* had them practically equal (47% with Heseltine and 46% with Major).[82] The *Independent on Sunday*'s NMR poll, however, showed Major in front at 48% Conservative support with him as leader compared to 47% with Heseltine.[83] The *Mail on Sunday*'s NOP poll of 52 marginal seats had Major with a two point lead on the question of Conservative party support (51% to 49%).[84]

By 27 November, the day of the second ballot, NOP in the *Independent* reported that a greater proportion of the electorate would be more likely to vote Conservative with John Major as leader than with Heseltine as leader.[85] The *Daily Telegraph*'s Gallup confirmed that Major had

> substantially improved his standing with the general public during the Conservatives' short leadership election campaign and now rivals Mr Michael Heseltine as the candidate most likely to win the next general election for the Conservatives.[86]

The poll showed that Major after being behind by five points two days

earlier now had a one point lead over his rival in Conservative voting intentions. It also revealed that Major was more appealing than Heseltine to
Conservative defectors; that Major had overtaken Heseltine in being seen to
be better at handling the NHS and education; and that he was regarded by the
public as equal to Heseltine in being 'prime ministerial material'.[87]

Michael Heseltine had been very adept at using public opinion polls
against Margaret Thatcher. But John Major had turned the tables and used
them against her tormentor. He had proved himself the equal of Heseltine on
precisely the grounds that Heseltine himself had chosen not merely to fight
for the premiership, but to establish his claim to undisputed supremacy in
public leadership. Heseltine both revealed and exploited the potency of an
explicitly popular campaign for what had been in the past a decidedly private
election, albeit with public ramifications. To all intents and purposes,
Heseltine had made the election into a public affair, deploying public strategies of campaigning and exerting public pressure to acquire support. Douglas
Hurd's discreet qualities of government experience, sober diplomacy and self-
effacing collegiality would have been formidable characteristics in an old-style
Conservative leadership campaign. In the hothouse atmosphere of November
1990, his candidacy visibly wilted *in* public – *because of* the public. It was
Major who took up Heseltine's challenge that leadership could make all the
difference. Major marketed himself as the individual who, in his own words,
had 'a very clear instinct for what the people in this country feel'.[88] His
implied intimacy with the drives and anxieties of the ordinary person paid off.
Major demonstrated that his leadership could make just as much difference as
Heseltine's leadership. This largely punctured Heseltine's claim of unique
leadership credentials. Heseltine had raised the bidding in the contest to one of
uniting the party by personal leadership and Major had matched him. As a
consequence, Heseltine's position began to falter while Major's candidacy
appeared to be on a rising curve. Once Major was seriously in contention,
Heseltine's public image suffered from comparison with the Chancellor. Major appealed to the public as warmer and friendlier than Heseltine. The
Chancellor was also seen as being more trustworthy, caring and sincere.
Heseltine by contrast was recognised to be more experienced and forceful than
Major, but he was also regarded as being vastly more ambitious for himself
and more willing to take risks as a politician.[89]

As his support began to decline, Heseltine was reduced to making desperate claims concerning which parts of the public he could attract to the
party. Like a presidential candidate openly engaged in pluralist coalition-
building, Heseltine insisted that his sectors of enhanced public support (i.e.
Scotland, the North of England, young people, and skilled manual workers)
were more pivotal than John Major's constituency to the electoral prospects of

the party. It was not convincing enough to the parliamentary party. The only presidential allusions employed on election day were those used to celebrate John Major's victory.

'Honest John' evoked the American folklore of a personal journey from log cabin to the White House. In what was a triumph of popular political campaigning, Major was feted as the new leader and as living proof of the Conservative conception of a classless meritocracy. Paul Johnson, for example, had no doubts that Major's rise to prominence from humble origins was an affirmation not only of his individual integrity and leadership potential, but of the liberty and opportunity of British society. To Johnson, the new prime minister had

> risen from nothing, entirely through his own efforts. More so perhaps than any other previous Tory leader, even Disraeli, he is a man of his own making. It makes one proud to think that Britain has a system which allows a man from such a humble background to climb to the top of the greasy pole … at so young an age.[90]

If Major had not realised before the contest the full extent of the political strengths and immunities that could be drawn from his personal background, he was left in no doubt after the election. His victory over Heseltine would not be the last time that Major would use his past for contemporary political effect.

It is commonly alleged that the decline of Margaret Thatcher and the corresponding rise of John Major amounted to the closure of an exceptional chapter in British politics. In one respect, this is quite true. Kenneth Baker was right to assert that 'we shall not see her like again'.[91] Being an exceptional person and an extraordinary leader is one thing, but employing that premise to arrive at the conclusion that Margaret Thatcher personified an utterly aberrational period of office is quite another. It is often claimed that the tumultuous events of November 1990 resulted in the immediate resumption of cabinet government, as if the latter represented a clearly definable and overriding norm of British political orthodoxy. Notwithstanding the question of whether cabinet government is quite so devoid of contested meanings as is customarily portrayed, the assumption, that the circumstances of Mrs Thatcher's fall from power affirmed her premiership to be a deviation from an allegedly central characteristic of British government, is a mistake. The picture of British government slipping effortlessly into a condition of traditional cabinet preeminence once the iron grip of the iron lady had been released is a distorted perspective. It conjures up a false dichotomy between prime ministerial government and cabinet government. It fosters the impression that Mrs Thatcher's problems in 1990 were reducible to the cabinet system somehow reasserting itself through dissent, challenge and ultimately, displacement. As a consequence, Mrs Thatcher was supposedly left stranded on her own outmoded structures of power. The cabinet eased her aside. It resumed its hegemony and defined the constitutionally contentious elements of central executive power by returning the issue to its customary state of dormancy.[92]

Nothing could be further from the truth. Far from nullifying the influence of presidential-style leadership politics in and around Number 10, both the prelude to the November contest and the campaign itself served in fact to confirm its presence and to demonstrate the extent of its development and penetration into the core of British politics. The period witnessed not the diminution of those forces that had fostered the centrality of personal leadership, but their continuation in altered circumstances. In the process, the degree to which high-level political dispute had become deeply ingrained with the varying dimensions and conceptions of leadership was dramatically revealed. Furthermore, their influence would remain just as evident and just as persistent in the period following John Major's much heralded reintroduction of cabinet government after November 1990.

CHAPTER 8

The post-Thatcher premiership and the 1992 general election

The resignation of Mrs Thatcher seemed at first to make all the difference both to the Conservative party and to the general character of British government. To a quite extraordinary extent, the party's abandonment of its high-profile leader led to a dramatic revival of party support. Even though the leadership contest had revealed the existence of divisions and tensions within the governing party, the departure of the figure who had been its chief electoral asset since 1979, appeared to provide a therapeutic effect in its own right. The Conservatives moved from a 12 point deficit in October 1990 to a $5^1/_2$ point advantage over Labour in December 1990. To many, the party's recovery was positive proof that the weight of personal controversy had been lifted from the government, and that in its place would be an altogether more conventional and less leadership-centred form of government.

Without Mrs Thatcher, the atmosphere at Westminster and Whitehall was considered to be radically different, Edward Heath, for example, was left in no doubt that John Major's presence in Number 10 had had a restorative effect on the party and the government.

> The change in the party has been quite remarkable. People are talking to each other now who haven't spoken for 15 years. They are no longer looking over their shoulders in the Smoking Room to see who's watching them or listening to them so they can rush off and report whether they are or are not 'one of us'. I think that Members of the Cabinet are now working together. The number of leaks seems to have almost dried up.[1]

Others agreed. Unlike Mrs Thatcher, John Major was sociable, accessible and accommodating. He kept in close contact with the back-benchers. Even after becoming prime minister he ate regularly in the member's dining room, where he would sit down with any group of Tory back-benchers and ask for their views on a range of issues. Taking their cue from the top, Tory MPs were noticeably more relaxed. One said:

> We have got back to Tory government. It's no longer personalised, one-person government. One can be cynical again and not feel anti-social.[2]

Another said:

> Have you noticed – people are talking to each other. They are not going around in little groups. That's the big change.[3]

Major's amiable and courteous regard for others was extended to the cabinet, where a new and genuinely collegiate outlook was said to have been inaugurated. One minister summed it up:

> With Mrs Thatcher, if you were Nicholas Ridley your views were always welcome, but for others it was more difficult. I find him much more approachable and easy to deal with. He invites opinions from around the table. He is a good chairman and always seems very aware of the dynamic of who is sitting around the table and what their views are.[4]

Major was widely reported as having united the cabinet through his own conviction in the virtues of collective decision-making. Unlike his predecessor, who sought to present her cabinet with fully worked out proposals for its approval, Major used the cabinet as a consultative device where ideas could be freely exchanged. Unconventional proposals were not foreclosed to discussion, but considered fully even to the point of being worked up as position papers. One survivor of the Thatcher cabinet concluded: 'It genuinely is a group now which reaches collective decisions'.[5]

The party's 'feel-good' outlook towards its new prime minister was further enhanced by the Gulf war. Although British forces had already been committed to the area by Mrs Thatcher, Major was installed in Number 10 when the attack against Iraq was launched by the international coalition. Major was therefore in a position to fulfil the role of war leader in what, to the West at the time, was a stunningly successful exercise in military organisation. As a consequence, Major was propelled on to the world stage and quickly acquired the stature of an international statesman. He not only developed his own personal rapport with President Bush, but used his new status to propose an internationally respected plan providing 'safe havens' for the Kurds, who were being persecuted by Saddam Hussein's army.

Within weeks of becoming the youngest prime minister this century, Major had come to personify national unity at a time of military engagement and to preside over an emphatically successful war effort. His honeymoon period had been spiced with the sort of unequivocal military triumph that very few British prime ministers have enjoyed. During the same period, Major was able to demonstrate further grace under pressure when the IRA launched a mortar attack on Number 10, Downing Street. The implicit kudos gained from a leader targeted for injury, or worse, was enhanced by Major's phlegmatic response to the blast, which blew in the Cabinet room windows – 'I think we had better start again somewhere else.'[6] The personal integrity of his leadership now seemed to be reassuringly matched by a personal toughness that confirmed him as prime ministerial material. At the end of January 1991, MORI reported that 61% of the public were satisfied with Major as prime minister with only 15% registering dissatisfaction. The differential of +46% was in stark contrast to the −46% rating of Mrs Thatcher in November 1990 when only 25% were satisfied with her performance as prime minister compared to 71% who were dissatisfied. Significantly, Major's rating was double that of Mrs Thatcher's best ever rating for MORI of +23% when the Argentinian forces surrendered at Port Stanley in June 1982. Major's level of public satisfaction was in fact the highest for any prime minister in the past fifty years – thus making Britain's new premier the most popular prime minister since Winston Churchill.[7]

Once the afterglow of the Gulf war had begun to fade back into the normality of party politics and government management, the transition from Thatcher to Major began to come under more critical scrutiny. In many respects, the war had acted as a screen during Major's introduction to the premiership. Political disputes on issues like the poll tax, the economy and the further development of the EEC, which could have caused serious divisions in the party, had been effectively suspended by the preoccupations of Operation Desert Storm. Close political scrutiny of the new prime minister had also been avoided by the compulsion to maintain national unity during the emergency. But with the resumption of domestic politics, sharp questions began to be asked about Major's government and about the prime minister himself.

The Conservative party in particular began to look introspectively at what post-Thatcherism might mean in respect to policy, substance and public style. As the unsustainably high opinion poll rankings for the prime minister began to fall and as the party's lead over Labour began to show ominous signs of diminishment, Conservative anxieties over the next general election became evident. By the spring of 1991, the party had become distinctly nervous over its condition to fight an election campaign. The Thatcherite wing, for example, complained that Major had deviated from the tenets of Thatcherism in the past (e.g. on the Exchange Rate Mechanism) and was showing alarming signs that he would do so in the future (e.g. on European integration and public spending). The implication was that he was not quite the trusted successor that Mrs Thatcher believed him to be in November 1990. If, as they believed, leadership was about principles and convictions confronting the insidious accommodation of consensus politics, then John Major's more even-handed approach to the office began to look, in the eyes of the Thatcherites, suspiciously like a simple lack of leadership. Mrs Thatcher herself was widely quoted in 1991 as saying that she found it difficult to know what Mr Major believed in. Since Mrs Thatcher had always claimed that beliefs were synonymous with leadership, the implied criticism of her successor was quite clear.

Other elements in the party were gratified that Major had softened the Conservative image by reducing some of the harsher features of the Thatcherite legacy. He had, for example, announced a review of the poll tax, eased the constraints on public spending and adopted a more positive attitude to the EEC. Nevertheless, doubts remained as to whether this more consensual approach by the prime minister was a refreshing and iconoclastic break with the past that pointed the party in a new direction, or just the net effect of an aimless patchwork of negotiations and compromises. He was accused, for example, of having a civil service approach to decision-making in which conflict was persistently avoided by way of prolonged consultation. 'To appear to be unable to choose is to appear to be unable to govern', complained the former Chancellor, Nigel Lawson, in March 1991. 'Consultation is an aid to government, but we are in danger of seeing consultation as a substitute for government.'[8]

Much of this open speculation on the operation and guiding principles of the Major government was caused by the circumstances of his elevation to Number 10. He was confronted by a potentially divided party, by difficult domestic and international issues, by the party's anxiety over its electoral chances of a fourth term. He was also haunted by the spectre of Michael Heseltine's political glamour and by continual intimations of disaffection on his flanks from retired cabinet ministers and from Mrs Thatcher herself. But the real force behind the intense interest in Major the man and Major the prime minister came from another source. It was conditioned and driven by the experience of the previous eleven years under Margaret Thatcher. Far from acquiring a release from the debates and disciplines of leadership, it was clear that in one important respect Major had not produced a break with the past. Even in the very act of seeking such a departure, Major found that the interpretations and assessments of him and his government were heavily dependent upon the Thatcherite conjunction of personal prominence, purposeful leadership and government direction.

Outside observers joined the party in seeking to fathom out the measure of the new prime minister. It soon became clear that they also were directly or indirectly dependent upon precisely those premises of leadership which had been most closely associated with Mrs Thatcher. The presumptive importance of leadership, combined with both its mercurial nature and the opaque personal qualities of John Major, led to a bewildering variety of revealing speculations. Very often the same evidence was used to support diametrically opposed constructions of the prime minister's leadership, or lack of it. For example, it was considered imperative that Major should not only be his own man but impress his individual authority in a demonstrative way. On the other hand, it was also thought that he should revive cabinet government by devolving responsibility upon his senior ministers. Soon after his accession to the premiership, it was widely asserted that he had indeed achieved this laudable objective. The question then raised was whether this development amounted to confirmation that he was not his own man and that the revival of the cabinet was synonymous with a lack of personal authority and leadership. Had the cabinet simply taken cabinet government back to itself through default? Was cabinet government just an extrapolation of the prime minister's passive personality? Or was it a calculated choice by John Major designed to strengthen his power base and enhance his leadership? Opinions varied.

In some respects, Major did appear to be a captive of his own desire to move forward by collective accommodation. According to this perspective, Major opened himself up to the charge of dithering by prolonged consultation and negotiation. Significantly, he was accused by those who had once been critical of Mrs Thatcher's style, for having no personal vision, for lacking individual drive and for radiating a sense of drift. According to this view, Major had not been tested by 'doing something difficult and unpopular'.[9] So far he had been 'making omelettes without breaking eggs'.[10] Rather than having made tough decisions, the new prime minister was thought to have succeeded merely in evading them: 'Almost everything has been a balancing act – the whip as prime minister.'[11]

Others disagreed. An alternative perspective viewed Major as adhering to the Thatcherite style of personal leadership but through different means. His advocacy of the virtues of cabinet government had to be tempered by what he may have acquired through a more collegiate style. Apart from the argument that a return to cabinet government through prime ministerial licence amounted to a contradiction in terms, Major was suspected of using the cabinet to solidify his own position. It was thought that like Ronald Reagan, his collegiality was a means of devolving difficult issues and controversy away from the chief executive. Michael Heseltine, for example, was given a senior position in the cabinet and with it the clear public responsibility to find a replacement for the poll tax. Major's personal preference for moving forward by discussion and consultation with colleagues also had the effect of producing a united and 'leak-free' cabinet which strengthened rather than weakened Major's position. For example,

> Ministers delayed the sensitive decision on the poll-tax replacement for longer than had originally been intended, while they consulted widely on how to

proceed. It paid dividends, however, when the whole Cabinet, and most backbench MPs, backed the formula for the council tax which was devised.[12]

As one member of the cabinet was quoted as saying: 'John's position is immensely stronger than his predecessor's because it's based on consent.'[13] Of course, the term 'consent', even where a replacement prime minister is concerned, has to be treated with caution, as the power of the office can directly contribute to agreement. As Douglas Hurd revealed in November 1991, cabinet meetings under John Major were a lot more informal than under Mrs Thatcher, but though the styles were different, their implications were similar: 'Now John lets people talk first, listening intently all the while and then expects everybody to agree with him.'[14]

In many respects, both party observers and political analysts were baffled by the new prime minister. His objectives and the means deployed to reach them remained in serious doubt. Sometimes he looked like a withdrawn and collegiate chairman; at other times he was declared to be a tough operator who did not suffer fools gladly. The party worried about his diffidence, amiability and courtesy. All were agreed that Major was a nice man, but they questioned the extent to which niceness was a resource in politics at this level.

> Niceness is, at best, a negative quality. People are not seriously praised by being called nice – as they are by being thought brave, clever or witty.[15]

On the other hand, 'niceness' made an attractive contrast to Mrs Thatcher, who had never aspired to such a characteristic.

In this regard, sceptics pointed to the way that the prime minister had gone to such lengths to brief and consult the opposition parties during the Gulf war.[16]

> Tory MPs were told not to embarrass Labour by stressing division in its ranks over military action. Debates were arranged with minimum time for Labour's opponents of war to complain – tactics, say many Tories, that would have been unthinkable under Mrs Thatcher.[17]

According to one of Major's colleagues, 'taking Kinnock and Ashdown into his confidence over the war was good politics as well as being in the national interest'.[18] Apart from being a deadly embrace that emasculated the opposition as an opposing force, it protected the war cabinet from domestic attack and allowed the prime minister to use consensus to his advantage and, thereupon, to the party's long-term benefit. To those who questioned the extent to which this style deviated from that of Mrs Thatcher, the response was that there were different ways of exerting leadership. Success in leadership had to be judged by strategic effects and not by operational tactics.

It was precisely these effects that came under close scrutiny in the months following the Gulf war, when the attention of the parties became increasingly dominated by thoughts of an imminent general election. The position of the Conservative party was mixed. On the debit side was a deepening recession that threatened the party's reputation in economic management, a collapse in the party's honeymoon lead following Mrs Thatcher's resignation, Conservative disunity over European union and a set of disastrous by-election results. On the credit side was the softening of the government's posture on social policy, the relaxation of public spending constraints and the declaration to review and then to replace the poll tax. Most significantly of all was the marked popularity of the prime minister himself. This was the one central and consistent factor in the polls and it gave party managers a source of relief from otherwise gloomy indicators. It also gave rise to hope that Major could hold the key to a fourth term of office for the Conservatives.

In many quarters, Major's popularity was said to be due to him being someone other than his predecessor. Although it was difficult to deny that at first Major's greatest strength was that he was *not* Mrs Thatcher, it was equally difficult to believe that Major's appeal remained wholly attributable to such an overriding and negative characteristic. Major was new, young and different. He was interesting in that he appeared to be so divorced from the previous regime, not least because of his lack of grandeur and pretension. Unlike Mrs Thatcher, he carried his modest roots with him quite openly and saw high office as simply another promotion rather than a personal metamorphosis. It was not simply that he was different because he was not Mrs Thatcher, it was that the Conservative party could not have found a leader who appeared to be more different from her. Even though Major had come from *her* cabinet, had been *her* chancellor and was *her* chosen successor, it was a tribute to his personal qualities that he was so quickly dissociated in the public mind from his patron and from the economic policies he had helped to put in place whilst in her government. Major's engaging temperament and his modest demeanour as the unaffected ordinary chap who had acquired a good job on merit, fostered the impression of a wholly new, and quite unconventional, prime minister. This in turn generated a sense that the Conservative government had changed in body and soul not merely by the departure of Mrs Thatcher, but by the emplacement of a genuinely different leader.

In other circumstances, and with a stronger sense of cabinet government, Major's accession to the premiership might have seemed like a board room shuffle. It quickly became evident, however, that it was a top-down transformation centred upon the person of John Major. He had given the government a new identity. For most of 1990, the Conservative party looked doomed to electoral defeat. But within weeks of John Major's entry into Number 10 the new prime minister appeared able to defy all prognostications of government decline. An exasperated Robert Harris found it difficult to comprehend that in May 1991, the Conservative and Labour parties were level pegging in the polls.

> When one considers the blunders and disasters of the past four years, it is the sheer resilience of Conservative support . . . demonstrated last week that it is astonishing. Apart, perhaps from Harold Wilson's fourth administration, 1974-76, I doubt if a worse government has presided over the nation's affairs since the war. By every rule of politics, the government should have shrivelled up and died of shame. Instead it is *neck and neck*.[19]

Labour insisted that on the fundamental issues which divided the parties, Major and Thatcher were one. As Major had been a leading member of Mrs Thatcher's government, then logically and ethically he should have accepted responsibility for any Conservative failures. But at the same time that Labour strategists tried to 'wrestle with the phenomenon of Teflon Man'[20] on whom nothing unpleasant ever stuck, Peter Jenkins observed that 'the country behaved as if last November [1990] there had been a change of government, and the new government had been given a remarkable honeymoon'.[21]

The precise extent to which Major's government was different to that of Margaret Thatcher will always remain open to dispute. But whether or not the changes were real or imagined; whether the varied reputations of the two leaders in 1991 were deserved or undeserved; and whether the popularity of the new prime minister owed as much to the public's negative view of Mrs Thatcher as it did to the positive attributes of her successor – one point became very clear in 1991. This was the agreement in the party that John Major had become its chief asset. It would be no exaggeration to say that to a government which in many ways had a public reputation for incompetence, disunity, fatigue and even callousness, the figure of John Major came to represent something of a life-support system. He was seen as a source of huge and untapped potential, and as the party's best – if not only – opportunity for re-election.

John Major had already achieved a position of prominence in the public domain. Articles and profiles showered analyses of the prime minister, his outlook and his policies. The figure of Mrs Thatcher may have gone, but the suppositions, expectations and bases of judgements had not. John Major was seen as the focus of government and his leadership was regarded as the motivating force behind his administration. Government problems were diagnosed, and Conservative prospects were evaluated, in terms of the challenges facing Major and his performance in Number 10. As interest and conjecture about the government became progressively reduced in perspective to the sphere of the leader, the links between the prime minister and his formative influences became subjects of journalistic investigation. John Major and his leadership became as newsworthy as Mrs Thatcher's leadership had been in the 1980s. Cabinet government may have returned, but the voracious appetite of the press was increasingly directed to what it believed was the more significant feature of British government – namely the prime minister. John Major himself was essentially a private person and did not take kindly to enquiries about his background, but as prime minister he quickly had to accept that he was a public commodity being probed and evaluated on a continual basis. Personal leadership was now confirmed to be a central feature in British politics. Simply being an inconspicuous chairman of the cabinet was not an option. Leadership had to be public and leaders were consequently the subject of public interest. The slightly incongruous figure of John Major in the power house of Number 10 proved to be irresistible to reporters and commentators. The rationale of a lengthy four page profile entitled 'The Greying of John Major' typified the outlook that looked for the answers to government in the personal puzzles of leaders.

> 'There are two surprising things about John Major. One is that he is Prime Minister; the other is that he seems embarrassed about his past. But the former makes the latter very intriguing.[22]

Given the public's high regard for John Major, together with its conditioned expectations of political leadership, there was never much doubt that the Conservative response to the general election would be 'to fight it as a presidential election'.[23] It would be the best way of maximising the windfall bequest of a prime minister with a remarkable capacity both to dissociate the party from its recent past and to unify the party around his ambiguous accommodations on Europe and public services. It also has to be acknowledged that the decision on a presidential-style campaign was not really a matter of choice. The Labour party was known to have reformed itself into a formidable electoral organisation under the dynamic leadership of Neil Kinnock. He was expected to exploit to the full the modern campaigning techniques that depended upon the central focus of the leader and which in turn enhanced the position of the leader into a public celebrity. For the Conservatives, not to have countered that strategy by giving maximum prominence to their own leader, would have given the impression that the party had so much to be defensive about that its leader was in relative hiding. Since the resurgent Liberal Democrats were also certain to engage in a concentrated drive for the media coverage of its new telegenic leader, the Conservative party strategists had to determine not whether but how Major would be given the presidential treatment.

Although the party concluded that Major should and would spearhead its campaign in such a way as to draw as closely as possible upon his personal qualities, this is not to say that the party did not harbour reservations about the strategy. Questions were raised not just about how it could be done, but whether it could be achieved at all. John Major was inexperienced as a national campaigner. His merits had a private interior character to them that might not translate well to public presentation. His courteous and assimilative qualities might be eclipsed against the oratorical skills and predatory partisanship of Neil Kinnock. What was more, his sensitivity to criticism could lead, in the abrasive atmosphere of a general election, to self-inflicted damage to his reputation as a calming and unifying influence upon British politics. There was concern, echoed in the media and amongst the public, that Major had no 'big ideas' or 'personal vision' that would provide the campaign with a set of guiding principles. Major was perhaps simply 'too unheroic and uncommanding a figure to be able to bank for long on public favour'.[24] Major was popular for being ordinary. The question was whether ordinariness could be marketed as a political resource that would motivate voters to opt for the Conservative party in preference to the programmes of more flamboyant leaders.

These and other anxieties circulated within the public and the party for much of 1991. John Major himself had no doubts that he was very much his own man and one not given to casting that independence into doubt by having to give public expression to it. He was widely thought to be psychologically withdrawn. In an interview with the prime minister in January 1991, Robin Oakley of *The Times* observed:

> Only one thing really fazes him: try discussing his image and he comes as close to squirming as he will ever do.[25]

In spite of these reservations and even objections, a discernible shift in Major's stature as prime minister took place during 1991. It was a gradual and at times equivocal and probably reluctant change, but the net effect was to make Major into a far more assertive and outwardly autonomous figure.

It can be argued that no real change took place and that it was nothing more than the extension of the prime minister's inherent characteristics into a more public setting. On the other hand, it is also possible to conclude that Major must have been forced into an uncharacteristically more visible and self-centred posture by the nature of modern leadership politics and by the imperatives of contemporary electioneering. The true position is difficult to determine, but what is clear is that in 1991 the unlikely figure of John Major rose to a position of personal pre-eminence in the government and the party. With the complicity of the party and the cabinet, Major assumed the personal licence and responsibility of public leadership. Any inhibitions he may have had at the beginning of his administration were dismissed as he went to considerable and conspicuous lengths both to impress himself visibly upon government and to deploy his office as an immediate point of contact between government and the public. He raised public consciousness in *his* government and *his* leadership in three ways that any contemporary American president would find familiar.

Incumbency

First, he used the power of incumbency to maximise the opportunities for acquiring a centre-stage position for himself. For someone whose prior disposition was to take the role of personality out of politics, Major openly exploited his position as prime minister to convey himself to as wide an audience as possible.

> Whoever heard of the chairmanship of the G7 Western industrialised nations being anything more than a three-day blaze of glory for the holder? Mr Major turned it into a six-month stroll on the world stage, which paid off handsomely during the August coup in Moscow, when he was rarely off the television screens.[26]

In January 1992, 'the Major-as-world-figure theme played fortissimo'[27] when the prime minister chaired an exceptional gathering of the UN Security Council. The summit had been called by John Major to discuss several important international issues, including the future composition of the Security Council itself. The meeting was due to begin on the final day that Britain held the rotating position of the UN presidency. The timing cast doubt on whether Britain should preside over the meeting. But, as David Hughes describes, the appetite of the British delegation for world attention was not to be denied.

> A combination of fast-moving world events, particularly in the former Soviet empire, and Rolls Royce diplomacy by Britain did the trick. As Major chaired the meeting, flanked by world leaders, Mr Kinnock was addressing Labour party candidates at the Greater Manchester World Trade Centre in Salford.[28]

At home, Major appeared to lose his entire inhibitions both about displaying the office and about projecting his occupancy of it. He not only adopted but developed Mrs Thatcher's Downing Street podium. It provided a stage for conducting open air press conferences and for addressing the public alongside world leaders. He unveiled what was couched as his Citizen's Charter. This involved the prime minister's full deployment of the Whitehall machine behind a measure that would be central to the Conservative's re-election campaign. It provoked criticism that 'civil servants had been used shamelessly to devise and launch the Citizen's Charter even though it was essentially the Conservative party manifesto in thin disguise'.[29] Objections were brushed aside as Major was now in full flight as prime minister. For a private man with a reputation for wishing to remain private, Major abandoned his privacy and began to exploit every opportunity for using the office for self-promotion. This change of outlook was epitomised in his agreement to take the nation through his childhood and inner thoughts on the fiftieth anniversary edition of the radio programme *Desert Island Discs* in January 1991.[30]

Outsider status

The second way in which Major sought to raise public awareness in his premiership was by protecting and cultivating his role as an outsider. Major had successfully demolished Douglas Hurd's prospects for the party leadership in November 1990 simply by allowing his meagre background to throw the Foreign Secretary's relatively privileged upbringing into sharp and damaging relief. Major now intended to use his own ordinariness as a weapon in a much larger conflict. To Major, his own rise from the lower middle classes was the decisive affirmation of his own principles in the importance of opportunities and choice in individual advance. In a quite unconceited way, Major was his own walking ideal and the validation of his conception of an open society. He had made it to the top, but there was no affectation of success or triumphalism of the self-made man worshipping his own creator. In fact, he was known to detest snobbery, pretension and arrogance. He had succeeded in the blue chip atmosphere of the Conservative party by judging people on their merits, in the same way as he expected to be judged by others. In many respects, he was an outsider in his party; a person who seemed genuinely surprised and even embarrassed by the perks of achievement. For example, when he became Chancellor and was shown around Number 11 Downing Street for the first time, he said to his friend who was accompanying him – 'God it's really beautiful. Of course, it's not for people like us.'[31] But it was this lack of pretension and his confident adherence to middle brow tastes and interests (e.g. C&A suits, Happy Eater meals, Chelsea Football Club) which made him such a formidable politician.

John Major appealed to a vast constituency of aspiration. His well publicised background together with his visibility as a prime minister, unaffected by being prime minister, made his example a much more tangible measure of life's possibilities than that provided by Mrs Thatcher and by Conservative party doctrines. Major had had direct experience of hard times. He had painful memories of his father's bankruptcy and of having to live on the fourth floor of a Brixton boarding house. The two room flat had a gas ring on the landing and a shared toilet on the ground floor. Major himself had been unemployed in his youth. His sympathy for those suffering from deprivation, therefore, seemed genuine and caring. He held high office, but in every other respect he appeared to remain an outsider, linked to that wider public which could identify closely with him and his principles. He showed every indication of being able to disarm his opponents with a populism of common sense attitudes and real life accounts of social mobility. To the Conservatives, it was essential that their exceptional leader should continue to be portrayed as an outstandingly ordinary person.

Major himself was 'wise enough to know that success can provoke envy rather than admiration, and that making hay out of one's early difficulties without seeming self-obsessed is not an easy harvest'.[32] Both Major and his party, however, were fully committed to exploiting his public status as the 'ordinary man in an extraordinary position'[33] for electoral effect. Major had shown in the past that he knew how to make 'skilful political use of this "ordinariness" on Labour's own class ground'.[34] His outsider appeal was so strong that it offered the prospect of providing the governing party with a distractive property that could turn attention away from its failures and mistakes. If Major was not exactly an anti-hero, he did provide an invaluable image that ran counter to much of the party and the government.

Spatial leadership

The third strategy adopted by Major was a classic exercise in spatial leadership. The new prime minister may have quickly developed a reputation for integrating himself within cabinet government, but it was not long before Major began to engage in sudden personal interventionism into government. His interventions were usually well publicised and designed to give the impression of an attentive prime minister breaking free from collective restraints and personally turning on some aspect of government policy or government machinery on behalf of the public.

His first venture in this role of prime minister as defender of the public came in December 1990 when he announced a £42 million settlement for 1200 haemophiliacs who had contracted the HIV virus through blood transfusions. The government's settled policy up to that point had been that no public money would be made available to such sufferers, as liability and compensation would have to be determined by the courts. In February 1991, Major played benefactor again by distancing himself from another set of government rules that threatened to produce charges of an unrepresentative government. Major stepped in to relax the rules on cold weather payments when severe weather conditions hit the country. Major waived the rules for two successive weeks. Although Mr Kinnock wrote to the prime minister accusing him of 'capricious government',[35] Major made it clear that he would continue to relax the eligibility rules as long as the freezing conditions prevailed.

On 4 July 1991, the *Guardian* reported that the prime minister, who had 'already put his personal stamp on further and higher education changes', had turned his attention to primary and secondary schools.

> John Major took personal political responsibility for the education service yesterday as he overturned existing plans for testing children at seven, 11, 14, and 16.[36]

The prime minister made it clear that it was time to stop the left wing 'canker in the education system' which had undermined 'common sense values, rejected proven teaching methods and debased standards'.[37] Major made known his strong personal preference for seven year olds to be taught the 'three Rs' and for them to have class-wide pencil and paper tests.

Major's free-wheeling interventionism became commonplace and spread to the outer limits of prime ministerial influence. Their wide-ranging character can be gauged by the headlines they generated in the press.

Major overturns plans for testing in schools' (*Guardian*, 4 July 1991)

Major cuts BR fares rise' (*Daily Mail*, 14 October 1991)

Major questions high food prices' (*Sunday Times*, 2 February 1992)

Major tells CBI wage increases must be earned' (*The Times*, 25 May 1991)

Major orders action to halt homes crisis' (*Sunday Telegraph*, 15 December 1991)

Major boost for gay rights (*Sunday Telegraph*, 1 March 1992)

This was not the same sort of interventionism as that practised in the past by premiers like Harold Wilson. It was different in scale, but more importantly it was different in nature. Wilson intervened to act for, or on behalf of the government. He acted to protect the political reputation of his administration by intervening to preserve and defend the government under Labour. Major on the other hand acted more as a guerrilla commander against the impersonalism and unresponsiveness of contemporary institutions. In his adopted role as the personal representative of broad public concerns, Major intervened as much to provide demonstrable evidence of his empathy with the ordinary person as it was to produce action. The act of intervention was important in its own right, irrespective of effect. It protected Major, and by extension his administration, because it allowed him to distance himself from the negative aspects of modern government and in the process to melt himself more into the public's own conception of its condition.

Major's most ambitious plan to act as an agent of popular complaint and as an instrument of redress was the Citizens' Charter. It was his flagship policy not just because it matched so closely John Major's outlook as prime minister, but because it was a way of patenting his interventionism on a mass basis. Its aim was to return power to the consumer by establishing performance standards, more effective complaints procedures and giving various rights of redress when public services broke their obligations. Major described it as the 'widest ranging and most comprehensive'[38] initiative ever undertaken by Government to raise quality, increase choice, secure better value and extend accountability of public services.

The sprawling quality of the Charter, which contained over 70 measures, was derided by those who regarded it as a pale substitute for a full bill of rights. Critics, however, misunderstood the intentions of the Charter. It was not an attempt at constitutional reform. Major had no interest in the latter and believed that his indifference was shared by the large mass of the British public, who, like him, had been brought up with a suspicion of such legal abstractions. The Citizen's Charter was not aimed at constitutional lawyers or at those who wished to unravel the British constitution. Its target was the mass public and its intention was avowedly populist in character. Even amongst those who felt that the Charter lacked finesse and substance were prompted to concede that Major had caught the public mood. The *Independent*, for example, believed that the Charter ought not to be lightly dismissed.

> Mr Major's workaday preoccupations are shared by millions of people. They are quietly furious at the incompetence and casual arrogance that has come to characterise producer-dominated public services and the privatised utilities.[39]

Peter Riddell in *The Times* agreed:

> It is easy to underestimate Mr Major, to dismiss him as a Mr Pooter with mundane concerns awkwardly expressed. But his 'ordinary man' approach masks one of the acutest politicians I know. In this respect the Citizen's Charter – Mr Major's Big Idea – reflects an appreciation of the public's frustration about distant services.[40]

'Distance' was the operative word. Major was intent upon opening up some space between himself and 'government', thereby identifying his leadership with the common good. This was made transparently clear in his televised address to the nation on the Citizen's Charter: 'I called it the Citizen's Charter because quite simply it's on your side – not on the side of the state, the politicians, the bureaucrats or the union bosses – on *your* side, the citizen's side.'[41]

All three elements of Major's leadership style were conspicuously fused together in his keynote speech to the Conservative Party conference on 11 October 1991. This was the first meeting of the party since Margaret Thatcher's downfall. It was also certain to be the last before the next general election.

The new leader was therefore expected to stamp his mark on the party and, in doing so, to give it a renewed sense of identity. Major used the occasion to full effect. Contrary to his mild and diffident exterior, Major made it clear that the party's new post-Thatcherite theme for the election would be based not so much on policy as on 'Reaganesque self-exposure'.[42]

'He invited people to identify in his personal mythology and to follow in his footsteps from Coldharbour Lane, Brixton to Number 10, Downing Street.'[43] He explicitly linked his present principles and programme to his own underprivileged background and his rise to prominence as an outsider. Because of his experience, the party – his party – was not indifferent to the plight of the unemployed: 'I know how they feel – I know what it's like for a family when a business collapses. What it's like when you're unemployed and when you have to search for the next job. I haven't forgotten – and I never will.'[44] Because of these hard knocks, he would 'never play fast and loose with the economy'.[45] His private difficulties in the past were now not only publicly aired by Major himself, but openly deployed to justify his occupancy of Number 10 and to vindicate the values of his party – 'the power to choose and the right to own . . . Ordinary values perhaps, but over which ordinary people have, in our time, fought an extraordinary fight.'[46]

Major was now prime minister ('I've got it. I like it, and with your help I'm going to keep it.'[47]) and, as such, he made it perfectly clear that he had used the office, and would continue to exert his incumbency, in the furtherance of his values. Although he acknowledged the cabinet was a form of collective leadership, Major gave emphasis to his own power. It was he who could be entrusted with its usage because of who he was and what he had been through. He claimed the right to be believed especially where the NHS was involved. It was 'unthinkable that I, of all people, would try to take that security away'.[48] As a consequence, there would be

> no charges for hospital treatment, no charges for visits to the doctor, no privatisation of health care, neither piecemeal, nor in part, nor in whole. Not today. Not tomorrow. Not after the next election. Not ever while I'm Prime Minister.[49]

It was precisely his background and character that would prevent his incumbency from becoming one of detachment and insensitivity. His memory of being just one of a crowd would always ensure a genuine, and electorally attractive, identity with the average person. He had not forgotten that as a young man thirty years before he attended his first party conference. He knew very few people and felt that it was a long road to the platform. He was now prime minister, but he knew his roots. To make sure the message was received inside, but more importantly outside, the hall, he broke with tradition. Instead of moving offstage at the end of his speech, he and Mrs Major left the hall in the same unconventional way as they had entered it – namely by moving through the crowd and circulating amongst the representatives. As he 'came down from the blue mountain and appeared among the people',[50] the impression of the outsider as leader was complete. As prime minister, the spectacle was of course carried to the public by a battery of television cameras. For a modest man, Major's exploitation of his personality had been extraordinary. In Hugo Young's view, the speech

> made clear that the Conservatives' visionary appeal is built, to a startling extent, around one model: himself. This was the unexpected coda to the Thatcher era. Mrs Thatcher was often charged with hubristic domination, and her conference speech was delivered and received as an annual consummation of one-woman government. But she was never so shameless in representing her own life as the proof of all she had to say.[51]

Major's transformation as an exponent of leadership politics was now complete. With the prime minister's personal ratings higher than those of his party and far in excess of those of the Leader of the Opposition, the party strategists had their chief asset in a position from which to strike, as leader, on the subject of leadership in the general election.

The Kinnock factor

What the Conservatives regarded as their 'Major factor' was very much the obverse of the 'Kinnock factor' in the Labour party. Whereas Major's strengths and weaknesses were translated into a net strength, Kinnock's merits and demerits were widely reduced to an alleged weakness. Although Major seemed to prevail over Kinnock in the public mind, what should not be overlooked is the extent to which Kinnock determined the Conservatives' strategy and forced Major into a position of explicit public leadership. Major had to compete on the grounds of leadership that Neil Kinnock and the Labour party had come to occupy during their period of opposition. These were the same grounds that they in turn had been forced to adopt during the period of Thatcher's ascendancy in the mid-1980s.

When Kinnock became opposition leader in 1983, the Labour party was in a state of disarray. The collapse of its share of the popular vote to a level of 27.6% in the election of that year, together with the effects of the internal convulsions it had suffered over policy and structure during the previous four years, prompted the party to engage in a long process of rehabilitation as an electoral organisation. With the breakaway of the Gang of Four, and the subsequent formation of the Social Democratic party, Labour's need to respond to changing political and electoral conditions became imperative. Its very existence as an alternative government was open to doubt. Kinnock was placed in the unenviable position of having to pull the party back from the brink of self-destruction.

A key component of this strategy, and a prime indicator of its chances of success, was the emulation of Mrs Thatcher's leadership of the Conservative party. At the same time that her leadership was being severely criticised by Labour, Kinnock was attempting to match its positive aspects – especially its associations with party unity, with policy coherence, and with personal strength signifying political direction and conviction. Indeed, in many respects, Labour's constant critique of Mrs Thatcher's leadership helped to build up an image of prime ministerial pre-eminence which the Labour leader felt constrained to imitate, in order to compete for power at the highest level. By the same token, the Conservatives were quick to exploit any divisions in the Labour party as indictments of Kinnock's leadership. A lack of leadership could be equated with a lack of control by the leader over the party. This could then be used to substantiate the proposition that the party was inherently uncontrollable and, therefore, unfit to govern. Whatever reservations the Conservatives might have about their own leadership, they knew that at the very least it could be used to throw the Labour leader's more provisional position, in what had always been a more democratically organised party, into sharp relief.

At first, Kinnock found it difficult to match Mrs Thatcher, especially at the Despatch Box. She would appear aggressively self-confident and speak in clear and clipped sentences. Kinnock was regularly outgunned. During this apprenticeship, he acquired a reputation for attempting to conceal his alleged lack of detailed knowledge and forensic skills with blustering rhetoric and garrulous digression. Although Kinnock's parliamentary performances improved, his reputation for personal incompetence was difficult to shake off. This was particularly irksome to Kinnock's supporters, as he was engaged in a battle on three fronts – against the Conservatives, the SDP and the Militant Tendency. He was showing considerable leadership, for example, on the issue of entryism in the Labour party. In 1985, he even risked disruption to the party, and to his position, by a public condemnation of the Liverpool City Council and its Militant leaders. Even though the stock of the Labour party improved under his direction, the position of the leader increasingly gave rise to controversy. The electoral strategy not just of the Labour party but also of the Conservative party became conditioned to what had become known as the Kinnock factor.

The extent to which the 'Kinnock factor' was a sign of weakness or strength is difficult to determine. The fortunes of the Labour party had been revived under Kinnock's leadership. Nevertheless there was concern in the party that as it rose in contention as an electoral force, Kinnock's personal limitations became more exposed and open to exploitation by the party's critics. The party leader, therefore, could be considered as both a stimulant and depressant at one and the same time. It was because of the importance of matching the strong leadership style of Margaret Thatcher and of the SDP's David Owen, that the Labour party went to such unprecedented lengths to personalise Kinnock's leadership and to use it as proof positive of Labour's electability and fitness to govern (see Chapter 4). The Kinnock factor was accordingly a product of his potential as a party leader. When the Conservative lead in the polls was threatened by Labour under Kinnock's leadership the attacks on him were renewed with the aim of reducing the credibility of the opposition by discrediting the leader.

In February 1987, for example, the Conservative lead had shrunk to 1.5%. Central Office responded with a booklet documenting Kinnock's 'failure of leadership'. Norman Tebbit, the party chairman, had already made clear his intention of countering Labour's attack on Thatcher and Thatcherism with an unremitting pre-election campaign against Kinnock in the expectation that he would 'crack' under the pressure. Senior Tories at Westminster took up the challenge and circulated three Commons motions openly attacking Kinnock in very personal terms. The first declared that

> Kinnock was unsuitable to be leader of the opposition, let alone hold a government post; accused him of being hostile to the monarchy because he once said that watching the Queen's coronation made him feel sick; cited his total lack of ministerial experience; lined him alongside the Militant Tendency and Arthur Scargill; and alleged that his involvement in a scuffle inside the Commons and a fight outside it, together with his 'frequent losses of temper at the despatch box', showed him to lack self-control.[52]

The second implied that he was a security risk. The third claimed he was guilty of deception, intolerance and extremism and that he was intellectually and administratively inadequate to become prime minister.

> Had the motions been tabled, Kinnock would have stood accused of a series of the gravest charges of personal incompetence and irresponsibility ever levelled at a party leader on the Commons order paper.[53]

In an unprecedented move, the Speaker refused, on grounds of prudence and taste, to allow the motions, even though they had been signed by over one hundred MPs. On the other hand, they had had their effect. Like all black propaganda, the objective was one of unanswerable suspicion. They helped to perpetuate the damaging suggestion that Kinnock was Labour's Achilles heel, insofar as he was personally and irredeemably flawed as a political leader. The self-serving intensity of such attacks in the name of the public interest, however, led to other suspicions. If Kinnock was quite so impoverished a leader as the Conservatives portrayed him as being in 1987, it is difficult to see why the governing party would risk giving him such extensive publicity, in order to condemn him.

In the event, Neil Kinnock had a very successful general election in 1987. Although Labour lost the election, he was widely credited with having won the campaign. He had reversed the party's decline, held off the attack by the Liberal–SDP alliance to displace Labour as the chief opposition grouping in the House of Commons, and silenced his critics by achieving poll rankings higher than those ascribed to Mrs Thatcher. Kinnock had proved himself to be not just a strong personal campaigner, but also a leader who could organise a formidable election campaign. He now set his sights on the next general election. He put in motion a large scale policy review of the party's policies with the intention of producing a modern social democratic manifesto to complement the party's proven strength as an electoral organisation. The battle strategy that Labour prepared for was to defuse enough of its policy weaknesses to enable its campaign team to confront the Conservative leadership head on.

While this revision of the party's policies and objectives was in process, Labour and its leader experienced the mixed blessing of Mrs Thatcher's decline. In one way, this was very much to Labour's benefit. It could be construed as a triumph for the opposition and as a vindication of its past condemnation of Mrs Thatcher and her policies. But in another way, it was to Labour's detriment. Labour had prepared for an election against the diminishing asset of Mrs Thatcher's leadership. It was important that she stay in her post. Labour's commitment to a sustained critique of her leadership for its own advantage was based on the assumption that she was irremovable at least before the next general election. When the edifice began to sway, Labour saw its electoral strategy faltering at the same time. As early as April 1991, it was reported that Neil Kinnock and his senior colleagues had

> decided to tone down their personal attacks on Margaret Thatcher because they believed she could be forced to stand down as prime minister.[54]

Party strategists urged the Labour front-bench team to

> switch their fire away from Thatcher and seek to pin the blame for the poll tax, high interest rates and rising inflation on the entire Tory cabinet.[55]

As one shadow cabinet source said at the time:

> We should do or say nothing that would give the Tories the opportunity to make a clean breast of it with the voters and make a new start with a white knight in shining armour.[56]

The net effect of Labour's successful assault upon Mrs Thatcher, therefore, was a new prime minister with assertions of a new government, and with Labour's large lead in the polls wiped out overnight. Although Kinnock's leadership ratings held steady, they were now dramatically eclipsed by those of John Major. In March 1990, Kinnock had been 16 points in front of Mrs Thatcher, but a year later he was 19 points behind Major. Within a matter of a few months, Kinnock's position had again become the subject of controversy. At the same time that the policy review succeeded in removing the party's electorally damaging positions on disarmament, European integration, nationalisation and trade union legislation, the leader who had inspired such a drastic remodelling found his own position open to attack. The party had come up with the weaponry. Now it was faced with doubts over its delivery system.

Labour's response was to close ranks, in order to protect its most important asset. It was now certain that whatever else the election would be about, it would feature a confrontation over leadership that might well be decisive to the result. While Labour had always planned for a presidential style election, the Conservatives given the state of the economy now had no alternative but to give maximum emphasis to John Major. Labour was already committed to Kinnock as it was now very much *his* party. In masterminding its rehabilitation, he had centralised power within the organisation around his office. The sense of order and discipline that he had injected into the opposition had raised its status in the public eye as a party prepared and competent to assume government. For the emphasis to switch away from Kinnock at this stage would be immensely damaging. It would suggest that the party leader was not in control and that the party's confidence in its leader was faltering. Since most of the criticism originated from outside the party, it would look as if the party was still too insecure in its own convictions to provide leadership. And given the extent to which personal leadership was now so central to party image, any doubts about the leader would be translated into doubts about the party as a whole. The party, therefore, was compelled to face a new and popular prime minister on his chosen ground of personal leadership.

This was no easy task for Kinnock as he was now the leader who had become vulnerable in the rapidly developing sphere of leadership politics. It is true that Kinnock was never a popular or even a sympathetic figure outside his own party. Many found him personally unpalatable. As a consequence, the venomous attacks upon his background, intelligence, temperament and integrity in the tabloid press found a receptive audience. Much of this sort of criticism could be ascribed to class or even ethnic prejudice. But not all of Kinnock's handicaps could be written off as purely figments of irrational and partisan spite.

For example, it was difficult to square Kinnock's message of new vision and innovation with the fact that he had been the opposition leader since 1983. It was also difficult to convey modernity and freshness as a party leader when he was confronted both by John Major and Paddy Ashdown who were facing their first election as leaders. Another problem was Kinnock's evident changes of position on such issues as unilateral disarmament, European integration and nationalism. In the past, Kinnock had made it clear that these were matters of personal and party principle. In ditching them as a necessary part of the party's refit, Kinnock laid himself open to the charge that he had compromised his leadership and the party's moral standing for electoral advantage.

A further weakness was seen to lie in the leader's background. To many neutrals, he was a Labour insider who had made his way up through the party apparatus, but in doing so was saddled with its diminishing identity. Kinnock was proud of his Welshness. He identified his integrity as a person and as a leader with what he took to be the integrity of a real community that would be recognisable to all. Its representativeness and general appeal was in doubt. To most floating voters, it may even have been quite alien to their experience. At a time when leaders were increasingly being expected to develop an identity with the general public, 'Kinnock conjure[d] up a world of working-men's clubs, bound by brotherhood, beer, rugby and community singing'.[57] As a consequence, 'his Labour roots in the South Wales industrial heartlands seemed curiously obsolete compared with the mobile, classless milieu of John Major'.[58]

Lastly, there remained the question of Kinnock's personal credentials to be prime minister. This was not simply confined to his lack of government experience, but embraced the nature of his prominence as leader. Kinnock's rise to power had been as a left wing rhetorician. The Kinnock the public saw was not the party manager, but still the emotive orator espousing causes, principles and moral outrage. It raised the concern that Kinnock might appear to be a little too well suited to being Leader of the Opposition and that, as a consequence, he risked disqualifying himself from the more sober responsibilities of being prime minister. His reputation for being highly emotional, excitable and undisciplined was a weakness that had been exploited by opponents in the past and could be used again in the future. Because of Kinnock's alleged gaucheness and lack of gravitas, the Leader of the Opposition helped to raise public interest in a concept of a fit between personality and the prime ministerial office that would always be to the direct advantages of the sitting tenant of Number 10.

Personal factors like these were once thought not to matter very much in the collective context of British government. Elections were traditionally contests between parties and programmes. They were not thought to be influenced by leaders or by the public's estimation of their qualities.[59] Nowadays the position is not so clear. Because of the prominence given to leaders, the issue of leadership has become something of a 'loose cannon' on the parties' decks. It should not be salient, but the constant fear is that it might be critical.

The public's estimation of a party leader's personal characteristics may not be fair, or accurate, or strictly relevant. Nevertheless, that does not prevent such appraisals from being believed capable of having a material effect on a party's public standing, on its electoral potential and on its basic morale. The 'Kinnock factor' was a prime example of the extent to which prima facie questions of personal appeal could be inflated into assertions of personal incompetence on the part of the leaders and, by extension, to claims that the party itself was unfit to govern because of its judgement in having selected such a leader. Even if such charges could be rebuffed, a leader like Kinnock could still be seen as something of a liability (i) for having prompted the charges in the first place; (ii) for drawing on the party's resources to counter the allegations; (iii) for disorientating the party's agenda away from topics sensitive to other parties; and (iv) for raising doubts about the leadership that might never be satisfactorily answered and might persistently recur. Where Kinnock was concerned, the reservations about his leadership took on a momentum of their own. Kinnock was vulnerable to being regarded as a poor leader because of the amount of adverse publicity he attracted. By the same token, because he drew such unfavourable comment, the public propensity to regard him as a poor leader increased in scale. Even though most of the charges may have been quite groundless, therefore, they acquired, by reputation and accumulation, a validity of their own. These had the capacity to damage the leadership enough to make the leader a sustainable issue not just outside the party but inside it as well. Once Kinnock had been saddled with a credibility gap as a person of doubtful prime ministerial material, he laid the Labour party open to bouts of aggressive leadership politics, designed and timed by its opponents to inflict the maximum disruption to the party.

The strategy and tactics behind the usage of the 'Kinnock factor', together with Labour's need to make a response in damage limitation were demonstrated to their fullest effect in September 1991. Using the pretext of reporting a marginal loss of public support for Labour in the latest opinion polls, the *Daily Mail* and the *Daily Express* suddenly launched an intense and sustained attack upon Neil Kinnock. This had occurred before but not with the same ferocity. Banner headlines proclaimed:

Fading Kinnock on Rack (*Daily Express*, 9 September 1991)

Labour Hit by Kinnock Crisis (*Daily Express*, 16 September 1991)

Kinnock Crisis of Confidence (*Daily Mail*, 17 September 1991)

Feature articles analysing Kinnock's change of policies in terms of a betrayal of principles appeared under such headlines as 'Why Kinnock Can Never Be Made Into a Winner'[60] and 'Bend It, Shape It, Anyway Kinnock Wants It'.[61] Kinnock was denounced in editorials as a 'rubberman . . . without any stiffening of long held beliefs'.[62] Labour was said to have been 'rattled to its roots' by the realisation that they had chosen a leader 'destined to be the principal architect of their continued humiliation'.[63] The repeated assertion that Labour was in serious disarray because its leader was 'now the party's biggest liability'[64] began to assume an air of authenticity, as reports of a leadership crisis radiated out into the broadsheets and into radio and television coverage. Senior Conservative figures like Norman Lamont and Tom King helped the controversy along by making public comments on the Labour leader that were then reported as lending further weight to Labour's difficulties. Whether the media had merely reported it, or had actively created it, the net effect of a week of such speculation was the public impression of a party with a chronic leadership problem.

From the Conservative standpoint, it seems clear that, notwithstanding the question of who or what began the critique, the party strategists were intent upon exploiting the situation to the full. With the prime minister considering the option of a November general election, it was tactically prudent to seek to discredit the Labour leader before he entered any purple patch of election campaigning. Even if Major were not to choose a November election, the attack might help to blunt the effect of the Labour party conference, which would be the opposition's best opportunity to acquire massive media exposure before the next general election. Furthermore, the revival of the 'Kinnock factor' would add lustre to John Major's premiership and to the various incumbency 'events', where the prime minister would be centre-stage. As the Conservatives were in some disarray over European union and the economic recession, the emphasis had necessarily devolved upon leadership which the party regarded as its strongest suit.

> Two weekend polls [14 and 15 September 1991] had shown the Tories 4 and 5 percent ahead. Both suggested that voters' doubts about Neil Kinnock were one of the main reasons for the Labour slump. The Tories, already geared up to make the Labour leader the prime target of the election campaign, decided it should be the main reason.[65]

In raising the leadership issue on the back of John Major, however, the party had to ensure that his chief opponent would not gain the initiative on this issue during an election. A pre-emptive strike was required on Kinnock who, during a parliamentary recess, was a much softer target than he would be when he had access to the publicity of the Despatch Box. As one senior Tory disclosed, it was a deliberate attempt to 'demoralise and destabilise' Kinnock.[66]

From the Labour standpoint, there can be little doubt that the party strategists were well aware of what the Conservatives were up to. But such knowledge did nothing to diminish the belief in the probable damage that had been incurred. Labour officials knew, along with Conservative managers, that Kinnock could not be dropped so near to an election. Apart from the constitutional problems that such a course of action would entail, it would utterly undermine the party's claims to unity, coherence, moderation and responsibility. Moreover, it was very much Kinnock's party in spirit and content. The programme on which Labour was committed to fight the election was one that had been devised and brought into existence by the leader. This is not to say that there were no rumbles of discontent, or speculations on the extent to which Kinnock had brought such problems on himself. Even in the midst of the crisis, Kinnock was thought to have made a tactical error in leadership politics. By defending himself in public ('I have been and am a very good captain of the team. You certainly don't drop winning captains'[67]), he merely confirmed that his leadership was in question. The way that Kinnock-bashing, however unwarranted, had so easily derailed the party's chosen agenda away from the recession and the NHS raised the question of whether the ability of a leader to prevent such unfavourable attention had now become a mark of modern leadership.

Polls published in September all added to the pressure on Kinnock. They showed that Kinnock was behind Major in nearly every category of leadership 'in many cases by a formidable margin';[68] that anxiety over Kinnock becoming prime minister headed the public's reservations about voting Labour; and were John Smith to be leader it 'would seriously enhance the party's chances of winning the next election'.[69] When Kinnock attended a shadow cabinet meeting at the Churchill Hotel in London on 17 September, 'he wondered whether he would be passed a revolver'.[70]

In the event, a gun was not made available to Mr Kinnock. The party knew it had to rally round its damaged leader to stand any chance of salvaging its position in the increasingly personalised, but also increasingly important, arena of leadership competition. To help rehabilitate its beleaguered leader, Labour strategists devoted a precious party political broadcast to publicising the personal roots and political integrity of Mr Kinnock. Hugh Hudson's film portrayed Kinnock as a man who was talked down by the press because he was, in the words of one member of the public, the 'one man who understands the problems of the people'.[71] The shadow cabinet did its best to allay concern over the leader by being filmed banging their fists on the table in support of Mr Kinnock – an expression of fealty as unlikely in Labour circles as a 'Tory cabinet throwing lager cans'.[72] And finally, the party in the final conference before the general election, gave its leader a massive vote of confidence by a series of standing ovations that bordered on mass adulation. Even though the party 'has a long tradition of animosity to the "cult of the individual"',[73] it buried such ambivalence in the overriding need to elevate its leader's public standing and to convey the impression that the party was effectively organised for government through the authority of its leader.[74]

The Liberal Democrats

The final closing of the circle around the issue of leadership was provided by the Liberal Democrats. Like Neil Kinnock, Paddy Ashdown had transformed his party. He was credited with having rescued it from the shambles that ensued when the Liberal–SDP alliance broke up after its failure to achieve a 'breakthrough' in the 1987 general election. In June 1988, public support for the Liberal Democrats was down to 7%. But by May 1991, it had risen to nearly 20%. The revival was widely attributed to Ashdown's energetic leadership. In Peter Jenkin's judgement, he had 'resurrected his party . . . in large part, through mastery of the political skills, by making himself a formidable platform speaker, a respected parliamentary performer, and a master of the sound bite'.[75]

Ashdown was also adept at choosing 'big issues' that suggested 'big leadership' – none more so than the theme of democratic renewal, which he made the subject of his final address to the party before the election in September 1991. He referred to new democracies in Eastern Europe and Russia as a spur to Britain's own quest for real citizenship.

> It is the right to a fair vote; the right to freedom under the law; the right to hold a government to account. So why is it that in Britain, Labour and the Conservatives think citizenship is only answering telephone calls on time and having less cones on the M1?[76]

By seeking to give the middle ground a radical and substantive identity, Ashdown attempted to place himself in the position of influencing the agenda of the election. He also sought to establish for himself a vantage point from which he could publicly monitor and evaluate what he portrayed as the two timorously conservative parties lying to the right and to the left.

As the election approached, Ashdown was convinced that he was the only party leader who could not lose. Both Major and Kinnock, on the other hand, had to prevail:

> They have to win, each of them, or the downside is very great, the bitterness of the attacks across the Dispatch Box reveals that. It has the character of High Noon: 'This town ain't big enough for the both of us.' I don't have to win to make progress.[77]

TABLE 8.1 *Public evaluation of party leaders; and public voting intentions*

Do you think that John Major is doing well or badly as Prime Minister?

Well	51%
Neither	17%
Badly	29%
Don't know	3%

Do you think that Neil Kinnock would do well or badly as Prime Minister?

Well	33%
Neither	17%
Badly	46%
Don't know	7%

Do you think that Paddy Ashdown would do well or badly as Prime Minister?

Well	41%
Neither	19%
Badly	25%
Don't know	15%

Voting intentions (excluding don't knows)

Conservative	38%
Labour	42%
Liberal Democrat	15%
Others	5%

SOURCE NOP poll in the *Independent* (21/2/1992).

Both parties had cause to be concerned at Ashdown's capacity for self-public-ity and at his potential not just for providing a home for the disaffected, but for generating large numbers of such volatile voters. Ashdown's strategy was leadership-centred because it was through the publicity he could attract as a dominant leader that the party's message could best be conveyed. He threat-ened to divert attention away from the two main parties and to provide the Liberal Democrats with an audacious sense of distinctiveness expressed through, and vindicated by, its evident provision of public leadership. It is also true that Ashdown embodied in an immediate sense the party's whole strat-egy for power. If the election were to produce a hung parliament, then Ashdown would direct the Liberal Democrats' coalitional negotiations. Should a deal be struck, and Ashdown be given a cabinet seat, then he would provide the physical evidence of the party's successful re-emergence as a national force in British politics.

Ashdown's formidable leadership skills were a problem for Labour because he consistently outranked Kinnock in the opinion polls. In the month before the general election, for example, NOP reported that Ashdown had a considerable lead over Kinnock in the public's estimation of their likely prime ministerial performance (see Table 8.1). Labour's defence of inferior leadership rankings to those of Major were based on grounds of prime ministerial incumbency and authority. Ashdown's high leadership results, therefore, were a source of public embarrassment for the chief opposition party. Ashdown showed that an opposition leader could develop a reputation comparable to that of the prime minister. He also demonstrated that an opposition leader was not destined to run behind his party like Kinnock (i.e. −5%) but could be far out in front of it (i.e. +20%). Ashdown's popularity was a potential problem for the Conservatives as well. First, Ashdown's leadership scores made Major's lead over Kinnock less spectacular and less valuable as a campaigning instrument. Second, Liberals in the past had a record of drawing votes away from the Conservatives. Since the 1992 general election promised to be a close leadership-dominated contest, Ashdown's appeal might be critical to the Conservatives' chances of re-election.

As far as both the main parties were concerned, Ashdown affirmed and extended the trend towards leadership politics. Even if one of the main party leaders might have preferred to assume a lower profile, Ashdown's activism would ensure that such a leader would be the odd one out. The likelihood would be that such an option would be interpreted as a retreat and as a failure of leadership.

The 1992 election campaign

For over a year before the election, the two main parties were observed as having moved to the centre. Major had sought to remove the abrasive radicalism of the previous administration. He was, for example, pressing for improvements in public services so that people would not wish to resort to private provision. Kinnock's team on the other hand had accepted the principle of European integration, the discipline of the ERM (the Exchange Rate Mechanism), the *fait accompli* of Conservative trade union legislation in place, and the need for only greater control, rather than public ownership, over newly privatised monopolies. Labour now recognised that the market was the chief engine of wealth creation. As early as March 1991, John Biffen concluded that the general election was likely to be

> fought by the three main parties on a closer policy consensus than at any time since the 'Butskellism' of the Fifties, when the Conservatives accepted Labour's post-war welfare state and planned economy.[78]

When the election campaign began in March 1992, the two main parties offered a choice, 'but a choice within limited parameters'.[79] As Conservative and Labour were also very close to one another in the opinion polls, the conclusion which was widely drawn at the time was the same one that commentators and analysts had reached over the long gestation period of the election – namely, that in such a close contest, and one that would be dominated to an unprecedented extent by the mass media, the party leaders might make all the difference to their parties' chances of victory or defeat. It was even possible that 'leadership could be the clinching factor'.[80] Hugo Young, for example, accepted both the prediction and the premise upon which it was based.

> This is an election about people. The people involved do matter, the leaders and their henchmen deserve close examination. The election is already charged with presidentialism and this is a just depiction. Personalising politics is frowned on only by those who misunderstand how politics really works. How the leader's juices move, including how he handles impudent scrutiny of the trivia of his life, is legitimate ground to search and judge.[81]

Leaders were expected to occupy a central role in the election not just because they would be spearheading their parties' campaigns, but because they would be personifying their parties to a mass audience. This was a time when both the main parties were 'groping in the centre ground, neither with much clear notion of its new frontiers, but there because the other side was'.[82] It was also a time when an estimated 18.8 million voters[83] (i.e. 44% of the electorate) were unattached to any of the parties and who were, therefore, open to conversion by the parties' chief persuaders.

As a consequence, party leaders were responsible both for cultivating the centre ground and also for giving their parties a sense of differentiation. They were seen as uniquely qualified for the latter in two senses. First, the concentrated attention given to leaders would expose personal qualities and dispositions that would be suggestive of each party's general demeanour and spirit as a whole. And second, the leaders would necessarily occupy and further enhance the arena of leadership politics, within which they would compete with each other on the meaning and provision of leadership. This would raise the salience of leadership as an evaluative category in political judgement and electoral strategy, and lead to an increased public interest in the type of features that always concern Americans in their choice of president –

> a man's record predicting whether he would be calm in a crisis, capable of overcoming bureaucratic inertia, good at selecting subordinates and able to handle criticism.[84]

THE MAJOR CAMPAIGN

Against this background, the Conservative party quickly moved their leader-centred campaign into high gear during the opening week of the campaign.[85] Its first party political broadcast set the tone. 'The Journey' was an evocation of Major's odyssey from Brixton to Downing Street and gave visible expression to the sentiments conveyed in his conference speech. Deploying the same mixture of 'equal parts self-effacement and self-promotion'[86] that he used before, he sought to translate his own personal experiences into qualifications for leadership and public office. In it, Major affirmed that his background was 'an asset not a disadvantage'. It was only when you had 'done something, or seen it, or been it or *felt* it' that you could understand what it meant and how it affected 'other people in their individual lives'.[87] The party's manifesto launch followed the same pattern. At the press conference, the prime minister, surrounded by the cabinet, assured the audience that the manifesto embodied *his* principles and *his* objectives. In order to prevent any misunderstanding, he lent emphasis to the point: 'It's all me, every last word of it is me.'[88] The occasion prompted one celebrated Thatcher-watcher to draw parallels between the two prime ministers. In his view, the comparison revealed the extent to which John Major had not merely emulated, but superseded his predecessor in the personalisation of the campaign.

> The Tories' projection of John Major as the prime issue in this campaign has a startling intensity . . . It is to be seen on the cover of the manifesto, the first the Conservatives have published where the image of the leader entirely dominates the words. Mrs Thatcher, for all her presidentialism, declined, out of prudence or fastidiousness, to wallow in such excess. Her face never appeared on the cover. Hers were years of austerity by comparison.[89]

The uninhibited drive for leadership projection was completed by the party's devices to take Major to the people. As the prime minister could not hope to compete with the platform oratory of Neil Kinnock, Conservative strategists sought to exploit Major's informality and in particular his ability to communicate well to small audiences. The strategy devolved into two main types of presentation. The first had Major sitting on a stool, taking question and answer sessions, amidst small groups of party supporters. The second, and much more important, device was a custom built £500,000 circular stage. It resembled a miniature coliseum coloured in shades of blue. The banked rows of circular seating gave emphasis to the focal point of the central stage. It also allowed Major to remain in intimate contact with his audience which, because of the seating arrangements, was almost devoid of any hierarchy of front and back rows or of central and side views. Apart from providing a setting tailored to the prime minister's conversational and undemonstrative style, the stage was intended to produce a visual simulation of incumbency. It attempted to do so firstly by providing a suitable arena for the prime ministerial podium from which Major could make his key campaign speeches; and secondly by screening around the back wall of the auditorium a tableau of video clips celebrating Major as prime minister. With the aura of incumbency in mind, Shaun Woodward – the party's Director of Communications – had also expressly intended the stage to produce a symbolic re-enactment of what he considered to be John Major's finest hour as prime minister. This definitive scene of the Major premiership was the occasion when he met, mixed with, and was subsequently surrounded by appreciative British troops in the Gulf.

Neil Kinnock was confronted with the task of leading the Labour campaign against an unpopular government with a popular leader. Labour had attempted to target Major for personal criticism before the election but its efforts had not met with much success. Even after a more than a year in office, Major was the Teflon prime minister. In an *Observer*/Harris poll in January 1992, for example, only 9% blamed Mr Major's government for the recession; 28% believed it was nobody's fault as it was an international slump, while 43% still believed that Mrs Thatcher's government was to blame.[90] Combined with the mercurial nature of his chief opponent, Kinnock suffered the additional handicap of his own lack of appeal, which was made ever more conspicuous by opinion polls, and the articles and graphics spawned by them. Only three weeks before the election was called, an *Observer*/Harris poll reported that the distaste for Kinnock headed the reasons why voters would not vote Labour. As many as 37% named Kinnock as an obstacle to supporting the party.[91] The poll led Nicholas Wapshott, the *Observer*'s political editor, to conclude that 'failure to overcome Mr Kinnock's negative public image could deprive Labour of victory at the election'.[92] Even more serious was the result of the Harris poll produced for the ITV's *Special Inquiry* programme screened on 15 March 1992 at the start of the election campaign. This asked what deterred *floating* voters, and therefore, those most likely to decide the election, from supporting the various parties. The prospect of Kinnock as prime minister headed their anxieties over Labour. It was mentioned by 47% of the sample. Even when the focus was narrowed to floating Labour voters (i.e. that portion of the floating voters already disposed to support Labour), 35% found Neil Kinnock to be an obstacle to choosing Labour.[93]

It is true that opposition leaders always find it very difficult to generate a favourable public impression when competing with the authority and pomp of an incumbent prime minister. But once the incumbency factor is diminished and public attention is more equally shared in an election campaign, then opposition leaders can be expected to reduce the deficit. Since Kinnock was a proven campaigner, it was always likely that he would make headway in the leadership polls, especially when the avowed partisanship of an election campaign would redistribute leadership support more in line with party voting intentions. The conspicuously high negative rating for Kinnock might also have been made artificially prominent through Labour's collective strength across a wide range of other issues. Alternatively, mentioning Kinnock as an obstacle to voting Labour may simply have been an 'easy option for those who had reservations about Labour'[94] all along. Whatever the likely diagnoses and prognoses, it became evident that the Labour leadership strategy would be a muted one. Kinnock would still front the party, but in a less personalised way than 1987. Kinnock now equated leadership with the ability to construct and manage a team of able colleagues. He offered his credentials as 'a man who had demonstrated over the years the ability to lead, to set sensible objectives (and) to involve people in a talented team'.[95] 'I think that does distinguish me from Mr Major', he said. 'Whatever his personal quality, he has demonstrated that he is not the most competent of team leaders.'[96] After seeking for years to emulate Mrs Thatcher's leadership qualities, Kinnock now changed tack. He implicitly conceded that Major had taken Mrs Thatcher's central place in government, but that this was neither a sign of leadership nor something to be condoned. In an interview with Robin Oakley, Kinnock explained that in the Tory years there had been too narrow a focus on the prime minister at the centre of all decision-making. This had undermined the British system. What was now required, in Kinnock's view, was a 'very substantial step away from that' to the 'strongly-led team government'[97] that he was offering to the British people. This was regarded as real leadership as it would take the government and the country into a genuine post-Thatcher condition. In accordance with this strategy, Kinnock acted as chairman of the board. He and his shadow cabinet concentrated on presenting a confident posture of an alternative government in waiting, content with their lead in the polls and in their conviction that they had wrong-footed the Conservative party again. 'We are selling the team rather than the individual' said a Labour source, quoted in the the *Sunday Times*: 'The Tories are trying to establish a new leader, fighting the same campaign we fought in 1987. We have moved on.'[98]

After two weeks of campaigning, neither of the two main parties showed any sign of a breakthrough. Frustration bred criticism. On the Conservative side, party supporters were beginning to condemn the campaign for its lack of direction, its negativity, and even its ineptitude. Since Mr Major dominated the campaign, mistakes and misjudgements were closely identified with the leader. His organisation at Central Office was drawing criticism for its inexperience and its lacklustre campaign. More disconcerting than anything else for the Conservatives was the realisation that they were faltering in the leadership politics – the one area where they were expected to prevail.

The first problem was that the Kinnock factor had not appeared. The Conservatives had relied upon Kinnock to expose his alleged vulgarities as a politician during the campaign. He had not done so. Labour's safety-first campaign had effectively ensured that whatever weaknesses Kinnock might possess were being neutralised by careful management. Andrew Neil in the *Sunday Times* might complain that Mr Kinnock was 'being kept hermetically sealed from any events to stop him shooting his mouth off'[99] but the Conservatives were beginning to fear that a self-inflicted gaffe by Kinnock might not make an appearance. This was a serious setback. The party planners had organised the campaign around a choice between the proven leadership of 'honest John' against the doomsday scenario of Kinnock's unfitness to be prime minister. But as Joe Rogaly reported at the time, the Labour party was not following the government's script.

> The Labour leader had spoiled the game. He has declined to play. Mr Kinnock's face is not on the Labour manifesto. His presence on TV is carefully controlled by members of his staff . . . The difficulty for the Conservatives is that Mr Major is running for president against a Labour party that is running for parliamentary control and a Labour leader who is running for prime minister. Mr Kinnock will not stand still to be compared with Mr Major.[100]

Charles Moore of the *Daily Telegraph* agreed. He regretted that John Major declined the Leader of the Opposition's invitation to a television debate. Major would then have been in a position to show that he was the 'best prime minister of the three, with the greatest grasp of policy and the clearest idea of what he wished to do'.[101] As Moore commented at the time,

> It is no good arguing that a British General Election is not presidential because nowadays it is.[102]

As a consequence, Major needed to engage Kinnock on a leader-to-leader basis, in order to force home his advantage as prime minister.

The evasiveness and reasonableness of the Labour leader led to the Conservatives' other problem in this area. Since Labour was refusing to fall on its sword, the responsibility for winning the election now fell squarely upon Major and his highly personalised campaign. But without the contrast of an accident-prone Kinnock, Major's own limitations as a campaigner came conspicuously to the fore. By the end of March, Conservative ambivalence was beginning to give way to quiet despair as party supporters, MPs and ministers speculated over whether the lacklustre campaign was the effect of a turgid Central Office or the reflection of a prime minister who was simply devoid of the passion required to conduct a national campaign. They pressed 'the Tory high command to adopt a more aggressive style although they did not want to prejudice Mr Major's popular image'.[103] The 'Kinnock factor' began to be displaced by the 'Major factor' as the Conservative chances of victory increasingly appeared to centre upon the nature and deployment of the prime minister's personality. To Ian Bell of the *Observer*, Major's own lack of identity seriously threatened that of the party. 'Niceness is now an issue', Bell pointed out.

> It works well in theory and in the polls, but the Tories plainly have no idea how to market it on the campaign trail.[104]

Paul Johnson in the *Sunday Telegraph* asserted that the usage of niceness was not the issue. What was required was for John Major to be altogether less nice and 'to go for the jugular'. Johnson continued:

> It is up to John Major now, this very morning, to take the Tory campaign by the scruff of its neck and shake it into action. He must shock the nation. . . . To win this election, he must campaign like a man possessed.[105]

But Trevor Fishlock in the same paper questioned whether Major was capable of depicting aggression.

> What you see is what you get. He is a genuine article. The packagers are promoting him as a decent man, which is what he is. . . . The campaign emphasis is entirely Major, his face and sincere smile the motif. But the managers have a problem because . . . they wanted him to be not only nice but also Basher Major. They wanted him to be more than life size. They have a leader, but they want more. They want a general, an inspirer, a rouser of crowds. But so far Major is Major.[106]

THE KINNOCK CAMPAIGN

Neil Kinnock also received criticism for his highly circumspect campaign. The presentation of an alternative budget, the portrayal of the shadow cabinet as the executive board of a multinational corporation, together with Kinnock's own offensive of double-breasted charcoal suits, his customised red rose jet aircraft and his VIP Daimler, all sought to give the impression of a prime minister and government in everything but name. The members of the shadow cabinet were allocated new titles to press home the effect. The shadow chancellor, for example, became 'Labour's chancellor of the exchequer'. Labour's treasury team posed for pictures on the steps of the Treasury to provide a sense of imminent, but also reassuring, change. But while all this emphasis on presentation may have helped to defuse doubts over Neil Kinnock's leadership, it was not producing a decisive breakthrough in the polls. The neutrality of the campaign began to cause disquiet amongst Labour supporters who feared that the party's potential was not being fully realised. While governments might for the most part win or lose elections, concern grew that on this occasion the huge opportunity for Labour, provided by a recession election, might be wasted through excessive caution at the top. Looking safe and responsible as a government in transition might not be enough. R.W. Johnson believed Labour's inhibition was a handicap:

> What Labour's campaign lacks, in a word, is populism. A yawning political gap exists for someone willing to promise undeniably popular things.[107]

Ian Aitken in the *Guardian* also began to have doubts about the lack of moral fervour and sense of purpose that he believed an opposition needed to displace even a tired government. He found it inexplicable that while Labour possessed 'the only contemporary politician capable of singing an uplifting song to which the nation could march', the party appeared

> determined to keep him under wraps, presumably in the belief that the opinion polls are right in portraying him as a liability rather than an asset.[108]

But to Mr Aitken, Kinnock was not a liability as a political campaigner.

> He is capable of matching Mrs Thatcher with that physical impression of commitment to an ideal. He looks like a man who believes in himself and his message, and he can convey that to vast audiences. It is time he was unleashed.[109]

THE ASHDOWN CAMPAIGN

For both the main party leaders, the 1992 campaign was massively complicated by the resurgence of the Liberal Democrats. They were using their general election exposure to maximum effect. Paddy Ashdown not only led his party's campaign but personified it, almost in its entirety. As the Liberal Democrats' chief electoral asset, Ashdown revelled in the sort of public attention that was generally denied to him at Westminster. It was through his ability to exploit the politics of leadership that the party acquired the appearance of at least being comparable to the two main parties. The furious pace of Ashdown's campaigning, combined with his skill in using the media to convey his party's ideals and objectives, made him a constant threat to Neil Kinnock and John Major.

Apart from the problems incurred by the prospect of a Liberal Democrat surge in marginal seats and of tactical voting in less marginal seats, the third party posed a number of other dangers. First, as the Liberal Democrats became squeezed in the increasingly crowded centre ground of the 'post-Thatcherite consensus', the party tried to wrong-foot its challengers by oscillating between the right and the left in its policy positions. For example, it wholeheartedly embraced market economics and dismissed Labour's redistributive taxation proposals whilst offering a series of radical reforms to local government finance, to education and, most importantly, to the constitutional structure of Britain. This eclecticism in policy was an attempt to carve out a particular identity for the party in the centre, while at the same time allowing it occasionally to outflank the opposition.

Second, the Liberal Democrats adopted a position above the area of normal political competition and, thereby, above the squeeze at the centre. From this vantage point, the party could appeal to those who were disaffected, not only by each of the two main parties, but also by the two party system itself. This lofty platform permitted the Liberal Democrats to engage in the kind of systemic, and apparently objective, criticism of British politics that threatened to generate a dissenting constituency of anti-politics. Lastly, the party built on its roots of local political activism to make a concerted effort to portray itself as moving in and amongst the people. It openly courted and encouraged 'people power' and actively dissociated it from party power. As leader, Ashdown plunged himself into an 18 hour a day schedule of open public campaigning designed to take himself bodily to the voters.

The Liberal Democrats' battle plan, therefore, was essentially a diamond-shaped strategy. The horizontal plane consisted of a liberated capacity to choose good policies, irrespective of ideological pedigrees. At the top of the vertical plane was a principled detachment from what was characterised as the 'punch and judy show' of Conservative and Labour vested interests. At the base of the vertical plane was a principled attachment to the public in its most immediate sense. Central to the coherence of the whole scheme was the leader. It was his 'vision' and his celebration of common sense that provided the substitute for ideology. It was his vitality as leader that symbolised the independence of a third force to emancipate Britain from outmoded political structures and practices, and to redeem the country from what Ashdown repeatedly referred to as forty years of failed leadership.

The two main parties may have taken comfort from the fact that the Liberal Democrats were not an alternative government and would in all likelihood be squeezed out of contention on polling day. Polls showed that the public was deterred from voting for the party because of its inexperience in government and because a Liberal Democrat vote was widely considered to be a wasted vote. According to this view, the party had been, and would continue to be, a staging post of dissent through which huge numbers of disaffected voters would pass before lodging their support with one or other of the two main parties. But despite the soft quality of the Liberal Democrat support, the polls also showed that Ashdown was proving to be a formidable campaigner. For example, two weeks into the campaigning, Gallup asked voters which leader and party had been the most impressive in its campaigning. Only 17%

chose Major's campaign. Over a quarter (28%) thought Kinnock's to be the best campaign. But it was Ashdown who headed the rankings with more than a third (34%) believing his campaign to be the most impressive.[110]

Ashdown may not have been in a position to win the election, but there was concern that he could derail the strategies of his opponents. For example, the Liberal Democrat campaign encouraged an increase in undecided voters. This made the Conservative and Labour strategists even more intent upon running tighter campaign ships, in order to ensure that floaters would have no reason *not* to vote for their respective parties. But with the greater number of undecideds in this election[111] and with the increasingly cautious outlooks of the Labour and Conservative leaders, Ashdown had the opportunity to play the maverick leader who could break out of the impasse and seriously embarrass the other leaders and their credentials for leadership. Ashdown used leadership as an issue, and as a mark of party differentiation, that gave a qualitative advantage to the Liberal Democrats to compensate for their quantitive handicaps. Arguably, it was the imaginative licence and rapid response of its leadership that enabled the Liberal Democrats both to address issues like the environment and European integration, which the main parties wished to ignore, and to embrace the dimension of constitutional change. In the view of the *Guardian*, for example, 'the only real winner of this campaign' was Mr Ashdown. The paper continued:

> The movement and the arguments and the actual switches in allegiance have all come from Liberal Democrat advance. They are the movers and shakers. And Mr Ashdown himself has indefatigably carried so much of the fight on his own shoulders.[112]

Although the two main parties complained that Ashdown's condescending and censorious attitude towards them was infuriatingly sanctimonious and self-serving, he nevertheless succeeded in raising the stakes of leadership politics. He fuelled doubts over the dynamics between the growing sector of undecided voters and the presence of two carefully packaged leaders in close proximity to one another.

Another way in which Ashdown threatened to disrupt the Labour and Conservative campaigns was by openly challenging the outsider status of Major and Kinnock. This issue had already aggravated Labour. It contested the view that Major was the archetypal 'ordinary man'. Far from giving weight to his avowed outsider credentials and his claims to spatial leadership, Major's critics believed that his background and personality contradicted his own icon – i.e. the average man, with unshakeable principles and extraordinary ability, acting as public champion. The Labour view was that Major was really what he seemed:

an identikit bank manager tendency Tory with an orthodox record of hard work, clubability and boot-licking. His CV to date reveals no achievements, no blunders, no interesting scraps, no distinctions, no character flaws and no strong opinions. He zig-zagged to the top by not being dogmatic and not being a threat to She Who Must be Obeyed.[113]

Even *The Economist* was keen to dispel any illusions that Major represented something other than a self-effacing administrator who 'emerged, blinking, into the daylight at the top of the skyscraper after years of smooth upward movement on a hidden elevator . . . Mr Major got on as an insider, part of a management elite – not as a leader.'[114] In comparison to Mr Kinnock, the prime minister was perceived by his critics to be incapable of providing a plausible, or even a desirable, model for the wider public. Blake Morrison of the *Independent on Sunday* described the contrast in the following terms.

> At best what Neil Kinnock means to people is roots and family and fighting your way up, whereas John Major, though as much a meritocrat, belongs in some self-effacing, self-erasing, gosh-how-did-I-get-to-be-here nowhereland. Mr Kinnock, on walkabouts, has a habit of asking people exactly where they live and/or grew up, a manoeuvre which may itself dwell in the realms of higher bullshit, but which makes people feel safer than they do in the faceless, rootless world of Majorism.[115]

In this battle to be Mr Everyman, the sheer scale of Ashdown's public engagement threatened to throw the more measured and cautious campaigns of Kinnock and Major into sharp relief. Ashdown's background and his own spell of unemployment was used to develop his status as a man apart from the establishments of both the right and the left. His adherence to his party was portrayed as a matter of conviction at the expense of power. 'He doesn't go where power would come easily, but where he can believe'[116] his wife told the *Sunday Times*. From this citadel of moral integrity, Ashdown could take up his watching brief on the restrictive practices of the two party system. Ashdown proffered independent commentary, open minded criticism, and a voice for the 'silent majority'. The very ostracism he had experienced at Westminster as 'a member of a club that had him under sufferance'[117] as a third party leader, he believed gave him an advantage in a general election. 'I'm an outsider' he said, 'trying to speak up for all the outsiders. All the people out there in this election are outsiders . . . If I have any strength out there it's because people don't regard me as a politician.'[118]

Election 92 and modern leadership politics

While the Leader of the Opposition was content to maintain his 'rose garden' campaign, it was the prime minister who felt compelled to change tactics. He was pressed by his party's deficit in the polls, by party criticism over an inept campaign, by the threat of the Liberal Democrats and by his declining lead over Kinnock that showed his popularity was 'not the electoral asset for the Conservatives it once was'.[119] As a consequence, Major became more aggressive towards his opponents. He sought to outflank them in their drive to displace his outsider status and his claims to spatial leadership. In the most richly symbolic move of the campaign, the prime minister appeared to dispense with the contrivances of modern campaigning in favour of immersing himself in the crowds and speaking with a loud-hailer on top of a soap box. Whether this was as contrived as the 'blue coliseum' remains open to argument. Whether it was born out of desperation or design is also debatable. What is clear is that on Saturday 28 March, Major rode into Luton, set up his soap box and began campaigning directly to the people. The national media were there to cover the spectacle. They reported it as a dramatic move by Major to break away from his handlers and to refute the public relations executives and market analysts of Central Office. Edward Stourton of ITN typified the coverage.

> Under pressure about his campaign, Mr Major today shook off the controlled style of the image-makers and took to raw electioneering, plunging into a crowd where supporters and opponents fought to make themselves heard. This was old-fashioned soap box electioneering that has not been seen from a prime minister for some thirty years.[120]

Major sought to relaunch his campaign by relaunching himself as a person, who by choice and motivation had a preference for real-life dialogue and unmediated contact with the public. Should this impression not be clear to the media, Sir Norman Fowler, who accompanied Major on the stump, was on hand to make the meaning of the event quite explicit. 'His strength comes from the people. He likes meeting the people and that is what this campaign exemplifies.'[121] The Luton experience was repeated on most of the remaining days of the campaign. On each occasion, it drew large crowds, generated demonstrations, and ensured extensive coverage. It was a spectacle that provided the excitement of the unexpected and unscheduled. It showed the prime minister being jostled and heckled. Abuse and eggs were hurled at him. It was a classic case of self-inflicted populism in which Major would appear as the non-conformist politician, breaking campaign norms, defying security, dropping his guard, and risking everything by trusting the people.

Critics like Edwina Currie complained that Major's new tactics were undermining his advantages as prime minister and making him look like a Leader of the Opposition – with the result that Neil Kinnock was increasingly made to resemble a prime minister designate. But such criticism only served Major's purpose. It strengthened the image of a leader acting against advice, secure in his own judgement and sense of purpose. It also lent weight to a notion that Major himself had initiated and was keen to give as much circulation as possible. This was the proposition that Major could only really be himself by being out and amongst the public. Far from being driven by political desperation, the soapbox to Major was a form of release. It was not a last resort so much as something he had wanted to do all along. This was certainly the impression conveyed by the television correspondents. John Simpson (BBC) observed that 'his new streetfighting tactics seemed to have liberated him'.[122] Peter Allan (ITN) agreed that 'prime ministerial or not this is the style with which Mr Major feels at ease . . . the style which he finds most agreeable'.[123] The message was that the prime minister remained in nature an outsider who could relate closely to the general public. The pointedly old-fashioned soapbox conformed to the integrity of his adopted role as that of a citizen politician defending 'you' the public from 'them' – large, unseen and threatening forces. The audacity of his unorthodox and even amateurish tactics also served to place Neil Kinnock's highly professional campaign in a bad light. Major's emphasis upon personal leadership in aggravated conditions provided a strong contrast to the collective caution of Labour's highly managed 'team' approach. His high-risk ventures not only cast doubts on Labour's softly softly strategy, but threatened to wrest the initiative in leadership politics away from both Kinnock and Ashdown. On 9 April the Conservatives won the election and John Major was acclaimed for having successfully defended his position as prime minister. What was just as clear was the extent to which leadership politics in this country had grown in scale, intensity and sophistication. The election demonstrated the extraordinary way that perceptions of leaders and leadership suffused the campaign. They penetrated discussions over political strategy and tactics, they pervaded estimations of the parties and they coloured the views of government records, party policies and electoral promises.

Professional analysts may have derided this fascination with leaders as vacuous, but they could do little to resist its effects. Anthony King, for example, reminded his readers in the *Daily Telegraph* that survey evidence always suggests that leaders are

> only one element in a larger mix. Like prospective diners in a restaurant, they are interested in the food, the decor and the standards of hygiene – not just in who happens to be head waiter.[124]

But having acknowledged this conventional wisdom, he nevertheless felt compelled, by public interest and the nature of leadership-centred electioneering, to devote considerable space to examining Gallup's leadership polls and to draw substantive conclusions from them. For example:

> Major/Kinnock contrast is a real one in many voters' minds and it works in the Tories' favour.[125]

> Gallup's findings suggest that he [Kinnock] remains a serious handicap to Labour. He appears to put off large numbers of potential Labour supporters.[126]

Newsworthy interpretations like these, drawn from over 50 polls published during the election period, helped to enhance the salience of leadership in the public's view of the political struggle. In the process, they also helped to increase the market for more elaborate leadership polls and for even more emphasis upon the results. Another feature of the 1992 election which served to illustrate the dynamics of leadership politics was the high level of 'leadership stretch'. Irrespective of whether the leaders wished to dominate or did dominate their respective campaigns, they were portrayed as doing so. Each leader was not only regarded as being responsible for his party's campaign, he was seen as personifying its principles, its programme and its general fitness to govern. This was largely as a result of the enormous media exposure that was given to the party leaders. Like all modern campaigns, the 1992 election was fought primarily through the medium of television. Party leaders depended upon television for public attention. Likewise, television relied upon the leaders' joint capacity to generate pictures, sounds and stories. The priority given to leaders was structural and self-perpetuating. If a leader wished to delegate national campaigning to another member of his party for a day, the likelihood was that his deputy would not receive either the same scale of coverage, or the same priority in the news reports. This was a frequent complaint of Paddy Ashdown when he was accused of being a 'one-man band'. To news organisations, party leaders were top billing. Viewers expected to see the leaders and how they had spent their day on the campaign trail.

An example of this dynamic in action was provided by the Labour party of Wales pre-election rally in Cardiff.[127] The meeting was attended by Neil Kinnock and five members of the shadow cabinet. All six gave a speech to the rally but the BBC and ITN cameras covered only Kinnock's address. The impression conveyed on both the BBC's *Nine O'Clock News* and ITN's *News at Ten* was that the rally had only been addressed by the party leader. The other five members of the shadow cabinet were neither shown on the platform, nor even mentioned.

This small example was repeated unremittingly during the four weeks of the campaign. Research by the Communications Centre at Loughborough

TABLE 8.2 *Number of broadcasting appearances[a] by main party figures*

Conservative		
John Major	175	
Norman Lamont	62	
Chris Patten	35	} 147
Margaret Thatcher	28	
Michael Heseltine	22	
Labour		
Neil Kinnock	162	
John Smith	55	
Roy Hattersley	21	} 112
Robin Cook	19	
John Cunningham	17	
Liberal Democrat		
Paddy Ashdown	152	
Des Wilson	46	
Alan Beith	18	} 88
David Steel	16	
Malcom Bruce	8	

[a]These are measured by the number of times each politician appeared on BBC 1 *Nine O'Clock News*, ITN *News at Ten*, BBC 2 *Newsnight* and BBC Radio 4 *Today* (between 8 am and 9 am) during the period from 9/3/1992 to 8/4/1992.

SOURCE Communications Research Centre at Loughborough University, published in the *Guardian*, (11/4/1992).

University showed that the extent of leadership stretch was considerable.[128] The number of broadcasting appearances[129] made by John Major (175), Neil Kinnock (162) and by Paddy Ashdown (152) were far in excess of the rest of the top five spokespersons for each party put together.

The Communications Centre's study of the length of time politicians spoke on the main television news programmes[130] also revealed a clear supremacy by the party leaders. Major accounted for 42% of the speaking time of all Conservative spokespersons. The equivalent figures for Neil Kinnock and Paddy Ashdown were 57% and 73% respectively. On the basis of these figures, it was possible to conclude that 'the focus on party leaders suggested an advanced degree of "presidentialisation" in the coverage'.[131]

The level of 'presidentialisation' was perhaps even greater than these figures imply. Such studies only measure the number of appearances or the precise amount of air-time absorbed in speaking. They do not take into account the time that the leaders are on camera, nor the running order and priority of news featuring the leaders. A small survey was undertaken for this study in an attempt to measure the extent of the leaders' domination of the campaign news in these respects. The survey covered the two main daily news programmes[132] over the final four days of the campaign. It measured the time devoted to the leaders, as a proportion of the campaign news.[133] The study revealed that the coverage of the leaders not merely speaking but also making public appearances and giving photo-opportunities, amounted on average to 73.6% of the daily campaign news reports. When this is combined with the fact that news of the leaders almost invariably came at the top of each programme's schedule, it greatly substantiates the impression of leadership stretch.

Closely related to leadership stretch was another facet of modern electioneering which became increasingly conspicuous during the 1992 contest. This is what might be called 'a sense of campaign'. This referred to the marked growth in the way the campaign itself became an object of observation and assessment. The coverage afforded to the strengths and weaknesses, and to the advances and setbacks, of the different party campaigns – combined with the near obsessional concern with opinion polls – had the effect of making the campaign a newsworthy story in its own right. In many respects, it became an issue in the election itself. Public awareness of the instrumentalities of political marketing and salesmanship was raised by numerous features on the techniques of the party's 'hidden persuaders'. Articles appeared, for example, on Saatchi's efforts for the Conservative party and on the contributions made by film directors like Hugh Hudson and John Schlesinger to their party campaigns. Television programmes like the BBC's *The Vote Race* series and special editions of Channel 4's *Dispatches* investigated the media strategies of the party image-makers. These and other contributions all helped to build up a sense that the campaign was a piece of political theatre with its own criteria for analysis and judgement. 'It is striking how commentators now analyse the campaign as an end in itself, almost as an art form',[134] remarked Professor Dennis Kavanagh. *The Economist* complained that the 'endless discussion of party tactics often replaced discussions of the policies the parties were putting forward'.[135] Polls on the qualities of the different party campaigns added further momentum to public discussion and to the public's awareness of 'spin doctors', minders and party strategists.

This 'sense of campaign' could lead to public disquiet over the ulterior motives, and even the reality, behind what was being portrayed to it by the parties. It also led to the same paradox as that experienced by American presidents. The more that politicians tried to reach people, the more they found themselves separated from them by a screen of handlers and media advisors. It was precisely this conundrum that Major sought to resolve by seeming to break out of his party's bubble of campaign management. He did so in public – equating an allegedly daring lack of contrivance with true and unmediated public relations. But the main effect of the 'sense of campaign' was the way it spawned a profusion of observations, arguments and theories on the subject of leadership and, in particular, on the relationship between leaders, and their parties' campaigns and electoral prospects. These views and debates were afforded extraordinary prominence. They were all predicated on the centrality of leadership to the parties' campaigns and on the existence of an indeterminate, but material, connection between each party's leader and its prospective performance on election day. Controversy surrounded questions like the nature of a good or bad campaign; the significance of prime ministerial appearance and behaviour; the problems involved in characterising a campaign as 'presidential' in the British context; the extent to which the criteria for an effective prime ministerial campaign were different to those for an effective campaign by an opposition leader; and whether leadership was distinguished more by positive or negative campaigning, or whether its essence in modern conditions was more related to defusing criticism of the party and to removing the leader from controversy.

John Major was the subject of several controversies surrounding the Conservative campaign. He was, for example, accused of running a tactically inept campaign that revealed his inexperience in leadership politics. After beginning a carefully conceived campaign in one style, the Conservative party was said to have changed tactics in a way that revealed a lack of faith in its own judgement. One of the Labour campaign team expressed dismay at the lack of sophistication at Central Office.

> They spend a year building up John Major as the polite soft-spoken, popular man of the people. He was supposed to be above the battle. Then, at the first sign of things going wrong, they throw all that over and get him snarling at the Labour party. If you draw up a strategy that you think is right, you have to stick with it.[136]

In a revealing review by a fellow leader, Paddy Ashdown thought that the prime minister had made an 'enormous tactical error'[137] in the leadership contest. He had not only mentioned his main opponent, but had actively and openly engaged in a negative campaign against him. Mrs Thatcher had always ignored the challengers to her position. She wished to deny them even the appearance of any comparability of status. To Ashdown, the prime minister's allusions to the nightmare on Kinnock street were a poor use of his resources as leader. Ashdown told Peter Jenkins that for Major,

> To lower himself to the business of attacking Kinnock devalued his greatest

assets as a nice, sensible man. He should have treated Kinnock with due disdain and prime ministerial superiority.[138]

But the example which best conveys the extraordinary range and intensity of the issues that swirled around the subject of political and campaign leadership in Britain was provided by Neil Kinnock.

The Labour party had built up the leadership, in order to increase public confidence in its coherence both as a party and as an alternative government. Kinnock himself had been instrumental in the transformation of Labour into a conspicuously leader-led party. His dominance of the party coincided with its revival as an electoral force. And yet, the closer the party came to full recovery, the more that Kinnock's qualifications for high office came into question. The 1987 campaign had been designed to build Kinnock up into an emphatically dominant party leader. The 1992 campaign was expected to be similar, but was in fact quite different. The party seemed intent upon building Kinnock down into a team captain figure.

This strategy generated a series of tensions that were to afflict the Labour party throughout the campaign. For example, Kinnock was obliged to meet the modern campaigning requirements for high-profile leadership, while at the same time seeking to keep to the party's game plan in which he was to be just a part of its collection of political talent. His previous existence as an attention-gathering orator was subordinated to his new role of looking and sounding 'prime ministerial'. This generated a sense of disjunction in which Kinnock acted as a party leader, but at the direct expense of developing his public leadership. A party's leadership has to be seen to have the ability to organise a campaign. Where Kinnock was concerned, he was being given credit for a sound party campaign, but at the same time he was being criticised for appearing to be a captive of the Labour strategy. The stark contrast in style between the 1987 Kinnock and the 1992 Kinnock fuelled fresh doubts about Kinnock's leadership credentials. If the packaging of the Labour leader was sufficient to portray a wholly different exterior to that which the public was accustomed to seeing, then it was also enough to raise suspicions that it might be concealing deficiencies. The more Kinnock tried to be prime ministerial, the more he was accused of only *appearing* to be prime ministerial, which was tantamount to not being prime ministerial at all. He was duly criticised for acting out of character and for failing to maximise the campaign potential of an opposition leader.

It became evident that Kinnock was being torn between being an 'up-front' public leader and what could only be described in the light of precedent and expectation as a 'down-front' team player. The disjunction was so great to a public that had become more conscious of the sophisticated techniques of political marketing, that questions began to be asked about which Kinnock was the real Kinnock. If the 'up-front' Kinnock was false, then it might be deduced that the leader really was being covered by, and carried by, the shadow cabinet. If the 'down-front' Kinnock was false, then Kinnock might be seen to be deliberately trying to pull the wool over the eyes of a nervous public. It would also suggest that the Labour team was as poor as its leader and that the party's policy programme might be similarly misleading. The competence of the campaign, therefore, could in itself be a sign of the leader's own incompetence. With the leader giving the appearance of concealing himself and with the party giving the appearance of complicity in keeping its leader from unscripted public contact, intense controversy was aroused over the Labour campaign and, in particular, over the role of the leadership within it. The public found it difficult to square Kinnock Mark I with Kinnock Mark II, or to reconcile either Kinnock with current Labour policies. The confusion of images suggested a hidden agenda, or worse, evidence of hidden incompetence.[139]

Labour's mass rally of party supporters at the Sheffield Arena was widely thought to have brought many of these strains to a head. On the same day that Labour's opinion poll lead stretched to what looked like a decisive 7 point margin,[140] the party staged a huge £150,000 spectacle of music, lights, fireworks, celebrity endorsements and political speeches. Brian Hanrahan of the BBC reported it to be 'the nearest British equivalent to an American style convention'.[141] Tim Ewart of ITN described it as 'an electronic extravaganza designed to portray Mr Kinnock as a president in waiting'.[142] And John Cole (BBC) referred to it as 'undoubtedly the most astonishing political meeting I have seen since Kennedy's attempt to win the Democratic nomination in New York in 1980'.[143] The celebration of imminent government was crowned by the appearance of Mr Kinnock. His helicopter's descent and landing was transmitted onto a giant video screen to the 11,000 ticket-holders inside the auditorium. With the shadow cabinet visibly in the shadows, Kinnock gave an address that in its passion and emotion was of vintage quality. Its reception, however, was mixed. Inside the hall, the party supporters were rapturous in their approval of it as a rallying cry for victory. Outside the hall in the wider public domain, Kinnock's Sheffield performance was widely construed to have been damaging both to his, and the party's, new image. In truth, the speech itself was torn on the one hand between a party leader's attempt to rally the troops and to defend socialism, and on the other a prime ministerial address giving emphasis to social consensus, community obligation and patriotic purpose. But the former detracted from the latter. The more uninhibited and jubilant Kinnock became, the more he aroused misgivings. He came near to undermining one leadership style with another. No matter how hard he tried to control the partisan sectarianism of the event with allusions to prime ministerial nationalism, he risked portraying himself as an insider who had risen within, and who embodied, the insider culture of the Labour party. He also risked giving weight to a widespread impression concerning the 'possible mismatch of his private and public personality, the feeling that despite the passion, he is somehow artificial'.[144] Finally, Kinnock's own propensity to overconfidence contributed to the rally's air of triumphalism that was regarded in many quarters as 'over-the-top',[145] 'undignified and presumptuous'[146] and even 'disgusting'.[147]

Arguments over whether Kinnock was the right leader with the wrong policies, or the wrong leader with the right policies, or quite simply the wrong leader with the wrong policies, pervaded the coverage of the election. David Marquand, for example, believed that there was a new Kinnock. He was 'the real hero of the campaign . . . Thanks largely to him, his party represented a coherent, intellectually respectable social and economic programme.' During the campaign, he had displayed 'reserves of imagination and flexibility I had not known he possessed'.[148] Stuart Hall, on the other hand, thought that the question of whether or not there was a new Kinnock was immaterial because no matter how Kinnock was presented, he could not avoid signifying the redundancy of the old Labour party.

> He embodied exactly those things that the constituency that Labour was trying to woo back – the new working class – is trying its damnedest to escape from. The welsh working-class bonhomie and the 'boyo' body language kept breaking through. Kinnock is resolutely of his place – principled, passionate, sentimental – and, by that token, he is not for these times.'[149]

The point about these many and varied debates was that they all proceeded on the same basic presupposition that leaders were central to electioneering and that leadership was important to each party's electoral prospects. The 'Kinnock factor' may have been the most prominent leadership issue, but it was by no means the only one. Paddy Ashdown's personality, his attention-grabbing campaign, his anti-politics appeal, and his success in placing proportional representation, constitutional reform and hung parliament scenarios at the top of the agenda, generated a huge amount of publicity and interpretive analysis. By the same token, Major's background, his soap-box, his political symbolism and his high-risk refusal to compromise on proportional representation and on Scottish devolution also served to enhance the reputation of leadership in electoral choice. Even though studies of voting invariably give maximum emphasis to the government's record and to the state of the economy in determining election outcomes, the performance of the party leaders acquires – through habitual examination and interpretation – the status of another significant factor in electoral choice. The assertions and controversies, the language and analysis, and, in particular, the suppositions of this leadership dimension in modern British politics were clearly visible in the 1992 election. Electoral descriptions and prescriptions were studded with references to leaders and to leadership. And these allusions were not confined to the tabloids. It was very noticeable that the quality broadsheets openly used leadership categories to appraise the parties' performances and to inform their editorial judgement on which parties warranted public support. *The Times*, for example, informed its readers that elections were 'about the selection of leaders for the immediate future on a calm assessment of merit'.[150] 'It is governors we are choosing this week . . . a choice of prime ministers'.[151] This being so, the paper gave its support to John Major since he had emerged 'as a likeable, competent and honest leader of his country'.[152] The *Sunday Times* also opted for Major but more because Mr Kinnock did not satisfy its criteria for the premiership.

> On all the major issues facing this country over the past four decades . . . Mr Kinnock has been wrong . . . At times of national crisis Mr Kinnock has been wrong in ways that would have spelt disaster for Britain had he been in power: during the Gulf war he spoke for dither and delay; during the Falklands war he spoke for nobody; during the cold war he spoke, unwittingly, for the Soviet Union. This is not a man whom Britain can afford to have as prime minister.[153]

The *Guardian*, on the other hand, felt that John Major had not done enough to deny the need for his party to be removed from government.

> The reasons to deny him a first, full term may be easily marshalled: He lacks any touch of destiny . . . he lacks a team with either energy or coherence . . . Above all, John Major lacks the vision to interpret and mould the Britain he superintends.[154]

These and other examples of influential papers in acts of editorial persuasion reveal an underlying conviction that leadership not only should, but actually does, motivate the public in its voting behaviour. There is little direct evidence that this is true in the stark terms in which it is mostly portrayed. It is far more likely that any substantive connection between leaders and votes will be found in conjunction with the public's view of each party's economic trustworthiness, its competence and its fitness for government. While professional analysts may well spend many years trying to distinguish the precise effects of leadership in the election, the verdict is already in from the media – the one sector which will be intent upon viewing high-level politics through the leadership dimension for the next five years.

The tone was set and the folklore was established directly after election day with a welter of reviews and post-mortems. It was John Major who had allegedly 'won a remarkable victory' and 'against the odds of historical precedent had brought the Conservative party home to its fourth election tri-umph'.[155] He had demonstrated a 'more natural rapport with the aspirations of the general public'[156] than the Labour leadership had managed to achieve. The Conservative party was reported as having benefited from the 'personal success of John Major in wooing substantial numbers of Labour's traditional supporters'.[157] The prime minister proved to be 'a national leader' who had 'risen to the challenge of combat'.[158] Mr Kinnock, on the other hand, had apparently been handicapped by an 'inability to present himself as a national leader'.[159] There were no doubts that Kinnock's shortcomings had had a direct effect upon the election. Nicholas O'Shaughnessy believed that in the end Labour had run

> its campaign principally as an American-style presidential election. This de-manded a starring role for Mr Kinnock, which encouraged voter doubts about him to surface – about his competence, circumlocutory evasiveness – as well as irritation at his overblown bonhomie.[160]

Others agreed:

> Certainly; the late swing towards the Tories suggested an unwillingness to see Kinnock as prime minister. (Allan Massie)[161]

> Major's success in winning an election . . . probably owes more to psychology than to psephology . . . That element of Neil Kinnock's personality which has always grated with floating voters was emphasised and those who had some-thing to lose under a Labour government began to think twice about continuing to punish the Tories for their errors. (Robin Oakley)[162]

> Voters . . . continued to perceive Neil Kinnock as a liability for Labour . . . having been on the wrong side of the argument on all the important issues of our age had in many voters' minds made him unfit to govern. (Andrew Neil)[163]

> When the voters were able to see through the gloss the party mangers had applied to Mr Major they liked what they saw...When the voters were able to see through Mr Kinnock's gloss, they did not like what they saw. In the end, then, it was Mr Major's victory. (*Sunday Telegraph* editorial)[164]

But probably the most revealing and significant reactions to the election came from the main protagonists themselves. When asked to comment on the election result, John Major quite unselfconsciously summed up the Conservative party victory in the first person.

> I'm delighted to have my own mandate. I think it is very important. I can now accept that the country have elected me in my own right to be Prime Minister.[165]

He continued:

> I now have a clear majority . . . I am prime minister of all this country, for everyone, whether they voted for me or not.[166]

Neil Kinnock, on the other hand, announced his intention to resign from the party leadership as quickly as possible. He knew that leadership politics in Britain had now become a continual process. His successor would need as much time as possible to prepare himself for the massive challenge of the next general election. But more importantly, the party could not afford to be without an individual fully and permanently engaged in the arena of leadership. Before any post-election policy review, it was the judgement of the party leader himself that the immediate priority lay in the provision of new leadership. He assured his supporters that the action he proposed taking was in its own right 'an essential act of leadership'.[167]

CHAPTER 9

The rise of the British presidency

This study was prompted by frivolity. To be more precise, it was motivated by the lack of seriousness surrounding the nature of prime ministerial power and the issue of political leadership in modern British politics. Suggestions of significant changes in the position of the premier, and in the forces exerted upon both the incumbent and the rival claimants to power, are almost invariably subsumed under the ancient 'prime ministerial power' versus 'cabinet power' debate. Once lodged in this familiar context, the assertions of change that give rise to analogies with the American presidency are then swiftly set aside by one or other of two basic methods.

First, the allusions to the presidency are seen as simply ways of drawing attention to the customary controversy over prime ministerial power. They become either a technique for dramatising the existence of the prime minister's singular position in the central executive, or, more often, a device for suggesting the progressive extension of executive power into the orbit of the prime minister's office. In both cases, the working assumption is one of a single dimension of political arrangements and conditions which varies from a diluted form to a concentrated form. When Peter Hennessy, for example, ruminates upon Mrs Thatcher's handling of the cabinet, he speculates on where she would be placed on a 'spectrum stretching from collective decision-making to "presidential" command'.[1] The latter is a clear misreading of the president's constitutional and political position insofar as the United States is concerned. The point to grasp, however, is that the use of the presidency in this context is to convey the idea of an extrapolated form of the prime minister's position. Just as the notion of prime ministerial power is, in many respects, taken to be a collective projection of the cabinet, references to a presidential form of power amount to a unitary conception of what is a store of pre-existing powers. As a consequence, to be presidential in Britain, therefore, usually means to be a prime minister in a condensed and highly potent form.

256

Having established a linkage between a presidential analogy and the idea of the cabinet's inherent pluralism collapsing into a clear cut monopoly of an Americanised prime minister, the presidential comparison is immediately compromised as implausible and invalid. The attempt to use a caricatured presidency to turn a prime minister into a gargoyle is always guaranteed to fail. It is easily picked off as a gross and unjustifiable disfigurement. After alluding to the presidential comparison, therefore, it is customary to discard it. This is done through an act of corrective 'realism' in which the most glaring structural and procedural differences between the British and American system are cited in such a way as to make the positions of both chief executives appear to be wholly incompatible with one another. The straw man of the presidential prime minister is threshed and milled by easy references to parliamentary support, party support, cabinet government, collective responsibility, sudden death votes of confidence and the absence of a separation of powers.

It is clear that in many cases, the presidential comparison is employed solely for the purpose of dismissing it and of vindicating the characteristics and the principles of traditional cabinet authority. In this light, the American presidency is regarded as a cautionary example – a repository of autocratic command thankfully absent in Britain. The American grotesque is then held up as the equivalent of what Britain's cabinet government would look like if its constitutional principles had been completely corrupted. The fact that the British prime minister cannot be equated with the American presidency is then taken as proof positive of the continued viability of cabinet government and of its interior capacity to prevent such American-style mutations.

The *second* method of setting aside the prime minister is less ethnocentric than the first but just as effective. It acknowledges that a prime minister like Mrs Thatcher, for example, was wholly exceptional as a leader. This was because she was a leader who occupied a position of leadership. It is well known that she held fewer cabinet meetings than her predecessors. She also bypassed the cabinet, reshuffled and reshaped it, and interfered persistently in the departmental work of cabinet ministers. Because she was engaged in an ideological mission to reconstruct Britain, her own leadership needed to be exceptional. After Thatcherism had percolated into the nation's consciousness, it was widely concluded that she and her leadership were outstanding in both senses of the word. It became commonplace to note that she was peculiar. She was said to be out of the ordinary and out of kilter with her predecessors. Because she was so extraordinary, she was also safe. Her astonishing prominence could be dismissed as a temporary aberration based upon personal idiosyncrasy. If 'her claim to rule was based on exceptionalism',[2] the exceptionalism of that 'rule' was necessarily peculiar to herself and to her administration.

257

Allegations of Thatcherite presidentialism followed one of two patterns. On the one hand, they were used to denote the existence of a set of governing conditions that could not accurately be characterised as cabinet government, or even as a derivative of cabinet government. 'She overflowed the boundaries of the office and consequently appeared to be presidential.'[3] According to this perspective, the term 'presidential' was synonymous with something that was distant from British traditions and working practices. In this guise, the Thatcherite premiership was designated presidential not only to capture its sense of iconoclasm, but also to assign it to a position of utter peculiarity. For presidential, read maverick; for maverick, read misrepresentative. Being cast in presidential terms, therefore, was a way both of acknowledging Thatcher's unusual position, and of dismissing any need to analyse or assimilate its significance. Like a president, hers was a personally constructed position. Like a president, such a position was not transferable to successors and would, therefore, rapidly decompose with her departure from office.

The other way of looking at Thatcher's presidentialism is less complacent and more analytical than the first, but possesses the same underlying assumption of insignificance. This perspective sees Thatcher's prominence in government as stretching and straining the boundaries of cabinet government, but never to the point of rupturing them. In fact, she is even used to affirm and to vindicate the processes of British constitutional constraint. In passages that evoke more the mechanical dynamics of America's checks and balances, commentators refer to Thatcher's decline as a consequence of an adventure in presidential deviancy that was predetermined to end in a revival of cabinet government. Mrs Thatcher is said to have 'certainly flouted the spirit of traditional cabinet government' even to the point of placing it 'temporarily on ice'.[4] What she could not do was to extinguish it. Moreover, she could not prevent the pendulum of power swinging back against her. In Ronald Butt's view, 'Mrs Thatcher's personal handicap had been her failure to see that she could not continue indefinitely to override and bypass her cabinet.'[5] Peter Hennessy agreed: 'The problems that had stored up under her style of Prime Ministerial leadership finally did come home to roost. An "over-mighty" premier had been unable to withstand them.'[6] And to Peter Madgwick, it was clear that 'Mrs Thatcher's fall from office showed the ultimate force of collective interest sorely tried, and striking back at arrogant prime ministerial power.'[7]

In retrospect, it is made quite clear that Mrs Thatcher's pre-eminent position was always as unsustainable as the allegations that she had incorporated a form of presidentialism into British government. According to this perspective, presidents never fall. To Alan Watkins, for example, it is 'an article of the presidential creed that a modern prime minister with a workable majority, in good health and in full possession of his or her faculties is irremovable'.[8] Following this assumption, Watkins could not disguise his satisfaction in the logical conclusion that 'Mrs Thatcher's fall dented recent theories of prime ministerial power.'[9] When Mrs Thatcher was forced to resign, Dennis Kavanagh posed the following question – 'Will the mobiliser be followed by a consolidator, and the presidential style by collective cabinet rule?'[10] It was evident that most commentators did not believe the question to be worth asking. The demise of Mrs Thatcher was simply equated with the resumption of cabinet government. It had never expired. It had been tested by Thatcher and had been reaffirmed as a matter of course by the fact of her succession.

There is a clear distinction between the two patterns of response to the presidential analogy in British politics. The first emphatically denies any reason for such comparisons. The second is more equivocal. It recognises the reason for presidential references being made. It even acknowledges that on occasions the maintenance of cabinet government has been a close run thing. In the end, though, it concludes that presidentialism in Britain is either an exaggeration, or a temporary aberration confined to special circumstances which always give way in the end to a basic condition of cabinet government. Although the two patterns are different from one another, they do share a common characteristic which is central to the British conception of executive government. In their different ways, the two sets of responses reflect and, in turn, reinforce this fundamental outlook. The perspective in question is the presumptive existence of collective cabinet rule. The 'cabinet' may be modified, adapted and even diminished, but it never disappears. It remains the pole star of British government. Views of it may change, but it is always assumed to be there as an active force and as a working principle of government. Analyses of central administration and executive power are dominated by the presupposition of a competitive body of ministers, who always have political resources at their disposal, and who always condition the prime minister's authority along the lines of a contingent and reversible level of political status.

The deterministic nature of the presupposition and the way it can inhibit analysis and deter efforts at discriminating appraisal is exemplified by George Jones's elastic band analogy. Jones sought to provide an understanding of prime ministerial power by equating the office with the properties of an elastic band.[11] It stretches to accommodate an activist prime minister and contracts with the arrival of a more quiescent chief executive. The more the rubber is stretched, the greater the force that is exerted upon the prime minister by the collective energies of the cabinet. Mrs Thatcher stretched the elastic but, in the end, she had to submit to its countervailing strength. It slipped effortlessly back into shape as she left Downing Street.[12]

There are many contentious aspects to such an analogy. For example, it assumes that the prime minister's office and powers have an objectively defined and, thereby, 'normal' shape. It assumes that the authority and style of different prime ministers constitute nothing more than a series of variations upon a single overriding theme. That theme of cabinet government is so rubbery and amorphous, it is capable of embracing almost any configuration of government in the name of collective decision-making and collegiate power-sharing. To this extent, the rubber band idea approximates to a truism that government is about more than one person.

Apart from the various tautological and self-validating aspects of such a notion, the elastic band analogy is significant in another and more fundamental respect. In spite of its deficiencies, or more likely because of them, Jones's elasticated device is a way not of explaining the relationship between prime ministerial power and the traditional norm of the cabinet, but of closing consideration of the issue down to an absolute and static minimum. To this extent, it is utterly symptomatic of the British constitution's aptitude for evading analysis and for suspending appraisal of its shadowy interior. The elastic band only appears to explain everything by appearing to cover everything. But it hardly explains anything at all.

It is possible to level all manner of charges against it. But the most important criticism is the widespread satisfaction that is induced by such a model. For such a complex and problematic issue as executive leadership to be reduced to such an impoverished, but nonetheless popular, form of analysis almost defies belief. While it is true that the elastic band conforms to the constitution's code of swathing difficult issues in an upholstery of corporate negligence, it is also true that the model epitomises those forces and habits which prevent a proper understanding of the centre of the British executive. It excludes notions of prime ministerial access to exclusive sources of power. It rejects presidential analogies as self-evidently inapplicable and logically inadmissible. In their place, it relies upon the casuistry of an iron law of elastic indeterminacy governed by a fixed attachment to a pre-existing and absolute form of cabinet government. In this sense, cabinet government acts as the core condition, the gravitational field, the home base – i.e. an entity which does not require explanation or even verification, and which successfully distracts attention away from areas of constitutional sensitivity.

The present study represents a reaction against this closed regime of observation and conception. It challenges the assumptions that lie at the heart of the two patterns of customary responses to the presidential analogy in British politics. Far from being an alien and mischievous distraction, the presidential analogy is in fact a valuable source of insight and interpretation. It is the superficial misuse and subversive trivialisation of the presidential perspective which is the main problem. The presidency is almost always employed in a facetious way. It is first turned into a bloated parody of itself and then deployed to affirm the absence of an implausibly autocratic form of central government in Britain. Even when the presidency is more carefully defined, the resultant comparison is still transformed into a turkey shoot of the very, very obvious dissimilarities between the two systems. It is only mutations like Mrs Thatcher who provoke misplaced interest in what John Hart contemptuously calls 'that misbegotten offspring' of the controversy over prime ministerial power – i.e. 'the debate about the "presidentialization" of British politics.'[13]

The problem with these images of the presidential frame of reference is that they are so wasteful. They corrupt and subvert the potential contribution that a more sensitive and measured grasp of presidential politics could provide in such areas as the development of the British premiership and the increasing significance of political leadership. It might even be said that the misuse of the presidential analysis acts as a barrier against a full realisation of the changes that have taken place in the higher reaches of the British system. It is ironic that at the time when studies of Britain's executive are becoming more expansive in scale and more sensitive in nature, the issue of the prime minister's comparability to the presidency should be discarded as an adjunct to the outmoded prime minister–cabinet debate. These studies of the centrifugal tendencies of Britain's 'executive territory' and of the centripetal efforts of the 'core executive' demonstrate the dynamic character of central government.[14] Set against the existence of intergovernmental agencies, 'policy communities', clientele groups, quangos, fragmentary and overlapping areas of decision-making, and a bureaucratic culture of departmentalism, the conclusion reached by such studies is that it is 'seriously misleading to assert the primacy of the cabinet'.[15] On the contrary, it is safer to claim that 'cabinet government itself has been marginalised or by-passed'[16] and that it would be more accurate to describe it as 'a residual executive'.[17] What holds for the cabinet, holds even more so for the prime minister. If the countervailing forces of the cabinet cannot withstand the dynamics of executive government, the prime minister's position is even less secure and the possibility of prime ministerial government even more remote – so remote in fact that far from being the 'hub of government', the prime minister's position can exemplify the 'hole at the centre'[18] of the British executive.

The exponents of core executive studies are quite right to challenge the arthritic institutionalism of the prime minister–cabinet debate which had always pivoted upon the contentious assumption that governmental autonomy necessarily rested either with the cabinet or with the premier. Modern analysis of the executive persuasively presses home the point that the debate is immaterial, as neither the cabinet nor the prime minister rules the roost. The problem with this sort of analysis is that its realism does not extend far enough. It is still bound by a residue of at least two aspects of the old controlling assumptions. First, it leaves behind the president comparison as an unwanted accoutrement of the discredited debate over prime ministerial power. The term 'presidential' is regarded as carrying connotations of a fictional convergence with a supposedly highly centralised system of government. The idea of a 'general trend explanation towards presidential government', in which Mrs Thatcher, for example, continued 'along a path already stamped out by her predecessors of increasingly centralized decision-making',[19] is taken to be a symptom of the misconceptions surrounding the prime minister. As a result, the potential of the presidential analysis for insights into British government is overlooked mainly because what is a misunderstanding of the presidency is used to prevent a more thorough understanding of Britain's executive territory.

Second, modern analyses of the British executive tend naturally to be concerned with the executive and, as a consequence, they have an inclination to underestimate those alternative dimensions of political power and influence that transcend the executive territory. Their concentration upon the distribution of executive power means that their analytical agendas can be blind to the extent to which a prime minister's political position is not drawn from the executive, and not measured by reference to executive policy decisions. In effect, there are other aspects to the prime minister's position which have to be taken into account, in order to acquire a fuller awareness of its integral properties and its position in modern British politics. These supplementary aspects not only throw additional light on the office and on the nature of the modern executive, but illuminate the political pressures, the opportunities and calculations of those who hold the office and of those who strive for Number 10.

This book has attempted to open up and to examine these different dimensions of the British premiership. Moreover, it has sought to do so by specific reference to comparisons and analogies with the American presidency. Far from misrepresenting the nature of the prime minister's position, the conviction that has guided this exploration is that the presidency can provide penetrating insights into the course and direction of what is a rapidly developing feature of British politics. Indeed, it is only by being aware of the contemporary character of the American presidency that it becomes clear how the position of the prime minister has undergone, and is currently experiencing, a series of substantial changes.

The changes in question are cumulative and mutually reinforcing in nature, and are far reaching in their consequences. They have led to a transformation in the way that political leadership is cultivated and exerted in

British political life. They also reveal the existence of deep-set shifts in the nature of the political system that have not only altered the standing and role of leadership in the dynamics of political relationships, but have allowed the personal nature of leadership to have a powerful bearing upon the wider fields of political perception, evaluation and discourse. These changes have been of an order and magnitude to make the comparison between the British prime minister's position and the American presidency far more pertinent now than it used to be. There is now more point to the comparison as there are now more analogies that can be drawn between the interior dynamics of both offices; and more characteristics that are common to both in terms of pressures, constraints and contingencies.

The previous chapters have attempted to demonstrate that the developments and forces underlying the changes in the political position of the British prime minister are not merely similar to those experienced in the White House, but are exemplified and illustrated most fully in their nature by the American presidency. The analytical and interpretive insights afforded by studies of the American presidency can, therefore, be exploited to great effect to increase further the understanding of contemporary developments in the British premiership and to illustrate the many political and social repercussions that flow from the intensification of these trends. This is not to underestimate the importance of the structural differences that exist between the two systems. But it is to draw attention to, and to recognise the significance of, the dramatic extent to which even within two such different contexts certain profound similarities have arisen. In spite of the clear contrast in institutional superstructures, the underlying points of resemblance are so exceptional that there is now evidence to support the contention that the similarities between the two offices are more revealing than their differences. Furthermore, these similarities are increasing in scale and importance all the time.

It is now a plausible contention to claim that the pressures and opportunities, the expectations and motivations, and the restraints and problems associated with the business of being and remaining a prime minister are sufficiently analogous to the equivalent conditions faced by an American president to justify the term 'president' being applied to the occupant of Number 10. In fact, it would be no exaggeration to assert that what this country has witnessed over the last generation has been the growing emergence of a British presidency.

It is important to point out that such an assertion is not implying a convergence of the British premiership with the American presidency. But neither does it carry the implication that the two positions are following diverging courses of development. What is being suggested is that they have come to move along parallel paths. Their separation is still significant, but the changes in the politics of the British premiership have now had the effect of pulling the conditions and properties of British political leadership in the same direction as the contemporary evolution of the American presidency. These forces underlying the presidency's development are now so clearly evident in the British context that they provide compelling grounds for establishing the existence of what is to all intents and purposes a *de facto* British presidency.

The reasons for such a conclusion formed the bulk of this study. They include:

• The rising phenomenon of 'spatial leadership', in which political authority is cultivated and protected by the creation of a sense of distance, and occasionally detachment, from government. The strategic invention of space between the prime minister and the government, and between leaders in general and their parent bodies, is seen not only as the mark of leadership – a visual expression of personal prerogative – but also as an instrument of leadership through its actual and symbolic connections to the public interest.

• The cult of the outsider and the strategies to acquire and maintain outsider status even within government and over extended periods of time. The need to develop a twin track approach to administration, in which a leader's professional and political competence is mixed with the ability to take an outsider's stance against government through criticism and personal intervention.

• The rise of a 'designer populism', in which leaders encourage and engage in self-inflicted forms of populist insurgency upon the structure, behaviour and policies of their own organisations. This has extended to government itself with prime ministers increasingly given to making highly publicised intercessions into the Whitehall machinery not in the style of a managing director, but more in the theatrical mould of a *deus ex machina* enhancing the political position of the premier at the expense of the organisational integrity of the government.

• The decline of the corporate ethos of party politics, assisted by the attributed exceptionalism and prominence of party leaders and by the personalisation of party differences. The intrusion of personal considerations and of leadership appraisal into the public's estimation of a party's fitness to govern.

• The way that expressing leadership through the public has come to give political leadership a distinctively public character. Public contact, or at least the 'common touch', used to be an important consideration in a prospective prime minister. With the emergence of a much less hierarchical social order, a leader's relationship with the public is now central and decisive. He or she must have the ability to appeal to the public's own criteria for leadership in an increasingly mass society. While leaders, in general, attempt to personify collective movement the prime minister in particular is expected to precipitate governmental movement in an administrative culture, which is often depicted as being so resistant to change that only an exceptional individual can make a difference.

• The importance of leaders in the creation of party images and of leadership in modern campaigning. The way that party leaders now uniformly have to try to maximise their independence from party structures in the presentation and promotion of the party. As parties are no longer reliable vehicles of public mobilisation in the more fluid conditions of dealigned and independent voters, they condone, and even exploit, the phenomenon of 'leadership stretch'. Each does so in order to increase its chances of translating the leader's intermediary position with the public into the party's point of access into government.

• A growing distinction between leadership and policy. The increasingly significant differentiation between the level of popular support for British leaders and the degree of approval given to the policies of their parties. The rise of publicly perceived and assessed 'leadership attributes' as separate and substantive categories of political evaluation.

• The increased dissociation of leaders from their party organisations and traditions. The ways in which the requirements of a public prominence and individual identity generate a nexus between the leader and the public that provides opportunities for new and independent sources of political authority that can be deployed inside a party by a leader and inside the government by a prime minister.

• The rise of a public dimension of leadership exposure and approval through media coverage, sustained opinion polling and the continual deployment of leaders by their parties into public settings of symbolism and spectacle. Just as the media gravitate towards the tangible entities of leaders, so leaders are drawn to the media for access to the public. The consequence is that competing leaders come to be judged just as much on grounds of leadership as on policy. By the same token, each leader has to affirm his or her public *raison d'être* by drawing widespread attention to himself as an expression of leadership and by encouraging the view that his party's competence to govern is related to its unity in being effectively and conspicuously led.

• The advent of a full-scale politics of leadership focusing not merely upon the relative merits and competitive behaviour of leaders, but the meaning, usefulness, value, sources and location of leadership within the political system. The growing significance of the 'big idea' to leadership and its relationship to a leader's personal background and experience. The way in which personal origins support a leader's claim to the right to propound a public vision, and the way in which formative influences and individual accomplishments are extrapolated into a personified essence of the vision itself.

• The refraction of issues through the lens of leadership figures. The extent to which leadership is moving from a position held by a person to one which is characterised by, and dependent upon, the idiosyncratic properties of the leader. The need for leadership to be personal in nature and public in form.

• The onset of self-sustaining and self-extending dynamics in leadership politics. For example, as leaders seek the public attention they require, they not only have to appear increasingly to be leaders in as full a sense as possible, they continually have to impress upon the public the need for leadership in British politics. Thereupon they each seek to satisfy in a particular way, the general need for leadership that they have collectively helped to arouse. When problems are commonly defined in terms of a lack of leadership, then they suggest their own solution and generate an ever intensifying competition to define what leadership is and who can provide it. Another example is provided by the persistent presentation of senior politicians as discrete individuals. As they are projected to the public on a personal basis, the populace is encouraged to equate the increasingly personal nature of political competition with the nature of the prizes on offer. Consequently, leadership is increasingly seen as possessing a distinctively individual character and the premiership, as the chief prize, is assumed to be not just the top job, but commensurately the most personalised office. As such, it encourages the idea that the contenders for high office can be known and assessed on intuitive grounds by members of the public exercising personal judgements about politicians, whose apparent accessibility as individuals grows with their burgeoning presence in the flickering living rooms of the country.

• The need for prime ministers to maintain their access to the public and their favourable dominance of the communication media, in order to retain the confidence of their party and the credibility of their claims to national leadership. Prime ministers can no longer afford to be displaced by other leaders in what has become a continual process of public engagement. Instead, they are propelled to acquire as much freedom of action as possible in order to optimise their party's political objectives.

• The effectiveness of leader-centred third parties in exploiting the opportunities for gaining national exposure and for acquiring the appearance of comparability with the two main parties. For example, David Owen's 'fast track' to the SDP leadership strengthened the impression of organisational slickness. It generated connotations of adaptivity and modernity by way of leadership, and exemplified through leadership. More recently, Paddy Ashdown's success in public leadership has been seen to have boosted the Liberal Democratic party and to have put it in a more competitive position with the mainline parties. Leadership has been used instrumentally and substantively to attack them. As leadership is boosted as an issue, it allows a lightweight third party like the Liberal Democrats to be seen to be led by a gifted leader with little organisational baggage to restrict his public movement, and, therefore, with personal licence to press home the need for national leadership. The consequent intensification of political dispute and party competition at the leadership level helps to turn normal politics into a permanent election campaign, in which leaders seek to outmanoeuvre each other in highly publicised displays of confrontation that in their turn make the political process even more leadership orientated.

• The onset of a presidential emphasis upon the nation and even upon a 'public philosophy' that can substantiate prime ministerial claims to represent the national interest and the general welfare. The way this strategy for maintaining and maximising the leader's influence and enhancing his or her *raison d'être* as leader further increases the sense of distance between the prime minister and both the party and the government.

• The importance of foreign policy in increasing the exposure and identity of a prime minister as a national leader. In particular, the rising prominence of international summitry in the public presentation of prime ministers openly performing the quasi-presidential role of speaking for the nation. A prime minister is seen most graphically to be a prime minister when set apart from party and cabinet in a collegiate arena of other leaders all exercising wide discretionary powers on behalf of their countries.

• The significance of the EEC and of Britain's position in it as a constant spur to the centrality of the prime minister in issues of national autonomy and cultural destiny. The association of personal negotiation and executive decision-making with constructions of an individual vision of European order and evolution. The onset of Europe as the archetypal challenge to domestic leadership in an increasingly interdependent world; and the corresponding rise of Europe as a leadership issue in both a party and a national context.

• The growing practice of viewing the prime minister and potential prime ministers as embodiments of national archetypes. The representation of a national tradition or form of social symbolism through leaders and leadership contenders. The direct cultivation of such personal encapsulations of social ideals and aspirations for political support. The rise of leadership to exemplify such characteristics and to validate their significance, and the concomitant effect of giving to a leader an identity demonstrably separate to that of the party.

• The prime minister's position and powers as a catalyst in the generation of the public's renewed consciousness of the content and value of constitutional principles. The way that the symbolic and actual representation of central executive power in concentrated form has helped to introduce a political debate and a political language similar to that which American presidents have long been accustomed to working with – namely, a close interest in the origins, location, legitimacy and distribution of power; a concern over the principles of its usage; and a desire to ensure that power is limited by legally enforceable restraints and by the existence of entrenched rights and liberties. In essence, the growing use of central executive power as the litmus test to assess the effectiveness of the constitutional ideal of a 'government under law'.

The British presidency is derived from a series of general developments and underlying dynamics. It is an emanation of conditions that approximate to a form of uninhibited presidential politics. This is exemplified by Britain's increasing preoccupation with the nature and role of political leadership. The properties, requirements and expectations of leadership have generated an entire medium of political exchange, in which a specialised vocabulary and set of evaluative categories has grown up through which leaders are observed and appraised. Leaders still remain utterly dependent upon parties for their formal position and initial platform as well as their access to government. And yet, it is also true to say that the leaders of the political parties in Britain increasingly occupy a world of their own.

This world might well be called 'leaderland'. It is dominated by the need for leaders to have leadership qualities, to have the opportunity to demonstrate them and to have them publicly appreciated. The net effect of all these imperatives is a uniform strategy adopted by leaders to maximise their chances of success by seeking a rapprochement with the general public. Leadership is watched, tested and assessed for its public qualities by a public increasingly interested in, and even absorbed by, the public performance of leaders. Leadership has now become an established political issue in its own right. The issue is played out in public, not least because it is this arena in which the issue is most significant. It is the arena in which the varying conceptions of leadership, and the differing estimations of leaders in fulfilling those conceptions, are discussed and debated. Not only are leaders constantly on show in such an arena, they have to be on permanent parade *in order* to remain leaders. To do this, they must acquire a high level of public visibility, continually advance the conception of a general public, and link their *raisons d'être* as leaders to that of the public's concerns and fears. Political leadership is now expected to be public leadership. It is no longer enough to be a political leader who merely appears in public. Leaders now have to possess the qualities to lead the public or at least to make a plausible assertion to be able to lead the public. They have to do well not just as party leaders but as public figures in the unrelenting exposure of leaderland, where they are judged not just by party criteria, but by more volatile public criteria generated by, and applied through, leaderland itself. As a result, the competition for Number 10 is increasingly a public contest about public leadership by public leaders.

British political leaders now have to lay claim to a communion with the public interest by way of a physical attachment to the public itself. Leaders continually have to give the impression to mass audiences that they identify closely with them. These efforts to establish a visceral immediacy with the public can be so intense that they amount to an attempt to establish public leadership by leaders insinuating themselves into the public itself and becoming a constituent part of it. So great is the pressure to acquire and to maintain a condition of public engagement that leaders have cultivated outsider strategies, techniques of spatial leadership and spectacles of personalised interventions.

Responding to, and intensifying, the same pressures for public leadership, the press and electronic media help to stretch the leaders away from their parent party organisations and, where the prime minister is concerned, from the government itself. Through their news coverage, their unremitting usage of opinion polls and their leader-oriented analyses of political developments, the media encourage the shift of interest towards party leaders and their leadership performance. They assist in the generation of a leadership agenda, an aroused consciousness of leadership characteristics and a differentiation of leaders from their parties in respect to both image and substance. This sense of distinction supports the sense of leadership. It also allows a leader considerable licence to appeal across already weakening party lines, to divert criticism away from the party or the government, and to develop multiple points of personal access to the broader constituency of the general public. Such opportunities are particularly useful for a prime minister. If he or she is skilful enough, he can cultivate his personal prestige with the public and deploy his incumbency advantage for national leadership both to increase his negotiating leverage inside government, and to enhance further his dominant position in the party and in the cabinet. But whether it is the prime minister or any other leader, they all seek to use their leadership positions to establish leadership as a political issue, as a separate criterion of political evaluation and, thereby, as a forum for personal advancement.

These are the sort of parallels between the contemporary development of the American presidency and the British premiership which support the contention that a British presidency has emerged – unannounced and unrecognised – into the mainstream in Britain's political life. It is worth reiterating at this point that the British presidency is not the same thing as the American presidency. The British premiership, and the political hinterland surrounding it, is not comparable to all the features associated with the American presidency. Significant and growing similarity is not the same as equivalence. In addition to the explicit structural differences like fixed tenures and separate elections, the British premiership is unlikely ever to share some of the more idiosyncratic features associated with the presidency.

For example, it is difficult to see how the prime minister's position could ever become as suffused as the American presidency is, in the pomp and pageantry of national symbolism and affirmation. The presidency is regarded as both an agent and an object of a history of national development and constitutional self-consciousness. This confers a teleological character upon the office which links executive leadership with the evolution of the state and the fulfilment of the moral idea of the American nation. It is almost impossible to imagine that the prime minister's office could reach a position which would rival the American presidency's centrality both in the country's view of itself and in the metaphysics of its cultural destiny and national vocation.

The British premiership may not be the American presidency, but neither is it the same as the old conception of the prime minister. In fact, it is now more accurate to say that the premier approximates far more to the presidency than it does to the traditional position of the prime minister. This study has sought to demonstrate that the emergence of a British presidency is not dependent upon the accommodation of those sorts of formal executive powers and prerogatives which are normally referred to in descriptions of prime ministerial power and especially in critiques of 'prime ministerial government'. These powers were certainly significant factors in the rise of the prime minister's official weighting in government, but it is misleading to attribute the onset of presidential status to the enlargement of formal responsibilities and official structures. In one sense it may be true, for example, that 'British prime ministers became more presidential as a succession of incumbents developed their own policy units inside Downing Street.'[20] But in another sense, statements like this fail to capture both the essence of presidentialism and the nature of the transition to it. Becoming more presidential in American appearances is not in the final analysis the same as becoming presidential in substance or becoming and being presidential in the British context.

The British presidency is not a pure derivative of formal transfers of power and authority. Its properties are not reducible to such constitutional sources or even to any tangible or observable rearrangements in the machinery of government. We are looking not at a set of extensions or at a settled pattern of growth, but at a qualitative change of form and interior substance – a metamorphosis in response to changes outside government in the wider environment of public opinion, social attitudes, national anxieties, communication techniques, electoral practices, popular interests, voting behaviour and political expectations.

The rise of the British presidency has been accompanied by a critical change in attitudes towards leadership. Previously, party leaders occupied positions of formal leadership. They were seen in essence to assume, rather than to construct, a centre of influence. A party leader might, thereupon, seek to personalise the position and even succeed in closely associating the office with his own individual characteristics and identity. But there were always strict limits to this sort of convergence. The leader remained a prominent yet integral element in a highly structured corporate organisation. The leader was the projection of the party – its chief spokesman and its senior representative tied to the party organisation by innumerable formal and informal cords. The leader was at the top only by being on top of the party's own hierarchy. The prime minister suffered from a double dose of institutionalisation insofar as he was a captive of both his party and of an office which was officially only first among equals. A prime minister was assumed to inherit the office rather than to fill it with himself. 'The first priority of a prime minister' was to 'do what was expected of him'[21] – i.e. to perform functions, not to provide performances.[22]

Now the limits are not so strict. The old moorings of institutionalisation have been stretched in response to the new context of personalised public leadership. As leaders increasingly stake their claim to leadership positions on the basis of personal characteristics and of a personal rapport with the public, the leadership positions themselves have changed to accommodate the altered outlook and dynamics of political leadership. A prime minister is still supported by the infrastructure of party and cabinet, but to an ever-increasing extent that support, and the executive authority derived from it, is clearly dependent upon his or her day to day performances as a personal leader of public stature operating in leaderland. A prime ministership is sustained more and more by the need both to attract public approval and to radiate it back to the populace. The public does not tend to demonstrate active approval for institutions or, at least, not in any sustained condition of agitation. But prime ministers and potential prime ministers are locked in a continual struggle for public approval and, as such, they personalise the contest for leadership as a public competition for personal leadership. The public is enticed and cajoled into giving or withdrawing approval from leaders on the basis not only of their public performance as leaders, but of the perceived relationship between their publicly revealed character traits and the provision of personal leadership.

This is not to suggest that British party leaders are becoming indistinguishable from their American counterparts. The latter's freedom of manoeuvre to engage in highly individualised campaigns, where personalities are marketed in an uninhibited way, is peculiar to the United States with its looser party structure and separate elections for the presidency. What is clear in Britain, however, is the emergence of a highly publicised matrix of leadership politics, in which leaders compete continuously with each other for public confidence in them as leaders. As repetitive opinion polls plot their progress and as the parties watch ever more closely the public watching their leaders, a new level and type of politics has developed. It has led to a pronounced emphasis upon leaders *being* their parties, and their parties' policies, in the public eye. In the past, leaders had always represented their parties' programme and political outlook. Today, they come almost physically to embody them through the presentation of themselves and their personalities. The leaders have to use their positions to satisfy the modern need to project their parties' messages and images to a wide audience. In doing so, each leader not only tends to reduce the party image to a visual form of personal components, but tends to become the physical expression of that party's public meaning.

A leader's success is no longer measured solely by his or her instrumental efficiency in acting for the party. It is also assessed by the leader's ability to personify the party, even to the point of translating that personification into a guiding vision and operational identity for the party – i.e. melting the party into himself or herself at the leadership level. Political leaders in Britain today are distinctive from their predecessors in this important respect. In order to survive and to compete effectively in the highly exposed and hostile environment of competitive leadership politics, leaders have to radiate themselves, their character and their background in any way possible to gain tactical advantages over other leaders. By projecting himself, a leader can not only look more like a leader in the singular individual sense. He can also assume the individual discretion (i) to match the presentation of personal properties to the public's changeable conceptions of his leadership and his party in particular; and (ii) to respond to the public's more general expectations of political leadership in modern conditions.

What these developments have led to is a widening sense of differentiation between the leaders and their parties. Leaders now stand out to a greater extent than before for reasons that are different from before. They are conspicuous because they have to be. They have to cultivate prominence both to capture public attention and to sustain it on the basis of approval. Their parties expect nothing less. Leaders also stand apart from their parties because they are in essence fighting a different campaign. They are competing with other leaders on grounds of leadership, together with all the distinct criteria and categories associated with it, for the opportunity to become prime minister. Just as leadership has become a political issue in its own right, so leadership has also become accepted as an indispensable function of modern British government. As a consequence, the office of the prime minister is now seen as a leadership role to be filled by individuals with proven credentials for leadership. Prime ministers, and aspiring prime ministers, are expected to be forceful personalities with demonstrable drive, independence, integrity and with 'big ideas' of their own.

Within the constraints of what is still primarily a party competition for government, therefore, the contest between leaders for executive honours has assumed an identity that is very much its own. It possesses its own rules of engagement, its own strategies and objectives and its own standards of assessment. The efforts of leaders to impress the public with their personal leadership, and the emphasis given to the value of leadership in the process, has led to the emergence of a distinctly presidential dimension in British politics. This is not an alternative construction or perspective of the traditional framework of party politics and party government which continues in much the same vein as it has in the past. The presidential dimension represents a separate and altogether different set of political dynamics. While it originated in the old party framework, it has taken on such a momentum of its own that it has diverged away from the established patterns of political exchange and evaluation. In doing so, it has generated its own form and style of politics that have grown to a position of central importance in British government.

Apart from explaining and promoting the popular interest in the substance and provision of political leadership, the presidential dimension fosters an ever closer convergence between connotations of the public and the nation on the one hand and the properties of individual leadership on the other. The increasingly presidential character of Britain's leadership specifications means that party leaders are significant not only because they can profoundly affect public confidence in their parties' competence to govern, but also because they work to insinuate themselves into the public's view of itself and of the nation's conception of its distinctiveness.

Leaders are no longer just party leaders. To be a prime minister, a leader has to prove in a most direct and immediate way that he or she is worthy of popular consideration as a leader of the British public as well as a leader of the British nation. Leading a major party is a necessary, but not a sufficient, condition to meet these requirements. A leader's claim to political leadership needs to be repeatedly verified and substantiated within a medium of competitive party politics, which is continuously broadening and deepening its suggestive conjunctions between executive office, public intimacy and personal leadership. Even recently, a party leader could be seen as primarily a salesman's boot in the public's door – gaining attention for the company's wares and seeking to put them in the best possible light. Today, a leader is not merely the boot. He constitutes some of the suitcase as well. He it is who must satisfy the public's aroused interest in the political agenda of executive leadership, impress his leadership credentials directly upon the populace, and raise public confidence in his party by virtue of its capacity to provide leadership.

With the advent of presidential politics comes an enhanced emphasis upon the office of the prime minister. In place of the largely understated and anonymous nature of the post, there has emerged a much more defined sense of its identity as an embodment of executive power. It has become evocative of the American presidency which embraces both the objective existence of a chief executive office and the physical presence of an individual who fills it, activates it, and contributes to it. The position of the British prime minister has increasingly assumed the same mix of conspicuous institutionalisation and of equally conspicuous informality and variation.

The 'prime ministership' used to be a rare and uncomfortable term, for the office, such as it was, amounted to only an informal summation of precedents and powers with no conscious or corporate identity of its own. It was institutionalised only to the extent that the prime minister's formal position under the aegis of the crown foreclosed the need for a separate identity or for a distinct conception of prime ministerial power. Today, the position is quite different. The office is talked about a great deal. It is an established term of reference in political debate and analysis. It is now almost universally referred to as the 'premiership', which implies the presence of a singular and separate office based firmly upon the notion of political priority and precedence. The meaning is amplified and authenticated by the evident association of such a singular office with a singular individual occupant. The individual incumbent has come to be in that position largely as a consequence of his performance within the medium of leadership politics. By the same token the image of the individual leader lends a tangible and unified quality to the position. It helps both to raise the status of the premiership as a distinct institution and also to lower its level of settled arrangements and boundaries. The premiership, therefore, has become at one and the same time far more prominent as an institutional entity and far more changeable in nature, as it varies openly and controversially with the differences and circumstances of individual incumbents. To this extent, the evolution of the British premiership conforms remarkably closely to the development of the modern presidency into its characteristic status of precarious eminence.

The rapidly developing dimension of presidential politics in Britain generates a profusion of intriguing questions concerning the sources, dynamics and ramifications of such a radical change in the position of British political leaders. For example, the precise nature of the relationships between spatial leadership and outsiders, between social outsiderdom and political outsiderdom, between leader detachment and public engagement, and between the electronic media and the creation of publicised gaps separating leaders from their organisations, are all subjects for future observation and extended analysis. It remains to be seen whether there is, for instance, a fundamental connection between the rise of leadership as a feature of British politics and the progressive decline of Britain's position in the world. It may well be that more interdependent global conditions generate a greater susceptibility to defiant cultural expressions in the form of enhanced leadership.

Other questions are of equal significance. It is possible to speculate whether one party is more structurally and culturally disposed towards exploiting, and in turn extending, the public's fascination with personal leadership. On the one hand, it might be argued that the properties of such conspicuous leadership have an inherent relationship with the populist impulses of the radical right. On the other hand, it is also quite plausible to contend that the appeal of spatial leadership against government and of outsider imagery should give primary advantage to any opposition party, irrespective of political persuasion. But what is plausible is not always realistic, especially in this new medium of presidential politics. At present, it seems more reasonable to conclude that the Conservatives have the edge. The party's electoral success, and the ability of its leaders to use the publicity advantages of incumbency to dissociate themselves from the effects of their own policy failures, point to a superior capacity to exploit the presidential dimension.

Taking current developments into account, the moderation of the Labour party's programme, through its policy review, can be interpreted as having been motivated as much by the need to strengthen Neil Kinnock's campaign for public leadership for the general election, as it was to reflect a collective change of internal opinion. The changes not only allowed Kinnock to match the party's outlook more closely to the prevailing configuration of public opinion, but gave the impression of a party being firmly, even forcibly, led by the personal qualities of its leader. Both the policies, which sought to eliminate any diversions to Kinnock's challenge to the Conservative government, and the imagery of party unity convincingly expressed through the leader and his programme, could be said to have optimised the Labour party's electoral position by optimising Mr Kinnock's position in the political struggle for national leadership. It might be concluded that after three election defeats, the Labour party had become only too painfully aware of the central importance of competing at the leadership level. It certainly went to extraordinary lengths to ensure that Mr Kinnock would not be disadvantaged by his party in his drive to acquire Number 10.

Further questions are raised in respect to the long-term implications of presidential politics in the British context. The most disquieting is the effect of the constant suggestions of a public lying outside the political process, requiring leaders to provide it with a form of access to its own government. This might be expressed/rationalised as a substitute for participation, or as an approximation to it, or as a form of compensation for its absence. The symbolism of the leaders' immediacy with the public, and of leaders making dramatic intercessions on behalf of some forgotten element of society, could encourage the view that government is necessarily distant, anonymous and separate from the public.

In these circumstances, the *raison d'être* of public leadership could become so tightly fused with the techniques of such public leadership that the very concepts of (the) government and public might increasingly be seen to be in tension with one another. This could easily lead to the growth in Britain of a negative form of popular sovereignty in which the public is excited by leaders into a sense of its own frustration and then agitated into accepting the need for leaders to relieve it. At the very least, extensive leadership projection carries with it the implication that there are profound reasons for leadership; that the need exists for extraordinary personal faculties to meet extraordinary public circumstances. When this form of electoral suggestion prior to government is combined with the 'in house' populism conducted within government itself over an established period of time, the consequence could well be a severe undermining of governmental authority. In sum, the development of the presidential dimension might introduce a change in the very nature of Britain's liberal democratic state.

One thing at least is quite certain. The dimension of the British presidency will continue to develop. The interconnectedness of its contributory factors and the self-generative nature of its dynamic will ensure that presidential politics will assume an increasingly greater prominence in the British system. Like the United States, questions about what leadership is, who has it and how they come by it will become central features of political debate. Controversies will abound over the relationship between leadership and public approval, between personalities and policies, between actual leadership and the appearances of leadership, between style and substance, and between the promise and actual provision of leadership. Political analysts will popularise debates over whether there is an optimum fit between the premiership and a particular personality type, and how such a fit might be arranged; over whether leadership is the equivalent of a political programme or a digressive substitute for one; and over whether the public can perceive, and assess through an individual's public persona, whether he or she is an effective leader.

The arguments are bound to be intense because leadership is such a potent, yet elusive, term to have in such common usage. It is a rubbery, nebulous and easily manipulative concept that excites strong feelings and high expectations. Americans are already thoroughly accustomed to the controversies over its ramifying meanings, usages and consequences. They are well aware of the problematic nature of leadership in a system geared so much to talking about it and acquiring it. To most ambitious politicians and, therefore, to most aspiring leaders, leadership is about mobilising the public, even to the extent of making it a political end in its own right. At the very least, it is about simply surviving in a highly exposed and competitive environment in which *not* incurring negative public reactions can be interpreted as the mark of a successful leader.

This is a far cry from the romantic rhetoric of leadership, but it is a characteristic of American presidential politics which is renowned both for elevated references to executive guidance and also for the harsh reality of public disillusionment, scepticism and humbled chief executives. The United States is known for the fervour which it attaches to the need for leadership and for the drive to capture it through public acclamation. It is also known for the limited political and constitutional opportunities for sustained pre-eminence and for the often self-fulfilling criticisms of failed presidential leadership. As a consequence, it is almost inevitable that presidential politics are marked by a series of deep disjunctions. They are expressed in the American public's deep ambivalence over the presidency. This leads to severe fluctuations in attitudes both towards individual presidents and towards the presidential office in general. Public sentiment can lurch from very high to very low approval ratings for a president. Similarly, conceptions of the office itself vary from one of command and institutionalised authority to one of weak provisional power conditioned by governmental restraints and political contingencies. Even the value ascribed to the presidency can oscillate violently between peaks of benevolence and troughs of malevolence. This pastiche of fluctuating outlooks and evaluations set in a political context of high-profile leadership and an advanced awareness of its problematic nature pervades the American presidency. There can be little doubt that as the leadership stakes are raised in Britain, the same syndrome of extravagant conviction and scepticism will increasingly come to characterise the politics surrounding the British presidency.

At present what is important is the recognition of a British presidency in formation. It is presidential because of its similarities with recent developments in the American presidency. But it is also very much a British phenom-enon. The presence of a *de facto* presidency in the British system has been occasioned by British circumstances and traditions. Furthermore, it has been assisted and supported by some of the most central components of the British system. Parties, for example, have come not only to sponsor the issue of leadership in political competition, but also to project their leaders as indi-vidual summations of public hopes, anxieties and ideals. Cabinets – filled as they are with professional politicians who know what is required for govern-mental and electoral viability in modern conditions – underwrite prime min-isterial prominence and leverage as the necessary instruments for remaining in office. Many of the prime minister's colleagues around the cabinet table will still aspire to his position, but their highest priority will be to remain in government. They will therefore condone and even encourage a prime minis-ter to go out and cultivate a presidential status in the public battle to provide high-profile popular leadership. This amounts to collective peer group pres-sure to a prime minister to breach the collective ethos of the cabinet and to assume both a public persona and an individual pre-eminence for the sake of the cabinet and the party as a whole. As Mrs Thatcher found to her cost, the pressure can work both ways. A prime minister whose stock declines in the public arena not only loses authority in the cabinet and the party, but risks being removed as party leader.

The British presidency is also distinctly British for another and more subtle reason. It is that its emergence has been almost wholly obscured by the traditional conviction that personal prominence is contrary to the spirit and working arrangements of the British political system. By reputation and custom, the properties as well as the language of leadership have no estab-lished place in the highly institutionalised nature of the British government. An exception like Winston Churchill may have occurred in the past, but as his ascendancy coincided with the extraordinary circumstances of World War II, he was reassuringly regarded to be an anomaly in what was an otherwise settled pattern of arrangements for collective government. The office of the British prime minister could safely be pictured as a rubber band – variable in size but always conforming to a basic shape that would invariably accommo-date the collegiate character of British government.

The influence of such closed traditions and visual devices has created an acute form of myopia, in which major developments in the form and nature of British politics can be completely overlooked. The British presidency is one such unacknowledged transformation. At present, it lies in a blind spot be-tween the traditional formalism of the British constitution and the equally conventional agendas of political analysis. On the one side, constitutionalists dismiss the presidential analogy out of hand because the prime minister is not a political head of state and, therefore, does not have the same responsibilities, political role, or need to adopt a position of public leadership. According to this perspective, the American presidency is a highly institutionalised *personal* office, while the prime minister is a highly institutionalised *impersonal* office. As a consequence, the latter is not studied much because it is not thought to be significant in isolation from the collective context within which it is set. In the words of Anthony King, 'the very force of the office, and its deep rootedness in history, seem in a paradoxical way to have led to its neglect by political scientists. It is not studied because it is simply "there", taken for granted, almost never, as an office, argued about.'[23]

Constitutional neglect has been matched by analytical indifference. Research into the relationship between government and the public has tended to be dominated by surveys of voting behaviour. The conventional outlook of such psephological research is that party leaders have a minimal significance upon the political allegiances of ordinary voters. This traditional premise coincides with the constitutional principle that the public is translated into government by collective means and that, as a result, 'electors vote for parties and not for candidates'.[24] Working on these assumptions, it becomes difficult to take account of the widening scope of the public competition for public leadership. Leaders are generally regarded as having no discernible electoral impact that is independent from generalised party images and party cues for voting. Leaders might make an impression by raising the public's consciousness of party differences,[25] but the impact is likely to be only marginal and, even then, it would be dependent upon a very large discrepancy between the popularity of the opposing candidates.[26]

According to most survey research, therefore, the competition for public leadership, and for a duly individualised executive office, is either a chimera, or else a side-show lacking electoral significance. This view, however, almost invariably underestimates the importance of political conduct between elections and away from voting. It undervalues the wider conditioning effects of changes in the conception and significance of the premiership. It also overlooks the political controversies raised by the office, the political issues translated through it and the contested criteria applied to it.

It is true that more recent psephological surveys have begun to question the earlier dismissal of leaders and leadership in voting studies. Several analyses have shown that a popular leader can exert an independent electoral influence sufficient to win or lose votes for his or her party.[27] Research conducted by Brian Graetz and Ian McAllister, for example, suggests that leader popularity is one of the two main causes of voters defecting from their normal party commitments.[28] In other research findings, Clive Bean and Anthony Mughan look at the relative appeal of different leadership qualities on party voting in the parliamentary systems of Britain and Australia. The uniformity of the response to different leadership characteristics, and especially the way that perceptions of leadership effectiveness dominate how voters respond to leaders, prompt Bean and Mughan to conclude that:

> prime ministerial candidates are judged against some kind of well-defined schema in the public mind and that they will have an electoral impact to the extent they conform to this mental image of what a leader should be like.[29]

As there is increasing evidence that American voters also evaluate their presidential candidates in relation to a similar structure of preferred characteristics,[30] Bean and Mughan find it is

> interesting to speculate that presidential and parliamentary elections may be converging not only with respect to the lesser role for party ideologies and the personalisation of television-dominated election campaigns, but also with respect to the way party leaders affect the vote. The 'presidentialisation' of British politics may have progressed further than many commentators and analysts suspect.[31]

Ivor Crewe for one is no longer prepared to dismiss the possibility of a growing electoral salience on the part of leaders. Writing in September 1991, he believed that the conventional wisdom on leaders and elections might have to be revised in the light of the forthcoming general election. This was not simply because television would dominate the election coverage of each party's campaign in terms of its leader's actions and statements. There were more substantial reasons

> the campaign is likely to turn upon the leaders' qualities more than before. The ideological gap between the Conservatives and Labour has never been narrower. The campaign will be devoted to questions of performance, not policy, and claims about performance amount to claims about the qualities of the party leaders. When Mr Kinnock argues that a Labour government would do things better, not differently, he is making a claim about his team's competence, and above all, his own. At the next election, uncommitted voters will have to judge the parties in terms of their leaders.[32]

These corrections and revisions do not, however, alter the basic implication of such studies – namely that the significance of public leadership as both a political issue and as a dimension of political activity is reducible to its effect on voting behaviour. This analytical self-limitation dovetails neatly with the constitutional oversight of leadership. Together, they provide a formidable wall to apprehending the sprawling and multi-faceted dimension of presidential politics and permanent personal electioneering that has developed in Britain. This is not to deny the importance of recent psephological research on leadership and public attitudes. Neither is it to derogate the significance of the calls for a 'more systematised and disaggregated analysis' into the 'attributes of political leaders such as their personalities and public images'.[33] Investigations into the relationship between individual leadership characteristics and popular prestige on the one hand, and on the constitutional position and political authority of the chief executive on the other would certainly be beneficial. Already Anthony Mughan has ventured to suggest that:

> the perception, if not the actuality, of a premier's indispensability to victory may help him or her to achieve presidential-style primacy in a parliamentary setting where government is formally a collective enterprise.... The great irony may thus be that the personalisation of parliamentary election campaigns in the party leader has been more consequential for governmental than for electoral politics; personal popularity may be useful for shaping more the behaviour of party colleagues and less that of voters.[34]

But at present, the general position is that the presidential wood cannot be seen for the old prime ministerial trees. The British presidency and its broad hinterland of presidential politics is for the most part missed by conventional analysis mainly because the sensory equipment deployed is too narrowly focused to register such a diverse collection of interrelated developments.

There is a further reason why the emergence of a British presidency has remained unacknowledged for so long. The British tradition of relying so much upon graduated evolutionary change in the constitution means that a transformation never seems like one. Paradoxically, for all its apparent experience in constitutional adaptation by practice and convention, the British system is poor at recognising change even when it occurs on a substantial scale. It can appear at times as if it is a constitutional convention not to engage in speculation over the extent to which the constitution has undergone alteration. Whatever the reason, change in the British system is out of all proportion to the extent of its recognition.

Nowhere is this more so than in the case of the prime minister. Despite the fact that evolutionary progression is a primary principle of the British constitution, there has been a marked reluctance to view the prime minister's office in evolutionary terms. While the rest of the system moves on, the position and conception of the prime minister remains in a timeless trough of wilful neglect. The little analysis that exists is distinctive because it possesses no real sense of evolutionary development. The variation of individual incumbents is presented as a form of random aimlessness surrounding an immutable central core of the 'prime minister's job'. The vacuous character of 'the job' serves to accommodate different prime ministers and also to suspend analysis into the nature of the post. In other words, the prime ministership is regarded as having an objective existence sufficient to substantiate the idea of a static entity. But at the same time, it is not worth studying because it is assumed to have no inherent nature and, therefore, nothing that can develop and evolve.

According to this traditional perspective, the prime ministership is nothing more than a derivative term formed from a succession of prime ministers doing a job in roughly similar ways. The norm is that prime ministerial things are done in prime ministerial ways and that the premiership is an abstraction which only arouses uncharacteristic and undesirable speculation into the British constitution. Even though Mrs Thatcher suddenly exposed the rich potential of the office and showed that such personal predominance was sustainable for a very extensive period, the analytical emphasis has still remained one of stasis. Mrs Thatcher's premiership has not been used to examine the underlying forces and dynamics which supported her ascendancy. On the contrary, more is drawn from her departure than from her incumbency. Peter Madgwick, for example, concludes that her 'ejection from office shows that prime ministerial government as practised by Mrs Thatcher is a deviant extension of the British form of executive government'.[35] By being forced from office, she has been rendered safe for the traditional study of the office. Just as Mrs Thatcher's personal style and influence can be written off as exceptional – especially by the manner and the fact of her departure – so her successor is instinctively assumed to have ushered in an effortless resumption of a previous, and thoroughly unnoteworthy, condition of cabinet government.

But evolution does not work along these lines. Evolution, even political and constitutional evolution, cannot turn the clock back. It cannot reverse itself because time is a generative force in its own right. If evolution means never escaping from the inheritance of the past, it also means that it is impossible to return to the conditions of the past. Present arrangements contain the accumulated consequences of the past, rather than the past itself. In this respect, John Major is probably far more significant than Margaret Thatcher. In seeking to break away from, and to act as an antidote to, the *grande dame*, he has in fact demonstrated the influence of her conditioning precedents. He arguably acted out of character, and contrary to expectations, to change the Thatcher government into a wholeheartedly Major government. He was obliged to replace one form of high-profile leadership with another. He personalised policy changes to give emphasis to the idea of a new administration taking its identity from the man at the top. He engaged in publicised interventions in government; he exploited international summitry to build up his personal reputation of leadership and governmental competence; and he came to embody and even to dramatise his own 'big idea' of the Citizen's Charter. In other words, he revealed the underlying evolutionary progression of the office. He showed that behind the surface fluctuations of individual incumbents, the position of the chief executive is developing in accordance with the compulsive inheritance of the past and with the present imperatives of a changing political environment.

It can be argued that a denial of evolution is quite consistent with the evolutionary process. The latter is supposedly a spontaneous and unconscious succession of changes that accumulate into adaptive transformation. Giving conscious recognition to such changes might be seen to be out of character with evolution. Certainly, Britain has a reputation both of dependency upon benevolent political evolution and of denying the onset of change. But a point comes when the scale of change is so extensive that even the British have to acknowledge it. That point has now been reached with the premiership. The political conditions and power relationships associated with the office are such that they can no longer be adequately accounted for by reference to historical rubber bands, or to any of the other devices intent upon insinuating implicit changelessness from explicit change. The British prime minister has evolved, and is evolving, away from what a prime minister used to do and used to be. As this study has attempted to show, the British prime minister has to all intents and purposes turned, not into a British version of an American president, but into an authentically British president.

Within months of the Conservative party's victory in the 1992 general election, the government experienced a series of crises and policy reversals[1] that threatened its existence and, at the same time, afforded a spectacular affirmation of the scale and dynamics of leadership politics in contemporary Britain. Following the election, it was customary to regard John Major's highly personalised election campaign as being pivotal to the Conservatives' win. Electoral analysts were characteristically more cautious, yet also conspicuously more prepared to accept that leadership evaluation 'played a significant role in the final decisions made at the polls'.[2] No such reservations affected the political commentators and columnists. To most, it was simply taken as read that Major's 'personal popularity ... made the difference between victory and defeat'.[3] It was an assumption that became increasingly self-evident with the passage of time.

> Winning votes turns on giving the impression that you are in charge and can change things. Mr Major ... conveyed that impression ... The Tories won because Mr Major appeared as the fresh head of a new government ... He gave people a reason to vote Tory.[4]

By the autumn of 1992, Major found that personalised leadership was a double-edged weapon. As a succession of failures and misadventures rocked the government, Major's position became markedly exposed to critical and even destructive personal scrutiny. In the same way that positive developments and events had earlier been tied both notionally and directly to John Major, so the process was now reversed, with failure transferred quickly to a prime minister who had always felt obliged to refer to government in the first person. Given the sheer scale of leadership stretch in British politics and the sophisticated techniques of personal warfare prevalent in 'leaderland', the effect was immense. The state of the party, the government, the economy and the nation became symbolically interchangeable with the state of the prime minister. Failures – often complex and globally induced failures – were reduced to a simple failure of leadership. And since leadership had become so inextricably linked to the personal qualities of the leader – i.e. an extrapolation of the man – then the failure of leadership was not merely the failure of John Major's leadership but the more personal failure of Major himself. The latter was an altogether more crushing and unanswerable indictment to which a large sector of the media was compulsively drawn in what can only be described as a frenzy of speculation concerning the prime minister's physical and psychological fitness for office.

Major was variously described as feeble, inflexible and incompetent; a prime minister who had lost his way and was 'mired in a sludge of temporisation whilst his party – and cabinet – drifted into ever greater disarray'.[5] For two weeks after the humiliation of Black Wednesday (16 September 1992), when the government effectively devalued the pound by withdrawing sterling from the European Exchange Rate Mechanism, reports were widespread that the government's authority had imploded around the collapse of Major's own authority as prime minister. As one senior government official said at the time: 'Nobody now believes that the prime minister has the will to crack down. We have become an engine without a driver.'[6] Repeatedly, the question raised was one of Major's personal authority together with the suggestion that he was 'neither decisive enough in … leadership or robust enough in confronting critics'.[7] His premiership and his administration were said to lack definition because of Major's own lack of fundamental beliefs. In Michael Ignatieff's words, there was 'a deep grey emptiness inside where the convictions necessary for policy should be found'.[8] Critics pointed not merely to the absence of an agenda or big idea, but to the poverty of imagination, language and expression that would always prevent him from producing a programme. Convinced that during his half-century in Parliament he had never seen the country worse governed than it was in the autumn of 1992, Roy Jenkins was equally sure where to lay the blame.

> Neither in breadth of personality, nor in depth of experience, is the Prime Minister up to the job. … The central weakness, it becomes increasingly clear, lies in the Prime Minister himself.[9]

The same target was identified and found time and time again. A political and economic crisis was effectively translated into a leadership crisis. Major was declared to be out of touch. It was said that his was a government which 'no longer understands how ordinary people think and feel'.[10] Strongly reminiscent of the criticism commonly lodged against incumbent American presidents, Major was roundly criticised for taking refuge in foreign policy. He was portrayed as being preoccupied with the civil war in former Yugoslavia and also with the Maastricht Treaty and the future development of the European Community – and all at a time when Britain's economic plight required the closest political attention. He was also thought to be out of his depth; in particular he did 'not possess the resilience to withstand the pressures of being a prime minister in a crisis'.[11] It was even feared that he might be so exhausted as to be nearly out of his mind. Charles Moore concluded that the 'psychological strain on Mr Major [had to be] acute' because he was being challenged not only on policy but on his 'entire approach to politics', which was 'based on friendship, and the power of personal persuasion'.[12] As Mr Major had 'built so much on personal influence, he [was] taking this crisis personally. His sense of personal injury [was] sharp'.[13] He was portrayed as living a lonely and unhappy existence in a small flat where his only square meal of the day was a breakfast fry-up. His dietary deficiencies, together with the strain of overwork, his lack of friends and a marked weight loss, fuelled speculation that he was near to cracking under the pressure.[14]

In the impulsive dash to convert personal achievement into personal culpability, the very traits that were once alluded to as personal strengths were now cited as the reasons for his decline. Pragmatism, conciliation, caution, sensitivity and 'niceness' were now derided as the obstacles to, rather than the ingredients of, effective leadership. His once valued dearth of zeal and core beliefs was dismissed as evidence of personal vacuity. And his penchant for compromise was now nothing more than a sign of insecurity. When he tried to act tough by threatening to resign and to call an election if his party's Euro rebels defeated the passage of the Maastricht Treaty, he only succeeded in looking misguided and unconvincing – even foolish.

Nothing exemplified this obsessive concern over leadership more than the way that the whole interpretive structure of Major's relationship with his cabinet shifted in response to the decline in his political reputation. During the early part of his administration, Major was said to have successfully revived collective cabinet government.[15] In place of the sychophancy and smouldering dissent of the Thatcher cabinets, Major's inclination towards open discussion and collegiate agreement was hailed as a successful technique in consensus building and a sign of the prime minister's political maturity and personal security. By November 1992, opinions had changed in the light of Major's perceived lack of leadership. Cabinet government was now condemned in some circles as a sign of weakness. The way in which senior ministers were effectively obligated to single positions by the very openness of discussions and by Major's habit of checking for dissent during cabinet meetings, was criticised as being insufficiently pluralistic in nature.

> Instead of the very lively intellectual discussion which had gone on in Mrs Thatcher's day, with people breaking ranks and going around saying 'rubbish', there was just a rather eerie silence … [It was] a conspiracy of silence, deepened by the fact that there [were] so many new ministers in the Government, with others hanging on to their jobs by the skin of their teeth.[16]

In this guise, a united cabinet was not so much a different way for a prime minister to achieve dominance as an indication of a prime minister's insecurity and need for the protective cover of senior ministers. Mr Major may have been able to ensure 'that all go along with the final decision'[17] but, as *The Times* made clear, this was precisely the problem.

286

He should chart his own route away from recession. At the moment, it seems, he can move nowhere without the support of cabinet members whose personal interests are not even in his survival. He looks weak. He is weak.[18]

John Major must have felt that he was in an impossible position because the crisis over his leadership led other critics to condemn him on the grounds that the cabinet was 'wreathed in collective irresponsibility'[19] According to this view, the prime minister had 'lost control of his cabinet. His colleagues neither respect nor fear him.'[20] Cabinet disunity, therefore, was also a symptom of lost leadership. Even when Major tried to assert himself with an unflinching decision on mining closures, he was universally condemned for his lack of consultation, for his failure to submit the plan to the full cabinet and quite simply for his ruthlessness. *The Times* disliked this side of the prime minister's performance as much as it disliked the clubbable 'chumminess' of a cabinet devoid of alternative strategies:

> Lady Thatcher was frequently excoriated for her high-handedness. Decisions were taken by cabinet committees packed with her supporters and then rubber-stamped by full cabinet. This was meant to change with her successor. ... Mr Major has quickly returned to the bad old ways.[21]

It was clear that there no longer existed even the pretense of a norm for prime ministerial–cabinet relations. The chief criterion and overriding political priority for a government was now the successful portrayal of its leader as an effective and popular prime minister – with or without the reputation of cabinet consultation.

So much now depends on a prime minister's mastery of the public character of leadership that the most dangerous feature of the crisis came with the impression that Major had lost touch with the public's frustrations and anxieties. Opinion polls soon revealed the seeds of the disenchantment. From being the most popular prime minister since Churchill in early 1991, Major's support slumped in October 1992 to a point where he became the most unpopular premier since polling began in the 1940s.[22] Anthony King observed that 'never since the Second World War had any government suffered such a precipitous drop in its political fortunes so soon after winning an election.'[23] With a dissatisfaction rating of over 70% and a Labour party lead stretching to twenty points, Major was now in a similar position to Mrs Thatcher when Tory MPs had felt compelled to replace her.

Polls on the prime minister's performance, together with the headline publicity given to them, possess a self-fulfilling property in this most public of offices. The dictum in Washington is that 'perception becomes reality' – or at least it will do unless perceptions are changed. In the period of September – November 1992, the collapse in the prime minister's public position generated a prodigious amount of diagnostic and prognostic speculation that centred upon the implications of such a slump. A MORI poll prompted the *European*, for example, to conclude that Major's unpopularity was as much a cause as an effect of government decisions. It 'explained the dramatic reversal of government policy ... on economic management and the slashing cuts in the coal industry'.[24] The paper believed that Major's unpopularity would 'further weaken his position' in insisting that his backbenchers support him on the Maastrict Treaty. His declining public stature would also 'reduce the effectiveness of his threat to resign if they [did] not support him'.[25] The possible consequences of Major's perceived weaknesses were enough to raise serious doubts as to his continued presence in Downing Street. The mainstream Tory press was so concerned about Major's hapless and inept performance that it turned against him. According to veteran former editors, 'the ferocity of Fleet Street's denunciation of the stature and competence of John Major as prime minister ... [was] unprecedented this century'.[26] Even the *Sun*, Major's praetorian guard during the 1992 election, asked in a front page splash, 'Is Major a goner?'[27]

Major might well have been toppled from the leadership if a serious alternative leader had been available. The prime minister regained some of the initiative he had lost with a series of measures designed to boost economic growth. After recognising that 'the umbilical cord between the government and the parliamentary party [had been] severed' after the election, he promised to repair the damage and to reinstitute a 'listening government'.[28] Major also stated his intention to maintain his populist crusade against slack standards in public services – 'chopping Goliath down to size',[29] he called it. He would achieve this objective by 'giving people the slings and stones to do it'.[30] In the event, the prime minister survived the crisis. He placed his trust in an economic recovery and in a revival of public confidence to redeem his premiership.

What the crisis showed was just how vulnerable even an apparently secure prime minister can be in the extraordinarily fluid conditions of leadership politics. Despite having been credited with winning an election for his party only months beforehand, the modern pressures by which social and international developments are correlated with the character and performance of a fully culpable leader, were sufficient to place Major's premiership in jeopardy. The crisis demonstrated very starkly the extent to which political analysis and evaluation had become permeated by references to personal leadership. The myriad complaints that Major was 'not up to the job' were founded upon the underlying premise that 'the job' in question was up to an individual and, thereby, personal in character. Condemnations of leadership were condemnations of Major's leadership, not leadership itself. Just as the problems of Britain were habitually reduced to the problem of leadership, so the solution presented was the idea and the promise of different leadership.

In Major's case, he was persistently instructed to change his style, in order to provide a change of leadership.

> He has lost his way. He needs to tear up the script and start again, casting himself as the Franklin Roosevelt of the decade. ...Unless Mr Major maps out a strategy for national revival, and implements it with conviction and the full force of all the powers at his disposal, the survival of his government cannot be taken for granted. (*Sunday Times* editorial)[31]

> Creating and stimulating hope is an essential part of successful leadership. ... Mr Major not only has to take grip over economic policy, but to be seen delivering the smack of firm government. (Peter Riddell)[32]

> Mr. Major must be seen to take charge. Reconstructing the cabinet will be difficult for a man who sets such store on friendship and loyalty. But, if to govern is to choose, as it is the fashion to assert, he must now choose to change. (Allan Massie)[33]

> Mr Major has been badly let down by his advisers at 10 Downing Street. ... Mr Major should reach out beyond Westminster and Whitehall for advice. (*Daily Express* editorial)[34]

> What is needed now is the definition and articulation of a clear strategy. ... It is that 'vision thing', to use President Bush's famous phrase – but without it he lost. (Kenneth Baker)[35]

> To deserve to survive he must show leadership. ... If a prime minister is to lead he has to be ahead. He needs a programme for the time before him. ... The country demands that the prime minister pull himself up and do the job that he sought so grimly last year. ... The country requires creativity, intelligence and new spirit. (*The Times* editorial)[36]

Doubts were openly expressed over whether Major was capable of imposing his own agenda upon government and inspiring a renewal of public belief in government. The task repeatedly placed before him as the criterion upon which he would be judged was the Thatcherite principle of leadership as a solution in its own right – i.e. personal leadership made into an instrument of popular mobilisation and political direction through the force of inner convictions, 'big ideas' and sense of the future.

Significantly, the same reproaches were levelled at the new leader of the Labour party. On 18 July 1992, John Smith had been elected leader by a margin of victory[37] that afforded him 'unprecedented power'[38] to compete effectively in the politics of national leadership. By the end of the year, he too was being widely criticised in his own party for what was seen to be his lack of leadership stretch and his lack of a party strategy. Labour insiders complained that they had no idea of what John Smith stood for. As a consequence, there was 'unease in the party about what was seen as a lack of direction, perhaps even a lack of vision'.[39] Concerned over the absence of new thinking or of any real alternative to government policy, criticisms were levelled at the leader for allowing the party to drift into what one respected MP described as 'a state of anaesthetised torpor'.[40] Smith was accused of not understanding the public dimension of leadership politics, or the constant requirement for self-promotion in what had become a condition of permanent electioneering. He was failing to exploit Major's 'prime ministerial weakness' which was now seen to be 'Labour's greatest opportunity'.[41] He was accused of having 'adopted too low a profile'[42] to be effective in the politics of national leadership. The leadership position was now understood to be so critical to the party's electoral prospects that Smith would be given only one chance to achieve victory. As a result, it was widely believed that he would need to change his style in order to fulfil his prime ministerial potential. 'He does need to inspire people more', admitted one adviser. 'He has got to speak passionately about change and what change to bring about.[43] To another colleague, it was clear that he had to 'spend more time projecting himself and his ideas to become prime minister'.[44] Quiet, if impressive, competence was no longer enough to remain party leader, let alone to acquire the premiership.

As both Major and Smith settle down to what will probably be a long haul leading up to the next election, they will have to become fully aware of the powerful undercurrents of presidential politics that now run through the British political system. On the one hand is the demand for prominence, creativity and the redemptive appeal of an autonomous individual with 'vision'.

> The demand for vision is sometimes nothing more than a demand for principles, but it is notable that 'vision' is said. 'Vision' ... is contingent upon a timely visionary. ... In an aside, one could say that vision is from Nietzsche rather than from the liberal Enlightenment. Somehow the democratic leader has acquired the task of taking the people towards a prophetic vision rather than minding the store and letting the people advance on their own.[45]

Harvey Mansfield's observations were prompted by the contemporary presidency in the United States, but they already have a clear resonance in Britain. Leadership, and especially visionary leadership, is celebrated in the same way. It is seen as a means of maintaining the appearance, or the prospect of, indigenous autonomy and national purpose in what is an increasingly interdependent world, where global markets and modern communications technology continually transcend and undermine national boundaries. By the same token, the familiarly American response to the cult of leadership is also increasingly discernible in British public life. The flamboyant panaceas of presidential candidates in the United States are regularly brought down to earth by a public with a hardened scepticism of, and impatience with, its leaders. A political culture geared to the search for leadership is complemented by an 'anti-leadership political system' in which 'others are out to get whomever is in authority'.[46] Whether it is because expectations are always inflated by leaders to politically unattainable levels[47] or whether it is because the abstract promise of leadership is always preferable to the actuality of a leader, the net effect is that America is as renowned for its 'anti-leadership' politics as it is for its leadership politics.

The events of 1992 suggest that Britain is rapidly developing its own version of this presidential dichotomy. As a consequence, whichever leader prevails at the next election will only have done so by enduring a highly volatile political process in which the impersonal is compulsively personalised with an ever-increasing intensity, universality and sense of validity. The essence of leadership will remain a highly nebulous and contested concept. Nevertheless, the public battle to persuade voters to believe that one party leader or another possesses leadership qualities – and with them a general competence to govern – will not only dominate party strategies and popular argument, but will also ensure a continual flux of wildly varying personal reputations at the centre of British politics.

Chapter 1

1 Bernard Crick, *The Reform of Parliament*, 2nd edn (London: Weidenfeld and Nicolson, 1968), p. 18.
2 Ronald Butt, 'The missionary in politics', *The Times*, 23 November 1990.
3 S. E. Finer, 'Thatcherism and British Political History', in Kenneth Minogue and Michael Biddiss (eds), *Thatcherism: Personality and Politics* (Basingstoke, Hants: Macmillan, 1987), p. 140.
4 Kenneth Minogue, 'Introduction: The Context of Thatcherism', in Minogue and Biddiss (eds), *Thatcherism: Personality and Politics*, p. xvii.
5 Hugo Young, 'To the Manner Born', in Hugo Young and Anne Sloman, *The Thatcher Phenomenon* (London: British Broadcasting Corporation, 1986), p. 12.
6 Hugo Young, 'Rough justice for a leader born to battle', *Guardian*, 23 November 1990.
7 *Ibid.*
8 Andrew Gamble, 'Following the Leader', *Marxism Today*, January 1991, p. 15.
9 Peter Hennessy, 'The Prime Minister, the Cabinet and the Thatcher Personality', in Minogue and Biddiss (eds), *Thatcherism*, p. 56.
10 Dennis Kavanagh, *Thatcherism and British Politics: The End of Consensus?*, 2nd edn (Oxford: Oxford University Press, 1990), pp. 246, 248.
11 Anthony King, 'Margaret Thatcher as a Political Leader', in Robert Skidelsky (ed.), *Thatcherism* (London: Chatto and Windus, 1988), pp. 57-8.
12 *Ibid.*, p. 56.
13 Peter Clarke, 'Margaret Thatcher's Leadership in Historical Perspective', *Parliamentary Affairs*, 45, no. 1 (January 1992), p. 11.
14 Butt, 'The missionary in politics'.
15 Joe Rogaly, 'Will the real Mr Major stand up', *Financial Times*, 28 November 1990.
16 Dennis Kavanagh, 'Prime Ministerial Power Revisited', *Social Studies Review*, 6, no. 4 (March 1991), p. 132.
17 William Rees Mogg, 'Haunted by the ghost of yesterday's leader', *Independent*, 15 April 1991.
18 Peter Jenkins, *Mrs Thatcher's Revolution: The Ending of the Socialist Era* (London: Pan Books, 1989), p. 174.
19 John Vincent, 'The Thatcher Governments, 1979-1987', Peter Hennessy and Anthony Seldon (eds), *Ruling Performance: British Governments from Attlee to Thatcher* (Oxford: Basil Blackwell, 1987), p. 288.
20 Jenkins, *Mrs Thatcher's Revolution*, p. 184.
21 Tam Dalyell, *Misrule: How Mrs Thatcher misled Parliament from the Sinking of the Belgrano to the Wright Affair* (London: New English Library, 1988), p. 17.
22 Ian Gilmour, 'The false doctrine of "Thatchocracy"', *Observer*, 30 July 1989.
23 For example, in a popular text on British politics entitled *Political Issues in Britain Today* (ed. Bill Jones, Manchester University Press, 3rd edn, 1989), the issue given the highest priority in the book was the editor's own appraisal of 'The Thatcher Style' (pp. 1-20).
24 'Fear and panic at the court of Queen Margaret', *Observer*, 29 October 1989.
25 John P. Mackintosh, *The British Cabinet*, 2nd edn (London: Methuen, 1968), chs 1, 18, 24; Intro. by R. H. S. Crossman, Walter Bagehot, *The English Constitution*, (London: Fontana, 1963), pp. 1-57.
26 Mackintosh, *The British Cabinet*, p. 624.

27 *Ibid.*, p. 627.
28 Crossman, Intro. to *The English Constitution*, p. 51.
29 *Ibid.*, p. 54.
30 See John Hart, 'President and Prime Minister: Convergence or Divergence?', *Parliamentary Affairs*, 44, no. 2 (April 1991), pp. 209-12.
31 Crossman, Intro. to *The English Constitution*, p. 51.
32 *Ibid.*, p. 56.
33 *Ibid.*, pp. 22-3.
34 Mackintosh, *The British Cabinet*, p. 428.
35 Crick, *The Reform of Parliament*, p. 25.
36 Brian Sedgemore, *The Secret Constitution: An Analysis of the Political Establishment* (London: Hodder and Stoughton, 1980), p. 66.
37 *Ibid.*, p. 66.
38 *Ibid.*, p. 66.
39 Tony Benn, 'Curbing the power of PMs', *Observer*, 15 July 1979.
40 James Margach, *The Anatomy of Power: An Enquiry into the Personality of Leadership* (London: W. H. Allen, 1979), p. 78.
41 *Ibid.*, p. 77.
42 Anthony King, 'The Prime Minister and Cabinet', *Contemporary Record*, 4, no. 1 (September 1990), p. 22.
43 Anthony King, 'Political Masters' (Review of Valentine Herman and James E. Alt (eds), *Cabinet Studies: A Reader*), *New Society*, 14 August 1975.
44 Harold Wilson, *The Governance of Britain* (London: Weidenfeld and Nicolson, and Michael Joseph, 1976), p. 20.
45 *Ibid.*, p. 20.
46 *Ibid.*, p. 21.
47 *Ibid.*, p. 22.
48 *Ibid.*, p. 15.
49 Richard Rose, 'British Government: The Job at the Top', in Richard Rose and Ezra N. Suleiman (eds), *Presidents and Prime Ministers* (Washington, DC: American Enterprise Institute, 1980), pp. 32, 25.
50 G. W. Jones, 'The Prime Minister's Power', in Anthony King (ed.), *The British Prime Minister*, 2nd edn (Basingstoke, Hants: Macmillan, 1985), p. 196.
51 *Ibid.*, p. 204.
52 G. W. Jones, 'The Prime Minister's Power', *Parliamentary Affairs*, 18, no. 2 (Spring 1965), p. 178.
53 Jones, 'The Prime Minister's Power', in King (ed.), *The British Prime Minister*, p. 213.
54 Anthony King, 'Men on the job' (Review of John P. Mackintosh (ed.), *British Prime Ministers in the Twentieth Century: Vol 1, Balfour to Chamberlain*), *New Society*, 11 August 1977.
55 Martin Burch, 'The British Cabinet: A Residual Executive', *Parliamentary Affairs*, 41, no. 1 (January 1988), pp. 4-48.
56 Vincent, 'The Thatcher Governments, 1979-1987', in Hennessy and Seldon (eds), *Ruling Performance*, p. 288.
57 Bob Jessop, Kevin Bonnett, Simon Bromley and Tom Ling, *Thatcherism: A Tale of Two Nations* (Oxford: Polity, 1988), p. 83.
58 Richard Holme, *The People's Kingdom* (London: Bodley Head, 1987), p. 125.
59 Gilmour, 'The False Doctrine of "Thatchocracy"', *Observer*, 30 July 1989.
60 Tony Benn, 'Power, Parliament and the People', *New Socialist*, September/October 1982.
61 G. W. Jones, 'Cabinet Government and Mrs Thatcher', *Contemporary Record*, 1, No.3 (Autumn) 1987, p. 8.

62 Kavanagh, *Thatcherism and British Politics*, p. 254. See also R. M. Punnett, *British Government and Politics*, 5th edn (Aldershot, Hants: Dartmouth, 1987), pp. 246-7.
63 Jenkins, *Mrs Thatcher's Revolution*, p. 185.
64 *Ibid.*, p. xvii.
65 G. W. Jones, 'Prime Minister and the Cabinet', *Wroxton Papers in Politics* (Wroxton College, 1990), pp. 5, 13.
66 G. W. Jones, 'Mrs Thatcher and the Power of the Prime Minister', *Contemporary Record*, 3, no. 4 (April 1990), p. 6.
67 Jones, 'Prime Minister and the Cabinet', p. 13.
68 Peter Jenkins, 'The real rebel of cabinet government', *Independent on Sunday*, 22 July 1990.
69 Frank Johnson, 'The Cabinet was in charge all along', *Sunday Telegraph*, 16 December 1990.
70 *Ibid.*
71 *Ibid.*
72 *Ibid.*
73 *Ibid.* For a similarly jaundiced view of what academics can contribute to the debate over prime ministerial power, see Alan Watkins, 'It's no good trying to be like Mrs Thatcher', *Observer*, 9 June 1991. Watkins refers to the way that 'several academics, whose closest acquaintance with Whitehall and Westminster was from the top deck of a number 11 bus, popularised the notion that we are living under a presidential system of government'. The most prominent had been John Mackintosh, who 'had worked out his views at the Universities of Edinburgh and Ibadan, Nigeria'.
74 Jones, 'Prime Minister and the Cabinet', p. 13.
75 Dennis Healey, quoted in Jones, 'The Thatcher Style', in Jones (ed.), *Political Issues in Britain Today*. p. 18.

Chapter 2

1 Taken from 'President Reagan's Inaugural Address, January 20, 1981', in *Congressional Quarterly Almanac*, 97th Congress, 1st Session, 1981, Volume XXXVII (Washington, DC: Congressional Quarterly, Inc., 1982), p. 11E.
2 Richard E. Neustadt, *Presidential Power: The Politics of Leadership* (New York: John Wiley, 1960), p. 185.
3 Thomas E. Cronin, *The State of the Presidency*, 2nd edn (Boston: Little, Brown, 1975), p. 84.
4 *Ibid.*, p. 84.
5 Clinton Rossiter quoted in Neustadt, *Presidential Power*, p. 152.
6 James Macgregor Burns, *Presidential Government: The Crucible of Leadership* (Boston: Houghton Mifflin, 1973), p. 351.
7 Bert A. Rockman, *The Leadership Question: The Presidency and the American System* (New York: Praeger, 1984), p. xvi.
8 Burns, *Presidential Government*, p. 346.
9 Robert S. Hirschfield, 'The Power of the Contemporary Presidency', in Robert S. Hirschfield (ed.), *The Power of the Presidency: Concepts and Controversy* (New York: Atherton, 1968), p. 245.
10 Samuel P. Huntington, 'The Democratic Distemper', in Nathan Glazer and Irving Kristol (eds), *The American Commonwealth 1976* (New York: Basic, 1976), pp. 9-38; Richard Rosecranz (ed.), *America as an Ordinary Country* (Ithaca, New York: Cornell University Press, 1976); Joel Krieger, *Reagan, Thatcher and the Politics of Decline* (New York:

Oxford University Press, 1986); James L. Sundquist, 'The Crisis of Competence in Our National Government', *Political Science Quarterly*, 95, no. 2 (Summer 1980), pp. 183-208.

11 See William Crotty and Gary Jacobson, *American Parties in Decline* (Boston: Little, Brown, 1980); Martin P. Wattenberg, *The Decline of American Parties, 1952-1984* (Cambridge, Mass.: Harvard University Press, 1986).

12 See Richard M. Scammon and Ben J. Wattenberg, *The Real Majority* (New York: Berkley Medallion, 1972); Walter Dean Burnham, 'The Turnout Problem', in A. James Reichley (ed.), *Elections American Style* (Washington, DC: Brookings Institution, 1987), pp. 97-133; Dean McSweeney and John Zvesper, *American Political Parties: The Formation, Decline and Reform of the American Party System* (London: Routledge, 1991), ch. 10; Martin P. Wattenberg, 'From a Partisan to a Candidate-centered Electorate', in Anthony King (ed.), *The New American Political System*, Second Version (Washington, DC: American Enterprise Institute, 1990), pp. 139-74.

13 See Nelson W. Polsby, *The Consequences of Party Reform* (New York: Oxford University Press, 1983); Jeane J. Kirkpatrick, *The New Presidential Elite* (New York: Sage, 1976); Everett C. Ladd, *Where Have All the Voters Gone? The Fracturing of America's Political Parties* (New York: W. W. Norton, 1982).

14 Larry Sabato, *The Rise of Political Consultants* (New York: Basic, 1981); John A. Ferejohn and Morris P. Fiorina, 'Incumbency and Realignment in Congressional Elections', in John E. Chubb and Paul E. Peterson (eds), *The New Direction in American Politics* (Washington, DC: Brookings Institution, 1985), pp. 91-116; Frank I. Luntz, *Candidates, Consultants and Campaigns: The Style and Substance of American Electioneering* (Oxford: Basil Blackwell, 1988).

15 Thomas E. Mann and Norman J. Ornstein (eds), *The New Congress* (Washington, DC: American Enterprise Institute, 1981); Michael Foley, *The New Senate: Liberal Influence in a Conservative Institution, 1959-1972* (New Haven, Conn.: Yale University Press, 1980); Steven S. Smith, 'New Patterns of Decision-Making in Congress', in Chubb and Peterson (eds), *The New Direction in American Politics*, pp. 203-34.

16 Hugh Heclo, 'Issue Networks and the Executive Establishment', in Anthony King (ed.), *The New American Political System* (Washington, DC: American Enterprise Institute, 1978), pp. 87-124.

17 Theodore Lowi, *The End of Liberalism: Ideology, Policy, and the Crisis of Public Authority* (New York: W. W. Norton, 1969).

18 Morris P. Fiorina, 'An Era of Divided Government', in Gillian Peele, Christopher J. Bailey and Bruce Cain (eds), *Developments in American Politics* (Basingstoke, Hants: Macmillan, 1992), p. 347. See also Charles O. Jones, 'The Voters Say Yes: The 1984 Congressional Elections', in Ellis Sandoz and Cecil V. Crabb, Jr. (eds), *Election 84: Landslide Without a Mandate?* (New York: New American Library, 1985), ch. 4; Walter Dean Burnham, 'The Reagan Heritage', in Gerald Pomper (ed.), *The Election of 1988* (Chatham, New Jersey, Chatham House, 1989), pp. 1-32. James L. Sundquist, 'Needed: A Political Theory for the New Era of Coalition Government in the United States', *Political Science Quarterly*, 103, no. 4 (Winter 1988-1989), pp. 613-35.

19 Harold M. Barger, *The Impossible Presidency: Illusions and Realities of Executive Power* (Glenview, Ill.: Scott, Foresman, 1984); Godfrey Hodgson, *All Things To All Men: The False Promise of the Modern Presidency*, rev edn. (Harmondsworth, Middlesex: Penguin, 1984); Hugh Heclo, 'The Presidential Illusion', in Hugh Heclo and Lester M. Salamon (eds), *The Illusion of Presidential Government* (Boulder, Colo.: Westview, 1981).

20 Paul Light, *The President's Agenda* (Baltimore, Md: Johns Hopkins University Press, 1982).

21 Barger, *The Impossible Presidency*, p. 7.

22 Theodore H. White, *The Making of the President, 1968* (London: Jonathan Cape, 1969); Richard Nixon, *The Memoirs of Richard Nixon* (London: Sidgwick and Jackson, 1978), pp. 295-414.

23 Quoted in David Graham and Peter Clarke, *The New Enlightenment: The Rebirth of Liberalism* (Basingstoke, Hants: Macmillan, 1986), p. 51.

24 Irving Kristol, *Two Cheers for Capitalism* (New York: Basic, 1978); Norman Podhoretz, *Breaking Ranks* (London: Weidenfeld and Nicolson, 1979).

25 Norman Mailer, *Miami and the Siege of Chicago: An Informal History of the American Political Conventions of 1968* (Harmondsworth, Middlesex: Penguin, 1969), pp. 9-80.

26 Philip E. Converse, Warren E. Miller, Jerrold G. Rusk, and Arthur C. Wolfe, 'Continuity and Change in American Politics: Parties and Issues in the 1968 Election', *American Political Science Review*, 63, no. 4 (December 1969), pp. 1083-1105.

27 Rowland Evans, Jr. and Robert D. Novak, *Nixon in the White House: The Frustration of Power* (New York: Vintage, 1972), p. 4.

28 Quoted in Theodore H. White, *The Making of the President, 1972* (New York: Bantam, 1973), pp. 292-3.

29 E. Howard Hunt, *Undercover: Memoirs of an American Secret Agent* (London: W. H. Allen, 1975), p. 156.

30 Theodore H. White, *Breach of Faith: The Fall of Richard Nixon* (London: Jonathan Cape, 1975); J. Anthony Lukas, *Nightmare: The Underside of the Nixon Years* (New York: Viking, 1976).

31 Clifton McCleskey and Pierce McCleskey, 'Jimmy Carter and the Democratic Party', in M. Glenn Abernathy, Dilys M. Hill and Phil Williams (eds), *The Carter Years: The President and Policy Making* (London: Francis Pinter, 1984), p. 128.

32 Jimmy Carter, *Why Not the Best?* (New York: Bantam, 1976), p. 168.

33 *Ibid.*, p. 171.

34 Jimmy Carter, *Keeping Faith: Memoirs of a President* (London: Collins, 1982), p. 23.

35 Gaddis Smith, *Morality, Reason and Power: American Diplomacy in the Carter Years* (New York: Hill and Wang, 1986).

36 Quoted in an interview with Ronald Kriss and Christopher Ogden, *Time*, 11 October 1982.

37 David S. Broder, 'Paradox in Carter's Future', *Washington Post Supplement* in *Guardian Weekly*, 1 December 1979.

38 James Fallows, 'The Passionless Presidency: The Trouble with Jimmy Carter's Administration', *Atlantic*, May 1979, p. 45.

39 *Ibid.*, p. 46.

40 *Ibid.*, p. 46.

41 George F. Will, *Statecraft as Soulcraft: What Government Does* (London: Weidenfeld and Nicolson, 1984), p. 16.

42 'Crisis of Confidence televised address, July 15 1979', in *Congressional Quarterly Almanac*, 97th Congress, 1st Session 1981, Volume XXXV (Washington, DC: Congressional Quarterly Inc., 1980), p. 46E.

43 Samuel Kernell, *Going Public: New Strategies of Presidential Leadership* (Washington, DC: Congressional Quarterly, 1986), p. 137.

44 Rowland Evans and Robert Novak, *The Reagan Revolution* (New York: E. P. Dutton, 1981), chs. 1, 12; Fred I. Greenstein, 'Reagan and the Lore of the Modern Presidency: What Have We Learned?', in Fred I. Greenstein (ed.), *The Reagan Presidency: An Early Assessment* (Baltimore, Md: Johns Hopkins University Press, 1983), pp. 159-87; Garry Wills, *Reagan's America: Innocents Abroad* (London: Heinemann, 1988), chs. 38, 40, 41; David Mervin, *Ronald Reagan and the American Presidency* (London: Longman, 1990), chs. 1-5, 8, 9.

45 Ronald Reagan, *Speaking My Mind: Selected Speeches* (London: Hutchinson, 1989), p. 98.

46 *Ibid.*, pp. 96, 414.

47 Ronald Reagan, *An American Life* (London: Hutchinson, 1990), p. 234.

48 *Ibid.*, p. 286.

49 *Ibid.*, pp. 286, 287.

50 *Ibid.*, p. 287.

51 David A. Stockman, *The Triumph of Politics: The Crisis in American Government and How It Affects the World* (London: Bodley Head, 1986).

52 James W. Ceaser, 'The Reagan Presidency and American Public Opinion', in Charles O. Jones (ed.), *The Reagan Legacy: Promise and Performance* (Chatham, New Jersey: Chatham House, 1988), pp. 174-93.

53 Louis Fisher, 'Reagan's Relations with Congress', in Dilys M. Hill, Raymond A. Moore and Phil Williams (eds), *The Reagan Presidency: An Incomplete Revolution?* (Basingstoke, Hants: Macmillan, 1990), p. 98.

54 Quoted in Kathleen H. Jamieson, *Eloquence in an Electronic Age: The Transformation of Political Speechmaking* (New York: Oxford University Press, 1988), p. 123.

55 Quoted in *ibid.*, p. 123.

56 Quoted in *ibid.*, p. 123.

57 Quoted in *ibid.*, p. 123.

58 Robert G. Kaiser, 'Ronald Reagan's America: An Intoxicating Myth for Our Time', *Washington Post Supplement* in *Guardian Weekly*, 4 November 1984.

59 Garry Wills, 'What Happened?' *Time*, 9 March 1987.

60 Wills, *Reagan's America*, p. 357.

61 Jane Mayer and Doyle McManus, *Landslide: The Unmaking of the President, 1984-1988* (London: Fontana, 1989), p. 31.

62 Quoted in Seymour M. Lipset, 'Beyond 1984: The Anomalies of American Politics', *PS*, Spring 1986, p. 228.

63 Everett C. Ladd, 'The Reagan Phenomenon and Public Attitudes Toward Government', in Lester M. Salamon and Michael Lund (eds), *The Reagan Presidency and the Governing of America* (Washington, DC: Urban Institute Press, 1984), p. 225.

64 Lipset, 'Beyond 1984: The Anomalies of American Politics, p. 229.

65 Ceaser, 'The Reagan Presidency and American Public Opinion', in Jones (ed.), *The Reagan Legacy*, pp. 197-8.

66 Quoted in Mayer and McManus, *Landslide*, p. 27.

67 Reagan, *Speaking My Mind*, pp. 415-16.

68 He had been US Ambassador to the United Nations, the first US envoy to China, Director of the Central Intelligence Agency and Chairman of the Republican Party.

69 'Fighting the "Wimp Factor"', *Newsweek*, 10 September 1987.

70 'Waving the Bloody Shirt: Good George, Bad George', *Newsweek*, 21 November 1988; John Cassidy, 'From Wimp to Winner', *Sunday Times*, 6 November 1988; Aaron Wildavsky, 'Making the Process Work: The Procedural Presidency of George Bush', in Aaron Wildavsky, *The Beleaguered Presidency* (New Brunswick, NJ: Transaction, 1991), pp. 302-6.

71 Quoted in John Cassidy and Mark Hosenball, 'Main event: battle is joined but the boxers land no punches', *Sunday Times*, 16 October 1988.

72 Michael Kinsley, 'Hypocrisy and the L-word', *Time*, 1 August 1988; Alexander Cockburn, 'The L-word in crisis', *New Statesman and Society*, 4 November 1988.

73 Michael Foley, 'Presidential leadership and the presidency', in Joseph Hogan (ed.), *The Reagan Years: The Record in Presidential Leadership* (Manchester: Manchester University Press, 1990), pp. 48-9.

74 Dan Goodgame, 'Plain Speaking', *Time*, 12 November 1990.
75 *Time*, 22 October 1990.
76 Quoted in Henry Miller and John Stacks, "Determined to Do What Is Right', *Time*, 7 January 1991.
77 Dan Goodgame, 'Read My Hips', *Time*, 22 October 1990.
78 *Time*, 25 May 1992.
79 Bert A. Rockman, 'The Leadership Style of George Bush,' Colin Campbell, SJ and Bert A Rockman (eds), *The Bush Presidency: First Appraisals* (Chatham, NJ: Chatham House, 1991), p. 20.
80 *Ibid.*, p. 28.
81 Lance Morrow, 'Voters Are Mad as Hell', *Time*, 2 March 1992.
82 Quoted in Joe Klein, 'Silent majority sends Bush an ultimatum', *Sunday Times*, 23 February 1992.
83 Quoted in Klein, *ibid.*
84 Quoted in Martin Walker, 'A child of the sixties claims his inheritance', *Guardian*, 29 February 1992.
85 Quoted in Peter Stodhard, 'Brown victory jolts Clinton bandwagon', *The Times*, 26 March 1992.
86 Quoted in James Adams, 'Punching Pat promises Bush a tough fight', *Sunday Times*, 9 February 1992.
87 Quoted in Andrew Stephens, 'Yahoos for George, his dog and wife', *Observer*, 19 January 1992.
88 Quoted in Mark Lawson, 'Candidate for a Cold Climate', *Independent Magazine*, 15 February 1992.
89 Quoted in Ian Brodie, 'A Texas folk-hero aims to join race,' *Daily Telegraph*, 23 March 1992.
90 Quoted in *ibid.*
91 Quoted in Martin Walker, 'The post-modernist saviour of America', *Guardian Weekly*, 7 June 1992.
92 Quoted in Walter Shapiro, 'He's ready, but is America ready for President Perot?', *Time*, 25 May 1992.
93 Quoted in Joe Klein, 'Goofy Bush chases rainbow in downpour', *Sunday Times*, 19 January 1992.

Chapter 3

1 Bert A. Rockman, *The Leadership Question: The Presidency and the American System* (New York: Praeger, 1984), p. 41.
2 Jim Prior, *A Balance of Power* (London: Hamish Hamilton, 1986), p. 117.
3 Hugo Young and Anne Sloman, *The Thatcher Phenomenon* (London: British Broadcasting Corporation, 1986), p. 30.
4 Prior, *A Balance of Power*, p. 99.
5 Quoted from Patrick Cosgrave, 'The stalking horse who romped home', *Independent*, 30 November 1989.
6 Kenneth Harris, *Thatcher* (London: Weidenfeld and Nicolson, 1988), p. 31.
7 Cosgrave, 'The stalking horse who romped home'.
8 Francis Pym, *The Politics of Consent* (London: Hamish Hamilton, 1984), p. 5.
9 Harris, *Thatcher*, p. 32.
10 Peter Jenkins, *Mrs Thatcher's Revolution: The Ending of the Socialist Era* (London: Pan, 1989), p. 14.

11 Anthony King, 'The Problem of Overload', in Anthony King (ed.), *Why is Britain Becoming Harder to Govern?* (London: British Broadcasting Corporation, 1976), pp. 8-30; Samuel Brittan, 'The Economic Contradictions of Democracy', *British Journal of Political Science*, 6, no. 2 (1975), pp. 129-60.

12 Samuel H. Beer, *Britain against Itself: The Political Contradictions of Collectivism* (London: Faber, 1982).

13 Robert Skidelsky, 'Introduction', in Robert Skidelsky (ed.), *Thatcherism* (London: Chatto and Windus, 1988), p. 10.

14 Jenkins, *Mrs Thatcher's Revolution*, p. 28.

15 *Ibid.*, p. 10.

16 Keith Joseph, 'Proclaim the Message: Keynes is Dead', in Patrick Hutber (ed.), *What's Wrong with Britain?* (London: Sphere, 1978), p. 105.

17 Margaret Thatcher, *The Revival of Britain: Speeches on Home and European Affairs, 1975-1988*, compiled by Alistair B. Cooke (London: Aurum, 1989), p. 3.

18 Michael Biddiss, 'Thatcherism: Concept and Interpretations', in Kenneth Minogue and Michael Biddiss (eds), *Thatcherism: Personality and Politics* (Basingstoke, Hants: Macmillan, 1987), p. 2.

19 Bob Jessop, Kevin Bonnett, Simon Bromley and Tom Ling, *Thatcherism: A Tale of Two Nations* (Oxford: Polity, 1988), p. 61.

20 Pym, *The Politics of Consent*, p. 5.

21 Harris, *Thatcher*, p. 62.

22 Julian Critchley, 'Mrs Thatcher's Tory Party', *The Listener*, 9 October 1980.

23 Edward Pearce, 'Fighter with a golden tongue', *Guardian*, 26 November 1990.

24 John Vincent, 'The Thatcher Governments, 1979-1987', in Peter Hennessy and Anthony Seldon (eds), *Ruling Performance: British Governments from Attlee to Thatcher* (Oxford: Basil Blackwell, 1987), p. 279.

25 Jessop, Bonnett, Bromley and Ling, *Thatcherism*, p. 82.

26 John Cole, *The Thatcher Years: A Decade of Revolution in British Politics* (London: British Broadcasting Corporation, 1987), p. 11.

27 Anthony King, 'Margaret Thatcher: The Style of a Prime Minister', in Anthony King (ed.), *The British Prime Minister*, 2nd edn (Basingstoke, Hants: Macmillan, 1985), p. 116.

28 Anthony King, 'Margaret Thatcher as a Political Leader', in Skidelsky (ed.), *Thatcherism*, p. 59.

29 Jenkins, *Mrs Thatcher's Revolution*, p. 184.

30 Quoted in Peter Jenkins, 'The real rebel of cabinet government', *Independent on Sunday*, 22 July 1990.

31 Robert Skidelsky, 'The pride and the fall', *Guardian*, 21 November 1990.

32 Peregrine Worsthorne, 'Whose party is it now?' *Sunday Telegraph*, 16 June 1991.

33 Peregrine Worsthorne, 'Who'll speak for England?', *Sunday Telegraph*, 25 November 1990. For more on Mrs Thatcher's overtly populist approach to politics and policy, see Vernon Bogdanor, 'Democracy is dying: long live democracy!', *Listener*, 17 April 1986; Desmond King, *The New Right: Politics, Markets and Citizenship* (Basingstoke, Hants: Macmillan, 1987).

34 King, 'Margaret Thatcher: The Style of a Prime Minister', in King (ed.), *The British Prime Minister*, pp. 117-18.

35 Quoted in Young and Sloman, *The Thatcher Phenomenon*, pp. 53-4.

36 John Gaffney, *The Language of Political Leadership in Contemporary Britain* (Basingstoke, Hants: Macmillan, 1991), p. 158.

37 Quoted in Young and Sloman, *The Thatcher Phenomenon*, pp. 95-6.

38 Noel Malcolm, 'Mrs Thatcher: Housewife Superstar', *Spectator*, 25 Febrary 1989.

39 Robert Harris, *Good and Faithful Servant: The Unauthorised Biography of Bernard*

Ingham (London: Faber, 1991), pp. 150, 93.

40 Ivor Crewe, 'The Policy Agenda: A New Thatcherite Consensus?', *Contemporary Record* 3, no. 3 (February 1990), p. 5.

41 Ivor Crewe, 'Values: The Crusade that Failed', in Dennis Kavanagh and Anthony (eds) *The Thatcher Effect* (Oxford: Oxford University Press, 1989), p. 250.

42 Ivor Crewe, 'Has the Electorate become more Thatcherite?' in Skidelsky (ed.) *Thatcherism*, p. 45.

43 *Ibid.*, p. 45.

44 William Rees Mogg, 'Imprecision, the latest vote loser for Labour', *Independent*, 7 May 1990.

45 Crewe, 'Has the Electorate become more Thatcherite?', in Skidelsky (ed.), *Thatcherism*, p. 44.

46 The average of 67.0% for Mrs Thatcher's policies was derived from the responses to a series of questions on 'specifically Thatcherite policies and decisions' presented in Crewe's article (*ibid.*, p. 41). The average of 39.0% for Mrs Thatcher's leadership is the figure given by Crewe (*ibid.*, p. 44). The differences between the public's view of Mrs Thatcher and her policies was also evident in Gallup's regular monthly questions of 'which party has the best leaders?' and 'which party has the best policies?' For much of the Thatcher period, there was often a clear discrepancy in preferences favouring Conservative leadership over Conservative policies. Although the response to leadership must have been based upon Mrs Thatcher's reputation for ascendancy, the public's favourable outlook was not extended to what were logically *her* policies. This disjunction was ever present during the nadir of the Thatcher era. In September 1990, for example, only 30% believed that the Conservatives had the best policies, while 39% thought Labour had the best policies. What was a -9% net rating on policy, however, turned into a +11% rating when the question changed to leadership, with 42% believing that the Conservatives had the best leaders and only 31% regarding Labour as the party with best leaders – *Gallup Political Index*, Report No. 361, September 1990.

47 James Alt, Ivor Crewe and Bo Sarlvik, 'Angels in Plastic: The Liberal Surge in 1974', *Political Studies* 25, no. 3 (September 1977), pp. 343-68.

48 The party changed its name to the Social and Liberal Democrat party following a merger with the majority faction of the SDP in 1987. It is now known simply as the Liberal Democrat party.

49 'The alliance's man of action: is he not charismatic?', *Sunday Times*, 31 July 1988.

50 Quoted in BBC Radio 3, *The Gang That Fell Apart*, Part 2, broadcast on 18 September 1991.

51 William Rodgers, 'Why merger must take place', *Observer*, 21 June 1987.

52 David Butler and Dennis Kavanagh, *The British General Election of 1987* (Basingstoke, Hants: Macmillan, 1988), p. 262.

53 *Ibid.*, p. 262.

54 David Owen, *Time to Declare* (Harmondsworth, Middlesex: Penguin, 1992), p. 701.

55 Anthony Howard, 'Why Foot has doomed Labour', *Observer*, 15 May 1983.

56 Robert Harris, *The Making of Neil Kinnock* (London: Faber, 1984), p. 138.

57 *Ibid.*, p. 184.

58 'Neil's niceness isn't enough', *Observer*, 1 October 1989.

59 Quoted in Richard Ford, 'Tory praises "outstanding" Kinnock revival', *The Times*, 27 May 1991.

60 Peter Kellner, 'Labour annuls its loveless marriage', *Independent*, 25 May 1990.

61 Tom Nairn, 'The future according to Benn' (Review of Tony Benn, *Parliament, People and Power: Agenda for a Free Society*), *Guardian Weekly*, 23 January 1983.

62 Martin Jacques, 'Labour needs to shed its old clothes', *Sunday Times*, 14 August 1988.

63 Michael Cockerell, 'Vote, vote, vote for Tony Benn', *Listener*, 25 June 1981.
64 Peter Kellner, 'A party no longer hounded by the left', *Independent*, 5 October 1990.
65 R. M. Punnett, 'Selecting the Leader and the Deputy Leader of the Labour Party: The Future of the Electoral College', *Parliamentary Affairs*, 43, no. 3 (April 1990), pp. 179-95.
66 Simon Hoggart, 'The Winner who must bear label of two-time loser', *Observer*, 12 April 1992.
67 Kenneth O. Morgan, *The People's Peace: British History, 1945-1989* (Oxford: Oxford University Press, 1990), p. 514.
68 *Ibid.*, p. 515.
69 Dennis Kavanagh, 'From Gentlemen to Players: Changes in Political Leadership', in William B. Gwyn and Richard Rose (eds), *Britain: Progress and Decline* (Basingstoke, Hants: Macmillan, 1980), pp. 73-93; Anthony King, 'The Rise of the Career Politician in Britain – And its Consequences', *British Journal of Political Science*, 11, no. 3 (July 1981), pp. 249-85; Anthony King, 'The British Prime Ministership in the Age of the Career Politician', *West European Politics*, 14, no. 2 (April 1991), pp. 25-47.

Chapter 4

1 Richard Rose, *The Postmodern President: The White House Meets the World* (Chatham, New Jersey: Chatham House, 1988), p. 35.
2 Ryan J. Barilleaux, *The Post-Modern Presidency: The Office after Reagan* (New York: Praeger, 1988), p. 134.
3 George C. Edwards III, *The Public Presidency: The Pursuit of Popular Support* (New York: St. Martin's Press, 1983), p. 5.
4 Bruce Miroff, 'The Presidency and the Public: Leadership as Spectacle', in Michael Nelson (ed.), *The Presidency and the Political System*, 2nd edn (Washington, DC: Congressional Quarterly, 1988), p. 272. See also Murray Edelman, *Constructing the Political Spectacle* (Chicago: University of Chicago Press, 1988).
5 Miroff, 'The Presidency and the Public', in Nelson (ed.), *The Presidency and the Political System*, p. 274.
6 *Ibid.*, p. 283.
7 James Ceaser, Glen E. Thurow, Jeffrey Tulis and Joseph M. Bessette, 'The Rise of the Rhetorical Presidency', in Thomas E. Cronin (ed.), *Rethinking the Presidency* (Boston, Mass.: Little, Brown, 1982), pp. 233-51.
8 *Ibid.*, p. 234.
9 *Ibid.*, p. 234.
10 *Ibid.*, p. 249. For a full exposition of the thesis, see Jeffrey Tulis, *The Rhetorical Presidency* (Princeton, New Jersey: Princeton University Press, 1987).
11 Samuel Kernell, *Going Public: New Strategies of Presidential Leadership* (Washington, DC: Congressional Quarterly, 1986), p. 223.
12 Joe McGinniss, *The Selling of the President* (Harmondsworth, Middlesex: Penguin, 1970); Nicholas J. O'Shaughnessy, *The Phenomenon of Political Marketing* (Basingstoke, Hants: Macmillan, 1990), ch. 9; Frank I. Luntz, *Candidates, Consultants and Campaigns: The Style and Substance of American Electioneering* (Oxford: Basil Blackwell, 1988), chs. 3, 5.
13 Theodore J. Lowi, *The Personal President: Power Invested, Promise Unfulfilled* (Ithaca, New York: Cornell University Press, 1985), p. 20. See also Aaron Wildavsky, 'The Plebiscitary Presidency, or Politics without Intermediaries', in Aaron Wildavsky, *The Beleaguered Presidency* (New Brunswick, NJ: Transaction, 1991), pp. 287-94.
14 Stephanie G. Larson, 'The President and Congress in the Media', *The Annals of the*

American Academy of Political and Social Science, 499 (September 1988), p. 66. See also Joynt Kumar and Michael B. Grossman, *Portraying the President: The White House and the News Media* (Baltimore, Md: Johns Hopkins University Press, 1981; Doris A. Graber, *Mass Media and American Politics*, 3rd edn (Washington, DC: Congressional Quarterly, 1989), pp. 235-54; Herbert Schmertz, 'The Media and the Presidency', *Presidential Studies Quarterly*, 16, no. 1 (Winter 1986), pp. 11-21.

15 Frank Cormier, James Deakin and Helen Thomas, *The White House Press on the Presidency: News Management and Co-Option* (Lanham, Md: University Press of America, 1983); Robert E. Denton, Jr. and Dan F., Hahn, *Presidential Communication* (New York: Praeger, 1986). In 1986 the Reagan White House produced an archetypal exercise in news management when it successfully transformed the diplomatic failure of the Reykjavik summit conference into a public relations triumph – see Donald T. Regan, *For the Record: From Wall Street to Washington* (London: Hutchinson, 1988), ch. 17; Jane Mayer and Doyle McManus, *Landslide: The Unmaking of the President, 1984-1988* (London: Fontana, 1989), pp. 406-11, 442.

16 Robert M. Entman, 'The Imperial Media', in Arnold J. Meltsner (ed.), *Politics and the Oval Office: Towards Presidential Governance* (San Francisco, Calif: Institute for Contemporary Studies, 1981), p. 94.

17 Kumar and Grossman, *Portraying the President*.

18 James Fallows, 'The Presidency and the Press', in Nelson (ed.), *The Presidency and the Political System*, p. 295.

19 David L. Paletz and Robert M. Entman, *Media Power Politics* (New York: Free Press, 1981), p. 21.

20 Michael J. Robinson, 'Television and American Politics, 1956-1976', *Public Interest*, 48 (Summer 1977), pp. 3-39; Thomas E. Patterson and Robert D. McClure, 'Television and Voters' Issue Awareness', in William Crotty (ed.), *The Party Symbol: Readings on Political Parties* (San Francisco, Calif: W. H. Freeman, 1980), pp. 324-34.

21 Fred Smoller, 'The Six O'Clock Presidency: Patterns of Network News Coverage of the Press', *Presidential Studies Quarterly*, 16, no. 1 (Winter 1986), pp. 31-49.

22 *Ibid.* See also Michael J. Robinson and Margaret Sheehan, *Over the Wire and on TV: CBS and UPI in Campaign '80* (New York: Sage, 1983).

23 Bruce Miroff, 'Secrecy and Spectacle: Reflections on the Dangers of the Presidency', in Paul Brace, Christine B. Harrington and Gary King (eds), *The Presidency in American Politics* (New York: New York University Press, 1989), p. 158.

24 Quoted in Michael Cockerell, 'The packaging of the President', *The Listener*, 8 November 1984.

25 Kathleen H. Jamieson, *Eloquence in an Electronic Age: The Transformation of Political Speechmaking* (Oxford: Oxford University Press, 1988), p. 13.

26 *Ibid.*, p. 117.

27 *Ibid.*, p. 117.

28 Charles W. Dunn and J. David Woodward, 'Ideological Images for a Television Age: Ronald Reagan as Party Leader', in Dilys M. Hill, Raymond A. Moore and Phil Williams, *The Reagan Presidency: An Incomplete Revolution?* (Basingstoke, Hants: Macmillan, 1990), p. 123.

29 Bert A. Rockman, *The Leadership Question: The Presidency and the American System* (New York: Praeger, 1984), pp. 139-40. See also C. Don Livingston, 'The Televised Presidency', *Presidential Studies Quarterly*, 16, no. 1 (Winter 1986), pp. 22-30.

30 Austin Rannay, 'Broadcasting, Narrowcasting, and Politics', in Anthony King (ed.), *The New American Political System*, Second Version (Washington, DC: American Enterprise Institute, 1990), p. 175.

31 Ceaser, Thurow, Tulis and Bessette, 'The Rise of the Rhetorical Presidency', in Cronin

(ed.), *Rethinking the Presidency*, p. 242.

32 *Ibid.*, p. 242.

33 Rose, *The Postmodern Presidency*, p. 132.

34 Ranney, 'Broadcasting, Narrowcasting and Politics', in King (ed.), *The New American Political System*, p. 187. See also, Robert Schmuhl, *Statecraft and Stagecraft: American Political Life in an Age of Personality* (Notre Dame, Indiana: University of Notre Dame Press, 1990).

35 Cockerell, 'The packaging of the President', For a study of the extraordinary attention given to public image in the Reagan White House, see Lawrence I. Barrett, *Gambling with History: Reagan in the White House* (New York: Penguin, 1983).

36 Jamieson, *Eloquence in an Electronic Age*, p. 175.

37 Jeb S. Magruder, *An American Life: One Man's Road to Watergate* (New York: Atheneum, 1974), ch. 5.

38 Bert A. Rockman, 'The Leadership Style of George Bush', Colin Campbell, SJ and Bert A. Rockman (eds), *The Bush Presidency: First Appraisals* (Chatham, NJ: Chatham House, 1991), pp. 1-35; George C. Edwards III, 'George Bush and the Public Presidency: The Politics of Inclusion', in *ibid.*, pp. 145-9; Dan Goodgame, 'Read My Hips', *Time*, 22 October 1990; Michael Duffy, 'A Case of Doing Nothing', *Time*, 7 January 1991.

39 Peter Pringle, 'Artful dodger enters danger zone', *Independent on Sunday*, 1 July 1990.

40 Quoted in Edwards, 'George Bush and the Public Presidency', in Campbell and Rockman (eds), *The Bush Presidency*, p. 145.

41 Quoted in Martin Walker and Simon Tisdall, 'Bush says sorry for the tax U-turn', *Guardian*, 4 March 1992.

42 Marcia Williams, *Inside Number 10*, rev edn (London: New English Library, 1975), p. 178.

43 Robin Day, *Grand Inquisitor* (London: Pan, 1990), p. 3.

44 Williams, *Inside Number 10*, p. 184. For the general influence of the mass media on British political leadership see Michael Cockerell, *Live from Number 10: The Inside Story of Prime Ministers and Television* (London: Faber, 1988); Colin Seymour-Ure, *The Political Impact of Mass Media* (London: Constable, 1974), ch. 8; Colin Seymour-Ure, *The British Press and Broadcasting since 1945* (Oxford: Basil Blackwell, 1991), ch. 8; Ralph Negrine, *Politics and the Mass Media in Britain* (London: Routledge, 1989); Bernard Ingham, *Kill the Messenger* (London: HarperCollins, 1991).

45 Quoted in BBC Radio 4, *The Wilson Years*, Part 1, broadcast on 3 October 1990.

46 Quoted in *ibid.*

47 Quoted in *ibid.*

48 Quoted in Day, *Grand Inquisitor*, p. 269.

49 Cockerell, *Live from Number 10*, ch. 10.

50 Dennis Kavanagh, 'The Heath Government, 1970-1974', in Peter Hennessy and Anthony Seldon (eds), *Ruling Performance: British Governments from Attlee to Thatcher* (Oxford: Basil Blackwell, 1987), p. 219.

51 Clive James, 'The Last Hurrah of Michael Foot', *Observer*, 29 May 1983.

52 Robert Fox, 'He was out-Saatchied at every turn', *The Listener*, 16 June 1983.

53 *Ibid.*

54 The Conservative lead over the second party in the popular vote was 14.8%. This made Labour's performance comparable to its record defeat in the 1935 general election. In terms of its overall share of the popular vote (27.6%), it was Labour's poorest performance since 1918.

55 Cockerell, *Live from Number 10*, p. 247. For a general survey of political packaging in Britain, see Brendan Bruce, *Images of Power: How the Image Makers Shape Our Leaders* (London: Kogan Page, 1992).

56 Cockerell, *Live from Number 10*, ch. 6; Max Atkinson, *Our Masters' Voices* (London Methuen, 1984), pp. 112-15.
57 Michael Cockerell, 'The marketing of Margaret', *The Listener*, 16 June 1983.
58 *Ibid.*
59 Quoted in *ibid.*
60 Patricia Hewitt and Peter Mandelson, 'The Labour Campaign', in Ivor Crewe and Martin Harrop (eds), *Political Communications: The General Election Campaign of 1987* (Cambridge: Cambridge University Press, 1989), pp. 49-54; Philip Gould, Peter Herd and Chris Powell, 'The Labour Party's campaign communications', in Crewe and Harrop (eds), *Political Communications*, pp. 72-86.
61 David Butler and Dennis Kavanagh, *The British General Election of 1987* (Basingstoke, Hants: Macmillan, 1988), p. 139.
62 Nicholas O'Shaughnessy, *The Phenomenon of Political Marketing* (Basingstoke, Hants: Macmillan, 1990), pp. 218-19.
63 Butler and Kavanagh, *The British General Election of 1987*, p. 144.
64 Ivor Crewe and Martin Harrop, 'Preface', in Crewe and Harrop (eds), *Political Communications*, pp. xiv-xv.
65 Cockerell, *Live from Number 10*, p. 323.
66 John Sharkey, 'Saatchi's and the 1987 Election', in Crewe and Harrop (eds), *Political Communications*, p. 65.
67 Rodney Tyler 'The Selling of the Prime Minister: How Mrs Thatcher Really Won the Election', *Sunday Times* 5 July 1987.
68 Simon Jenkins, 'The Designer Campaign' (Review of David Butler and Dennis Kavanagh, *The British General Election of 1987*), *Sunday Times*, 24 April 1988. For a dispassionate evaluation of political marketing in Britain see Martin Harrop, 'Political Marketing', *Parliamentary Affairs*, 43, no. 3 (July 1990), pp. 277-91.
69 Quoted in Rodney Tyler, *Campaign: The Selling of the Prime Minister* (London: Grafton, 1987), pp. 221-2.
70 Butler and Kavanagh, *The British General Election of 1987*, p. 157.
71 Tyler, *Campaign*, p. 240.
72 *Ibid.*
73 *Sunday Times*, 5 July 1987.
74 John Kingdom, *Government and Politics in Britain* (Oxford: Polity, 1991), pp. 328-9.
75 O'Shaughnessy, *The Phenomenon of Political Marketing*, p. 220.
76 Kingdom, *Government and Politics in Britain*, pp. 329-30.
77 This was dramatically demonstrated in Mr Kinnock's controversial denunciation of the Militant leaders of the Liverpool City Council during the 1985 Labour party conference: 'Comrades, the voice of the people – not the people here – the voice of the *real* people with real needs is louder than all the boo's that can be assembled. Understand that please comrades … in your commitment to those people'. Quoted in BBC Radio 3 *The Gang That Fell Apart*, Part 3, broadcast on 18 September 1991.
78 R. W. Johnson, 'The president has landed', *New Statesman and Society*, 30 November 1990.
79 Michael Cockerell, 'Vote, vote, vote for Tony Benn', *The Listener*, 25 June 1981.
80 Johnson, 'The president has landed'.
81 *Ibid.*
82 O'Shaughnessy, *The Phenomenon of Political Marketing*, p. 212.
83 Lord Beloff, quoted in *ibid.*, p. 209.
84 McGinniss, *The Selling of the President*, p. 35.
85 Quoted in Cockerell, *Live from Number 10*, p. 247.
86 Quoted in Butler and Kavanagh, *The British General Election of 1987*, p. 254.

87 Richard Rose, 'British Government: The Job at the Top', in Richard Rose and Ezra N. Suleiman (eds), *Presidents and Prime Ministers* (Washington, DC: American Enterprise Institute, 1980), p. 18.
88 *Ibid.*, p. 22.
89 *Ibid.*, p. 44.
90 Rose, *The Postmodern Presidency*, p. 132.
91 *Ibid.*, p. 272.
92 *Ibid.*, p. 272.
93 Rose, 'British Government: The Job at the Top', in Rose and Suleiman (eds), *Presidents and Prime Ministers*, p. 46.
94 Richard Rose, 'From Soapbox to the Box' (Review of Nicholas J. O'Shaughnessy, *The Phenomenon of Political Marketing*), *Times Higher Education Supplement*, 3 August 1990.
95 Richard Rose, *Politics in England: Persistence and Change* (London: Faber, 1985), p. 229.
96 Rose, *The Postmodern Presidency*, p. 273.
97 Dennis Kavanagh, 'The Heath Government, 1970-1974', in Peter Hennessy and Anthony Seldon (eds), *Ruling Performance: British Governments from Attlee to Thatcher* (Oxford: Basil Blackwell, 1988), p. 218.

Chapter 5

1 William Leith, 'The jaw-jaw of Ashdown's war', *Independent on Sunday*, 3 March 1992.
2 *Ibid.*
3 *Ibid.*
4 *Ibid.*
5 David Butler and Dennis Kavanagh, *The British General Election of 1987* (Basingstoke, Hants: Macmillan, 1988), p. 249.
6 Colin Seymour-Ure, 'Political Television: Four Stages of Growth', *Contemporary Record*, 4, no. 2 (November 1990), p. 22.
7 Michael Cockerell, *Live from Number 10: The Inside Story of Prime Ministers and Television* (London: Faber, 1988), p. 287.
8 Quoted in *ibid.*, p. 287.
9 Quoted in BBC Radio 3, *The Gang That Fell Apart*, Part 2, broadcast on 18 September 1991.
10 Richard Rose, 'British Government: The Job at the Top', in Richard Rose and Ezra N. Suleiman (eds), *Presidents and Prime Ministers* (Washington, DC: American Enterprise Institute, 1980), p. 20
11 Columns 1 and 2 of Table 5.1 as a percentage of columns 3, 4 and 5 gives a figure of 104%.
12 Columns 1 and 2 of Tale 5.1 as a percentage of columns 3, 4 and 5 gives a figure of 184%.
13 Caroline Lees, 'Major column inches ahead', *Sunday Times*, 5 January 1992.
14 The newspapers surveyed were: *The Times, Guardian, Daily Telegraph, Financial Times, Independent, Today, Scotsman, Northern Echo, Sunday Times, Sunday Telegraph, Observer, Independent on Sunday, Lloyd's List* and *The European*.
15 Butler and Kavanagh, *The British General Election of 1987*, p. 145.
16 Barrie Axford, 'Leaders, Elections and Television', *Politics Review*, 1, no. 3 (February 1992), pp. 17-20.
17 *Ibid.*, p. 18.
18 Richard Rose, 'British Government', in Rose and Suleiman (eds), *Presidents and Prime Ministers*, p. 21.
19 Butler and Kavanagh, *The British General Election of 1987*, p. 145.

20 David Butler and Dennis Kavanagh, *The British General Election of October 1974* (London: Macmillan, 1975), p. 143.
21 David Butler and Dennis Kavanagh, *The British General Election of 1983* (Basingstoke, Hants: Macmillan, 1984), p. 160.
22 Butler and Kavanagh, *The British General Election of 1987*, p. 145.
23 *Gallup Political Index*, Report No. 361, September 1990, p. 10.
24 *Gallup Political Index*, Report No. 369, May 1991, p. 11.
25 Anthony King, 'Picture poll shows Front-Bench fame is underdeveloped', *Daily Telegraph*, 13 May 1991.
26 G. W. Jones, 'Prime Minister and the Cabinet', *Wroxton Papers in Politics* (Wroxton College, 1990), p. 12.
27 *Ibid.*, p. 12.
28 Patrick Dunleavy, G. W. Jones and Brendan O'Leary, 'Prime Ministers and the Commons: patterns of behaviour, 1868-1987', *Public Administration*, 68 (Spring 1990), p. 137.
29 R. K. Alderman, 'The Leader of the Opposition and Prime Minister's Question Time', *Parliamentary Affairs*, 45, no. 1 (January 1992), p. 67.
30 Quoted in BBC Radio 4, *Analysis*, broadcast on 25 November 1990.
31 For more on how Prime Minister's Questions has drawn 'the prime minister away from his or her natural parliamentary base', see Colin Seymour-Ure, *The British Press and Broadcasting since 1945* (Oxford: Basil Blackwell, 1991), p. 182. In particular, Seymour-Ure speculates on the way that '"question time" might move figuratively away from Westminster even if the cameras had moved literally in there. It would become a kind of modified American presidential press conference, with MPs playing the part of journalists' (p. 182).
32 The figures for the other network news broadcasts ranged from 23% to 25%. Study produced by Professor Jay G. Blumler and others of the Parliamentary Research Group of the Institute of Communications Studies, University of Leeds for the Select Committee on Televising the Proceedings of the House. Figures quoted in Brian Tutt, 'Televising the Commons: a full, balanced and fair account of the work of the House', in Bob Franklin (ed.), *Televising Democracies* (London: Routledge, 1992), p. 132.
33 Tutt, 'Televising the Commons', in Franklin (ed.) *Televising Democracies*, p. 133. See also Michael Ryle, 'Televising the House of Commons', *Parliamentary Affairs*, 44, no. 2 (April 1991), pp. 194-205.
34 Figures quoted in Tutt, 'Televising the House of Commons', in Franklin (ed.), *Televising Democracies*, p. 133.
35 Peter Kellner, 'Major wins back the commanding heights', *Independent*, 15 July 1991.
36 Peter Kellner, 'Party fortunes hang on leaders' trial of strength', *Independent*, 26 April 1991. It should be pointed out that Peter Kellner is only being cited in this context as a representative example of what is a general analytical priority.
37 Robin Oakley, 'Labour regains poll lead but Lib Dems take Tory support', *The Times*, 8 July 1991.
38 Anthony King, 'Major's popularity with voters is key to Tory fortunes', *Daily Telegraph*, 5 July 1991.
39 Peter Kellner, 'Labour back to 10-point lead', *Independent*, 21 June 1991.
40 Anthony King, 'Double blow for Major as Labour widens lead', *Daily Telegraph*, 7 June 1991.
41 Peter Kellner, 'Liberal Democrat support surges', *Independent*, 15 March 1991.
42 Nicholas Wapshott, 'Major's gang of four lifts Tories', *Observer*, 21 July 1991.
43 David Hughes, 'Tories take poll lead as Major flies to Moscow', *Sunday Times*, 1 September 1991.

44 Nicholas Wapshott, 'Labour now 10 points ahead', *Observer*, 16 June 1991.
45 Anthony King, 'Major's popularity with voters is key to Tory fortunes', *Daily Telegraph*, 5 July 1991.
46 NOP in *Independent*, 26 April 1991.
47 Harris in *Observer*, 21 July 1991.
48 *Gallup Political and Economic Index*, Report No. 366, February 1991, p. 20.
49 For example, see Peter Kellner who despite giving pronounced emphasis to the leadership ratings in his monthly analyses of the NOP's BBC 2 *Newsnight/Independent* polls, reserved his position on the electoral significance of leadership in a separate article. In 'What the papers didn't say about Mr Kinnock' (*Independent*, 20 September 1991), Kellner affirmed that 'voters plump for parties they think will deliver effective policies, not for leaders they find personally attractive'.

Chapter 6

1 Richard E. Neustadt, *Presidential Power: The Politics of Leadership* (New York: Wiley, 1960), p. 10.
2 *Ibid.*, p. 10.
3 James D. Barber, *The Presidential Character: Predicting Performance in the White House* (Englewood Cliffs, NJ: Prentice-Hall, 1972), p. 445. See also Michael Nelson, 'The Psychological Presidency', in Michael Nelson (ed.), *the Presidency and the Political System*, 2nd edn (Washington, DC: Congressional Quarterly, 1988), pp. 185-206.
4 Arthur L. George, 'On Analysing Presidents', *World Politics*, 26, no. 2 (1974), pp. 234-82; Arthur L. George, 'Assessing Presidential Character', in Aaron Wildavsky (ed.), *Perspectives on the Presidency* (Boston, Mass.: Little, Brown, 1975), pp. 91-134; Erwin C. Hargrove, 'Presidential Personality and Revisionist Views of the Presidency', *American Journal of Political Science*, 17, no. 4 (November 1973), pp. 819-35; J. H. Qualls, 'Barber's Typological Analysis of Political Leaders', *American Political Science Review*, 71, no. 1 (March 1977), pp. 182-211.
5 Richard Rose, 'British Government: The Job at the Top', in Richard Rose and Ezra N. Suleiman (eds), *Presidents and Prime Ministers* (Washington, DC: American Enterprise Institute, 1980), p. 44.
6 *Ibid.*, p. 44.
7 Dennis Kavanagh, *Thatcherism and British Politics: The End of Consensus?*, 2nd edn (Oxford: Oxford University Press, 1990), p. 244. The clear significance of leadership in British politics is combined with a cultural inhibition in considering its properties. John Gaffney expresses this mixture in a penetrating sentence: 'Political personalism is a complex and influential phenomenon in British political life which affects both the electorate and party organisation but which – possibly because of the near taboo placed on the discussion of leadership because of the European experience of Fascism in the twentieth century – has been little considered outside analyses of totalitarianism on the one hand or "personality politics" on the other, which associates the projection of political leadership with the selling of soap powder.' *The Language of Political Leadership in Contemporary Britain* (Basingstoke, Hants: Macmillan, 1991) p. 11. For a representative example of how the British distaste for taking leadership very seriously can lead to a contemptuous attitude in which the role of personality in politics is ridiculed and, thereupon, dismissed, see Edward Pearce on Michael Heseltine. 'He is everywhere praised for charisma. I always thought of charisma as a South American dance rhythm. But one observes that the most desirable rulers – Cavour, Guizot, Peel, Truman, Attlee, Monet and Kohl – have been without it. Michael Heseltine admires J. F. Kennedy, a crashing

error of taste which suggests that from a Heseltine government we shall have charisma the way we otherwise have chips' ('Fighter with a golden tongue', *Guardian*, 26 November 1990). 'For elections we require personalities who, in turn, need charisma. The result will be a festival of eager self-promotion, the parade of dwarves on tiptoe … Charisma is an odd word. I always think if it as a three beats-to-the-bar Latin American dance rhythm vaguely associated with Edmundo Ros. "Down São Paulo way, this is how we do the charisma". It suggests a shake of maracas and spangles in the hair; and nowhere is this more the case than when Michael Heseltine does the charisma' ('Cash 'n' carry charisma', *Guardian*, 26 February 1992). What this outlook often leads to is an assumption that since personality and politics can be dismissed as merely 'charisma', 'normal' leadership in British Government is, thereby, devoid of personal considerations.

8 Anthony King, 'Psychic roots', (Review of Bruce Mazlish, *Kissinger: The European Mind in American Politics*), *New Society*, 13 October 1977.
9 Nelson W. Polsby, *British Government and its Discontents* (New York: Basic, 1981); Andrew Gamble, *Britain in Decline: Economic Policy, Political Strategy and the British State* (London: Macmillan, 1980); Anthony King (ed.), *Why is Britain Becoming Harder to govern?* (London: British Broadcasting Corporation, 1976); Samuel H. Beer, *Britain Against Itself: The Political Contradictions of Collectivism* (London: Faber, 1982).
10 Michael Foley, *The Silence of Constitution: Gaps, 'Abeyances' and Political Temperament in the Maintenance of Government* (London: Routledge, 1989), p. 103.
11 Anthony King, 'Margaret Thatcher: The Style of a Prime Minister', in Anthony King (ed.) *The British Prime Minister*, 2nd edn (Basingstoke, Hants: Macmillan, 1985), p. 118.
12 Philip Norton, 'Prime Ministerial Power', *Social Studies Review*, 3, no. 3 (January 1988), pp. 108-15; Leo Abse, *Margaret, Daughter of Beatrice: A Politician's Psycho-Biography of Margaret Thatcher* (London: Jonathan Cape, 1989); Hugh Berrington, 'Review Article: The Fiery Chariot: British Prime Ministers and the Search for Love', *British Journal of Political Science*, 4, no. 3 (July 1974), pp. 345-69; Anthony Clare, 'National Trauma: A Doctor Writes', *Sunday Correspondent*, 25 November 1990; Donald Macintyre, 'Badgered Major tries to close "Schoolgate"', *Independent on Sunday*, 21 April 1991; Bruce Anderson, *John Major: The Making of the Prime Minister* (London: Fourth Estate, 1991).
13 Thomas Cronin, *The State of the Presidency*, 2nd edn (Boston, Mass.: Little, Brown, 1975), p. 2.
14 Barbara Hinckley, *The Symbolic Presidency: How Presidents Portray Themselves* (New York: Routledge, 1990), p. 12.
15 *Ibid.*, p. 11.
16 John E. Mueller, *War, Presidents and Public Opinion* (New York: Wiley, 1973); Jong R. Lee, 'Rallying around the flag: Foreign policy events and presidential popularity', *Presidential Studies Quarterly*, 7, no. 3 (Fall 1977), pp. 252-6.
17 Michael Howard, *War and the Liberal Conscience* (Oxford: Oxford University Press, 1981), p. 116.
18 Louis Hartz, *The Liberal Tradition in America: An Interpretation of American Political thought since the Revolution* (New York: Harcourt Brace Jovanovich, 1955), p. 286.
19 Stephen Burman, *America in the Modern World: The Transcendence of United States Hegemony* (Hemel Hempstead, Herts.: Harvester Wheatsheaf, 1991), ch. 8; Paul D. Erickson, *Reagan Speaks: The Making of an American Myth* (New York: New York University Press, 1985), ch. 6; David Mervin, *Ronald Reagan and the American Presidency* (London: Longman, 1990), ch. 7.
20 Quoted in Stanley W. Cloud, 'Exorcising an Old Demon', *Time*, 11 March 1991.
21 A *USA Today* poll (1 March 1991) returned an approval rating level at a record 91%.
22 Quoted in John Cassidy, 'A bit of unfinished agenda', *Sunday Times*, 3 March 1991.

23 George F. Will, 'How Congress shaded in our picture of the President', *Daily Telegraph*, 4 August 1987.
24 Margaret Thatcher, *The Revival of Britain: Speeches on Home and European Affairs, 1975-1988*, compiled by Alistair B. Cooke (London: Aurum, 1989), p. 164.
25 Sarah Benton, 'Tales of Thatcher', *New Statesman and Society*, 28 April 1989.
26 *Ibid.*
27 Kenneth W. Thompson, *The President and the Public Philosophy* (Baton Rouge, La: Louisiana State University Press, 1981).
28 David Marquand, *The Unprincipled Society: New Demands and Old Politics* (London: Fontana, 1988), p. 11.
29 Quoted in an interview with Kenneth Auchinloss and David Pedersen, *Newsweek*, 15 October 1990.
30 Thatcher, *The Revival of Britain*, p. 259.
31 *Ibid.*, p. 260.
32 Kenneth O. Morgan, *The People's Peace: British History, 1945-1989* (Oxford: Oxford University Press, 1990), p. 515. See also Paul Rich, 'The Quest for Englishness', *History Today*, June 1987, pp. 24-30; Raphael Samuel (ed.), *Patriotism: the Making and Unmaking of British National Identity, Volume 1: History and Politics* (London: Routledge, 1989); Ghita Ionescu, *Leadership in an Interdependent World: The Statesmanship of Adenauer, De Gaulle, Thatcher, Reagan and Gorbachev* (Harlow, Essex: Longman, 1991) pp. 167-82.
33 While the British may be reconciled to greater European integration, survey evidence shows that they do not identify closely with Europe. For example, to the question 'Does the thought ever occur to you that you are not also British but also European', 69% said never (*New Statesman and Society*, 22 June 1990). In another poll conducted for the *European* (21-23 June 1991), 66% of British respondents answered no to the question 'Do you feel more a European citizen than you did five years ago?' This was by far the highest negative response in the six nations surveyed (Italy, France, Germany, Spain, Denmark and Britain). See also the ICM poll in *Guardian*, 14 November 1991.
34 Ellen R. Gold, 'Politics by Wordpower,' *Times Higher Education Supplement*, 28 October 1988. See also Erickson, *Reagan Speaks*, passim; William K. Muir, 'Ronald Reagan: The Primacy of Rhetoric,' in Fred I. Greenstein (ed.), *Leadership in the Modern Presidency* (Cambridge, Mass.: Harvard University Press, 1988), pp. 260-95.
35 Benton, 'Tales of Thatcher'.
36 Richard Rose, *The Postmodern President: The White House Meets the World* (Chatham, New Jersey: Chatham House, 1988); Ghita Ionescu, *Leadership in an Interdependent World*, chs. 3, 4.
37 Harvey C. Mansfield, *Taming the Prince: The Ambivalence of Modern Executive Power* (New York: Free Press, 1989), p. 291. See also Edward S. Corwin, *The President: Office and Powers, 1787-1984*, 5th edn (New York: New York University Press, 1984); Louis Henkin, *Foreign Affairs and the Constitution* (Mineola, New York: Foundation, 1972); Foley, *The Silence of Constitutions*, chs. 3, 5; Louis Fisher, *Constitutional Conflicts between Congress and the President* (Princeton, New Jersey: Princeton University Press, 1985); Christopher H. Pyle and Richard M. Pious (eds), *The President, Congress and the Constitution: Power and Legitimacy in American Politics* (New York: Free Press, 1984).
38 Arthur M. Schlesinger, Jr., *The Imperial Presidency* (London: André Deutsch, 1974), p. 275.
39 Harold H. Koh, *The National Security Constitution: Sharing Power After the Iran-Contra Affair* (New Haven, Conn.: Yale University Press, 1990), p. 204.
40 Theodore J. Lowi, 'Presidential Power: Restoring the Balance', *Political Science Quarterly*, 100, no. 2 (Summer 1985), p. 189.

41 Foley, *The Silence of Constitutions*, p. 88.
42 *Ibid.*, p. 89.
43 Nicholas Ridley, *My Style of Government: The Thatcher Years* (London: Hutchinson, 1991); William Whitelaw, *The Whitelaw Memoirs* (London: Aurum, 1989); Norman Fowler, *Ministers Decide: A Memoir of the Thatcher Years* (London: Chapmans, 1991); Bernard Ingham, *Kill The Messenger* (London: HarperCollins, 1991).
44 Peter Hennessy, *Cabinet* (Oxford: Basil Blackwell, 1986), p. 122.
45 Tam Dalyell, *Misrule: How Mrs Thatcher has Misled Parliament from the Sinking of the Belgrano to the Wright Affair* (London: New English Library, 1988), p. 36.
46 See Michael Heseltine's resignation statement, *The Times*, 10 January 1986.
47 Quoted in Robert Harris, *The Making of Neil Kinnock* (London: Faber, 1984), p. 206.
48 Quoted in *ibid.*, p. 206.
49 'Lady Muck', *Daily Mirror*, 27 July 1989.
50 Quoted in K. D. Ewing and C. A. Gearty, *Freedom Under Thatcher: Civil Liberties in Modern Britain* (Oxford: Oxford University Press, 1990), p. 4.
51 Marquand, *The Unprincipled Society*, p. 194.
52 *Ibid.*, p. 194.
53 Patrick McAuslan and John E. McEldowney, 'Legitimacy and the Constitution: The Dissonance between Theory and Practice', in Patrick McAuslan and John E. McEldowney (eds), *Law, Legitimacy and the Constitution* (London: Sweet and Maxwell, 1985), p. 17.
54 *Ibid.*, pp. 32, 13.
55 Ewing and Gearty, *Freedom Under Thatcher*, p. 255.
56 *Ibid.*, p. 255.
57 *Ibid.*, p. 7.
58 Peter Clarke, 'Margaret Thatcher's Leadership in Historical Perspective', *Parliamentary Affairs*, 45, no. 1 (January 1992), p. 12.
59 Ewing and Gearty, *Freedom Under Thatcher*, p. 7.
60 *Ibid.*, p. 7.
61 Cosmo Graham and Tony Prosser, 'Introduction: The Constitution and the New Conservatives', in Cosmo Graham and Tony Prosser (eds), *Waiving the Rules: The Constitution under Thatcherism* (Milton Keynes, Bucks: Open University Press, 1988), p. 12.
62 Quoted in the Prologue to *Charter 88*.
63 *Ibid.*
64 For example see the evidence produced by the Rowntree Trust's 'State of the Nation' polls supporting the contention of a widespread public demand for a new constitutional settlement. Polls presented in Patrick Dunleavy and Stuart Weir, 'Ignore the people at your peril', *Independent*, 25 April 1991; Patrick Dunleavy and Stuart Weir, 'They want to see it in writing', *Independent*, 2 October 1991.
65 '"We, the People ..."': Towards a Written Constitution', *Liberal Democrats Federal Green Paper No. 13* (Hebden Bridge, Yorks: Hebden Royd, 1990).
66 Rodney Brazier, *Constitutional Reform* (Oxford: Oxford University Press, 1991), p. 7.
67 *Ibid.*, p. 103.

Chapter 7

1 David Selbourne, 'Strident heroine of the corner shop who fought for hard-headed virtues, *Sunday Times*, 25 November 1990.
2 David Hughes and Margarette Driscoll, 'The Duel for the Crown', *Sunday Times*, 18 November 1990.

3 There were 3 absentees, 24 spoilt ballots and 33 votes for Sir Anthony Meyer. The 60 MPs who failed to support Mrs Thatcher amounted to 16% of the parliamentary party. See Philip Norton, 'Choosing a Leader: Margaret Thatcher and the Parliamentary Conservative Party', *Parliamentary Affairs*, 43, no. 3 (July 1990), pp. 249-59.

4 Robin Oakley, 'Tories all in a dither over the right time to challenge leader', *The Times*, 18 November 1990.

5 *The Times*, 29 October 1990.

6 *Independent*, 2 November 1990.

7 Quoted in David Hughes, 'Out Come the Knives', *Sunday Times*, 4 November 1990.

8 Christopher Barder, 'The Fall of Mrs Thatcher', *Politics Review*, 1, no. 1 (September 1991), p. 31.

9 Peter Jenkins, 'Now she faces a fight for her life', *Independent*, 14 November 1990.

10 *Independent*, 2 November 1990.

11 *Ibid.*

12 *Ibid.*

13 Quoted in Hughes and Driscoll, 'The Duel for the Crown'.

14 *Independent*, 2 November 1990.

15 *Ibid.*

16 Michael Helseltine's resignation statement, *The Times*, 10 January 1986.

17 Michael Helseltine's announcement of his decision to stand in the leadership contest, *Guardian*, 15 November 1990.

18 *Ibid.*

19 'The chance of a choice for the nation', *Guardian*, 19 November 1990.

20 'Lesser of two evils', *Sunday Correspondent*, 18 November 1990.

21 *Ibid.*

22 *Ibid.*

23 'The Tories Choose', *The Economist*, 24 November 1990.

24 'The Ego Has Landed', *Spectator*, 17 November 1990.

25 'Heseltine: Man of Honour', *Mail on Sunday*, 25 November 1990.

26 Robert Harris, 'Thatcher is for burning now – win or lose', *Sunday Times*, 18 November 1990.

27 Robert Harris, 'Credo of a Tory exile', *Sunday Times*, 11 November 1990.

28 *Ibid.*

29 Quoted in an interview with Christopher Huhne, *Independent on Sunday*, 25 November 1990.

30 Margaret Thatcher, 'Remain true and we shall win again', *Daily Telegraph*, 19 November 1990.

31 Quoted in an interview with Simon Jenkins, *The Times*, 19 November 1990.

32 *Ibid.*

33 Charles Laurence, 'Pitch, polish – and duck the hostile questions', *Daily Telegraph*, 21 November 1990.

34 *Ibid.*

35 *Ibid.*

36 'Heseltine: The man of honour'.

37 Andrew Grice, 'Polls say Tories would do better under Heseltine', *Sunday Times*, 18 November 1990.

38 In the *Sunday Times* (18 November 1990), MORI showed that, with Heseltine as leader, the Conservative/Labour split would move from 37%/48% to 44%/43%.

39 In the *Observer* (18 November 1990), Harris showed that, with Heseltine as leader, the Conservative/Labour split would move from 34%/49% to 44%/43%.

40 In the *Independent on Sunday* (18 November 1990), NMR showed that, with Heseltine as

leader, the Conservative/Labour split would move from 42%/44% to 49%/39%.

41 In the *Mail on Sunday* (18 November 1990), NOP showed that, with Heseltine as leader, the Conservative/Labour split would move from 36%/48% to 47%/40%.

42 Under Thatcher, 14% thought the economy would improve. Under Heseltine, the figure rose to 32% – see MORI poll, *Sunday Times*, 18 November 1990.

43 Gallup poll, *Sunday Telegraph*, 18 November 1990.

44 Quoted in an interview with Brian Walden in ITV, *Walden*, broadcast on 18 November 1990.

45 Harris poll in the *Observer*, 18 November 1990.

46 Gallup poll in the *Sunday Telegraph*, 18 November 1990.

47 Ivor Crewe, 'Leadership Fight Revives Tory Vote', *Independent on Sunday*, 18 November 1990.

48 John Benyon, 'The Fall of a Prime Minister', *Social Studies Review*, 6, no. 3 (January 1991), p. 106.

49 Quoted in George Jones and John Hibbs, 'Fifty Tory MPs hold key to leader's future', *Daily Telegraph*, 19 November 1990.

50 Quoted in an interview with Robin Oakley, *The Times*, 27 November 1990.

51 Quoted in an interview with Nicholas Wapshott, *Observer*, 25 November 1990.

52 Quoted in an interview with Brian Walden in ITV, *Walden*, broadcast on 25 November 1990.

53 Harris, 'Credo of a Tory exile', *Sunday Times*, 11 November 1990.

54 'The chance of a choice for the nation'.

55 'Best of Three', *The Times*, 27 November 1990.

56 Quoted in an interview with Charles Moore and George Jones, *Daily Telegraph*, 19 November 1990.

57 Hugo Young, 'She's finished anyway', *Guardian Weekly*, 25 November 1990.

58 Cassandra Jardine, 'The other half of the ticket', *Daily Telegraph*, 24 November 1990; Margaret Driscoll, 'Images of a first lady in waiting', *Sunday Times*, 25 November 1990.

59 Ben Fenton, 'Hurd taps iron fist in the velvet glove', *Daily Telegraph*, 27 November 1990.

60 Quoted in an interview with Max Hastings, *Daily Telegraph*, 26 November 1990.

61 *Ibid.*

62 Quoted in an interview with Ivan Fallon, *Sunday Times*, 25 November 1990.

63 'Best of Three'.

64 Quoted in an interview with Jonathan Dimbleby in BBC 1, *On The Record*, broadcast on 25 November 1990.

65 Quoted in an interview with Robin Oakley, *The Times*, 27 November 1990.

66 Quoted in an interview with Max Hastings, *Daily Telegraph*, 26 November 1990. This point was amplified further in an interview with Jon Snow on *Channel Four News* (23 November 1990). In it, Heseltine made it clear that if he were to become leader the main *raison d'être* of such a position would be to exert himself fully in pursuit of a general election victory for the Conservative party. That being the case, both Hurd and Major could remain in their current positions. The evident implication was that Heseltine believed the election would be so leadership-centred that the lack of turnover in the two most senior cabinet posts would be immaterial both to the party's new image and to its electoral potential.

67 Ian Aitken, 'Tightrope act of a bookie and healer', *Guardian*, 26 November 1990.

68 Hella Pick and Alex Brummer, 'Pastless, presentable, future PM?', *Guardian*, 27 November 1990.

69 Nicholas Wapshott, 'John Major: Who I am and whence I came', *Observer*, 2 December 1990.

70 Joe Rogaly, 'Will the real Mr Major stand up', *Financial Times*, 28 November 1990.

71 Quoted in an interview with Max Hastings, *Daily Telegraph*, 26 November 1990.
72 Quoted in an interview with Stephen Glover, *Independent on Sunday*, 25 November 1990.
73 Quoted in an interview with Ivan Fallon, *Sunday Times*, 25 November 1990.
74 *Ibid.*
75 Edward Pearce, Fighter with a golden tongue', *Guardian*, 26 November 1990.
76 *Ibid.*
77 MORI poll, *The Times*, 18 November 1990.
78 MORI poll, *The Times*, 24 November 1990.
79 Gallup poll, *Sunday Telegraph*, 25 November 1990. Gallup divided the question on the economy into two parts – first a general question on who could best handle the economy and secondly a more specific question on who could best handle the issue of inflation. While Heseltine had a lead over Major (39% to 23%) on the general question of the economy, Major had a substantial lead over Heseltine (45% to 24%) in what could be regarded as the most critical problem facing the economy (i.e. inflation). These figures should perhaps be taken in conjunction with the results of MORI's poll for the *Sunday Times*, 25 November 1990. MORI asked the single question of which of the contenders would be best at handling the economy. The result was a clear lead for Major (43%) over Heseltine (29%) and Hurd (12%). It was the only one of the seven subject categories that Major outranked both his rivals.
80 Harris poll, *Observer*, 25 November 1990.
81 Gallup poll, *Sunday Telegraph*, 25 November 1990.
82 ICM poll, *Sunday Correspondent*, 25 November 1990.
83 NMR poll, *Independent on Sunday*, 25 November 1990.
84 NOP poll, *Mail in Sunday*, 25 November 1990.
85 NOP poll, *Independent*, 27 November 1990.
86 Anthony King, 'Major rivals Heseltine as candidate most likely to lead Tories to victory', *Daily Telegraph*, 27 November 1990.
87 Gallup poll, *Daily Telegraph*, 27 November 1990.
88 Quoted in an interview with Charles Moore, *Daily Telegraph*, 26 November 1990.
89 Gallup poll, *Daily Telegraph*, 27 November 1990.
90 Paul Johnson, 'A Winner to put the Tories on top again', *Daily Mail*, 28 November 1990.
91 *The Times*, 27 November 1990.
92 Most of the popular accounts of John Major's rise to power resonate with these sorts of assumptions. They presuppose that her decline could be accounted for by the manoeuvrings of the party's interior hierarchy; that the collegiate manner of her fall somehow explained the real nature of her eleven year pre-eminence; and that the way in which John Major succeeded to the office would predetermine how he would perform as prime minister and use the premiership thereafter. See Anderson, *John Major*; Edward Pearce, *The Quiet Rise of John Major* (London: Weidenfeld and Nicolson, 1991); Alan Watkins, *A Conservative Coup: The Fall of Margaret Thatcher* (London: Duckworth, 1991).

Chapter 8

1 Quoted in Julia Langden and David Wastell, 'Major's one hundred days in the hot seat', *Sunday Telegraph*, 3 March 1991.
2 Quoted from Colin Brown, 'Happy days are here again ... ', *Independent*, 17 December 1990.
3 Quoted from *ibid*.
4 Quoted in Stephen Castle, 'A year in politics is a considerable length of time',

Independent, 24 November 1990.

5 Quoted in Michael White, 'Mr Nice Guy and his chums', *Guardian*, 28 November 1991.

6 Quoted in Anthony Bevins, 'Bomb landed near leading Tory figures', *Independent*, 8 February 1991.

7 David Hughes and Andrew Grice, 'Major is Britain's most popular PM since Churchill', *Sunday Times*, 27 January 1991.

8 Quoted in Robert Morgan, 'Stop consulting, start deciding, Lawson advises government', *The Times*, 26 March 1990.

9 Michael White, 'The 100-day crash course', *Guardian*, 7 March 1991.

10 Peter Jenkins, 'Nice PMs must break eggs too', *Independent*, 6 March 1991.

11 Robin Oakley, 'Major's balancing acts break with Thatcher style', *The Times*, 29 November 1991.

12 David Wastell, 'The Year of Living', *Sunday Telegraph*, 24 November 1990.

13 Quoted in White, 'Mr Nice Guy and his friends'.

14 Quoted in Charles Lewington, 'One year on and it's curry and children at Number 10', *Sunday Express*, 17 November 1991.

15 John Casey, 'What price niceness', *Sunday Telegraph*, 17 March 1991.

16 See for example Frank Johnson, 'Mr Major comes to Mr Kinnock's aid', *Sunday Telegraph*, 17 February 1991.

17 Toby Helm, 'The man they just can't nail', *Sunday Telegraph*, 24 November 1991.

18 Quoted in Michael Jones, 'One hundred days in No 10', *Sunday Times*, 3 March 1991.

19 Robert Harris, 'How bad must the Tories get before Labour pulls ahead', *Sunday Times*, 5 May 1991.

20 John Hibbs, 'Opponents show signs of battle fatigue', *Daily Telegraph*, 29 November 1991.

21 Peter Jenkins, 'A vital U-turn for Mr Major', *Independent*, 7 March 1991.

22 Cal McCrystal, 'The Greying of John Major', *Independent on Sunday*, 21 April 1991.

23 Robin Oakley, 'Major's balancing acts break Thatcher's style', *The Times*, 29 November 1991.

24 David Selbourne, 'One of Us?' *Sunday Times*, 8 March 1992.

25 Robin Oakley, 'Gulf will never be the same', *The Times*, 31 January 1991.

26 David Hughes, 'Major plugs into the power of office', *Sunday Times*, 2 February 1992.

27 *Ibid.*

28 *Ibid.*

29 Robert Harris, 'Ruthless grip on the levers of power gives Tories the edge', *Sunday Times*, 2 February 1992.

30 *Desert Island Discs*, BBC Radio 4, broadcast on 26 January 1991.

31 Quoted in Barbara Amiel, 'The Man Who Would be Major', *Sunday Times*, 29 March 1992.

32 Quoted in *ibid*.

33 Robin Day, quoted in *ibid*.

34 David Selbourne, 'Left, right, here comes the all-purpose Major', *Sunday Times*, 13 March 1992.

35 Quoted in Nicholas Timmins and Alex Renton, 'Heating payment rules waived', *Independent*, 13 February 1991.

36 James Meikle, 'Major overturns plans for testing in schools', *Guardian*, 4 July 1991.

37 *Ibid.*

38 Quoted in George Jones, 'Major pledges power for the consumer', *Daily Telegraph*, 23 July 1991.

39 'Major catches the public mood', *Independent*, 23 July 1991.

40 Peter Riddell, 'An idea that will make Major's mark', *The Times*, 31 January 1992.

41 Party Political Broadcast, 25 July 1991.
42 Harvey Thomas, 'Hero of suburbia', *Guardian*, 12 October 1991.
43 Peter Jenkins, 'Just a Brixton boy made man of the people', *Independent*, 12 October 1991.
44 Quoted in *Independent*, 12 October 1991.
45 Quoted in *Guardian*, 12 October 1991.
46 Quoted in *Independent*, 12 October 1991.
47 Quoted in *Guardian* 12 October 1991.
48 Quoted in *Independent*, 12 October 1991.
49 Quoted in *Guardian*, 12 October 1991.
50 Jenkins, 'Just a Brixton boy made man of the people'.
51 Hugo Young, 'Surprising egotist proves he is more equal than others', *Guardian*, 12 October 1991.
52 Michael Jones, 'The Politics of Abuse', *Sunday Times*, 22 February 1987.
53 *Ibid.*
54 *Ibid.*
55 *Ibid.*
56 *Ibid.*
57 'The Prime Minister Remembers', *Independent on Sunday*, 12 January 1992.
58 Donald Macintyre, 'Kinnock: How the man became the issue', *Independent on Sunday*, 22 September 1991.
59 See chapter 9, footnotes 24-26.
60 Paul Johnson, 'Why Kinnock Can Never Be Made Into a Winner', *Daily Mail*, 17 September 1991.
61 John Ingham, 'Bend It, Shape It, Anyway Kinnock Wants It', *Daily Express*, 10 September 1991.
62 'The contortionist', *Daily Mail*, 9 September 1991.
63 'Delight and danger for Mr Major', *Daily Express*, 16 September 1991.
64 Johnson, 'Why Kinnock Can Never Be Made Into a Winner'.
65 Macintyre, 'Kinnock: How the man became the issue'
66 Quoted in *ibid.*
67 Quoted in *ibid.*
68 David and Anthony King, 'Kinnock trails in popularity race', *Sunday Telegraph*, 22 September 1991.
69 *Ibid.*
70 Quoted in Andrew Grice, 'Oh, When Will I Be Loved', *Sunday Times*, 22 September 1991.
71 Party Political Broadcast, 25 September 1991.
72 Simon Hoggart, 'The winner who must bear label of two-time loser', *Observer*, 12 April 1992. After the 1992 general election, it was revealed there had indeed been two attempts by senior Labour figures in the autumn of 1991 to replace Kinnock with John Smith, the shadow chancellor. Rumours of a leadership switch were strongly denied at the time, but in the aftermath of Labour's defeat, it was disclosed that John Smith had been approached by disaffected sectors of the party. Apart from the prodigious constitutional difficulties in changing the leader, the attempt to replace Kinnock was thwarted by John Smith's refusal to be a party to any plots against the leader. See Nicholas Wapshott, 'Labour's top men twice tried to oust Kinnock', *Observer*, 21 June 1992.
73 Barrie Axford, 'Leaders, Elections and Television', *Politics Review*, 1, no. 3 (February 1992), p. 20.
74 Kinnock won only a short reprieve. The cycle of hostile press coverage resumed in February 1992 with a series of allegations concerning Kinnock's links with Soviet

government officials, and a comprehensive indictment of Kinnock's change of policy positions and political outlook. Michael Jones, 'Soviet files reveal Labour's private dialogue with Kremlin', *Sunday Times*, 2 February 1992; Tim Sebastian, 'Dialogue with the Kremlin', *Sunday Times*, 2 February 1992. See also Jones, 'Kinnock: The Flight from Conviction', *Sunday Times*, 16 February 1992; Jones, 'Class War: The Tunes of Glory', *Sunday Times*, 23 February 1992; Jones, 'Chameleon Kinnock's right turn towards voter respectability', *Sunday Times*, 1 March 1992.

75 Peter Jenkins, 'Man of history for the Nineties comes of age', *Independent*, 13 September 1991.
76 Quoted in *Independent*, 13 September 1991.
77 Quoted in Nicholas Wapshott, 'Ashdown relishes poll shoot-out', *Observer*, 8 September 1991.
78 John Biffen, 'A contest between like minds', *Independent*, 6 March 1991.
79 Peter Riddell, 'Vision of the Brixton boy', *The Times*, 19 March 1992.
80 Peter Jenkins, 'Foul play as the political gets personal', *Independent on Sunday*, 9 June 1991.
81 Hugo Young, 'Why this election matters', *Guardian*, 12 March 1992.
82 Peter Jenkins, 'A choice that's much constrained', *Independent*, 12 March 1992.
83 According to MORI, 44% of the electorate at the start of the campaign could be classified as floating voters – well above the figure in previous elections. See *Sunday Times*, 29 March 1992.
84 'From here to the White House', *The Economist*, 15 February 1992.
85 Party Political Broadcast, 'The Journey', BBC 1, broadcast on 18 March 1992.
86 Hugo Young, 'Surprising egotist proves he is more equal than others'.
87 Party Political Broadcast, 'The Journey'.
88 Quoted in Michael White, 'Modest plans fail to fire campaign', *Guardian*, 19 March 1991.
89 Hugo Young, 'Mr Major and his albatross', *Guardian*, 19 March 1992.
90 *Observer*, 19 January 1992.
91 *Observer*, 16 February 1992.
92 Nicholas Wapshott, 'Tories losing confidence of voters on the economy', *Observer*, 16 February 1992.
93 *Special Inquiry*, ITV, broadcast on 15 March 1992.
94 Peter Riddell, 'Misunderstood Mr Kinnock', *The Times*, 2 March 1992.
95 Quoted in Patrick Wintour, 'Kinnock unveils himself as winning factor', *Guardian*, 12 March 1992.
96 Quoted in Robin Oakley, 'Why my team can run Britain', *The Times*, 26 March 1992.
97 Quoted in *ibid*.
98 Quoted in Michael Jones, David Hughes and Andrew Grice, 'Tory Tremors', *Sunday Times*, 22 March 1992.
99 Andrew Neil, 'Round one to Labour', *Sunday Times*, 22 March 1992.
100 Joe Rogaly, 'The Kinnock factor', *Financial Times*, 24 March 1992.
101 Charles Moore, 'Making up for lost time', *Daily Telegraph*, 23 March 1992.
102 *Ibid*.
103 Robin Oakley, 'Kinnock team leaps every hurdle in dash for the line', *The Times*, 28 March 1992.
104 Ian Bell, 'Pleasant John gives the Tories an identity crisis', *Observer*, 22 March 1992.
105 Paul Johnson, 'Now Mr Major must go for the jugular', *Sunday Times*, 22 March 1992.
106 Trevor Fishlock, 'Major's High Noon', *Sunday Telegraph*, 22 March 1992.
107 R. W. Johnson, 'Neil should have a modern Nye Bevan', *Observer*, 16 February 1992.
108 Ian Aitken, 'Time to turn Kinnock loose as lack of uplift leaves electorate feeling flat', *Guardian*, 27 March 1992.

109 *Ibid.*

110 The 'Don't Knows' amounted to 20%. *Daily Telegraph*, 26 March 1992. Ashdown's campaign also impressed the voters for running what was deemed to be a 'clean campaign', in contrast to the negative tactics employed by the two main parties. In a NOP poll for the *Independent* (6 March 1992), voters were asked whether they thought any of the parties were engaged in 'dirty tricks'. While 36% believed all the parties were generally guilty of using these tactics, 31% narrowed the charge down to the Conservatives, 27% named the Labour party as being solely responsible for dirty tricks, while only 2% believed the Liberal Democrats to be the only party engaged in such activities.

111 See Ivan Fallon, 'Soapbox Major fails to satisfy', *Sunday Times*, 5 April 1992.

112 'Campaign winner Ashdown', *Guardian*, 6 April 1992.

113 Ben Pimlott, 'Victory from the jaws of wisdom', (Review of Edward Pearce, *The Quiet Rise of John Major*), *Guardian Weekly*, 25 April 1991.

114 'The art of followership', *The Economist*, 22 February 1992. See also Allan Massie, 'The Triumph of Mr Ordinary', *Sunday Telegraph*, 24 November 1991.

115 Blake Morrison, 'Belong to Them?', *Independent on Sunday*, 5 April 1992.

116 Quoted in Barbara Amiel, 'Paddy's Body Politics', *Sunday Times*, 15 March 1992.

117 *Ibid.*

118 Michael Ignatieff, 'Outsider who wants to be in', *Observer*, 22 March 1992.

119 Ivor Crewe, 'Democrats gain at Tories expense', *The Times*, 23 March 1992.

120 ITN *News at Ten*, broadcast on 28 March 1992.

121 BBC 1 *Nine O'Clock News*, broadcast on 1 April 1992.

122 BBC 1 *Nine O'Clock News*, Broadcast on 1 April 1992.

123 ITN *News at Ten*, broadcast on 1 April 1992.

124 Anthony King, 'Contrast between party leaders is failing to sway the public', *Daily Telegraph*, 3 April 1992.

125 Anthony King, 'Why Major must stay in the trenches', *Daily Telegraph*, 23 March 1992.

126 Anthony King, 'Turnout may favour the Tories', *Daily Telegraph*, 9 April 1992.

127 The meeting was an all-ticket pre-election rally organised by the Welsh Labour Party. It took place at Cardiff City Hall on 28 February 1992.

128 Data from Loughborough University's Communications Research Centre were presented in Peter Golding, 'Economy and polls hogged coverage', *Guardian*, 11 April 1992.

129 The analysis of broadcasting appearances was based on a study of the following programmes between 9 March 1992 and 9 April 1992: BBC 1 *Nine O'Clock News*, ITN *News at Ten*, BBC 2 *Newsnight* and BBC Radio 4 *Today* (between 8.00 am and 9.00 am).

130 This analysis was conducted on the same data base as that used in the measurement of broadcasting appearances.

131 Golding, 'Economy and polls hogged coverage'. Even though the Conservative party was thought to be committed to a slightly more collegiate approach to electioneering than that practised during the Thatcher years (see Robin Oakley, '"A-team" shares party burden', *The Times*, 14 March 1992), the figures confirm that Major's predominance in the 1992 election campaign was on a par with that attained by Margaret Thatcher in her campaign.

132 BBC 1 *Nine O'Clock News* and ITN *News at Ten*.

133 Campaign news refers quite specifically to news about each day's campaigning. It avoids background information and features on such themes as Scottish devolution, social policy briefings, the problems of Northern Ireland and the state of the old left. It also excludes the presentation and analysis of opinion polls. It concentrates instead on the coverage given to politicians actually engaged in electioneering – e.g. press conferences, factory visits, meet the people sessions, photo-opportunities, 'walkabouts', speeches etc.

134 Dennis Kavanagh, 'Wedded to the hack pack', *Guardian*, 7 April 1992.

135 'Getting the medium across', *The Economist*, 11 April 1992.
136 Quoted in Philip Webster, 'Kinnock's campaign veterans eager to build on flying start', *The Times*, 23 March 1992.
137 Quoted in Peter Jenkins, 'I don't think the phone will ring', *Independent*, 2 April 1992.
138 Quoted in *ibid*.
139 The problem of Labour's incompetence and untrustworthiness was featured in the party's own post-mortem of its election failure. In his report on Labour's performance, Larry Whitty, the party's General Secretary, recognised that a late shift in public attitudes had drained support away from the party. Private polling indicated that, in the last three days of the campaign, the party had suffered a massive loss of 11 points in its competence as a potential government. 'It is difficult to escape the conclusion', Whitty reported, 'that, at the very end of the campaign, the electorate was just too apprehensive about Labour and the more evident it became to them that Labour would win, or there would be a hung parliament, fears of high tax, plus the general unease about our economic competence or general distrust of the party and its leadership took their toll'. Quoted in Patrick Wintour, 'Labour sifts through the dust of defeat', *Guardian*, 17 June 1992.
140 The MORI poll published in *The Times* on 1 April 1992 had Labour at 42% and the Conservatives at 35%.
141 BBC 1 *Nine O'Clock News*, broadcast on 2 April 1992.
142 ITN *News at Ten*, broadcast on 2 April 1992.
143 BBC 1 *Nine O'Clock News*, broadcast on 2 April 1992.
144 'Kinnock ran a good race: Now what is to be done?' *Independent on Sunday*, 12 April 1992.
145 Robin Oakley, 'Over-the-top rally left Kinnnock exposed', *The Times*, 11 April 1992.
146 Nicholas Wapshott, 'John Major's discreet charm to the British bourgeoisie', *Observer*, 12 April 1992.
147 Matthew Parris, 'Election Sketch', *The Times*, 2 April 1992. After the election, it was generally recognised by Labour itself that the Sheffield rally had left an unfavourable impression. Larry Whitty's report to Labour's National Executive Committee (see note 139) said that had 'probably' been a mistake and had generated 'some negative impact' (quoted in Nicholas Timmins, 'Labour begin post-mortem on election defeat', *Independent*, 30 April 1992).
148 David Marquand, 'Searching for mutual courage to ditch the stifling history', *Guardian*, 11 April 1992.
149 Stuart Hall, 'No new vision, no new votes', *New Statesman and Society*, 17 April 1992. Whitty's report (see note 139) also echoed these sentiments. In it he alluded to the 'serious concern about the Labour party as a party of the past, and one which holds back aspirations and tends to turn the clock back' (quoted in Wintour, 'Labour sifts through the dust of defeat').
150 'Major versus Kinnock', *The Times*, 14 March 1992.
151 Simon Jenkins, 'A question of character and leadership', *The Times*, 7 April 1992.
152 'Major's First Test', *The Times*, 8 April 1992.
153 'Britain HAS changed', *Sunday Times*, 5 April 1992.
154 'The five years that form the test', *Guardian*, 7 April 1992.
155 'Mr Major's "100 days"', *The Times*, 11 April 1992.
156 'Will the real John Major please stand up', *Observer*, 12 April 1992.
157 Wapshott, 'John Major's discreet charm to the British bourgeoisie'.
158 'Mr Major's "100 days"'.
159 Allan Massie, 'On the big day, he could only strike air', *Daily Telegraph*, 11 April 1992.
160 Nicholas O'Shaughnessy, 'Why a "flawless" campaign flopped', *Independent on Sunday*, 12 April 1992.

161 Massie, 'On the big day, he could only strike air'.
162 Oakley, 'Over-the-top rally left Kinnock exposed'
163 'Socialism RIP', *Sunday Times*, 12 April 1992.
164 'A Mandate for Major', *Sunday Telegraph*, 12 April 1992.
165 Quoted in *Guardian*, 11 April 1992.
166 Quoted in *The Times*, 11 April 1992.
167 Quoted in *Guardian*, 14 April 1992.

Chapter 9

1 Peter Hennessy, *Cabinet* (Oxford: Basil Blackwell, 1986), p. 121.
2 Robert Skidelsky, 'The pride and the fall', *Guardian*, 21 November 1990.
3 Bill Jones, 'The Thatcher style', in Bill Jones (ed.), *Political Issues in Britain Today*, 3rd edn (Manchester: Manchester University Press, 1989), p. 17.
4 Hennessy, *Cabinet*, p. 122.
5 Ronald Butt, 'A missionary in politics', *The Times*, 23 November 1990.
6 Peter Hennessy, 'How Much Room at the Top? Margaret Thatcher, the Cabinet and Power Sharing', in Philip Norton (ed.), *New Directions in British Politics? Essays on the Evolving Constitution* (Aldershot, Hants: Edward Elgar, 1991), p. 34.
7 Peter Madgwick, *British Government: The Central Executive Territory* (London: Philip Allan, 1991), p. 238.
8 Alan Watkins, 'It's no good trying to be like Mrs Thatcher', *Observer*, 9 June 1991.
9 *Ibid.*
10 Dennis Kavanagh, 'Woman who set out to wrench Britain on to a new course', *The Times*, 28 November 1990.
11 George Jones, 'Mrs Thatcher and the Power of the PM', *Contemporary Record*, 3, no. 4 (April 1990), pp. 2, 5, 6.
12 George Jones, 'Prime Minister and Cabinet', *Wroxton Papers in Politics* (Wroxton College, 1990), p. 13.
13 John Hart, 'President and Prime Minister: Convergence or Divergence?', *Parliamentary Affairs*, 44, no. 2 (April 1991), p. 219.
14 Madgwick, *British Government: The Central Executive Territory*; Martin Burch, 'The British Cabinet: A Residual Executive', *Parliamentary Affairs*, 41, no. 1 (January 1988), pp. 4-48; Patrick Dunleavy and R. A. W. Rhodes, 'Core executive studies in Britain', *Public Administration*, 68 (Spring 1990), pp. 3-28; John Greenaway, 'All Change At The Top', *Social Studies Review*, 6, no. 4 (March 1991), pp. 136-40.
15 Dunleavy and Rhodes, 'Core Executive Studies in Britain', p. 3.
16 *Ibid.*, p. 19.
17 Burch, 'The British Cabinet: A Residual Executive', *passim*.
18 Greenaway, 'All Change At The Top', p. 139.
19 James Barber, *The Prime Minister since 1945* (Oxford: Basil Blackwell, 1991), p. 128.
20 Joe Rogaly, 'Will the real Mr Major stand up', *Financial Times*, 28 November 1990.
21 Richard Rose, 'British Government: The Job at the Top', in Richard Rose and Ezra N. Suleiman (eds), *Presidents and Prime Ministers* (Washington, DC: American Enterprise Institute, 1980), p. 44.
22 It should be pointed out that this remains the view held by most of the leading scholars in the field. Anthony King, for example, believes that the 'person who walks for the first time through the door of Number 10 as prime minister does not create or recreate the prime ministership: the job, to a considerable extent, already exists' (p. 31). Prime ministers, therefore, 'just acquire the job and do it' (p. 45). Consequently, scholars need to

study, 'not *the* prime minister but prime minister*ships*' (p. 43). See Anthony King, 'The British Prime Ministership in the Age of the Career Politician', *West European Politics*, 14, no. 2 (April 1991), pp. 25-47. See also Peter Hennessy, 'Finding a job for the prime minister', *Independent*, 8 July 1991.
23 King, 'The British Prime Ministership in the Age of the Career Politician', p. 25.
24 Ivor Jennings, *Party Politics* (Cambridge: Cambridge University Press, 1961), pp. 260-1. See David Butler and Donald Stokes, *Political Change in Britain: Forces Shaping Electoral Choice* (London: Macmillan, 1969), chs. 16, 17; Bo Sarlvik and Ivor Crewe, *Decade of Dealignment: The Conservative Victory of 1979 and Electoral Trends in the 1970s* (Cambridge: Cambridge University Press, 1983), pp. 130-33; David Denver, *Elections and Voting Behaviour in Britain* (London: Philip Allan, 1989), pp. 89-93.
25 David Butler and Donald Stokes, *Political Change in Britain: The Evolution of Electoral Choice*, 2nd edn (London: Macmillan, 1974), ch. 17.
26 *Ibid.*, pp. 362-8.
27 Anthony Mughan, 'Electoral Change in Britain: The Campaign Reassessed', *British Journal of Political Science*, 8, no. 2 (April 1978), pp. 245-53; Brian Graetz and Ian McAllister, 'Party Leaders and Election Outcomes in Britain, 1974-1983', *Comparative Political Studies*, 19 (1987), pp. 484-507; Clive Bean and Anthony Mughan, 'Leadership Effects in Parliamentary Elections in Australia and Britain', *American Political Science Review*, 83, no. 4 (December 1989), pp. 1165-79; Marianne C. Stewart and Harold D. Clark, 'The (Un)importance of Party Leaders: Leaders Images and Party Choice in the 1987 British Election', *Journal of Politics* 54, no. 2 (May 1992), pp. 447-70.
28 Graetz and McAllister, 'Party Leaders and Election Outcomes in Britain, 1974-1983'.
29 Clive Bean and Anthony Mughan, 'Party Leaders and the Vote', *Contemporary Record*, 4, no. 2 (November 1990), p. 25.
30 Donald R. Kinder, Mark D. Peters, Robert P. Abelson and Susan T. Fiske, 'Presidential Prototypes', *Political Behaviour*, 2 (1980), pp. 315-37; Arthur Miller, Martin P. Wattenberg and Oksana Malanchuk, 'Schematic Assessments of Presidential Candidates', *American Political Science Review*, 80, no. 2 (June 1986), pp. 521-40.
31 Bean and Mughan, 'Party Leaders and the Vote', p. 25.
32 Ivor Crewe, 'How much do leaders matter', *The Times*, 19 September 1991.
33 Dunleavy and Rhodes, 'Core Executive Studies in Britain', p. 24.
34 Anthony Mughan, 'Candidate Affect and the "Presidentialization" of Parliamentary Elections', paper presented to the Political Studies Association conference at the University of Lancaster, 6 April 1991.
35 Madgwick, *British Government: The Central Executive Territory*, p. 249.

Epilogue

1 Chief among these was the government's abandonment of the European Exchange Rate Mechanism and, with it, the collapse of John Major's entire economic strategy for the country. Other crises included the scandal surrounding John Major's close friend and cabinet colleague, David Mellor; the style and substance of the government's precipitous decision to close thirty-one coal mines, together with its subsequent decision to review its own policy in the light of the massive outcry against the 30,000 job losses; the prime minister's choice to risk a split in his own party and to place both the government and his premiership in jeopardy over the approval of the Maastricht Treaty; the protracted disarray and lack of economic direction following the ERM debacle, set against a backdrop of rising unemployment, bankruptcies and closures; the charges of duplicity and dishonesty surrounding the arms to Iraq affair which centred on the behaviour of government

ministers in the trial of three former executives of the Churchill-Matrix company; and the myriad troubles of the Chancellor of the Exchequer, Norman Lamont, whose personal credibility was progressively eroded not just by the state of the economy, but by a series of personal revelations that cast doubt on his competence (e.g. overdue payments on his Access credit card) and on his probity (e.g. the receipt of government and party funds to pay the legal expenses incurred in evicting a sex therapist from one of his properties).

2 J. Andrew Brown, 'The Major Effect: Changes in Party Leadership and Party Popularity', *Parliamentary Affairs*, 45, no. 4 (October 1992), p. 551. According to Brown, preliminary evidence suggests that the 'leadership war ... seemed to be a crucial factor in the casting of a sizeable number of votes' (p. 560). The prime minister 'outstripped Kinnock in terms of general image and, more importantly, the public's belief in his prime ministerial ability' (p. 561). As a consequence, both 'Major and Kinnock effects were in operation as voters went to the polls' (pp. 561–2). David Saunders is more cautious. Major's superior showing in the public's satisfaction ratings of party leaders 'may well have played some part in some people's voting decisions, though the precise extent of any such effect is almost impossible to specify' (David Saunders, 'Why the Conservative Party Won – Again' in Anthony King *et al.*, *Britain at the Polls, 1992* (Chatham, New Jersey: Chatham House, 1993), p. 192. Nevertheless, there is 'evidence that "the Kinnock factor" harmed Labour's political fortunes' (p. 193). To Ivor Crewe, 'it was not the parties' organisational strength or electioneering skills that made the difference, [but] ... it may well have been the leaders' ('Why Did Labour Lose Yet Again?', *Politics Review*, 2, no. 1 (September 1992), p. 6.). A Gallup post-election survey asked who would have made the best, or alternatively the worst, prime minister. From the combined 'best' and 'worst' scores, Crewe concludes that 'Kinnock (-37) was a serious electoral liability while Major (+30) and to a lesser extent Ashdown (+5) were assets. Moreover, compared with 1987, Major was a bigger bonus to the Conservatives than Margaret Thatcher, and Kinnock a bigger drag on Labour' (p. 7). This is not to say that the leadership differences were decisive, but that they were a significant factor, especially in conveying an impression of general governing competence.

3 David Wastell, 'Major's Second Front', *Sunday Telegraph*, 22 November 1992.
4 Peter Riddell, 'An alarm bell called Bush', *The Times*, 21 December 1992.
5 'The black hole of Major indecision', *Guardian*, 30 September 1992.
6 Quoted in Wastell, 'Major's Second Front'.
7 Philip Stephens, 'It hasn't been a piece of cake', *Financial Times*, 28–29 November 1992.
8 Michael Ignatieff, 'The grey emptiness inside John Major', *Observer*, 15 November 1992.
9 Roy Jenkins, 'Major is not up to the job', *Observer*, 18 October 1992.
10 Allan Massie, 'A government sadly in need of a candid friend's advice', *Daily Telegraph*, 30 November 1992.
11 Paul Johnson, 'Why the prime minister should go', *The Times*, 28 October 1992.
12 Charles Moore, 'Major is an honourable man – and look where that's got us', *Daily Telegraph*, 2 October 1992.
13 *Ibid.*
14 Graham Patterson and Andrew Pierce, 'Can Major take the strain?', *The Times*, 21 October 1992.
15 See Philip Norton, 'The Conservative Party from Thatcher to Major', in King *et al.*, *Britain at the Polls, 1992*, pp. 61–2.
16 Graham Turner, 'The Clubbable Cabinet', *Sunday Telegraph*, 9 August 1992.
17 Peter Riddell, 'Tory bandages torn apart', *The Times*, 5 October 1992.
18 'The Prime Minister', *The Times*, 16 October 1992.
19 'The black hole of Major indecision'.
20 Johnson, 'Why the prime minister should go'.

21 'Cabinet, What Cabinet?', *The Times*, 17 October 1992.
22 See the Gallup poll in the *Daily Telegraph*, 5 October 1992; the MORI poll in the *European*, 22–25 October 1992; and the MORI poll in *Sunday Times*, 1 November 1992.
23 Anthony King, 'Major suffers collapse in popularity', *Daily Telegraph*, 5 October 1992.
24 'Major sinks to rock bottom with the voters', *European*, 22–25 October 1992.
25 *Ibid.*
26 Brian MacArthur, 'Press makes it Major's Black Sunday', *The Times*, 19 October 1992.
27 *Sun*, 17 October 1992.
28 Quoted in Andrew Grice, 'Major: I'll learn from my mistakes' *Sunday Times*, 20 December 1992.
29 Quoted in Anthony Bevins and Colin Hughes, 'Major ready to chop down "Goliath" of bureaucracy', *Independent*, 7 June 1992.
30 Quoted in *ibid.*
31 'New Deal for Britain', *Sunday Times*, 18 October 1992.
32 Peter Riddell 'Why the shrewd man has to turn into action man', *The Times*, 16 October 1992.
33 Massie, 'A government sadly in need of a friend's advice'.
34 'Show them who's boss', *Daily Express*, 21 October 1992.
35 Kenneth Baker, 'The new year calls for a new vision from Mr Major', *Daily Telegraph*, 22 December 1992.
36 'The Prime Minister'.
37 The scale of John Smith's victory over his challenger, Bryan Gould, was overwhelming. He won over 91% of the votes in the electoral college used to choose Labour's leadership.
38 BBC Radio 4, *Nine O'Clock News*, 19 July 1992.
39 Bryan Gould quoted in Patrick Wintour, 'Smith leadership under fire', *Guardian*, 9 December 1992. See also Martin Kettle, 'Whatever is the matter with John Smith?', *Guardian*, 5 December 1992.
40 Nick Raynsford quoted in Andrew Grice, 'Plain John Smith: Too Plain for Words?', *Sunday Times*, 22 November 1992.
41 Bryan Gould, 'The Tories' only hope is that Labour fails to attack the home front', *Sunday Times*, 18 October 1992.
42 George Jones, 'Where is he going wrong?', *Daily Telegraph*, 9 December 1992.
43 Quoted in Grice, 'Plain John Smith: Too Plain for Words?'
44 Quoted in *ibid.*
45 Harvey Mansfield, 'The vision thing', *Times Literary Supplement*, 7 February 1992.
46 Kerry Mullins and Aaron Wildavsky, 'The Procedural Presidency of George Bush', *Political Science Quarterly*, 107, no. 1 (Spring 1992), p. 58.
47 For an excellent discussion on the 'politics of expectation', see Henry Fairlie, *The Kennedy Promise: the Politics of Expectation* (New York: Doubleday, 1972).

Minogue, Kenneth, 3
Miroff, Bruce, 90
Mitchell, George, 53
Moore, Charles, 238, 285
Morgan, Kenneth O., 86
Morrison, Blake, 243
Mughan, Anthony, 279-81

nationalism (British), 158-63, 207-8,
    236, 267, 270
nationalism (U.S.) 45-8, 72-3, 100, 155-
    8, 270
Neave, Airey, 61-2
Neil, Andrew, 238
Neustadt, Richard, 149-50, 152, 154, 168
New Deal, 25, 28-9, 38, 46
New Frontier, 27
Nixon, Richard, 33-6, 68, 100, 164

Oakley, Robin, 143, 215, 237
opinion polls (Britain), 76, 82, 130-47,
    116-17, 191-3, 202, 206, 208, 226,
    231-3, 236, 241-2, 245-87, 287-8
opinion polls (U.S.), 45-6, 50, 52, 54, 57
O'Shaughnessy, Nicholas, 112, 115, 254
Owen, David, 79-80, 86, 121-2, 125, 266

Parkinson, Cecil, 130
Pearce, Edward, 201
Perot, H. Ross, 56, 58, 102-3
Peyton, John, 62
poll tax, 176, 202, 208-10
Powell,Enoch, 132, 169
presidential election (1960), 34 (1972),
    35; (1984), 48; (1988), 49-51;
    (1992), 52-8
prime ministerial government, 8-15, 20,
    71-3, 165-74, 182, 209-12, 237, 257-9
Prime Minister's Questions, 132-4
Pringle, Peter, 102
Prior, James, 8, 60-1
Pym, Francis, 8, 68

Reagan, Ronald, 25, 39-48, 51, 68, 73,
    76, 90, 95-6, 98, 100-1, 156
Reece, Gordon, 109
Rees-Mogg, William, 75
Riddell, Peter, 220, 289
Rockman, Bert, 52

Rodgers, William, 79-80
Rogaly, Joe, 6, 200, 238
Roosevelt, Franklin D., 25, 289
Rose, Richard, 117, 124, 151

Scargill, Arthur, 3, 72
Sedgemore, Brian, 10
Sherman, Alfred, 64
Shore, Peter, 74
Simpson, John, 245
Skidelsky, Robert, 65
Smith, John, 230, 289
Smoller, Fred, 95
Social Democratic party, 78-9, 222
Spencer, Stuart, 48
Steel, David, 78-80, 125
Stourton, Edward, 244

Tebbit, Norman, 113, 117, 125, 130,
    192, 224
Thatcher, Margaret, 2-8, 11, 14-22, 59-
    64, 66, 77, 85-7, 108-14, 116-17,
    132, 134, 146, 153-4, 158-9, 160-
    2, 167-74, 175-84, 186-8, 205,
    212, 237, 257-9, 282, 286-7
Thorpe, Jeremy, 78
Tsongas, Paul, 53-4
Tyler, Rodney, 113-14

Vietnam, 27, 158
Vincent, John, 69

Wapshott, Nicholas, 200, 236
Watergate, 164-5
Watkins, Alan, 258-9
Westland crisis, 168, 182-3, 186
Whitelaw, Willie, 61
Williams, Marcia, 104-6
Williams, Shirley, 122
Wills, Garry, 45
Wilson, Harold, 11, 13, 76, 103-6, 116, 219
Wilson, Woodrow, 90
Woodward, David, 96
Woodward, Shaun, 236
Worsthorne, Peregrine, 73

Young, Hugo, 3, 195, 222, 234
Young, Lord David, 113
Yugoslavia, 285